GREEK TRAGEDY
IN NEW TRANSLATIONS

GENERAL EDITORS
Peter Burian and Alan Shapiro

FOUNDING GENERAL EDITOR
William Arrowsmith

FORMER GENERAL EDITOR
Herbert Golder

THE COMPLETE SOPHOCLES, VOLUME I

The Complete Sophocles, Volume I

The Theban Plays

Edited by
PETER BURIAN
and
ALAN SHAPIRO

OXFORD
UNIVERSITY PRESS

2011

OXFORD
UNIVERSITY PRESS

Oxford University Press, Inc., publishes works that further
Oxford University's objective of excellence
in research, scholarship, and education.

Oxford New York
Auckland Cape Town Dar es Salaam Hong Kong Karachi
Kuala Lumpur Madrid Melbourne Mexico City Nairobi
New Delhi Shanghai Taipei Toronto

With offices in
Argentina Austria Brazil Chile Czech Republic France Greece
Guatemala Hungary Italy Japan Poland Portugal Singapore
South Korea Switzerland Thailand Turkey Ukraine Vietnam

Published by Oxford University Press, Inc.
198 Madison Avenue, New York, New York 10016

www.oup.com

Oxford is a registered trademark of Oxford University Press

Library of Congress Cataloging-in-Publication Data
Sophocles.
   [Selections. English. 2010]
   The complete Sophocles. v. 1, The Theban plays / edited by Peter Burian and Alan Shapiro.
      p.   cm. — (Greek tragedy in new translations)
   Includes bibliographical references.
   ISBN 978-0-19-538879-4 (acid-free paper)—ISBN 978-0-19-538880-0 (pbk. : acid-free
paper) 1. Sophocles—Translations into English. 2. Mythology, Greek—Drama.
I. Burian, Peter, 1943– II. Shapiro, Alan, 1952– III. Title. IV. Series.
   PA4414.A2B87 2010
   882'.01—dc22

9 8 7 6 5 4 3 2 1

Printed in the United States of America

EDITORS' FOREWORD

"*The Greek Tragedy in New Translations* is based on the conviction that poets like Aeschylus, Sophocles, and Euripides can only be properly rendered by translators who are themselves poets. Scholars may, it is true, produce useful and perceptive versions. But our most urgent present need is for a *re-creation* of these plays—as though they had been written, freshly and greatly, by masters fully at home in the English of our own times."

With these words, the late William Arrowsmith announced the purpose of this series, and we intend to honor that purpose. As was true of most of the volumes that began to appear in the 1970s—first under Arrowsmith's editorship, later in association with Herbert Golder—those for which we bear editorial responsibility are products of close collaborations between poets and scholars. We believe (as Arrowsmith did) that the skills of both are required for the difficult and delicate task of transplanting these magnificent specimens of another culture into the soil of our own place and time, to do justice both to their deep differences from our patterns of thought and expression and to their palpable closeness to our most intimate concerns. Above all, we are eager to offer contemporary readers dramatic poems that convey as vividly and directly as possible the splendor of language, the complexity of image and idea, and the intensity of emotion and originals. This entails, among much else, the recognition that the tragedies were meant for performance—as scripts for actors—to be sung and danced as well as spoken. It demands writing of inventiveness, clarity, musicality, and dramatic power. By such standards, we ask that these translations be judged.

This series is also distinguished by its recognition of the need of nonspecialist readers for a critical Introduction informed by the best recent scholarship, but written clearly and without condescension. Each play is followed by notes designed not only to elucidate obscure references but also to mediate the conventions of the Athenian stage as well as those features of the Greek text that might otherwise go unnoticed. The notes are supplemented by a glossary of mythical and geographical terms that should make it possible to read the play without turning elsewhere for basic information. Stage directions are sufficiently ample to aid readers in imagining the action as they read. Our fondest hope, of course, is that these versions will be staged not only in the minds of their readers but also in the theaters to which, after so many centuries, they still belong.

A NOTE ON THE SERIES FORMAT

A series such as this requires a consistent format. Different translators, with individual voices and approaches to the material at hand, cannot be expected to develop a single coherent style for each of the three tragedians, much less make clear to modern readers that, despite the differences among the tragedians themselves, the plays share many conventions and a generic, or period, style. But they can at least share a common format and provide similar forms of guidance to the reader.

1. Spelling of Greek names

Orthography is one area of difference among the translations that requires a brief explanation. Historically, it has been common practice to use Latinized forms of Greek names when bringing them into English. Thus, for example, Oedipus (not Oidipous) and Clytemnestra (not Klutaimestra) are customary in English. Recently, however, many translators have moved toward more precise transliteration, which has the advantage of presenting the names as both Greek and new, instead of Roman and neoclassical importations into English. In the case of so familiar a name as Oedipus, however, transliteration risks the appearance of pedantry or affectation. And in any case, perfect consistency cannot be expected in such matters. Readers will feel the same discomfort with "Athenai" as the chief city of Greece as they would with "Platon" as the author of *The Republic*.

The earlier volumes in this series adopted as a rule a "mixed" orthography in accordance with the considerations outlined above. The most familiar names retain their Latinate forms, while the rest are transliterated; -os rather than Latin -us is adopted for the termination of masculine names, and Greek diphthongs (as in Iphigeneia for Latin Iphigenia) are retained. Some of the later volumes continue this practice, but where translators have preferred to use a more consistent practice of transliteration or Latinization, we have honored their wishes.

2. Stage directions

The ancient manuscripts of the Greek plays do not supply stage directions (though the ancient commentators often provide information relevant to staging, delivery, "blocking," etc.). Hence stage directions must be inferred from words and situations and our knowledge of Greek theatrical conventions. At best this is a ticklish and uncertain procedure. But it is surely preferable that good stage directions should be provided by the translator than that readers should be left to their own devices in visualizing action, gesture, and spectacle. Ancient tragedy was austere and "distanced" by means of masks, which means that the reader must not expect the detailed intimacy ("He shrugs and turns wearily away," "She speaks with deliberate slowness, as though to emphasize the point," etc.) that characterizes stage directions in modern naturalistic drama.

3. Numbering of lines

For the convenience of the reader who may wish to check the translation against the original, or vice versa, the lines have been numbered according to both the Greek and English texts. The lines of the translation have been numbered in multiples of ten, and these numbers have been set in the right-hand margin. The (inclusive) Greek numeration will be found bracketed at the top of the page. The Notes that follow the text have been keyed to both numerations, the line numbers of the translation in **bold**, followed by the Greek lines in regular type, and the same convention is used for all references to specific passages (of the translated plays only) in both the Notes and the Introduction.

Readers will doubtless note that in many plays the English lines outnumber the Greek, but they should not therefore conclude that the translator has been unduly prolix. In most cases the reason is simply that the translator has adopted the free-flowing norms of modern Anglo-American prosody, with its brief-breath-and-emphasis-determined lines, and its habit of indicating cadence and caesuras by line length and setting rather than by conventional punctuation. Even where translators have preferred to cast dialogue in more regular five-beat or six-beat lines, the greater compactness of Greek diction is likely to result in a substantial disparity in Greek and English numerations.

ABOUT THE TRANSLATIONS

The translations in this series were written over a period of roughly forty years. No attempt has been made to update references to the scholarly literature in the Introductions and Notes, but each volume offers a brief For Further Reading list that will provide some initial orientation to contemporary critical thinking about the tragedies it contains.

THIS VOLUME

Sophocles' three "Theban plays" do not constitute a trilogy in the formal sense of a set of tragedies written at one time to be presented as a unit. Assuming that the traditional date of *Antigone* (442 BC) is correct, that play is almost four decades older than *Oedipus at Colonus*, written at the very end of Sophocles' long life, in about 406; *Oedipus the King*, although of uncertain date, in all likelihood falls roughly halfway between the two. Each is an independent work, originally produced with other dramas entirely, and we should not expect complete consistency in characterization or narrative detail. Nevertheless, putting these three tragedies together in one volume is an easy choice. Whether they are read in narrative order as segments of the myth of Laius' troubled line or, as presented in this volume, in the order of their composition, the collocation provides important insights into their interconnections and differences, and into the larger contours and meaning of the myth itself. How lucky we are that these three plays have survived to give us the fruits of Sophocles' return to the terrible and fascinating tale of Oedipus and his children at three different moments of his own life and of legendary history!

For us, inevitably, part of the fascination of the Oedipus story derives from the Freudian claim that it is, however unique and bizarre it may seem, the story of every man's repressed desire for his mother and urge to destroy and replace his father—the Oedipus complex. And yet, readers or spectators new to the dramas themselves can hardly fail to notice how deeply the fate of Oedipus and his children is implicated in the social and political world they inhabit. Oedipus becomes a king by unknowingly slaying his predecessor, and thereby threatens to destroy the state for whose well-being he is responsible. In *Oedipus at Colonus* the apparently helpless former ruler struggles to keep his body from the power of a state that had cast him aside and now needs him again, and finds in Athens a defender and champion. In *Antigone*, Oedipus' daughter enters the public sphere by defying the order of the new king, Kreon, in order to bury her brother Polyneices, and she loses her life when her intransigence falls afoul of his. So, although self-knowledge is a crucial theme of all three plays, it is always presented in the context of a larger nexus of family and community, and that, too, is part of its fascination.

The plot of *Oedipus the King* is perhaps too well known to require introduction. It has often been regarded as the first detective story, and there is truth in that, since Oedipus relentlessly and against all advice pursues his father's murderer, at last convicting himself. But the play is no whodunit. Its intended audience, and audiences everywhere today, know from the start who the guilty party is, and that superior knowledge is precisely what makes the tragic irony for which the play is famous so effective. It is interesting to imagine how the play would work if performed for an audience who had no more idea than Oedipus himself seems to of who he really is. The effect of the discovery would no doubt be very striking, but completely different from what we take it to be now, or what we assume the Athenian audience experienced in its own day.

Unable to create suspense about the outcome of Oedipus' investigations, Sophocles nevertheless can articulate its progress in ways that are both surprising and disturbing. Initially, he shows us an Oedipus beloved by the people of Thebes, revered as almost godlike for his defeat of the murderous Sphinx. Deeply concerned for his city's welfare, Oedipus promises to find a remedy for the terrifying plague that now besets it, saying, with an ironic truth he cannot even guess at, that he knows what they suffer, and himself suffers more than those who are ill, since: "my whole being wails and breaks / for this city, for myself, for all of you" (84–85 / 63–64). When Oedipus at last confronts the knowledge of his own identity, the monstrous and essential truth that has always eluded him, we may suppose this knowledge will save his city, but by the time it arrives the play has left the plague far behind. Oedipus stands revealed for all to see as a polluted pariah who killed his father, then married his mother.

This is how we knew it would be, and yet the final scenes of the play seem designed to deprive us of our privileged knowledge, to replace tragic irony with tragic uncertainty. The play has carefully led us to expect that Oedipus, once he is known to be the pollution that besets

Thebes, will be expelled from the city. Early in the play, Oedipus himself curses anyone involved in the death of Laius to exile, and later, when he begins to suspect his own responsibility, he remembers his curse and recognizes with horror that he may have condemned himself to banishment. Teiresias twice emphatically foretells Oedipus' exile for Oedipus, and once Oedipus has discovered the truth at last, he himself repeatedly begs to be cast out of Thebes. In a forceful plea, Oedipus names the proper, seemingly inevitable site for his banishment:

> As for me
> never let this city of my fathers see me here in Thebes.
> Let me go and live on the mountain, on Kithairon—the mountain
> my parents intended for my grave
> Let me die the way they wanted me to die.   (1883–87 / 1451–54)

Exile becomes Oedipus, it would seem, as much as mourning becomes Electra. But the final scene instead denies or at least defers Oedipus' wish, for Kreon, Oedipus' brother-in-law who succeeds him as ruler) insists that the fallen king be hidden from view in the palace that saw his ill-fated birth and incestuous marriage, at least until the gods show some further sign. There were many ways of telling Oedipus' story, and Sophocles does not give his audience—or his tragic hero—any certainty about what the future will bring. We, who have known all along what Oedipus did not, must in the end accept they we do not know the whole story or its whole meaning either. To put it another way, as we watch Oedipus led away blind and helpless, we must be satisfied with his own dark yet unmistakably proud prediction:

> And yet this much I know—
>   No sickness,
> No ordinary, natural death is mine.
> I have been saved, preserved, kept alive
> For some strange fate, for something far more awful still.
>   (1899–93 / 1455–57)

Toward the end of his life, Sophocles decided to revisit the figure of Oedipus and give us his own version of the hero's "strange fate." The result is a stunning drama that brings Oedipus at last to the release of death, but as something more than a blind, infirm, disgraced old man. *Oedipus the King* has often been compared to *Hamlet*; *Oedipus at Colonus* might in a similar vein be called Sophocles' *King Lear*. In Sophocles' late work, we witness the same stubborn, relentless, overbearing Oedipus, weighted down now by years of privation and suffering, transcend his fated fall and indeed the bonds of mere mortality to end his life as a sacred hero. He finds rest at last in Attic soil, where his bones will become a continuing source of strength to his friends and harm to his enemies. Despite this reversal of the arc of the action, however, Sophocles establishes an emphatic relation between the two through the inverse parallelism of their structures.

An initial sign that *Oedipus at Colonus* is to be understood as a sequel to its predecessor comes when Oedipus learns that he has wandered into a grove sacred to the Eumenides near Athens. With a thrill of recognition, he connects this apparent chance to the original oracle of Apollo,

> who
> when he foretold the horrors that lay ahead
> said that in the fullness of time I'd fine rest
> when I reached a country I could stop in at last
> in a shelter for strangers, a sanctuary
> of the Holy Ones. (99–104 / 87–90)

Oedipus has entered the scene as a beggar, apparently helpless and utterly dependent on his daughter Antigone, the sole companion of his exile and wandering. Now he declares himself a suppliant of the Goddesses, to whom he looks for safety. The contrast with the Oedipus of the earlier play, the masterful and self-reliant ruler to whom his people turn as suppliants for safety, could hardly be more marked. Beginning with this moment of recognition, Oedipus will gain the inner strength and prophetic knowledge to curse his enemies, whereas in *Oedipus the King* he unwittingly curses himself and only later learns the truth about his own past.

In the earlier drama, Oedipus seeks out those who know the truth (Teiresias, the Shepherd) and forces them to speak; in *Oedipus at Colonus*, he is sought out by and crushingly rebuffs those who want to use him for their own ends, Kreon (spelled "Creon" in the translation offered here) and Polyneices. At the end of *Oedipus the King*, Oedipus blinds himself in punishment of his terrible transgressions, and as we have seen begs for banishment but is forced to enter the palace as an outcast among gods and men; at the end of the later play, Oedipus gains an inner sight that permits him to lead the way to the final home that he alone can recognize. At last he achieves the proximity to the gods wrongly attributed to him before his fall by the people of Thebes:

Remember your love for Thebes. Your skill was our salvation once before.
For this Thebes calls you savior.
Don't let us remember you as king—godlike in power—
Who gave us back our life, then let us die.   (*Oedipus the King* 68–71 / 47–50)

For now, it is the gods themselves who call him to them:

For again and again a god calls him,
echoing from every direction at once:
You! You there! Oedipus! Why
do we put off our departure like this?   (1798–1801 / 1626–28)

Oedipus' passing is a mystery and a moment of extraordinary beauty, peace, and love in a life fraught with so much violence, ugliness, and hatred. But this must not allow us to forget that he also curses his sons to mutual slaughter for having mistreated and neglected their father after his fall. Cursing as well as blessing is the prerogative of the sacred hero, but the final exchange of the play brings a subtle but jarring reminder that these powers cannot easily be kept separate. Oedipus' daughter Antigone, faithful to her father but full of love for the sons he so despised, asks to return to Thebes, in hopes that "we may yet, somehow / stop the slaughter rushing toward our brothers" (1969–70 / 1770–72). Athenians knew, as do all who know Sophocles' *Antigone* today, how that would turn out. Oedipus' hatreds will in the end sweep away his loved ones as well.

Antigone, the earliest of the plays in this volume, is divided between two central figures, Antigone and Kreon, whose conflict generates one of the richest and still most controversial of surviving Greek tragedies. Hegel's view of the two antagonists as embodying real but partial rights (roughly those of the family and those of the larger community) long ago laid the groundwork for debates about the play. On the one hand, his view cannot simply be right, for both in obvious ways make very bad representatives of the rights they are said to embody. Creon becomes more and more tyrannical, less and less willing to listen to other voices, until finally he identifies the state itself with his own will. His son Haimon tells him, "You'd do well as the single ruler of some deserted place" (799 / 739). And Antigone makes a deeply anomalous representative of family right, daughter as she is of an incestuous bond between mother and son. Antigone treats her loving sister Ismene as an enemy for refusing to take part in what Antigone regards as a pious duty, and chooses marriage to death over an appropriate marriage to her cousin

Haimon. In defying Creon, Antigone defies not only her ruler but her uncle and guardian. By insisting on burying her brother, Antigone sacrifices the endogamous marriage that would preserve her house, destroys herself, and precipitates the deaths of her prospective bridegroom and mother-in-law.

With so many distortions of kinship and state, it might seem hard to claim that the play is centered on figures representative of anything but themselves. With equal clarity, however, *Antigone* is not simply a tragedy of two individuals whose conflict sweeps others into its path, or even just the final act of the drama of the House of Laius. It is a play deeply enmeshed in questions about the polis and about the role of women in it. What are the limits of the claims the polis makes on its? What of those who are excluded from full participation in civic life? How far can a ruler go in defiance of popular will? What right do individuals have to oppose the actions of government that they regard as wrong? Who has that right? All these questions are raised in the play.

Antigone, who as a woman is excluded from the public sphere, invades it by defying Creon's decree. (This indeed was one of Hegel's crucial and foundational insights.) That was not presumably the original purpose of her act, which was simply to bury her brother, as she had buried her family's other dead. Challenging Creon, however, was inevitably part of that act; Creon's decree made her deed a public issue, a crime, and in the play she finds a voice to defend herself before Creon and her city. It is of the utmost moment that the person who claims this bold act of defiance is a woman. The play shows us again and again the strain caused by Antigone's challenge not only to Creon's decree, but to the logic of patriarchal authority—a terrible strain on her, on him, on their loved ones, and on the community. Thus, the struggle of an individual against the power of the state is intensified and made more threatening by the willingness of a woman to stand up to a man—her guardian and ruler at that.

It would be easy at a certain level to say that Antigone is rightly punished for her resistance, for taking on the role of citizen instead of the role the polis offers her, and in various ways it has been said; but the play still asks what those who are not citizens can and should do if the state tramples on what they hold holy. Ismene says, we women can do nothing. Antigone acts and dies. Most of us would be Ismenes, but few would prefer Ismene to Antigone. Antigone's action has consequences for the city, whose male-dominated order it calls into question; Creon's has consequences for the family, the value of whose stability and solidarity it calls into question. The interpenetration of public and private, civic and familial is everywhere in this extraordinary drama.

The translations in this volume were first published between 1978 and 2004. STEPHEN BERG, well known both as a poet and as the co-founder and co-editor of *American Poetry Review*, is the author of numerous volumes of poetry. His practice includes a major component of translation, in which poems from many languages and cultures are reinvented in striking contemporary idiom. Recent examples include *Rimbaud Versions and Inventions:... still unilluminated I...* and *The Elegy on Hats*, a collection informed by Baudelaire (both 2005). REGINALD GIBBONS is a poet, fiction writer, translator, literary critic, artist, and Professor of English and Classics at Northwestern University. He has published some thirty books, including eight volumes of poetry, and he was for many years editor of *TriQuarterly*, an international magazine for new writing. In addition to *Antigone*, he collaborated with Charles Segal on a translation of Euripides' *Bacchae*, also for this series. EAMON GRENNAN, an Irish poet long resident in the United States, is Dexter M. Ferry, Jr. Professor of English at Vassar College, has published a number of collections of poetry, including the recent *The Quick of It: Poems* (2005), *Matter of Fact* (2008), and *Out of Sight: New and Selected Poems* (2010). He is also the author of a translation of selected poems of Giacomo Leopardi (1997), and his criticism includes *Facing the Music: Irish Poetry in the Twentieth Century* (1999).

DISKIN CLAY is RJR Nabisco Professor of Classical Studies, Emeritus, at Duke University and the author of a number of distinguished books and monographs on classical literature and ancient philosophy, including *Paradosis and Survival: Three Chapters in the History of Epicurean Philosophy* (1998), *Platonic Questions: Dialogues with the Silent Philosopher* (2000), and *Archilochos Heros: the Hero Cult of Poets in the Greek Polis* (2004). Among his published translations is Euripides' *Trojan Women* (2005). RACHEL KITZINGER, Professor of Classics and the Matthew Vassar, Jr. Chair at Vassar College, specializes in Greek tragedy, the plays of Sophocles in particular. Among her Sophoclean studies is the monograph *The Choruses of Sophokles' Antigone and Philoktetes: A Dance of Words* (2007). She has often been involved as well in productions of Greek tragedy, both in English and in the original Greek, using the restored pronunciation. The late CHARLES SEGAL taught at a number of major universities and at the time of his death was Walter C. Klein Professor of Classics at Harvard University. Segal was a prolific and versatile scholar; among his many books and articles on subjects ranging from Homer to twentieth-century reception of the classics are influential studies of Sophocles (including the magisterial *Sophocles: Tragedy and Civilization: An Interpretation of Sophocles*, 1981) and Euripides. His other contribution to this series is a translation of Euripides' *Bacchae*, also in collaboration with Reginald Gibbons.

CONTENTS

CONTENTS

ANTIGONE

Translated by

REGINALD GIBBONS

and

CHARLES SEGAL

PREFACE

The final stages of my work on the play overlapped with a Fellowship from the National Endowment for the Humanities, which was awarded for another project, but nevertheless contributed to the efficient completion of the book. I am deeply grateful to the Endowment for their support.

I completed work on this volume at a time when Antigone's lament about being between upper and lower worlds took on an intensely personal meaning as I faced a life-threatening illness. I cannot list all the friends, colleagues, and students, past and present, who offered their help, encouragement, and prayers, but they are all gratefully remembered. I would like particularly to thank my Harvard colleagues for their many kindnesses, especially Kathleen Coleman, Albert Henrichs, and Richard Thomas, chair of the department. I am deeply grateful to the medical professionals whose expertise and concern enabled me to finish my share in the volume and indeed to continue looking on the light of the sun: Drs. Christopher Colie, Keith Stuart, and David S. Rosenthal and Ms. Judith Podymatis, RN. My collaborator, Reg Gibbons, not only made several long trips so that we could work together in the best possible way, by face-to-face discussions, but remained a steadfast and involved friend on whom I could also count for support. I am grateful to George Steiner for taking the time to read the manuscript at a time when he was busy delivering the Norton Lectures at Harvard. To my wife, Nancy Jones, my gratitude for her ever-present love and devotion at a period of particular adversity goes beyond what words can express.

CHARLES SEGAL

INTRODUCTION

For the nineteenth-century idealist German philosopher Hegel, *Antigone* is "one of the most sublime, and in every respect most consummate, work[s] of art human effort ever produced. Not a detail in this tragedy but is of consequence."[1] Hegel's dazzling accolade is typical of the high esteem for the play in the early nineteenth century.[2] For Hegel, *Antigone* plays a major role in the evolution of European consciousness, one of whose early stages is exemplified by *Antigone*'s conflict between State and individual, or more accurately between "the public law of the State and the instinctive family-love and duty towards a brother." This division in turn is an aspect of a larger conflict between Nature and Spirit and so a step toward the emergence of Spirit (*Geist*). The individual bearer of such consciousness is essentially tragic because he or she enters into the division between the divine law, embodied in the *polis* or state, and the human law, embodied in the family, and in entering into that division is destroyed. And yet "it is precisely this destruction," as George Steiner explains Hegel's view, "which constitutes man's eminent worth and which allows his progression towards the unification of consciousness and of Spirit on 'the other side of history.'"[3] In terms of Hegel's emphasis on action and his conception of fate in Greek tragedy, Antigone, rather than Kreon, is the full bearer of the tragic because she self-consciously decides to act and therefore chooses the path of her destiny.[4] The "classical" perfection of *Antigone* lies not only in the clarity and purity with which it develops this conflict but also in its representation of divinity, which goes beyond the horrific chthonic gods

1. G. W. F. Hegel, *Philosophy of Fine Art*, quoted from the Osmaston translation (London 1920), in Anne and Henry Paolucci, eds., *Hegel on Tragedy* (Garden City, N.Y., 1962), 178.
2. See George Steiner, *Antigones* (Oxford, 1984), 1–19.
3. Ibid., 31.
4. Ibid., 36.

of the old myths and the old religion to more impersonal gods, who do not appear on the stage as anthropomorphic beings and are more important for the principles they endorse than for any visual effects.

The weaknesses of Hegel's reading have long been clear.[5] It is as simplistic to identify Kreon with "the law of the State" as it is to identify Antigone with individualism *tout court*. Even Antigone's devotion to family love, or *philia*, is problematical, given the incestuous bonds within this family and her harsh treatment of her sister, Ismene. Antigone, to be sure, may be identified with the emergence of an individual ethical consciousness that resists the domination of certain laws that have been imposed by Thebes' present ruler, but the play calls into question whether these laws may be associated with an abstract, impersonal Law of the State. It is questionable to identify a small fifth-century city-state or *polis* with the modern abstract notion of State. The *polis* of *Antigone* is rather the total civic space in which the religious and the political, the private and the public are closely intertwined, and the fact that they are so intertwined creates the tragedy. Each protagonist sees only half of the whole, and each acts as if the two realms are independent of the other.

Nevertheless, Hegel's influence should not be taken lightly, and his articulation of his position in his earlier work offers a more nuanced and profound reading. In Hegel's dialectical thinking of this period, the position of human and divine changes places. The family, in its honoring of the dead, can also embody the divine law, while the city-state's law, as the creation of human beings and as the visible regulator of day-to-day affairs, can embody the human. In the fact that the two sides share in both human and divine law lies the irreconcilably tragic nature of the conflict. And this conflict is also gendered between the "feminine-ontological" and the "masculine-political," between the woman's domestic world of hearth and home and the man's public world of civic assemblies and legislative bodies.[6]

Political, historical, and social considerations add further nuances. Antigone is opposing not the city's Law (*nomos*) as a totality, but rather Kreon's specific "decree" forbidding the burial of her brother's body. She is primarily the champion not of the individual against the State but of the ties of blood and birth that rest on the solidarity of the family.

---

5. Among the earliest criticism is Goethe's, in J. W. von Goethe, *Conversations with Eckermann*, trans. John Oxenford (1850; reprint New York, 1998), 174–78 (March 28, 1827). For further discussion see, e.g., Steiner, *Antigones*, 49–51; T. C. W. Oudemans and A. P. M. H Lardinois, *Tragic Ambiguity* (Leiden, 1987), 110–17.
6. Steiner, 34–35.

More specifically, she opposes to Kreon's authority the traditional authority of the old aristocratic families to honor and bury their dead. The care for the dead was especially the prerogative of women, and it was increasingly restricted in Athens in the sixth and fifth centuries as the democracy sought to limit the power of the aristocratic clans, but it was nevertheless widely respected.[7] The Athenian institution of the public, city funeral for warriors who died in battle, established around the middle of the century, sharpened the conflict between the family's mourning and the public ceremony, and this conflict is doubtless in the play's background.[8] Against Kreon's laws (*nomoi*) Antigone sets the "unwritten laws" that pertain to the burial of the dead, which are also the "custom-laws" (another meaning of *nomoi* or *nomima*) that have a place within every city and rest on the sanctity, as she says, of "Justice, who resides in the same house with the gods below the earth" and on the authority of Zeus himself (translation 495–501 / Greek 450–55).[9] Thus, while she is so human and moving in the fragile strength of her defiance of the ruler, she has on her side the weight of religious tradition, the universal recognition of the rights of burial, and the performance of those offices for the dead that traditionally belong to women in the *polis* and in the family.

Viewed more broadly, *Antigone* brings down to earth and to purely human characters some of the conflicts of Aiskhylos' *Oresteia*. Antigone's position has some affinities with that of the Furies in Aiskhylos' conflict between Olympian and chthonic, upper and lower worlds, in the last play of the *Oresteia*, the *Eumenides*. Here the newer and younger Olympians, Apollo and Athena, who belong to the reign of Zeus, are identified with the male-dominated political institutions of the city, whereas the ancient gods, the Erinyes or Furies, daughters of primordial Night, defend the bonds of blood and birth and the rights of the mother and of Earth in their vengeful pursuit of the matricide, Orestes. To be sure, the issue of *Antigone* is burial, not vengeance; the cosmic order is in the background, not the foreground; and the focus is on the family as a whole and not on the rights of the father as against those of the mother. *Antigone* also presents the conflict in terms of the

---

7. For the importance of female lament in the play see my *Sophocles' Tragic World: Divinity, Nature, and Society* (Cambridge, Mass., 1995), 119–20, 125–27, 135–36.

8. This aspect of the play is stressed by William Tyrrell and Larry Bennett, *Recapturing Sophocles' Antigone* (Lanham, Md., 1998), especially 5–14, 115–17.

9. Bernard Knox, *The Heroic Temper* (Berkeley and Los Angeles, 1964), 97, shows that the (literally) "unwritten and secure custom-laws (*nomima*) of the gods" of which Antigone speaks in 500–501 / 454–55 refer primarily to the sanctity surrounding burial rites. Yet her word *nomoi*, literally "laws," in 498 / 452, also indicates that broader issues are involved.

more impersonal "eternal laws of the gods" rather than through the awe-inspiring mythical presences of the Furies. Nevertheless, the framing of this conflict between male and female and between civic order and primordial religious tradition bears comparison with the *Oresteia*. Antigone, too, looks for support from the divinities of the lower world (in the lines cited above; also in 593 / 542), and her vindication comes, finally, from Hades and the Furies (1145–47 / 1074–75).

Comparison with the *Oresteia*, however, also reveals how poorly the Hegelian scheme of thesis-antithesis-synthesis fits the play. *Antigone* has none of the resolution that ends the *Eumenides*, where the Furies finally accept the Olympian persuasion of Athena and consequently are reconciled with the *polis* of Athens and transform themselves into the more benign and acceptable Eumenides, the "Kindly Ones." In *Antigone* the conflict between the blood ties within the family, to which the women are particularly devoted, and the realm of political action that belongs to men is played out almost entirely on the human level. The gods appear only as the remote agents of retributive justice; and the mortal representatives of family ties and civic duty respectively both suffer a terrible doom, Antigone by the despairing suicide of her death in her cave-prison, Kreon by the blows that leave him disoriented, isolated, and totally crushed at the end.

The Hegelian notion, however, that both sides have some degree of right on their side—or, as A. C. Bradley will later rephrase it, that there is a division in the ethical substance with a resultant "violent self-restitution of the divided spiritual unity"[10]—has the merit of getting us into the fundamental issues of the play. Conflict is the heart of this work, which is so structured that each protagonist can act only by attacking and destroying the central values of the other. The play offers conflicting definitions, explicit or implicit, of the basic terms of the human condition: friend and enemy, citizen and ruler, father and son, male and female, justice and injustice, reverence and irreverence, purity and pollution, honor and dishonor, and even (in the Ode on Man) conflicting judgments of what is *anthrôpos*, a human being—powerful or helpless, something "wonderful" or "terrible" (both of these, meanings of the same word, *deinon*). Not only are the definitions in conflict, but the terms themselves become ambiguous or (as in the case of Antigone's "holy wrongdoing") paradoxical.[11] Antigone and Kreon use the same

---

10. A. C. Bradley, "Hegel's Theory of Tragedy" (1909), in Paolucci (above, n. 1), 385.

11. On these conflicts and ambiguities in the larger context of the nature of Greek tragedy, see Jean-Pierre Vernant, "Tensions and Ambiguities in Greek Tragedy," in J.-P. Vernant and Pierre Vidal-Naquet, *Myth and Tragedy in Ancient Greece* (1972, 1986), trans. J. Lloyd (New York, 1990), 29–48, especially 41–43.

words to mean different things, like *philos* and *ekhthros*, "dear one" and "enemy," or *nomos*, law. Antigone's incestuous birth complicates these ambiguities of language by confusing the basic terms of kinship: in the family of Oidipous, son and husband, brother and son, sister and daughter horribly coincide. What in fact sets the plot into motion is the mutual slaughter of the incestuously begotten sons/brothers, Polyneikes and Eteokles, who are simultaneously too close in their claims on the inherited throne and too distant in their murderous struggle, simultaneously the nearest of "dear ones," *philoi*, and the most bitter of "enemies," *ekhthroi*. The play's obsessive harping on words for "self-," "common," "one another" is the verbal expression of this deadly fusion of same and opposite that underlies the tragedy of the house of Oidipous.

The ambiguities of *philia*, being near-and-dear, in this house are enacted in the opening scene between the two sisters. The language of intimate kinship in Antigone's opening address to Ismene is painfully fractured by the end of that scene, and Antigone's virtual identification with her sister in the opening line, with its untranslatable juxtaposition of *koinon autadelphon*, literally, "shared/sharing self-sister," has turned to scorn and near hatred by the time the two young women leave the stage.

In this opening scene Antigone not only sets out the main issues but also displays all the contradictions and dangers that define her character: her intensity of feeling, the single-mindedness of her devotion to family, her unbending will, her readiness to defy the entire city in the name of what she believes, her involvement with the dead, and her willingness to face death if necessary. With sarcasm she shows her independence and bitterness when she recounts that "the noble Kreon has proclaimed" his order against the burial of Polyneikes (39–43 / 31–34), while at the same time she personalizes the conflict and dramatizes its immediacy and the consequent need to act decisively. She has a visceral sense of Polyneikes' exposed corpse—she not only recounts that "no one may hide it inside a grave, wail over it or weep for it," but she also pictures it as horribly desecrated by vultures, "a sweet-tasting treasure that birds will spy and feed on with their greedy joy" (34–38 / 27–30). That this image is distinctive, we see from comparing Kreon's otherwise similar description of his decree later (229–35 / 203–6).[12]

The paradox of what Antigone calls her "holy crime" (90 / 74) shows her understanding of her isolation but also signals the moral complexity

---

12. Kreon says "eaten by birds and dogs" and adds the epithet "shameful for anyone to see" (or literally the detail of "disfigurement" or "outrage"), but he does not use Antigone's more vivid expression.

of her forthcoming act.[13] When Ismene refuses to help, Antigone turns abruptly from affection to hatred. She openly accepts the folly of her own resolve, and she is determined to die the "noble death" of the male warrior, on the model of the Homeric hero. Her claim to the honor that she will win from her deed, her determination to "lie beside" her brother in death in her "holy wrongdoing," and her open defiance of the city at a time of crisis, would almost certainly alarm the audience of male Athenian citizens, accustomed to the view that women do not challenge men (as Ismene states in 76–77 / 61–62), especially in the all-male areas of politics and public life.

The ensuing ode, sung by the Chorus of Theban elders, reveals the one-sidedness of Antigone's position in the context of the city's fears and so sets the stage for an initially sympathetic view of Kreon. The Chorus describes the battle of the preceding night in images of animality, blood, madness, and fire that show the horror of what the city might have suffered had the fierce enemy warriors broken through the walls. Entering directly after the ode, Kreon vehemently denounces Polyneikes, the attacker who came to "burn their country and the temples with columns around them and the offerings inside" (328–29 / 285–87). On the other hand, the absolute refusal to bury a traitor's body, though legally justified, could be perceived as harsh. A traitor's corpse was often cast outside the city walls, where family members might bury it and where the danger of pollution to the city would be avoided. This is in fact the punishment specified for Polyneikes' corpse by Aiskhylos in *Seven against Thebes* and by Euripides in *Phoinikian Women*.[14] Elsewhere, too, in Greek tragedy the refusal of burial is regarded as cruel and impious, as in Sophokles' *Aias* and Euripides' *Suppliants*.[15] In the latter play, Theseus, the civilizing hero and model king of Athens, heeds his mother's plea to defy Kreon and the victorious Thebans, bury the fallen Argive warriors, and thereby "stop them from overturning the

13. With 90 / 74 see the similar phrasing of 990–91 / 924 and 1011 / 943.
14. Aiskhylos, *Seven against Thebes*, 1013–25; Euripides, *Phoinikian Women*, 1629–30. See Patricia E. Easterling, "Constructing the Heroic," in Christopher Pelling, ed., *Greek Tragedy and the Historian* (Oxford, 1997), 26–28, who argues that Kreon's punitive treatment does not correspond precisely to any known historical situation in the fifth century. The Aiskhylean version, however, though specifying burial outside, does nevertheless include exposing the body to dogs (no birds, however) and the prohibition against burial by the family (*Seven*, 1013–15). The date of the ending of the *Seven*, however, remains controversial, and it may have been influenced by Sophokles: see Appendix 2. For further discussion of the problem of the justification of Kreon's decree, see Steiner, *Antigones*, 114–20, and Oudemans and Lardinois, *Tragic Ambiguity*, 101–2, 162–63.
15. For Euripides' *Suppliants* see the Note on 1153–58 / 1080–83. In *Antigone*, 1133–61 / 1064–86, Teiresias is probably referring to the tradition that Theseus, King of Athens, intervened against Kreon for the burial of the exposed corpses of the attacking Argive warriors: see Griffith's note on Greek lines 1080–83.

custom laws (*nomima*) of all Greece" (*Suppliants* 311–12). The Kreon of *Antigone* even seems to relish his punitive authority as he dwells on the details of exposing Polyneikes' corpse and on his specific steps to ensure that the body will remain unburied (**230–35** / 203–6, **248** / 217, **451–58** / 408–14). He gives four lines (in the Greek) to the honors due to Eteokles, nine to the defiling of the traitor's body (**217–35** / 194–206)—a touch of a cruelty that will be seen again later when he sends Antigone to her death.[16] The repeated first-person statements of his opening speech too, though innocuous enough in their context, also sound a note of authoritarian willfulness and self-important sententiousness that will emerge more ominously later (**214–15** / 191, **223–24** / 198, **238–40** / 209–10).[17]

Both protagonists turn out to have a relation to the city-state (*polis*) different from what the opening scenes might suggest. Kreon's view of *nomos*, law, one of the crucial words in the play, proves to rest on too narrow a vision of the city. The word *nomos* also means "custom" and can refer to "practice" or "convention" so embedded in society that it has virtually the authority of the "laws" that derive from formal legislation. (The two meanings of *nomos* are particularly important in Sophokles' time, in democratic Athens of the fifth century, which is very much aware of the sovereign power of the assembled citizenry, the *dêmos*, to create new laws, abolish old, and replace or modify traditional "laws," and thereby codify as statute or written decree what had been more loosely defined as "custom-law.")

Both protagonists, however, assume that the gods defend their *nomos*. Kreon increasingly regards the law of the city as an extension of his own authority and assumes, erroneously, that the order of the gods is congruent with what he sees as the order of the *polis*. Antigone, in defying Kreon's laws on the grounds of the "unwritten laws" of the gods, opens up the definition of both law and the city in directions that Kreon does not understand. The city does, in fact, have obligations to the dead and to the chthonic divinities who protect them and watch over the rituals that separate the dead citizens from the living and move them to their appropriate realm in Hades. Later in the play the prophet Teiresias will announce the dire effect of violating these "unwritten laws" (**1133–61** / 1064–86); and he will show that Kreon's attempt to absorb ritual practice and the politics of the gods into his own politics of the city rests on a one-sided vision of both the city and the gods.

16. See, e.g., **838–42** / 777–80 and **944–50** / 885–90, and the Notes on these passages.
17. On the reservations that the language of Kreon's opening speech may cause the spectator, see Felix Budelmann, *The Language of Sophocles* (Cambridge, Eng., 2000), 75–78.

If Antigone seems initially to disregard the legitimate claims and needs of the *polis*, the course of the action dissipates the sympathy for Kreon aroused by the first ode and by the civic sentiments of his opening speech. The turning point is the scene with Haimon, who, for the first time, allows other voices in the city to be heard (747–55 / 692–700). Antigone, defying Kreon to his face earlier, had said that the elders of the Chorus shared her view but had their mouths sealed by fear of Kreon, whose rule she describes as *turannis*, "one-man rule" (556–58 / 506–7). The word does not yet carry the full associations of our word "tyranny," but it does connote autocratic power, the absolute rule of a single man, and it begins to undercut Kreon's claims to represent the city as a whole. Knowing his father, Haimon cannily begins with a declaration of loyalty and obedience but then endorses Antigone's position with increasing force. He might be thought a biased reporter of the citizens' sentiments when he echoes Antigone's words and defends her as one who merits "golden honor" (754 / 699). Teiresias' warnings, however, will validate this other voice and give it the authority of the gods.

In condemning Antigone to death, Kreon callously disregards her marriage with Haimon. "It's Hades who will stop this wedding for me," Kreon says to Ismene (626 / 575). But Hades in fact fulfills this marriage, later, in its way; as the messenger recounts, Haimon "in the end has had his wedding ceremony—but in the house of Hades" (1325–27 / 1240–41). "It's Hades who desires these laws" for the living and for the dead, Antigone says earlier, in defending herself before Kreon (570 / 519). Yet Kreon begins with confidence in his power to use Hades—that is, death—as an instrument of political control. However, Hades' laws operate more terribly on living and dead than even Antigone had imagined. "Only from Hades will he not procure some means of escape," the Chorus had sung in their ode on the achievements of human civilization (403–5 / 361–62), and their pronouncement is spectacularly fulfilled in Kreon's doom.

Kreon carefully arranges Antigone's death to leave himself and his city free of pollution. But her suicide in the cave doubly undoes his schemes. She takes control of her own death and turns it into a polluting death after all.[18] She thereby initiates a cycle of pollutions in Kreon's house parallel to the pollutions that his nonburial of Polyneikes has brought to the city. At the end, when Kreon's wife's suicide leaves him totally bereft, he cries out, "Ah, Harbor of Hades never to be purified! Why, why do

---

18. On Antigone's polluted death, see Nicole Loraux, *Tragic Ways of Killing a Woman* (1985), trans. Anthony Forster (Cambridge, Mass., 1987), 31–32.

you destroy me?" (1371–72 / 1284–85). His house has now taken on the pollutions from Hades that he had tried to avoid for the city, and these will not be cleansed.

In his prophecy, Teiresias explains how Kreon has done violence to his own favored realm of the gods above, the Olympians, because he kept on earth what did not belong to them (1140–44 / 1070–73). As a result, the "late-punishing" avengers, the Furies of both Hades and the gods, lie in ambush for him (1145–47 / 1074–75). Like Antigone, he now suffers an immersion, while alive, in the realm of Hades, for he enters the tomb and sees her dead and his son mad with grief, and then also dead; and, like Antigone, Kreon suffers the deaths of his closest kin. This man of the city is left, like Oidipous, in a house emptied by the suicide of a wife and the bloody deaths of two sons. Kreon's wife, Eurydike, in her dying curse, calls him "killer of sons" and so makes him, like Oidipous, responsible for the death of his two sons (1391–92 / 1304–5).[19] In his first speech Kreon had referred to his intimate kinship with Oidipous as the basis for the legitimacy of his rule (194–95 / 173–74), but this close tie with Oidipous' house takes on a sinister meaning by the end of the play. In the tragic irony of his reversal, Kreon gains not just the city of Oidipous but the house of Oidipous as well.

Antigone, silenced by her being immured in the cave, is symbolically present at both stages of Kreon's doom, first in the recognition of the symmetries between upper and lower worlds in Teiresias' prophecy, which hark back to her defiant speech to Kreon on the Justice that dwells with the gods below (495–518 / 450–70), and later in the cries of lament that Eurydike utters over her last son, for these echo Antigone's cries over the body of her last brother.[20] Antigone's suicide, too, both anticipates Eurydike's suicide and motivates Haimon's. Yet the gods who have vindicated Antigone's chthonic Justice and her demand for the equal burial of both her brothers do not intervene for her as an individual. Their absence suggests Sophokles' deeply tragic worldview, which includes the remoteness and inaccessibility of the divine beings who

---

19. Although Oidipous' curse on his two sons is not explicitly mentioned in the play, it is a familiar feature of the myth from at least the sixth century BCE on and is dramatized by Sophokles in his *Oidipous at Kolonos*. It was also prominent in Aiskhylos' *Seven against Thebes*. In our play Antigone also alludes to the curse in her opening lines, and it is probably also in the background of the third ode (642–50 / 594–603). The "Fury in the mind" mentioned here (650 / 603) also suggests the curse, as parents' curses on children are regularly fulfilled by the Erinyes or Furies. Compare Teiresias' prediction later that the "Furies, who avenge Hades and the gods" (1146–47 / 107–76), will lie in wait for Kreon.

20. Compare 1389 / 1302 and 1402 / 1316 (of Eurydike) with 35–36 / 28 and 468–72 / 422–27 (of Antigone).

permit the catastrophic waste and loss of the courageous and passionate young people who have championed their cause.

In retrospect, Antigone's unyielding commitment to her beliefs and the dignity and courage of her defiance of Kreon are perhaps the only things that illuminate the darkness of this tragic world. Hence to many, influenced by the highly politicized versions of Jean Anouilh and Bertolt Brecht in the 1940s, the history of the play is "the history of the European conscience."[21] And yet, in Sophokles' play, Antigone's very intensity of commitment has triggered the disaster. Given her devotion to her family and her passionate nature, the fact that she responds as she does bears the Sophoklean stamp of tragic inevitability. She resembles other Sophoklean tragic protagonists—Aias, Elektra, Philoktetes: admirable in her inner strength and integrity, but also dangerous to herself and to others in her one-sidedness, violent emotions, and unbending will.[22] Kreon, of course, is just as rigid as Antigone. Fresh in his authority, eager to display his full control of a crisis barely averted, and determined to assert his newly gained power, he cannot afford failure in this first challenge to his command. To be faced down by a woman, and in public, is particularly humiliating. He has, however, more options than Antigone, more space for yielding or finding areas for compromise. But in these heated circumstances and between these two personalities, no compromise is possible.

Interpreters of the play after Hegel have often idealized Antigone for her heroism and love of family. Jebb's remark, in the preface to his great commentary, is typical: "It is not without reason that moderns have recognized her as the noblest, and the most profoundly tender, embodiment of woman's heroism which ancient literature can show." Some half a century later, Cedric Whitman offered a brilliant reading of Antigone as the exemplar of an existential hero who holds bravely to her integrity and her grandeur of spirit in total isolation.[23] "In a world of hollow men, she is real." More recent critics, however, have increasingly questioned Jebb's alleged "tenderness" and stressed her darker side.

21. See Pierre Vidal-Naquet, *Le miroir brisé: Tragédie athénienne et politique* (Paris, 2001), 47–51; also Steiner, *Antigones*, 170–71, 193–94. See also Maria-Grazia Ciani, ed., *Sofocle, Anouilh, Brecht: Variazione sul mito* (Venice, 2001).

22. On these and related qualities in the Sophoklean hero, see Bernard Knox, *Heroic Temper*, 10–27, especially 16ff.

23. C. H. Whitman, *Sophocles: A Study in Heroic Humanism* (Cambridge, Mass., 1951), 88–91. The following quotation is from p. 90. In order to save Antigone's heroic perfection, however, Whitman has to delete lines 905–12 of the Greek text. See the Notes on 967–79 / 905–15. For views of Antigone similar to Whitman's, see Oudemans and Lardinois, 107–10.

With her "heart that's hot for what is chilling" (105 / 88), she is more involved with her dead relatives than with her living sister or fiancé. In the grandeur of her unshakable certainty she towers above everyone else in the play, but as Bernard Knox has emphasized, she shares the harshness and intransigence of most Sophoklean protagonists, and precisely because of her nobility and integrity she brings terrible suffering to herself and those around her.[24]

One can agree with the later Hegel that Kreon (initially, at least) may have some "right" on his side, but the tragic situation consists in the intertwined, interactive responsibility of both protagonists. The play, like most of Sophokles' extant plays, as we now increasingly acknowledge, has not one but two foci of tragic concern.[25] In the uncompromising sharpness of her personality, and the brazenness and stiffness of her defiance, Antigone undercuts whatever hope of compromise there might have been and calls forth from Kreon a complementary intransigence that destroys them both. The passions of the young—Antigone's all-absorbing family loyalty in this moment of loss and Haimon's love and despair—meet the stubbornness and inflexibility of their elders at a crisis when the city's safety has only just been secured. Interpreters who view Kreon as a champion of civic values and communal solidarity stumble against his increasingly autocratic behavior and the final judgment of the gods. Their intervention, as expounded by Teiresias, retrospectively clarifies and supports Antigone's instinctive knowledge of what she had to do and why.

As always in Sophokles, the interaction of human circumstances and human character are sufficient to account for the tragedy. Sufficient, perhaps, but not final—for in Sophokles' tragic view, human life is always part of a larger continuum, which includes the natural world and the divinities whose power, immanent in the world, makes it what it is. Antigone follows and reveres her values with an intensity for which she is ready to pay with her life. Yet she lives in a world defined by the needs of a city that she rejects. Both antagonists have limited horizons, but Kreon ultimately proves to be more disastrously limited, and he must finally yield to Teiresias' larger prophetic vision. His power buckles, but too late for Antigone to be saved.

---

24. Knox, *Heroic Temper*, chapter 1, especially 19–23, and also 62–67; R. P. Winnington-Ingram, *Sophocles* (Cambridge, 1980), 128–29, 135.

25. This important point is established by Albert Machin, *Cohérence et continuité dans le théâtre de Sophocle* (Hauteville, Québec, Canada, 1981), especially 366–76. See my review in *American Journal of Philology* 107:3 (1986), 594–99.

DRAMATIC STRUCTURE

In the prologue Ismene sets out the weakness of Antigone's position. Should she persevere in her plan to bury Polyneikes, she, a mere woman, with a woman's weakness, will be defying men and the male authority of the city (75–79 / 61–64). We should keep in mind that for fifth-century Athens political life is an area of male autonomy, freedom, and control. Women are excluded from direct political activity, may not control or administer property (including their own property), cannot enter into contracts or represent themselves in a court of law, and remain subject to the authority of their male relatives (which of course does not mean that they were without respect, rights, and influence of other kinds).[26] Except for religious festivals, they are expected to remain inconspicuously in the house (*oikos*), which is their domain.[27] The *polis* is a male work of art, an artificial system of rules, limitations, and eligibilities of man's own making, a creation of intellect and conventions, located within its natural setting, to be sure, but also separate from it in the special kind of secondary order that the city imposes on its world by its walls, temples, monuments, and of course its institutions. Yet the city also depends on the order of nature for its fruitful and harmonious relation with the land, and it depends on its women for the procreation of new citizens.[28] With procreation come sexual desire, maternity, and the strong ties of family. All these have an important role in *Antigone* and shape its tragic form.

Kreon's *polis* proves to be not so autonomous after all, and his role as father and husband throws him back into the network of the unpredictable, biological bonds that his construction of his world and of himself would exclude. Although he harshly rejects the ties of blood and marriage that connect him to his niece, Antigone, and views her "crime" solely in terms of the law she has violated, he cannot escape the power of those bonds of blood. As his wife's last words show (as reported by the Messenger at 1387–92 / 1301–5), Kreon has lost his elder son, Megareus,

---

26. This is not to say that women were completely without rights or various forms of personal power and influence. For a good survey of women in fifth-century Athens see Elaine Fantham, Helene Foley, Natalie Kampen, Sarah Pomeroy, and Alan Shapiro, eds., *Women in the Classical World* (Oxford, 1994), chapter 3, especially 74–75, 79–83; Roger Just, *Women in Athenian Law and Life* (London, 1989), especially chapters 2 and 3.

27. It remains controversial whether women were allowed to attend the dramatic performances at the City Dionysia, the festival in honor of Dionysos. See the discussion and references in my *Oedipus Tyrannus: Tragic Heroism and the Limits of Knowledge*, second edition (New York, 2001), 21–22, with n. 8, p. 23.

28. The "interconnectedness" of man and nature, with the latter's uncontrollable ambiguities, in contrast to their rationalistic separation, is a main theme of Oudemans and Lardinois, e.g., chapters 3–4.

who, presumably, sacrificed himself, or was sacrificed, to save the city.[29] Kreon never speaks of this loss, but the silenced grief returns in the sorrow of the mother, first in an oblique hint (**1265–66** / 1191) and then in the outburst of emotional and physical violence with which she ends her life. And everywhere in the background is the house of Oidipous, destroyed by just those bonds of blood that Kreon dismisses. The power of the tragic reversal, as we have observed, consists in part in the fact that Kreon's house comes increasingly to resemble that of Oidipous.

Like many tragedies of divine retribution, the action has an hourglass shape (though not completely symmetrical) as the power flows from Kreon to Antigone. He is tested by a series of challenges until he is completely destroyed in the last scene. The encounter with Haimon brings the challenge closer to home as his own son questions his authority over both city and house. In sending Antigone to her death in the cave, Kreon reasserts his power, but the entrance of Teiresias shifts the balance back to Antigone. The reversal (peripeteia) reaffirms the two areas that Kreon has tried to subordinate to his civic authority, the underworld and family ties. He enters the dark cave where he has ordered Antigone immured and where both she and Haimon kill themselves. He thereby makes a symbolical journey to the underworld, parallel to Antigone's, and this subterranean space now wreaks its vengeance on him and fulfills Antigone's parting curse (**992–96** / 925–28).

The crushing blow comes from the house and particularly from female mourning and sorrow within the house. His wife, Eurydike, whom he never actually confronts alive within the play, comes on stage from the house just long enough to hear the news of Haimon's death.[30] Her subsequent suicide inside the house demonstrates the power of everything that Kreon had disvalued in his single-minded exaltation of civic values: women's emotions and their intense involvement in the bonds of family and in pollution, lament, and death itself. The last third of the play centers on Kreon; yet his collapse is implicitly measured against the absent Antigone's strength and integrity.

Kreon's entrance immediately after the first ode consolidates the weight of authority that now rests on him as commander-in-chief of a city that has survived a deadly attack. His presence intimidates the elders of the Chorus, and he obviously savors his new role as leader of the city and spokesman for the civic ethos, on which he moralizes expansively in

---

29. See the Note on 1387–92 / 1301–5.

30. Eurydike is presumably played by the same actor who played Antigone. For her role at the end, see my *Tragedy and Civilization* (Norman, Okla., 1999), 194–95, and my *Sophocles' Tragic World*, 133–36.

his platitudinous opening speech. The Guard who arrives soon after with the bad news of the "burial" of Polyneikes—in fact, a ritual sprinkling of dust—is also terrified of Kreon's power but not entirely cowed. When the Guard returns with Antigone as his prisoner after the first stasimon (the second ode), he is relieved to escape any further expression of Kreon's wrath, although he also has a small word of sympathy for Antigone (481–84 / 436–39).

Antigone's defiance of Kreon in the following scene contrasts with the submissiveness of both the Chorus and the Guard. Her rejection of Ismene's attempt to claim a share in the crime increases her isolation. If, with the manuscripts, we assign to Ismene line 619 / 568, in which she asks if Kreon will "kill [his] own son's bride-to-be," then the implication of this line is that Antigone is so completely absorbed in her determination to bury her brother, despite the threatened punishment by death, that she herself seems to have no thoughts of Haimon. At this crisis of her spiritual life, Haimon lies below the horizon of her moral vision. We admire Ismene's courage, too, for Kreon, in response to her expressed solidarity with her sister, quickly arrests her as a co-conspirator and will not release her for some two hundred lines (830–31 / 770–71). But Ismene's gesture does nothing to help Antigone and in fact separates her even further from her one remaining blood relative.

Haimon's entrance after the second stasimon brings the first open defense of Antigone's position, and for the first time stymies Kreon in his attempt to suppress opposition. His encounter with Haimon formally resembles his encounter with Antigone. In both scenes, initial statements of principle are followed by sharp antithetical debates in the line-by-line exchange known as stichomythia. In the previous scene, that statement of principle was Antigone's powerful assertion of her reverence for the gods below, which Kreon answered by asserting the authority of the city's and his laws (495–518 / 450–70 and 521–47 / 473–96, respectively). Haimon's challenge strikes more deeply at Kreon's basic conception of himself. Kreon is pleased and relieved at his son's opening expression of loyalty, which encourages him to make a characteristically expansive speech on his favorite virtues, after the manner of his first speech in the play: Kreon's view of the proper order in the family exactly matches his view of the proper order in the city, for both rest on hierarchy and absolute obedience (686–95 / 639–47, 709–34 / 659–80). The young and impetuous Haimon, however, is very different from the timid Chorus of elders. He sketches an image of the city that infuriates his authoritarian father—a city that holds and utters voices and opinions antithetical to Kreon's.

The angry exchange pushes Kreon to his revealing statement, "Isn't the city held to be his who rules?" to which Haimon replies, "You'd do well as the single ruler of some deserted place." Kreon rebuts him with "It seems this man is fighting on the woman's side!" (798–800 / 738–40), extending his authoritarian principles to another area of hierarchy, the subordination of female to male with which he had ended his previous tirade on obedience (731–34 / 677–80).

Haimon's open challenge to Kreon's rule in fact exposes the latter as very close to the *turannos*, the man who seizes sole power in the city and concentrates it entirely in his own hands. Kreon is not actually a "tyrant," for he has gained his authority legitimately, through inheritance, not through force or trickery. Yet his behavior emerges increasingly as that of a *turannos* in his identification of the *polis* with himself and his obsession with obedience, conspiracy, and money.[31] (Some interpreters have suggested that Sophokles has thus expressed an underlying criticism of Perikles' control over Athens, which technically was shared with the other elected officials, but in fact approached autocratic power.[32] In a famous passage of his *History of the Peloponnesian War* Thukydides describes Athens under Perikles as "in word a democracy but in deed rule by the first man" [2.65.10].) Kreon makes no attempt to engage in a serious discussion of Haimon's arguments. Instead he unleashes a series of *ad hominem* insults, culminating in the threat that Haimon will never marry Antigone while she lives (810 / 750), an ironic foreshadowing of the marriage-in-death that will in fact occur.

The scene begins and ends with fatal misunderstandings.[33] Although Haimon explicitly begins by putting his father ahead of his fiancée (684–85 / 637–38; cf. 801 / 741) and never appeals to the marriage as an argument for saving Antigone, Kreon, finally, can see his son only as Antigone's betrothed. Kreon's response escalates the violence to a new level. Taking an oath by Olympos, he orders his guards to lead Antigone out and kill her at once, "beside her bridegroom" (821 / 761). This cruel order, although not carried out, both provokes and foreshadows the couple's subsequent marriage-in-death.

Haimon begins with praise of his father's counsel and ends by accusing him of madness (824–25 / 765). It adds to the irony that he urges

---

31. On Kreon's concern with money as characteristic of the *turannos*, see Richard Seaford, "Tragic Money," *Journal of Hellenic Studies* 118 (1998), 132–34. For Kreon as *turannos*, see Winnington-Ingram, *Sophocles*, 126–27.

32. For this view and other aspects of Kreon's possible connections with Perikles, see Victor Ehrenberg, *Sophocles and Pericles* (Oxford, 1954), 95–98, 145–49.

33. For good comments on the misunderstandings in this scene, see David Scale, *Vision and Stagecraft in Sophocles* (Chicago, 1982), 97–98.

Kreon to yield in terms that are not wholly dissimilar from Kreon's own statements to Antigone about a stubborn will being broken (cf. 521–28 / 473–79 and 768–75 / 710–14). Haimon's nautical metaphors also hark back to Kreon's sententious posturing in his opening speech (cf. 775–77 / 715–17 and 212–13 / 189–90). But passion, not reason, now dominates, and no voice of calm and clarity will be heard again—until it is too late.

A scene that opened with broad generalizations about obedience and submission ends with wild threats whose meaning will be revealed only later. Sensitive to any questioning of his authority, Kreon misconstrues as a threat to his own person Haimon's promise that Antigone's death will kill someone else.[34] When Haimon exits, the Chorus comments, "The man has gone off quickly in his anger! The mind, at his age, can become weighed down by grief" (826–27 / 766–67), unknowingly fore-shadowing Haimon's probable meaning, suicide, for elsewhere in Sophokles the verb translated here as "he has gone," *bebêke*, often refers to death; and the mind "weighed down," or "heavy" or "resentful," foreshadows the ominous silent exit of Eurydike (1342 / 1256).[35] Kreon, however, remains impervious to criticism. Although he agrees to release Ismene, he continues with his intended execution of Antigone, and he ends with a cruel remark that "she'll learn at last what pointless waste of effort it is to worship what is down below with Hades" (840–42 / 779–80).

Eros is the subject of the immediately following ode. Eros is not "love" in our sense but the dangerous, irresistible, elemental force of passion. The ode stands at the midpoint of the play and sets the tone for the rest. The irrational forces of the previous ode, on the sufferings in the house of Oidipous, now become dominant. Begun as an ode sung by the Chorus, the Eros ode leads directly into a lengthy lyrical exchange (known as a *kommos*) between the Chorus and Antigone. This song echoes the play's opening exchange between Ismene and Antigone and, to a lesser extent, the debate between Kreon and Antigone, but it takes those previous exchanges to a new register of emotional intensity. Antigone now expresses the pathos of what it means to become "Hades' bride." She will leave this world unlamented by any friends or family (935–41 / 876–82)—exactly the fate that she has tried to prevent for Polyneikes at the cost of her life.

34. Haimon's threat at 811 / 751 is in fact left somewhat ambiguous, for at the end he does attack Kreon with his sword, presumably to kill him (1316–17 / 1232–34).
35. Cf. the similar ominous exit of Iokasta in *Oidipous Turannos*, 1073–75, and the similar phrasing in the account of Deianeira's death in *Trakhinian Women*, 813–14 and 874–75.

Still intimidated by Kreon, the Chorus offers only grudging and fleeting sympathy.[36] They cannot hold back their tears at the sight of the girl about to be led off to the cave to die, but they continue to identify themselves with the collective political consciousness of the city. In the one place where they acknowledge her "reverence," they contrast it with the "power" of the ruler, which must not be transgressed (931–34 / 872–75). Kreon, who probably reenters just as Antigone is finishing her lament, hardheartedly dismisses her mournful song as an attempt to delay the inevitable, and his brusque response deepens the pathos of her isolation (942–43 / 883–84). He sends her to her death satisfied that he is ritually "pure," that is, unpolluted by shedding the blood of kin; but the ending will show his failure to escape so easily from pollution.

Antigone's last speech, once more in the dialogue meter of iambic trimeter, is addressed to the cave/tomb/bridal chamber that she is about to enter. Cut off from the human world, she turns to her dead family members in Hades. She addresses Polyneikes three times, once by name (964 / 902) and twice by the untranslatable periphrasis, literally "head of my brother" (960–61 / 899, 978 / 915), a phrase that echoes her address to Ismene in her opening line and so serves as another measure of her present isolation from the living. She already looks back at her mortal existence from the perspective of death. Forgetting Ismene, she sees herself as the last of her family whom Persephone, queen of the dead, has received in the underworld (954–56 / 894–96).

In the context of her absorption into the world below, Antigone makes the famous assertion that she would not have sacrificed her life to bury a husband or a child but only a brother, for with her parents dead she can have no other siblings. This is the *nomos*, the "law" or "custom," she says, by which she dared to become a criminal in Kreon's eyes (976–79 / 913–15). This "law" seems very different from those eternal, god-given, unwritten laws on which she based her earlier defiance of Kreon (495–518 / 450–70). The apparent contradiction between the two statements has troubled interpreters, some of whom, following Goethe's romantic reading, would excise the lines as a later interpolation based on a similar line of argument in Herodotos.[37] But Antigone's two accounts of her

---

36. Some scholars have thought that Kreon is present on stage during this ode, but it seems to us unlikely that he is there during Antigone's lament, which follows directly upon the ode: see the Note on 838–42 / 777–80.

37. Herodotos, *Histories*, 3.119. Goethe objected that the passage was unworthy of Antigone's "noble motives ... and the elevated purity of her soul" and that it "disturbs the tragic tone and appears to me very far-fetched—to savor too much of dialectical calculation." He also says, "I would give a great deal for an apt philologist to prove that it is interpolated and spurious": *Conversations with Eckermann* (above, n. 5), 178 (March 28, 1827). Goethe has found many champions, and these

motives are complementary, not contradictory. Now she reveals that more personal, emotionally vulnerable side that she had already expressed in the preceding lyrical exchanges with the Chorus.[38]

That more intimate tone is also appropriate to her present situation. Not only is she on the verge of death, but she is addressing her dead kin, particularly her mother and brothers, whom she expects to join imminently in the underworld. In the poignancy of these last, reflective moments, she finally expresses her bitterness and sorrow at her loss of marriage and children. The speech obviously wins sympathy for her as the young victim of cruelty and injustice. In this loneliness and despair, she even questions the gods, who have thus let her die, when her "reverence has earned [her] charges of irreverence" (990–91 / 924), but she does not forget her anger as she asks the gods to make her enemies suffer no more, and no less, than they have made her suffer (992–96 / 925–28).

In this final moment when we see her alive, Antigone reveals again her capacity for hatred and steely determination alongside her softer side of devotion to the intimate bond of *philia* or family love. We recall the curses of other Sophoklean good in their last moments, notably Aias as he commits suicide.[39] Her curse, though uttered at her lowest ebb of despair, also looks ahead to the shift in the balance of power that will take place when the gods, through Teiresias, do in effect answer her plea for vengeance and justice. But evidently they will not act on behalf of the girl who has served them. Antigone leaves the stage, and the mortal world, with a final, hopeless appeal to the city and citizens of Thebes, once more singing in lyric meter to the Chorus (1005–11 / 937–43). Her isolation is total as she regards herself, again as if Ismene did not exist, as the only survivor of "the royal house" of Thebes (1008–9 / 941). At the end of her previous speech, in the dialogue meter of iambic trimeter, she looked to the gods for justice (992–96 / 925–28). Now she

---

lines have often been regarded as a later interpolation based on Herodotos. But, as Herodotos was working on his *History* in the late 440s, there is no serious chronology problem with his priority. See the Note on lines 967–79 / 905–15. The authenticity of the lines is also supported by the citation of part of the passage in Aristotle, *Rhetoric*, 3.1417a29–33. For a cogent defense of the authenticity of the lines see Knox, *Heroic Temper*, 104–7. Some authoritative contemporary scholars still regard them as spurious, e.g., Winnington-Ingram, *Sophocles*, 145, with n. 80.

38. On Antigone's more vulnerable and so sympathetic side in this scene and the preceding lament, see Winnington-Ingram, *Sophocles*, 138–46.

39. Sophokles, *Aias*, 835–44. Cf. also Oidipous' curse on his sons in *Oidipous at Kolonus*, 1370–96, and Polyphemus' curse on Odysseus, *Odyssey*, 9.528–35.

looks for sympathy to the human world that has punished her for her "pious impiety," her third use of such an expression and her last utterance in the play. Yet in all of her long lament she expresses sorrow but no regret and no weakening of resolve.

The following ode, the fourth stasimon, is one of the most complex and controversial in Sophokles. The Chorus continues to distance itself from Antigone, but its mythical exempla have a potential multiplicity of meanings that is appropriate at this critical moment in the action. All three of the myths the Chorus alludes to illustrate imprisonment and so can easily point to Antigone. Yet all three also have implications that extend to Kreon as well.

The enclosure of Danae in her tower of bronze seems clearly enough to refer to Antigone. Yet the moral drawn from it, the inevitable power of the gods, will also come to refer to Kreon, particularly as Danae's myth includes the destruction of the powerful older king, Akrisios, who imprisoned her.[40] The Chorus' next example, the Thracian king Lykourgos who persecutes Dionysos and is punished with a madness in which he kills his own son, has even stronger relevance to Kreon, whose anger and folly cause the death of his son. The third myth, a less familiar tale of jealousy between a wife and an ex-wife that results in the bloody blinding of two sons, evokes the sufferings of the house of Oidipous, but it also has implications for the doom that is about to overtake the house of Kreon, in which an angry, vengeful wife will wreak self-destruction with a bloody instrument. The Chorus, of course, does not know what is going to happen and does not understand the full implications of their mythical exempla. As often in Sophokles, and in the Greek tragedy generally, the Chorus members say more than they know; and the full meaning of their words appears only later, in retrospect.

The ode's closing reference to "the Fates, that live long ages" sets the tone for the entrance of the old blind prophet of Thebes, Teiresias, led on stage by a young boy or slave. After previous scenes with the Guard, Antigone, and Haimon, Kreon now meets a fourth challenge to his authority, but this time from an older rather than a younger man, and from the gods rather than from mortals. The prophet's opening address, "Lords of Thebes" (1050 / 988), like Antigone's last address to the leaders of Thebes (1008 / 940), in itself implies a less autocratic view of the city's government than Kreon had assumed, as he has been addressed earlier

---

40. For the death of Akrisios at the hands of Danae's son by Zeus, Perseus, see Apollodoros, *Library of Mythology*, 2.4.4.

as the single "lord" of the land (e.g., **254** / 223, **319** / 278).[41] Kreon responds to Teiresias, as before to the previous challenges, with angry and defensive accusations of bribery and conspiracy (cf. **321–59** / 280–314). Teiresias, however, is not Kreon's subordinate, but truly an authoritative spokesman for the divine order, and he replies to Kreon's insults with a prophet's foreknowledge, which takes even Kreon aback (**1133–72** / 1064–97). For the first time Kreon acknowledges weakness ("my mind is confused," **1179** / 1095), asks for advice, and submits to another's advice: "What must I do? Tell me! I will obey" (**1174** / 1099).

Even in yielding to the divine message, however, Kreon still gets his priorities wrong. The Chorus' advice is clear: first release Antigone, then bury the body (**1175–76** / 1100–1101). With a misplaced concern for the political rather than the personal and for the soldier rather than the girl, he attends to the corpse first. By the time he reaches Antigone, it is too late.[42]

Kreon exits with the promise to release Antigone: "I am afraid it's best to observe the established laws through all one's life, to the end" (**1189–90** / 1113–14). These "established laws" look back to the religious laws (or customs) pertaining to burial that Antigone had cited in her great speech of defiance (**495–501** / 450–55), and in Kreon's mouth the word "laws" now tacitly acknowledges her victory. Yet the phrase "to the end" is ominous and foreshadows the horror that is approaching. (In contrast to Antigone, who remains steadfast, Kreon is afraid and "gives way." True heroism, of the unbending Sophoklean type, rests with her, not with him.[43] Her last words are about piety, his about fear.)

The fifth stasimon, the sixth and last regular ode in the play, is a prayer to Dionysos for help and purification at this time of crisis for Thebes. Dionysos is a major divinity of Thebes, his birthplace; but the ode also

---

41. Kreon himself addresses the elders of the Chorus merely as "men," *andres*, whereas Antigone calls them "citizens of my native land" (**866** / 806), "men of the city, with all your possessions" (**902–3** / 843–44), and "you rulers of Thebes" (**1008** / 940). It may be that she does not want to address Kreon, from whom she can expect no sympathy, and wants to empower those whom she still has some hope of moving; but she also seems to envisage a government more broadly shared among the Thebans than Kreon's autocratic or tyrannical model.

42. Kreon's reply inverts the order of events but nevertheless suggests that he might in fact go first to Antigone while his attendants go to bury Polyneikes (**1183–90** / 1108–14). As we learn later, however, he accompanies his attendants first to Polyneikes' corpse and then goes to Antigone's cave (**1271–83** / 1196–1205). F.J.H. Letters, *The Life and Work of Sophocles* (London, 1953), 157–59, attempts to defend Kreon's choice on the grounds that Teiresias' prophecy has emphasized the importance of burying Polyneikes for the welfare of the city. But this view does not take account of the advice of the elders, who are equally concerned with the city, nor that part of Teiresias' prophecy that includes the burial alive of Antigone as part of the disruption of the relation between upper and lower worlds (**1133–44** / 1064–73).

43. See, in general, Knox, *Heroic Temper*, 62–75, 109–10.

invokes the god's broader association with Italy and Eleusis, associations that point to mystery cults that promise initiates happiness in the afterlife. The allusion to Dionysos' maenads, his frenzied female worshipers (1201–5 / 1126–30), also reminds us of the female emotions that Kreon has tried to suppress by violence and imprisonment. It is as if these Dionysiac figures, like the murderous wife of the previous ode, become nightmarish projections of the female "madness" that Kreon attributes to Antigone and Ismene (see 542–43 / 491–92; 612–13 / 561–65). In the myths about these maenads, such as that of Pentheus dramatized in Euripides' *Bakkhai*, the god's female followers eventually triumph over resistance from a king. The Chorus ends with a characteristically Dionysiac prayer for the god's epiphany, calling to him: "O You that lead the dance of the stars that breathe out fire, You that watch over the voices sounding in the night" (1218–20 / 1146–48). They thus point toward the powers of nature, the gods, and the world-order beyond human control.

In the play's first ode the Chorus invoked Dionysos primarily as the local god of Thebes, to be honored in the all-night choruses of the citizens' victory celebrations (171–73 / 152–54). But the Dionysos of the last ode reaches far beyond the city of Thebes. His all-night choruses consist not of Theban citizens but of the fiery stars in the heavens. The fire-bearing enemy Kapaneus, trying to scale Thebes' walls in the first ode, was compared to a bakkhant in the madness of his wild rush against the city (152–55 / 134–37); but the fiery bakkhantic madness of this last ode belongs to the god and will not be driven away from the city. The bright ray of the sun that heralded Thebes' salvation in that first ode is now answered by nocturnal dancers outside the city; and the whole city, far from enjoying victory (167 / 148) or salvation, is in the grip of a "sickness" that may cause its doom (1214–15 / 1140–41).[44]

Once Kreon acknowledges his mistake, events move rapidly. The answer to the Chorus' prayer for release from pollution is the Messenger's entrance with the news of a polluting death within Kreon's own house. Kreon is now in a state of living death (1238–40 / 1166–67), a fitting punishment for one who confused the relation between the living and his dead (cf. 1137–44 / 1068–73). At first the Messenger gives only the barest account of Haimon's suicide, until Eurydike, Kreon's wife, enters from the palace. Sophokles has carefully contrived this scene so that the Messenger makes his full report not to the Chorus but to Eurydike. He thus makes us witness the bloody violence in Antigone's cave through

---

44. The contrast between the first and last odes is also suggested by the earlier joyful invocation to "Nike, the goddess of victory, with great name and glory" (167 / 148), in a mood very different from the desperate invocation to Dionysos here as the "god of many names" (1191 / 1115).

the eyes of the mother and wife who will soon become the instrument of completing Kreon's tragedy.

The Messenger's narrative is one of the most powerful in Greek tragedy, and it vividly brings before us the ruin of Kreon's house. Having buried Polyneikes first, Kreon and his attendants approach Antigone's cave. He enters and finds her dead and Haimon in a frenzy. Now in the role of supplicant (1313 / 1230), not an all-commanding father, Kreon begs his son to leave the cave; but the boy, looking "wildly at him with fierce eyes," spits in his face, lunges at him with drawn sword, and, after he misses, stabs himself. He then falls in a dying embrace on Antigone's lifeless body, matching, as bridegroom, her role as a bride of death itself (1317–23 / 1234–39).

Antigone's defiance of Kreon is now fulfilled in Haimon's, and it is a defiance that utterly undoes Kreon's authority over his son, over Antigone, and over his city. Kreon prided himself on his patriarchal authority, his good sense, his rational approach to life, and his superiority to women. Haimon overturns all these principles. He rejects the father for the promised bride, surrenders to the wild passions surrounding love and death, and chooses the cave's Hades-like prison of a condemned woman over the *polis*-world where he should succeed his father in ruling the city. The two houses, Kreon's and Antigone's, are joined together by a fearful marriage-in-death; and it is as if with that union Antigone, the heiress, transfers to the house of Kreon all the pollutions in the house of Oidipous: the suicide of the mother, the death of two sons, and the fulfillment of a terrible prophecy.[45]

The Messenger concludes with a generalization about the dangers of foolish behavior, but Eurydike makes no reply. She slips away in silence, like "Iokaste" in *Oidipous Turannos*, and it is a silence that strikes both the Messenger and the Chorus as ominous. But before they can absorb its meaning, Kreon enters with the body of Haimon, either actually in his arms, as the Chorus says (1344 / 1258), or on a bier or wagon that Kreon accompanies with his arms around his dead son. It is a mournful tableau, and the contrast with Kreon's first entrance is shocking. Instead of making authoritative civic pronouncements in the proud bearing of a victorious ruler, he utters cries of lament and misery. Instead of generalizations about statecraft he sings a funeral dirge, the traditional task of women, punctuated by sharp cries of grief, indicated in the Greek text by *aiai aiai, oimoi,* or *pheu pheu* (1354 / 1267, 1358 / 1271, 1362 / 1276). This is

---

45. On hearing the cry from the cave Kreon had exclaimed, "Am I a seer?" (1291 / 1212; cf. 1252 / 1178).

also the first time in the play that he sings extensive lyrical passages, accompanied by the *aulos*, the double wind instrument (probably with a reed, like a clarinet or oboe) that was felt by the Greeks of Sophokles' era to be particularly emotional.[46] This change of musical and emotional registers marks his shift from absolute power to total helplessness, and he continues to sing in lyrics to the end of the play.

More suffering lies in store. The Messenger returns from the royal house to announce the death of Eurydike. The manner of her end intensifies Kreon's pain, for she has killed herself in a particularly horrible way, stabbing herself at the household altar in the courtyard, cursing her husband as the killer of both his sons—Haimon and an elder son who died earlier, here called Megareus, who is left obscure but is possibly to be identified with the Menoikeus of Euripides' *Phoinikian Women*, who leaps from the walls of Thebes to fulfill a prophecy that only the voluntary death of a descendant of Thebes' autochthonous inhabitants could save the city.[47]

Eurydike's curse turns the two generative roles in the house, maternity and paternity, toward death, the appropriate punishment of one who has interfered with the basic ties of family in Antigone's house. The Messenger calls her *pammêtôr nekrou*, literally "the all-mother" of the corpse, the mother in the fullest sense of the word ("mother absolute," at 1368 / 1282).

Also, Eurydike's final, suicidal lament recalls the cries of Antigone over the body of Polyneikes at the moment when she was caught, and in fact Sophokles uses the same verb of both women's cries (468 / 423, 1389 / 1302). Again like Antigone, Eurydike combines lament with curse (473 / 427 and 1391–92 / 1304–5). The close verbal parallels bring Kreon's suffering into direct causal connection with his actions in a way that is expressive of the retributive justice that the Greeks call *dikê*. Taking full responsibility for the deaths that he has caused, Kreon now sees himself as "no more than nothing" (1408 / 1325). The man who spoke in metaphors of keeping things straight and upright now finds his whole world awry: he says, "everything is twisted in my hands" (1425–26 / 1342).

---

46. Prior to this passage, Kreon has only two short anapestic exchanges with the Chorus about sending Antigone into the cave (999–1000 / 931–32, 1003–4 / 935–36); otherwise, he speaks only in iambic trimeters.

47. See Griffith's note on 1302–3 and our Note on 1387–92 / 1301–5. Eurydike's accusatory epithet for Kreon, "killer of sons," may refer only to the death of Haimon, but the passage can also be read as implying that Eurydike holds Kreon responsible for the deaths of both sons.

MYTHS AND ODES

The six odes of the play are among the most poetically elaborate of those in the extant Sophokles and provide a commentary parallel to the main action on the ambiguities of Kreon's controlling power and the atmosphere of doom surrounding Antigone.[48] The parodos, as we have noted, celebrates the city's victory over its enemies and so sets the stage for Kreon's entrance. Yet its Dionysiac language and the all-night civic choruses return with very different meanings in the last ode, when something of the emotional violence and frenzy that also belong to Dionysos make their appearance.

The first stasimon, sometimes called the Ode on Man, is one of the most famous passages of all Greek literature (377–416 / 332–75).[49] Its triumphant list of the achievements of human civilization is often read as a hymn to the confidence, humanism, and rationalism of the Periklean Age, which saw so many advances in the arts and sciences. Yet the opening words, "At many things—wonders, terrors—we feel awe, but at nothing more than at man," are deeply ambiguous, as the translation of the word *deinon* implies, for *deinon* means "wonderful" but also "fearful," "strange," "terrible," "uncanny." Antigone uses it, for example, of the "terrible" suffering that she is ready to undergo for defying Kreon (114 / 96) and the Guard of the "terrible" things he fears from Kreon (278 / 243). The ode's opening, furthermore, echoes the beginning of a famous ode of Aiskhylos' *Libation Bearers* on the destructive passions and crimes of evil women (*Libation Bearers* 585ff.).

It is tempting to associate with Kreon the Ode on Man's attitude of proud, rationalistic domination of the world. Yet both he and Antigone, in different ways, embody the quality of the "wonderful/terrible" with which the ode begins; and both protagonists ambiguously shift between being "high in his city" and "outside any city" (412–13 / 370). Many of the items listed as the proud achievements of humanity return later with their meaning reversed. The human conquest of earth, sea, and the birds of the skies returns later as a human failure to control. The conquest of disease, for example, comes back ominously in the disease of pollution with which Kreon's acts afflict the city (1079 / 1015; cf. 1215 / 1141 and 467 / 421). The juxtaposition of "inventive" (literally "all-devising") and "without invention" or "device" 401–2 / 360 points to the paradoxical collocation of the human strength and weakness enacted by both protagonists. The qualification of human power in the next line, "Only

---

48. For the place of the odes in the rhythm of the action, see my *Tragedy and Civilization*, 197–206.
49. For further discussion and references, see my *Tragedy and Civilization*, 152–54.

from Hades will he not procure some means of escape" (403–5 / 361–62), looms large in a play so much concerned with the underworld and the ways in which the dead destroy the lives of the living. Kreon's tragedy in particular follows a trajectory from his confident assertion of authority over love and marriage ("It's Hades who will stop this wedding for me," 626 / 575) to his miserable cry that his house is a "harbor of Hades" whose pollution he cannot cleanse (1371 / 1284). The ode's insistence on human cleverness and intellect contrasts, of course, with the bad judgment of the ensuing action. In their closing lyrics, the members of the Chorus blame the absence of "good sense" for the tragic outcome (1427 / 1348, 1431 / 1353).

The taming of "Gaia, the Earth, forever undestroyed and unwearying, highest of all the gods" (382–83 / 337–39) by agriculture comes early in the ode, paired with the conquest of the sea. However, it is not Earth as highest but as it is associated with both the realm of the dead below and with the dust of burial that determines the course of the tragedy. When Antigone is apprehended performing burial rites for Polyneikes' body, a mysterious whirlwind, as the Guard describes it, lifts the dust from the earth as a "storm of trouble high as heaven," which "filled up the whole huge sky," so that those watching the body suffer a "supernatural plague" (462–67 / 415–21), as if some divine power were inverting upper and lower realms. The next ode describes the murderous curse in the house of Oidipous in the bold metaphor of the "blood-red dust of the gods under the earth" (if we can trust the manuscript text) reaching up to "reap" "the last rootstock of the House of Oidipous" (647–50 / 599–602). This second stasimon begins by associating the dark sand stirred from the depths by violent storms at sea with the doom of the house of Oidipous (633–44 / 582–95) and then contrasts that submarine turbulence with the immutable radiance of Zeus high above on Olympus (651–57 / 604–10). At the peripeteia or reversal, Teiresias traces the spread of pollution to Kreon's inversion of what belongs above and below the earth (1133–48 / 1064–76).[50]

In fact, the mood of this second stasimon is virtually the reverse of that of the first stasimon. The Ode on Man begins with the conquest of the sea; but the second stasimon, as we have noted, uses the sea as a metaphor for exactly the opposite meaning, associating the dark, stormy Thracian sea with the irrational sufferings that have afflicted Antigone's family. Taking the afflictions of the ancient house of Oidipous as its paradigm, this ode dwells on the irrational aspects of mortal life. Its tone

---

50. For the upper/lower axis in the play, see my *Tragedy and Civilization*, 170–73, 178–79.

proves justified, for the Chorus immediately introduces Haimon (673–77 / 626–30), who is now the bearer of the uncontrollable passions in Kreon's own house.

From this point on, the odes run parallel to the increasing emotional and physical violence of the action. The third stasimon (fourth ode), on the invincible power of Eros, forms the transition between the fatal quarrel of Haimon and Kreon and Antigone's final lament with the Chorus. It thus joins the two destructive forces operating in the background, Eros and Hades, love and death. The complex fourth stasimon (fifth ode), as we have already noted, narrates myths of passion and violence that are applicable, in different degrees, to both protagonists. Finally, the Dionysiac themes of the last ode, suggesting a possible fusion between the city and the natural world, are different from the views of both the parodos (the first ode, on Thebes' victory) and the Ode on Man. Dionysos' maddened female worshipers here (1222–24 / 1150–52) also anticipate the release of dangerous female passion in the play's closing movement, the suicides of both Antigone and Eurydike.

If Kreon implies that he sees the sisters as something like maenads, maddened or running wild (see 542–43 / 491–92 and 630 / 579), Antigone on the contrary sees herself as a bride of Hades, that is, as Kore, the Maiden, who is also called Persephone, carried off to the underworld.[51] Young women who die before marriage are conventionally regarded as "marrying" Hades. For Antigone, however, the motif of wedding Hades is part of a dense network of associations. She will not just wed Hades figuratively, for by the manner of her death she will actually go underground, entering Hades while alive. And there in fact a marriage of sorts will be enacted in Haimon's bloody embrace of her corpse as he dies from his self-inflicted wound. Her death as a bride of Hades makes horribly literal what is only a convention of speaking. She is being sent to her Hades-like cave, moreover, because she has valued the dead and their gods above her life on earth; and, as we have observed, she is vindicated by Teiresias' accusation of Kreon's interference with the relation between upper and lower worlds.

As a bride of Hades, Antigone is a Persephone carried off violently by the god of the lower world. Yet she is a Persephone who will remain unmarried and will never return to the upper world in the seasonal

---

51. For the role of Persephone and Demeter in the mythical background of the play, see my *Tragedy and Civilization*, 179–81. For the fusion of marriage and death in tragedy, see Richard Seaford, "The Tragic Wedding," *Journal of Hellenic Studies* 107 (1987), 106–30; Gail Holst-Wahrhaft, *Dangerous Voices: Women's Laments and Greek Literature* (London and New York, 1992), 41–42; Rush Rehm, *Marriage to Death* (Princeton, 1994), especially 59–71.

alternations of winter and spring that are essential to the Demeter–Persephone myth, as told in the *Homeric Hymn to Demeter*. "Go send the girl (*korê*) up from her deep-dug house," the Chorus advises Kreon when he finally gives in to Teiresias (1175–76 / 1100–1101). Their word, "send up," evokes the motif of Persephone's ascent when Hades must return her to Demeter with the return of the earth's fertility in the spring.[52] Yet the Kore/Persephone that Antigone envisages is a goddess of death, not of renewed life, she who "has received [Antigone's] dead among the shades" (954–55 / 893–94).

Antigone's role as an unrisen Persephone parallels that of Haimon as the young man who dies "out of season," *aôros*, a term that is used of youths who will not make the transition between the bloom of adolescence and adulthood but will die before their time. In this respect the two suicides are symmetrical in their perversion of the normal pattern of life-generating marriage. Antigone remains too close to her house of origin. Instead of going to the house of the bridegroom—the usual pattern of patrilocal marriage in classical Athens—she goes to the Hades that holds her parents and brother. She thereby reenacts the introverted kin ties characteristic of the house of Oidipous.[53] Marrying Hades, staying in her house of origin, and being the child of an incestuous marriage are all in a way equivalent aspects of Antigone's tragic situation, her sacrifice of the normal progression to womanhood to the bonds of family and to devotion to the dead. The incest of her parents is the inverse of her nonmarriage, but it belongs to a similar failure of "normal" family life. The excessive closeness of incest (same staying with same) short-circuits the union of same and other in normal marriage and so parallels Antigone's refusal to separate herself from her natal family in a union with a bridegroom of another house. Haimon, analogously, undoes all the expectations of the groom. He not only goes to his bride's "house" (instead of bringing her to his) but also attacks his father (recalling Oidipous' patricide) and then consummates the marriage in an act of reverse penetration that leads to the spilling of his blood, like the maiden's, instead of seed.

52. In the Homeric *Hymn to Demeter* the verb "send up" describes Demeter's allowing the grain to grow on earth (lines 307, 332, 471).
53. For the way in which the house of Oidipous is characteristic of a Theban pattern of introverted family ties, see Froma I. Zeitlin, "Thebes: Theater of Self and Society in Athenian Drama," in J. J. Winkler and F. I. Zeitlin, eds., *Nothing to Do with Dionysus?* (Princeton, 1990), 130–67, especially 150–52.

In Antigone's long lyrical lament as she prepares to enter the cave, she looks to another female model from the realm of myth, Niobe, the grieving mother who weeps incessantly for her lost children and is turned into a rock from which streams of water flow perpetually (883–93 / 823–33). The Chorus objects that Niobe is a god and Antigone a mere mortal, and in response Antigone feels pain at what she takes to be mockery (899ff. / 839ff.). There is irony, too, in the fact that Niobe is the mother of many children, Antigone of none. Yet Antigone can identify with the eternity of lament into which this *mater dolorosa* is frozen forever. Both the eternity and the stony end speak to her condition. The image of Niobe is also a negation of the fruitful aspect of the mother figure in the Demeter-Persephone myth. It evokes Demeter's role as a mother of sorrows, lamenting her lost daughter, Persephone, as she wanders over the earth in her desperate search for the abducted girl. This is also the aspect of Demeter that applies to the other mother figure in the play, Kreon's wife, Eurydike, whose name, literally "of broad justice," or "wide-ruling," is also an epithet for the queen of the dead. As the "all-mother" of the dead Haimon, as we have noted, she is associated with grieving maternity. Antigone, doomed to die childless, is also drawn into the model of the grieving mother when she laments over the body of Polyneikes like a mother-bird that finds her nest emptied of fledglings (469–71 / 423–25). The simile of grieving motherhood once more points to the unfulfilled life of this bride of Hades. She is a Persephone who will not ascend and a sorrowing Demeter/Niobe who will always lament.

The images of the mother in this play, in fact, are all of the mourning, dying, or murderous mother, not the fertile mother. This is true even of the fourth stasimon's myth of Danae, imprisoned like Antigone and "made to exchange the light of the sky for a dark room bolted with bronze" (1012–14 / 944–47). She will, of course, be impregnated by Zeus' golden shower and bear his son, Perseus (1017–18 / 950), but the ode dwells rather on her imprisonment and on the ineluctable doom given her by the Fates or Moirai (1018–20 / 951–53). The final strophe of the ode tells the story of another imprisoned mother and centers on the blinding of her two sons by the jealous stepmother. And in the background is Iokaste, who "violently disfigured her own life" by suicide (67–68 / 53–54) but by whom Antigone feels loved and whom she hopes to see soon in the underworld (960 / 898).

Of the six formal odes, only the first stasimon, the Ode on Man, seems to have no immediate connection with the events enacted on stage. Yet on further reflection it has profound implications for the meaning of the play as an interpretation of the human condition.[54] The ode's celebration of the confident domination of nature by human intelligence and technology is undercut by the themes of the subsequent odes and by the subsequent actions. Sophokles' contemporaries might well read this contrast as a critique of the human-centered rationalism of Athens' Periklean Age. The achievements of this extraordinary period include the high classical art and architecture that extol the human form (especially the male body) as the standard of beauty and a rationalistic view of religion, law, medicine, history, language, and the founding of cities, and so on, as creations of human intelligence and progress, not gifts of the gods. Influential here are the theories of the Sophists, such as Protagoras or Hippias, and of scientists and philosophers, such as Anaxagoras, Parmenides, or the atomist Leukippos, and of medical writers such as Hippokrates.

While it would be simplistic to identify this spirit of scientific inquiry with Kreon, the play does insist on his materialism and shallow rationalism. In the face of events that might have a supernatural cause, like the initial burial of Polyneikes, where there are no signs of human or animal presence (284–94 / 249–58), or Teiresias' announcement of widespread pollution, Kreon's first response is an accusation of bribery and conspiracy. Men, he assumes, always act for "profit," one of his favorite words. But in Antigone, as later in Haimon and Teiresias, he encounters motives that cannot be reduced to material gain or to his mode of reasoning. Antigone dismisses all calculation of personal advantage, including life itself. "If I die before my time," she says in her speech of defiance to Kreon, "I count that as my profit" (508–10 / 461–62). Until he finally backs down in the face of Teiresias' prophecy, Kreon assumes that he understands the ways of the gods and that their values coincide with his. Hence his anger and scorn at the Chorus' suggestion that the gods might have buried Polyneikes (319–20 / 278–79), a possibility that the play in fact leaves open.[55] Such, too, is his confidence in the narrow

---

54. For further discussion, see my "Sophocles' Praise of Man and the Conflicts of *Antigone*," in my *Interpreting Greek Tragedy* (Ithaca, N.Y., 1986), 137–61. Noteworthy is Martin Heidegger's celebrated existentialist interpretation of the ode as a reflection on the mysterious and "uncanny" nature of our humanness, which makes us both violent and creative, both citiless outcasts and all-powerful conquerors of a world that, nevertheless, eludes and defeats us as we are "tossed back and forth between structure and the structureless," between order and the ultimate nothingness of death: Martin Heidegger, *An Introduction to Metaphysics*, trans. Ralph Manheim (New Haven, 1959), 146–65, conveniently accessible in Thomas Woodard, ed., *Sophocles: A Collection of Critical Essays* (Englewood Cliffs, N.J., 1966), 86–100. The quotation is on 97. See also Steiner, *Antigones*, 174–77.
55. On the much discussed question of the so-called double burial, see H. D. F. Kitto, *Form and Meaning in Drama* (London, 1956), 138–44, 152–54, and my *Tragedy and Civilization*, 159, with the references cited in n. 25, 442–43. In favor of possible divine intervention are the absence of any marks

legalism of putting Antigone to death in a manner that avoids pollution to the city (in contrast to his original threat of punishment by public stoning, 46–47 / 36), his bold assertions of what can and cannot bring pollution, and his use of death or Hades as an instrument of political control.

All these views turn on him with terrible consequences. The Ode on Man warns that death is the one thing that humankind's technological progress cannot overcome. The marriage that Kreon thinks Hades will stop (626 / 575) takes place in the Hades-like cave, from which comes the final wave of death and pollution that submerges Kreon's life. The association of Eurydike's name with the underworld, noted earlier, further suggests that death and Hades, far from being something that Kreon can inflict on others, are already deep within his own house. The Ode on Man suggestively links Kreon's attitude of domination and control with a larger worldview in which nature is an inert resource to be exploited by human technology. The ode's description of yoking the horse, for example, echoes Kreon's metaphor of the yoke for power over the Thebans (336 / 291–92). His first response to Antigone's speech of defiance is also a metaphor of tempering iron by fire and taming horses with the bit (521–28 / 473–79). When Haimon offers alternative images of trees by a flooding river that bend with the current or ships that slacken sails in high winds instead of fighting the winds (768–77 / 710–17), Kreon responds with anger at being chastised by a younger man (786–87 / 726–27).

The sharpest opposition comes, of course, from Antigone, who values the invisible world of the dead over the surface, material world that Kreon would dominate as the plow of the Ode on Man wears down the surface of the inexhaustible earth and renders it serviceable for

of human agency, the fact that the first watch of the day (288 / 253) finds the body while Ismene and Antigone are still speaking in "this very night" (21 / 16), and Antigone's return to bury the body on the occasion when she is caught, even though the first "burial" would suffice for the funerary ritual (290–93 / 255–56). On the other hand, interpreters have argued that Antigone's response when she sees the body uncovered and her curses on those who have uncovered it (468–73 / 423–28) imply her having performed the initial burial: see Winnington-Ingram, *Sophocles*, 125, with n. 31. Yet Sophokles' language even here is vague enough to leave open other possibilities. In any case, the gods seem to be working through Antigone, even if they do not intervene directly, and the play offers a double perspective on the events in the contrast between the mysterious details in the background and Kreon's insistence on what is visible and tangible: so Seale, *Vision and Stagecraft*, 87–91. Kitto, 154, suggests that the gods and Antigone "are working on parallel paths." Analogously, Ruth Scodel, *Sophocles* (Boston, 1984), 55–56, suggests that the gods may not directly intervene in either burial but help Antigone's success in performing the rites on both occasions. In any case, the Chorus' explicit suggestion of divine intervention (319–20 / 278–79) is particularly important, for it strongly signals the possibility of divine interaction. It suffices for the play that the possibility is raised and has some plausibility, even if the play offers no definitive answer.

humankind. Kreon translates his political and legal conflict with her into a conflict of genders, male versus female. He may be reflecting some of the anxieties of Greek males about strong women's assertion of power; but he also reflects a deeper polarization of worldviews.[56] Where Kreon stresses differentiation by political allegiance, Antigone stresses the unifying bonds of kinship, notably in her famous exchange of 562–76 / 511–25. Where he insists on the political labels of "friend" or "enemy" as the defining terms, Antigone insists that both her brothers have an equal right to burial under "Hades' laws," and asserts, "My nature's not to join in hate but to join in love" (574 / 523).[57]

In comparing herself to Niobe, as we have seen, Antigone conveys her image of eternal devotion to family, lament for dead kin, and funerary ritual. But her comparison also suggests a dissolution of the barrier between the human form and the natural world. Niobe is a grieving mother whose body has now become an ivy-covered mountain from which the waters flow as tears would flow down a human face. In Antigone's insistence on the sanctity of death, she also affirms, indirectly, the sanctity of life and the value of those bonds within the family that derive from generation and blood kinship, not political and legal institutions.[58] Yet if Kreon forgets that the civic institutions also rest on smaller, more intimate units like the family, Antigone equally forgets that the family is also part of the city. That the ties within her own family are so fraught with the double pollutions of incest and fratricidal self-slaughter is one of the play's deep tragic ironies. Her convoluted family ties, as the second stasimon, on the house of Oidipous, indicates, belong to what is dark, mysterious, and irrational in human life. The Chorus' first two odes celebrate, respectively, the victory of the city over wild, bakkhantic aggression and of human intelligence over the physical and animal world. But the play ends with the darker vision of catastrophe

---

56. On the male-female conflicts in the play, see my *Tragedy and Civilization*, 183–86. Helene P. Foley, "Antigone as Moral Agent," in Michael S. Silk, ed., *Tragedy and the Tragic* (Oxford, 1996), 49–73, drawing in part on the work of Carol Gilligan, suggests that the two protagonists represent contrasting notions of moral responsibility; she contends that Antigone thinks in terms of specific and personal contexts, involving "care and responsibility," whereas Kreon operates with more abstract and impartial notions of rights and justice (64). See, however, the critique by Michael Trapp, ibid., 74–84, and Mark Griffith, "Antigone and her Sister(s): Embodying Women in Greek Tragedy," in André Lardinois and Laura McClure, eds., *Making Silence Speak: Women's Voices in Greek Literature and Society* (Princeton, 2001), 117–36, especially 126–35, on the range and fluidity of the female voice in tragedy and the problems of constructing a model of "female" behavior or language.

57. See the Note on 574 / 523.

58. Steiner, *Antigones*, 287, remarks of the play, "No poet or thinker, I believe, has found a greater, a more comprehensive statement of the 'crime against life.' "

unleashed by the uncontrollable passions of grief and love, bad judgment, and irreverence.

The final lines on good sense, piety, cautious speech, and learning wisdom by great suffering in old age offer little comfort. Kreon's old age is the bleakest possible; but the tragedy has also afflicted the young, the new generation of the two houses, who come together only for violent death, whether at the gates of Thebes, as do Polyneikes and Eteokles, or in the Hades-like cave of perverted union, as do Haimon and Antigone. Ismene, of course, is still alive, but she has not been mentioned for some six hundred lines (since 830–31 / 770–71), and her survival hardly counts.

The Chorus' closing advice, far from offering consolation, implies a world hedged about by dangers and limits, a world that is far removed from the triumphant domination of nature in the Ode on Man. The Hades that seemed only a secondary qualification or an afterthought in the Ode on Man is now frighteningly near, and the "gleaming marble heights" of Olympos, where Zeus rules in his timeless power, hopelessly remote (651–57 / 604–10).[59]

To return to Hegel, the play does not show any synthesis of two antithetical positions, but it does reveal the terrible wholeness of a reality of which Kreon and Antigone separately perceive only a part. Each ignores the modicum of truth that the other's worldview might hold. And yet Antigone has a reverence for the hidden powers of the divine world that Kreon increasingly flouts, carried away as he is by the arrogance of his human power, until his open defiance of the spokesman of the divine order provokes the curse that seals his punishment. Indeed, Antigone speaks of the gods more than does any other character in the play.[60] Unshaken in her convictions, she is cast in the mold of the true Sophoklean hero. Kreon, when we see him last, is a broken man. The emptiness that surrounds him at the end contrasts with the spiritual fullness of Antigone's death, lonely and despairing as it is.[61] It is interesting to compare his cries of utter misery at the end with those of Oidipous in the Oidipous Turannos, written a decade or so later. Oidipous gives voice to similar utterances of despair and misery at the moment of tragic reversal, but these are not his final words. His play,

---

59. The "weariless passing of the months" (653–54 / 607), or more literally, "the untiring months" (*akamatoi mênes*) associated with these remote, eternal gods, may evoke Earth the "unwearying" (*akamatan*) of the Ode on Man (383 / 339). The succession of the months is beyond human control and thus a sign of the ultimate human frailty rather than human power. See also the similar description of the Olympian realm in the second stasimon of Oidipous Turannos (863–72).

60. See Budelmann, *Language of Sophocles*, 175–79.

61. See Karl Reinhardt, *Sophocles* (1947), trans. H. and D. Harvey (Oxford, 1979), 93.

unlike Kreon's, continues for another 300 verses, in which he discovers a new kind of strength and a new kind of heroism. No such discovery awaits Kreon.[62]

The ending justifies Antigone, but too late to save her life; it brings learning to Kreon but too late to protect him from the polluted "Harbor of Hades" into which he has fallen. "Good sense is the first principle of happiness," the Chorus moralizes as it moves toward closure (1427–28 / 1347–48). But whatever "good sense" Kreon has learned "in old age," in the play's final lines, contains no trace of happiness, only the dazed, barren, and lonely old age into which we see him frozen as his attendants lead him offstage.

CHARLES SEGAL

---

62. Compare especially 1403–26 / 1317–46 with *Oidipous Turannos* 1307–68. For further discussion, see my *Oedipus Tyrannus: Tragic Heroism and the Limits of Knowledge*, 132–33.

ON THE TRANSLATION

Some nuances of the text of *Antigone*, as of every Greek tragedy, must have been thrown into view by performance, especially since this was so stylized—the language markedly different from speech, many passages chanted or sung to accompanying music and dance, the dialogue exchanges punctuated by commentary within the play itself in the form of the choral odes. And the actors' masks would have shifted all facial expressiveness to the voice and body. The very artificiality of ancient performance could not help calling attention to the language itself rather than to action or the apparent personalities of the characters (something in which we take more interest than did the ancient Greek poets, for whom the play was an exploration not so much of character as of ultimate questions of human fate and freedom). We do not know how ancient audiences reacted to the theatrical convention of actors changing roles, yet surely the stagecraft would have had some effect on the audience's sense of the language they were hearing. For example, how could one not listen very keenly to such remarkably staged moments as the beginning?—when, as George Steiner concisely describes it, "the masked male actor who impersonates Antigone addresses the masked male actor who impersonates Ismene" (206). Then it is very probably the actor who plays Antigone who also returns as her betrothed, Haimon— and then as Teiresias, and then as Haimon's mother, Eurydike! This *actor*'s changing of roles *enacts* a striking idea: that each *character* who in vain challenges Kreon brings back on stage the futile challenges of the others. This theatrical practice is scarcely ever repeated today, nor, on the page, is there any way to "translate" the effect of that actor appearing in different roles, or of the actor playing Ismene returning as the Guard and the Messenger. Or to "translate" the strange stubbornness of role of the one actor who plays only the stubborn Kreon: he remains on stage for most of the play, while the other figures appear and disappear around him. (The Greek text includes no stage directions, but in this translation we provide them to give the reader our conjectures about what is likely to be happening on stage.)

LANGUAGE AS AN ELEMENT OF STRUCTURE

Antigone opens after the slaughter and fright of war have come to the very gates of Thebes but have been kept outside. The heroine's two brothers have already killed each other, one heroically defending their native Thebes, the other cruelly attacking it. These life-and-death bodily conflicts are an emblem of the intense conflicts of words and beliefs with which the play begins and continues—which is only to say that *Antigone* (like all Greek tragedy) includes much argument, and that the argument arises from, and leads to more of, an inordinate amount of dying and death and suicide. Warfare has left rotting bodies outside the city walls, and then come the suicides of three of the six main characters of the play—Antigone, Haimon, and Haimon's mother Eurydike. (Still alive but offstage at the conclusion are Ismene, of whom we see nothing in nearly the last two-thirds of the play, and Teiresias, the seer; on stage at the end is Kreon, whose self-satisfaction in his rule and whose emotional investments in life have been utterly destroyed.)

Returning again and again to dire confrontations and conflict, and to descriptions of appalling acts, the play repeatedly returns also to certain ideas and words. Some of the individual words themselves are sites of struggle between the new ruler Kreon and his series of antagonists, as he and they fight from opposite points of view to control the meaning of the language they use. For instance, Kreon and Antigone argue over who can properly be called "friend" and who "enemy," over what is just and honorable and reverent, and what is unjust and dishonorable and irreverent. Sometimes the characters launch competing words at each other, so that, for example (in the words of Mark Griffith):

> [W]e can trace an implicit struggle for validation between the calculating "intelligence," "counsel," and "thought"...recommended by Kreon and other (male) characters, as against Antigone's intuitive "knowledge" and "certainty"...and among the male characters, we may contrast Kreon's emphasis on "calculation" and rigid "straightness" with Haimon's and Teiresias' recommending of "learning" and "bending." (42)

(I have translated the Greek word here represented by "bending" as "yielding" and also "giving way.")

The play is not a long text, and its diction is repetitive, so as Sophokles draws out the complexity of meaning in attitudes, beliefs, and words, many of the associations and connotations around each key Greek word are eventually brought to light, sometimes with grim and sorrowful tragic irony. The structural effect of such language is of a highly deliberate wovenness (a favorite ancient metaphor for poetry) that is both intellectually beautiful and artistically effective; to achieve an analogous effect in translation, the translator can try to repeat an English word to match the repetitions of a particular Greek word. For example: "You'd do well as the single ruler of some deserted place," Haimon bitterly tells his father (799 / 739), using the same word (erêmos) that Sophokles will just afterward give to Kreon, both when he plans to "lead [Antigone] out to some deserted place" (833 / 773) and when he specifically orders her to die "alone, deserted" (946 / 887); finally Sophokles gives the word to Antigone herself, who laments that she has been "deserted by those close" to her (984 / 919).

However, working against the translator is the dispiriting historical fact that any particular word in contemporary English has its own associations and connotations that have nothing whatever to do with the Greek ones, but instead are the traces of centuries of use in other times and cultures, and of our own particular, present-day linguistic environment. The word that is repeated several times in Greek, turned by Sophokles this way and that to reveal the nuances and implications of its use in different phrases and circumstances, is necessarily represented by a word in English without those nuances and implications and with a number of new implications that are irrelevant. However, there is no other way but repetition—when this is possible without forcing English to be unidiomatic—to signal Sophokles' method of bringing words back in new contexts to show which underlying ideas are relevant to a moment of struggle between characters. Fundamentally, the repeated words structure the play both in that weaving way I mentioned earlier and also in setting out the binary oppositions between which Sophokles dramatizes a conflict of belief, feeling, and real power. (For example, when Kreon utters with contempt the word "woman," an ideological axis of the play comes immediately into view.)

Standing on the shoulders of Charles Segal and the scholarly editions of Antigone, I offer below just a few key words with some of their connotations and associations in Greek—on which I myself am far from being an authority.

(1) It turns out to be impossible to echo consistently in English the repetitions of the several words derived from or related to Greek philos. "Loved," "beloved," "those close to us," and so on, are among the

different articulations of this idea in English that I have used for the same word in Greek, because no one word in English is adequate. As Griffith notes, "Given the wide semantic field occupied by *philos*—covering 'family member,' 'loved one,' 'friend,' 'ally,' even 'one's own' (limbs, etc.), and extending even further with the usage of [related words]—contradictions constantly arise, as members of the same family or political group (= *philoi*, by definition) become 'hateful/hostile' to one another as a result of their behavior" (40–41). Kreon even uses a derivative of *philos*, translated as "money-loving," when accusing Teiresias of greed (see point 5, below). And to Kreon—whose character Sophokles convincingly portrayed, even if character as such was not foremost among the poet's interests—a form of *philos* can quickly suggest its opposite: hatred and the enemy.

(2) The famously untranslatable first line of the play uses three of the often repeated key words of the play: *koinos*, meaning what is shared in common; *autadelphon*, a word for sister or brother that includes as prefix the root word *autos*, meaning "self"; and *kara*, a noun meaning "head," but used idiomatically as an elevated periphrasis expressing endearment and emotional involvement. Every use of the word "self" in the translation—such as "self-killing," "self-will," "he himself," and so on—echoes Sophokles' use of some form of *autos* in the Greek, as I tried to represent Sophokles' restless inquiry into how much of suffering is brought on oneself by one's own decisions, as opposed to how much is ordained by the gods. In this translation, *koinos* is represented by the words "shared" and "common" singly or together (and these English words are not used to represent any other Greek word); and the noun *kara* by the adjectives "dear" or "true," as when Antigone calls the dead Polyneikes her "own dear brother" (978 / 915).

(3) The polar opposites that I have rendered as "reverence" and "irreverence," and related forms, appear often, but if my goal had been to achieve variety in the diction of the translation, the Greek words could have been translated at least some of the time as the opposites "pious" and "impious." Kreon believes it is impious or irreverent with respect to the gods of the city—presumably Dionysos and Zeus, among others—to give funeral rites to Polyneikes, because the latter made himself an enemy of the city, while Antigone believes it is irreverent or impious to the gods of the underworld, Hades their chief, *not* to give proper ritual burial to the dead. However, the action of the play finally implies that Kreon has been blasphemous; since Kreon is destroyed, we do not doubt that some of the gods, at least, are punishing him.

(4) I have used the words "right" and "straight" and related words to represent the Greek word *orthos* and its derivations (and have not used "right" otherwise). *Orthos* is one of Kreon's favorite words. In following his "straight" course, Kreon manifests his rigid and stubbornly mistaken thinking. He claims he stands for what is "right" and he tries to establish the authority of his concept.

(5) Kreon is convinced that the reason people do what they do is for *kerdos*, "profit," material gain. His reiterations of this word, sometimes even when it does not appear to be relevant, make it seem that Sophokles wished to show how, as we might say in our day, Kreon keeps attributing to others a motive of his own that he keeps secret, even from himself; perhaps he is excited that he may profit from his having come into the position of ruler of Thebes. We cannot know; the play is not psychological in this way. Antigone counters that her profit, by contrast, is *not* material but instead is a noble or honorable death (508–12 / 462–64). Perhaps the idea of profit is on the mind of the culture itself, so to speak. After all, even though Teiresias was not present earlier to learn of Kreon's rage at the guards' presumed willingness to be bribed, the seer happens to conclude his opening speech by urging Kreon to accept a metaphorical "profit" from good advice. Kreon, though, takes the word literally and he bitterly accuses everyone, including Teiresias himself, of profiting somehow by betting on his decisions. With a devastating turn, the word *kerdos* is used last by the Chorus, who in effect say to Kreon (1409 / 1326): you were obsessed with profit; well, your own has finally come, but only in the form of your agonized and belated understanding.

(6) A Greek word for the worst of fates is *atê*. Griffith glosses it this way: "*Atê* is a rich and evocative term, especially in tragedy, suggesting both *outcome* ('delusion,' 'ruin,' 'misery'), and *cause* (often a mixture of human folly and supernatural sabotage)" (121). Later, Griffith adds that *atê* is an "inescapable complex of delusion, error, crime and ruin" (219). Since the idea of the *cause* of ruin effectively implicates human decisions, whether these seemed bad or even good when made, *atê* also suggests the emotional state, the mistaken impulse, the ill-advisedness or foolishness, that leads someone to ruin. Yet the ancient Greeks often regard this bad impulse as having been sent, for sometimes unknowable reasons, by the gods. I have used "ruin" to represent *atê* throughout.

(7) The idea of human folly leads me to two other structures of polar opposites informing the play that deserve brief comment. In *Antigone*, events seems to turn on whether decisions by a man—or a woman—are sensible or foolish. A large family of words denoting these ideas is based on the Greek root *boul-* but cannot be translated so as to echo a single root word in English. The repeated echoing of *boul-* in various forms in

Greek, I have had unfortunately to disperse in the translation into disparate English words, but I hope that the polarity of concept—well-advised versus ill-advised, good counsel versus bad, and so on—remains visible. In fact, in the repetition of the large number of Greek words for mind, thought, judgment, ascertainment, and so on, we seem to see a cultural preoccupation different from our own.

Another structure of opposites has to do with freedom versus slavery. For example, Kreon relegates women to the status of slaves when he speaks contemptuously of how Antigone's ambition to violate his order is not only wrong but also inconceivable, since she is not a man (526–28 / 478–79). Again, Antigone argues passionately that the brother who died and still lies unburied outside the city walls "was no slave" (568 / 517). But although the same Greek word for enslaved war captives may be used also for the servants and attendants of Kreon and his wife Eurydike, I have translated many instances as "servant" or simply "man" in the sense of "Kreon's man" (or "men"), because while slavery was a notable part of the social and political fabric of Sophokles' Athens, the complex differences between Athenian and American slavery make it unwise to imply in the American linguistic, historical, and political context an easy identification of these two "peculiar institutions."

RHYTHMS

One great problem of translating ancient Greek poetry is that, for unavoidable historical and cultural reasons, the language we ourselves speak and write no longer makes any use of a poetic lexicon—a special register of word-choice that is generally felt to be "poetic." So a translator can create scarcely any effects at all that are *analogous* to those that the ancient poets created for their audiences (and conversely, some of the effects created by the translation would be unrecognizable to ancient audiences). Also, we live in a world of print and media images that can override our sense of the rich complexity of linguistic expression; compared to the consciousness of the ancient Greeks, our consciousness is saturated proportionally less by the rhythms of language spoken *between* living human beings and more by language aimed by media *at* passive listeners. Furthermore, for the translator, the difficulties of representing the intensity and liveliness of the language of the ancient Greek stage, and of particular words or kinds of words, are really only first problems; next comes the problem of the different manner of speaking of each of the characters in the ancient play, and then the problem of differences between sorts of stage language in general—dialogue, chanted lines, and sung lines. Sung lines appear both in odes and in certain scenes, when

it's as if the sheer intensity of feeling—in Antigone, as she is about to
be sealed up alive in a tomb, and then in Kreon, after the deaths
of Haimon and Eurydike—pushes them from agitated speech into anguished singing.

In this play, especially, *agôn*, contest, is nearly everything—a debate,
after war, for new life-and-death stakes. When the characters are speaking to each other in one-line utterances (the stichomythia), I would have
liked to produce iambic lines all of the same length, but this was
impossible because of the extraordinary compression of ancient Greek
in general and especially of Sophokles' language. For the sake of faith-
fulness to the pace of the play in Greek, I have kept all these utterances
to one line in English, too, but the length of that line varies from five to
six or occasionally seven metrical feet. And the stichomythia is not the
only contest of words in the play—the characters, each using a particular
tone and diction, dispute each other in longer speeches also. In these,
Sophokles sometimes creates structural symmetries—two lines from one
character are answered by two from another, or forty-two spoken by
Kreon answered by forty-two spoken by Haimon, and so on. To preserve
the symmetries of the number of lines in the briefer exchanges, I have
sometimes lengthened lines to fit everything in, but in longer speeches
I considered instead that the consistent rhythm of blank verse was
more important than the precise length of the speech.

The ancient dynamic of argument points to a larger difference between Greek tragedy and the modern theater (although psychologically,
Antigone does seem among the most "modern" of all the surviving
tragedies), which is the way the Greek writers saw the play as both an
action on stage and also as word-work, the performance of language.
Andrew Brown notes that Sophokles and Euripides almost always include a messenger speech in their (surviving) plays, and says that
these, "with their opportunities for vivid and exciting narrative, were
deliberately cultivated by the tragedians, and not regarded as regrettable
necessity imposed by the limitations of the Greek stage" (217). These
narrative passages require a rhythm at least distantly related to epic
poetry, but the odes sung by the Chorus, and the sung portions of
the play's final moments, require a markedly different rhythm, and
they, too, are composed and structured rhythmically, thematically, and
by diction and symmetries of length. I have put the rich and densely
figurative lines of sung passages into free verse, using hemistichs, or half-
lines, to produce more opportunities in English for word-emphasis
and more vigorous rhythmic movement. I have also reproduced symmetries of stanza-size and a few other symmetries in the pairs of matching ode-stanzas called *strophe* and *antistrophe*.

LANGUAGE LITERAL AND SENSUOUS

Of the odes, Griffith writes, "If it is characteristic of lyric poetry in general to be dense and ambiguous, these odes must be counted among the most opaque—as well as the most adventurous—in all of Greek tragedy" (18). Sophokles is known for the compression of his effects, both of metaphor and syntax. (Rather than calling some of his most difficult metaphors "mixed"—which is what we could call them, given our contemporary expectations of poetic practice—classicists call them "bold," since they belong to a somewhat different, ancient, aesthetic. And yet the wonder is how much of Sophokles' practice as a poet—apart from meter—is immediately comprehensible, in technical terms, to us, 2,500 years after he composed the play.) What has struck me most about Sophokles' language is its density of metaphor and image— its cognitive boldness, to be sure, but also at other moments its literalism of effect—especially when words (either abstract or concrete) are brought back to achieve also that effect of wovenness. Perhaps when classicists themselves do not always translate very literally, it is because they believe some of the metaphors in the Greek to have been already dead in Sophokles' time or because they are intent on conveying to readers of their translations the general sense of an utterance rather than its texture. (An example is that word *kerdos*, profit, mentioned earlier. In rendering the moment at the end of the play when the Chorus turns this word against Kreon as a metaphor, two of the classicists on whose great scholarship I have depended resort to paraphrases that entirely lose the effect of this devastating reiteration.) Even more complicated is Sophokles' use of metaphor in the odes.

My goal in translating metaphors was not to smooth out the language of the play but to get as close to the Greek as I could, in an English that can reproduce at least some of the poetic qualities of this magnificent long poem-for-performance. An example: at the beginning, after Antigone has slipped out of the city in the dark and Ismene has reentered the royal house, the Chorus of Theban elders see Kreon approaching and they wonder why he has assembled them. At Greek line 158, literally they say, "What plan [or counsel or thought] does he stir-as-with-an-oar?" Sophokles frequently makes use of metaphors that are this vivid if taken literally, but yet are ordinary in his linguistic context; these are difficult to catch hold of in our contemporary American English, which has almost completely lost touch with the immediacy of the pre-technological physical world that was the basis of ancient Greek figures of speech. For this line, Sir Richard Jebb gives us in his marvelous 1900 edition of the play: "What counsel is he pondering?" Mary Whitlock Blundell, in her excellent scholarly translation, writes, "What plan is he plying?" To provide more information, she annotates the line—an option that literary translators must avoid if they want to produce a text that is playable. Like Blundell, two other classicists preserve the oar's movement, but not with the implication of an oar, specifically: Andrew Brown offers, in the literal version accompanying his edition of the Greek, "What plan is he putting in motion?" (and he annotates the line) and Elizabeth Wyckoff (in David Grene's well-known edition of 1954) translates, "What plan ... beats about his mind?" So what is the translator to do with that stirring-as-with-an-oar? Is it worth trying to keep hold of?

The problem with the stirring or rowing lies not only in its vital immediacy in ancient Greece, where the sea was the path of the Athenians' trade and military conquests, but also in its lack of immediacy in our lives. Merchant ships and naval triremes had both oars and sails, but in our epoch sails belong to pleasure boats and oars are mostly thrown underneath beached, overturned aluminum rowboats awaiting an energetic vacationer. To put the word "rowing" or "oar" into the translation of the Greek line is to try to catch hold of something both vigorous and solemn, something *telling*, in Sophokles, and simultaneously to throw that meaning away because of the bathos of *our* oar. The translator is always translating both *out of* and *into*, and the lack of a fit can be found on either end of the transaction, or on both at once.

I say solemn, because after the Chorus has thought of the stirring of water when the oarsman propels his boat or turns it, Kreon immediately launches (182 / 162) his own principal metaphor—his ship of state—for the seriousness of what faces Thebes in the aftermath of the failed attack by the traitorous Polyneikes. (Note also that following this scene—in which Kreon hears from the newly arrived guard that Polyneikes' body has been given a funeral ritual, although not a full burial, against Kreon's orders and under penalty of death—the stasimon that follows [the Ode to Man], one of the great poems in all of ancient Greek, says of man that among his wondrous accomplishments is that in his ships he courageously "sails the gray- / White sea running before / Winter storm-winds, he / Scuds beneath high / Waves surging over him / On each side.") And in Kreon's ship of state, everyone must pull at the oars together and in the same direction, especially through dangerous waters. But Antigone refuses to do so, or even to use this kind of language.

Later, Sophokles writes for Ismene, in the scene when Antigone, Ismene, and Kreon are all on stage, a line of pained fellow-feeling for her sister that brings that ship and that rowing back into our minds; Ismene uses another nautical verb (592 / 541) when she says, "But amidst your troubles I am not ashamed / To sail beside you through your suffering." (The verb is in an untranslatable number, neither singular nor plural but dual—meaning that only she and Antigone have done this, against all others.) So we would not want to have missed, in English, the sense that the earlier "stirring-as-with-an-oar" evokes seafaring, for out of echoes like this Sophokles builds the language of his play. My own solution (178–79 / 158), as much to avoid "oar" and "rowing" as to capture the idea of a boat, is merely like Blundell's: "What course does he plan to steer?"—all I have done is point the metaphorical sense of the line toward the ocean, so that Kreon can then imagine his metaphorical ship of state sailing across dangerous seas, and thus initiate in English, too, Sophokles' *sequence* of nautical metaphors. This sequence will lead eventually to Haimon's metaphor of a sailing ship that has capsized and must be captained upside down (775–77 / 715–17). In fact, once Kreon's house has been turned upside down by death, he is incapable of serving as captain any longer. In an outburst of anguished metaphor that concludes Sophokles' nautical sequence, Kreon sees Hades as a harbor clogged with the bodies of the dead (1371 / 1284).

There is an important contrasting metaphor that is all too easy to leave buried. (And in a play about burial, a translator should think twice about what should be buried and what most certainly should not—Antigone should not be buried at all, much less alive, nor should the living vividness of Sophokles' language. A translator is tempted to say that Antigone the character is, among other things, a figure for the very livingness in language, which is an irrepressible gesture of resistance— in this case, Antigone's resistance to Kreon's attempt to control not only her life but also her language and thought.) Hugh Lloyd-Jones translates the Chorus' line about thinking as a kind of rowing (the same Greek line I have just discussed) as "What plan is he turning over?" But if "turning over" suggests anything in the physical world, it is not the oars reaching out from the sides of a Greek ship, feathered as the oarsmen turn them before attacking the water on the next stroke, but rather the plow that turns over the soil. Yet for what the Chorus says, an implicitly landlocked image about Kreon could not be more wrong, for the soil is associated by Sophokles with Antigone and her fierce allegiance to the gods of the earth—as, for example, when she is described as having poured handfuls of dust on the dead body of her brother Polyneikes, or when she thinks of the reiteration of the doom of her father as (literally) "thrice-plowed" (of which, more later), or even when she is associated in Kreon's mind with the passivity of cultivated soil; he uses a brutal metaphor when, with Ismene and Antigone standing before him, he says—echoing language of the ancient patriarchal Athenian marriage-contract, according to Griffith (216)—that Haimon can find another bride: "There are other furrows he can plant" (620 / 569). Antigone's *tripolistos* (919–20 / 859), "thrice-plowed," is often rendered in English translations as "repeatedly." Even if this metaphor is already dead in Sophokles' time, he revives it: the word "thrice" numbers the generations of Antigone's family who have borne an apparent curse of the gods; and the word "plowed" suggests the gods of the earth, of dirt and dust, to whom Antigone gives reverence. To me it would seem a mistake to erase this repeated plowing with the generality "repeatedly." After all—to refer once more to the Ode to Man—the play says that one of the characteristics of this strange creature, man, who is so ingenious at both good and evil, is that the most ancient of the gods, Gaia (who deserves greatest reverence from men because without her there is no world at all), is also for man merely dirt to be plowed again and again, as if he sought to wear Her out (382–86 / 337–41).

I describe these few word-motifs to emphasize that a poetic translation usually cannot afford to go right through a metaphor as if it were transparent and arrive at some general sense behind it. It is bad enough that the intricate patterns of the play of sounds in ancient Greek are far beyond any possible translating. To lose also most of the metaphorical compression and synthesizing of ideas, themes, motifs, and so on would be to drain the lifeblood out of the poem. It seems to me that when translating, metaphor above all is what has to be lifted safely past a tempting explanatory, general language, for it to be grasped in its vividness and multiple signifying. It is a common practice of scholarship and criticism, in general, to read poetry for the ideas, themes, even information, that it contains, but readers turn to poetry for pleasures—of being engaged with language that signifies richly through its diction, its rhythms and sound, and the ways it is structured—pleasures of language that heighten our somber reflection on even the most tragic of subjects. This play, above all—which for 2,500 years, for all sorts of readers, has resisted giving away a definitive sense of how to resolve the conflict between Antigone and Kreon—would be travestied if one cared only about decoding the positions that Sophokles gives to his characters, or guessing what he himself, behind them, believes. The complexity of the characters' stances is in the very density and beauty of the language, which is not just an aspect of the play but is itself the meaning of the play—the difficulty of the language continually enacts at the level of word and syntax and rhythm the uncertainty and acutely competing forces represented by the play as a drama.

I could unfortunately give many more examples of metaphors of literal and sensuous immediacy in Greek that I could not quite unbury in English, any more than Haimon—or even Kreon, once his mind was able to think right again—could rescue Antigone.

METHOD AND SOURCES

Working with Charles Segal, first on Euripides' *Bakkhai* and then on Sophokles' *Antigone*, has led me in a new way to the deep pleasures of artistic problems. Our method was for me to produce successive drafts of the translation, to each of which Charlie brought suggestions, corrections, nuances, and clarities of interpretation, while also pointing out verbal reiterations in the Greek that were too subtle or distant from each other for me to have noticed on my own. Together we wished to produce a translation as "fine-woven" (1303 / 1222) as Antigone's fatal veil. There were some problems we could not solve—one was the frequently repeated interjections (*ômoi, pheu, iô,* and so on) for which almost nothing in contemporary English will do, since the choices are between the outdated "alas!" and many contemporary expressions lacking gravity. Another unsolved problem is the reliance of the language of tragedy on relatively few words, often repeated, for people who have been ruined, are miserable, wretched, ill-fated, and so on. Scarcely any of the available words in English for a bad fate have the ring of deeply felt, ultimate misfortune—partly because our sense of "unhappy" no longer includes anything of fate in it, but instead refers to feeling. Another problem is avoiding the chance occurrence in English of words sounding too much alike—which is why, since the translation must often use the word "profit," I did not use "prophet" but "seer," and why I tried to minimize the use of the word "counsel," an idea which is so necessary to the play, because it sounds like "council."

As in translating Euripides' *Bakkhai,* I have preferred to use transliterations of Greek for proper names except for the most familiar Latinized names and the occasional word, like "chorus." For help with the Greek text I relied above all on Charles Segal, but I also drew on sources to which he sent me: Griffith, Jebb, and Brown, cited at the head of the Notes, and Hugh Lloyd-Jones' edition and translation (*Sophocles II,* Cambridge, Mass., 1998), and Mary Whitlock Blundell's translation of *Sophocles' Antigone* (Newburyport, 1998). I have also consulted Charles Segal's masterful *Sophocles' Tragic World* (Cambridge, Mass., 1995), his *Tragedy and Civilization* (1981; reprinted Norman, Okla., 1999), and separate essays. Also important to my understanding of the play, and of what might be made of it today, was George Steiner's remarkable *Antigones* (Oxford, 1984). Although Charles Segal provided me with characteristically wise and kind counsel regarding every aspect of meaning and interpretation, and of course made all necessary decisions regarding textual problems and variants, whatever flaws of sense and sound that may remain in the translation should be ascribed solely to me.

I end this brief essay with thanks—to good fortune, to Oxford University Press, and to series editors Alan Shapiro and Peter Burian for the opportunity to translate the play with a scholar of such great learning and wisdom. Much too soon after finishing his introduction and notes to this *Antigone*, and after he and I had completed our work together on the translation, Charles Segal died on January 1, 2002. I have known no one else who achieved a longer, more Sophoklean view of human life and death, or who gave more thoughtful attention to those around him; Charlie believed that the value of scholarship and poetry was deep and that at their best these have added wise counsel, humane ideals, and intellectual beauty to our entire civilization, and will continue to do so. In a way, this book is a most fitting memorial to Charlie, for it represents by his example the good of seeking to understand and revivify elements of the human past that belong to us all. This is a good in which Charlie believed wholeheartedly. Our *Antigone* also exemplifies Charlie's supreme learning and intelligence and his gift for bringing Sophokles to light for others.

REGINALD GIBBONS

ANTIGONE

Translated by

REGINALD GIBBONS

and

CHARLES SEGAL

CHARACTERS

ANTIGONE   a young woman of about sixteen to eighteen years of age, daughter of Oidipous

ISMENE   her sister, probably younger

CHORUS OF
ELDERLY
THEBAN
MEN   citizens who counsel Kreon, sometimes speaking singly, sometimes together

KREON   ruler of Thebes, maternal uncle of Antigone and Ismene

GUARD   a low-ranking soldier

HAIMON   the young son of Kreon, betrothed to his cousin Antigone

TEIRESIAS   an aged, blind seer

MESSENGER   one of Kreon's men

EURYDIKE   the wife of Kreon and mother of Haimon

VARIOUS
MALE
ATTENDANTS   servants; slaves

Line numbers in the right-hand margin of the text refer to the English translation only, and the Notes beginning at p. 119 are keyed to these lines. The bracketed line numbers in the running heads refer to the Greek text.

ETEOKLES and POLYNEIKES, *sons of self-blinded* OIDIPOUS, *have been at war,* ETEOKLES *having refused to alternate the rule of Thebes with his brother, as he had promised, and* POLYNEIKES *having led an army of military allies from Argos against the city.* OIDIPOUS *had put a curse on his two sons that they would kill each other, and in fact, on the day before the play opens, amidst battles surrounding the city, these two older brothers of* ANTIGONE *and* ISMENE—ETEOKLES, *defending one of the seven gates of Thebes, and* POLYNEIKES, *leading the attack against him— have fought and killed each other. Now, well before dawn in Thebes, the sisters* ANTIGONE *and* ISMENE *are standing—surprisingly—outside the great main doors of the house where they were born and where, under the guardianship of their uncle,* KREON *(their dead mother's brother), they have again been living since the death of* OIDIPOUS. POLYNEIKES' *Argive alliance has now retreated during the night and abandoned the war and its dead warriors, whose bodies lie on the plains outside the walls of Thebes.*

ANTIGONE Ismene, my own true sister, Oh dear one,   1
                 Sharing our common bond of birth, do you know
                 One evil left to us by Oidipous,
                 Our father, that has not been brought down on
                 The two of us by Zeus, while we still live?
                 Among our woes, both yours and mine, there's
                      nothing
                 Painful to us, nothing that's not weighed down
                 By ruin, no shame and no dishonor, that I
                 Have not already seen. And now, what is
                 This proclamation they say the general   10
                 Has issued for all the citizens—the men?
                 Have you heard anything? Or have you not
                 Noticed that evils of our enemies
                 Are marching now against our friends and dear ones?

ISMENE No talk of friends we love has to me,
                 Antigone—neither welcome nor painful,

Since that moment when we two sisters were
Dispossessed of our own two brothers—killed
On one day by twin blows of each other's hands.
And since the Argive army went away   20
This very night, I know no more, nor whether
I'm closer to good fortune or to ruin.

ANTIGONE I thought so! That's why I called you outside
The courtyard gates, alone, to listen to me.

ISMENE What is it? It's certain your words will be as dark
as dye.

ANTIGONE But hasn't Kreon honored only one
Of our two brothers with a tomb and dis-
Honored the other? They say he has covered
Eteokles with earth, as justice and law
Require, so down below among the dead   30
He will be honored. But the body of poor
Polyneikes, who died so miserably—
They say a proclamation has been cried
To all the citizens that no one may
Hide it inside a grave, wail over it
Or weep for it, it must be left unmourned,
Unburied, a sweet-tasting treasure that birds
Will spy and feed on with their greedy joy.
And this is the very order that they say
The noble Kreon has proclaimed to you   40
And me—to me, to me he says it!—and then
To make it clear to those who don't yet know,
He's coming here, and he does not treat this
As some small matter: anyone who does
What he has now forbidden will be put
Before the people and by public stoning
Murdered.
         There you have how things stand, and soon
You will show whether you are noble, or—
Despite high birth—are low and cowardly.

ISMENE   Oh my poor sister!—but if things are knotted up   50
         This way, then how could I unravel them?

ANTIGONE Think about joining in my action and my burden!

ISMENE   What sort of dangerous act? What have you decided?

ANTIGONE Will you join with this hand of mine to lift the body?

ISMENE   What? You're thinking you will bury him,
         When this has been forbidden to the city?

ANTIGONE My brother, yes—and yours—if you don't want to!
         I will not be caught betraying him.

ISMENE   Hard, headstrong girl!—even though Kreon bans it?

ANTIGONE It's not for him to keep me from my own.   60

ISMENE   Oh! But sister, you must understand—
         Our father, after beating out his eyes
         Himself, with his own self-striking hand, then died
         Infamous and detested, because of crimes
         That he himself discovered he'd committed!
         Then his mother and wife—the woman had
         Two titles—with a twisted loop of rope
         Violently disfigured her own life.
         Third, our two brothers on a single day,
         A wretched pair, with hands aimed at each other,   70
         Killing themselves have shared a doom in common.
         And now we two, the last ones left—consider
         How much worse death will be for us if we
         Defy the law and flout the rulers' vote
         And power—we must keep in mind that first,
         We're born as women, we're not brought into being
         To war with men; and second, that we are ruled
         By those whose strength is greater, and we must yield
         To this—and to much that's worse than this. So I

Will plead with those under the earth to feel 80
For us and pardon us, because I'm forced
To act as I do, and I'll obey the rulers,
For it makes no sense to do things that are futile.

ANTIGONE I won't insist. And even if you wished
To do this, now, it wouldn't make me happy.
So be as you decide to be—but I
Will bury him. For me it's noble to do
This thing, then die. With loving ties to him,
I'll lie with him who is tied by love to me,
I will commit a holy crime, for I 90
Must please those down below for a longer time
Than those up here, since there I'll lie forever.
But you, if that is what you decide, then leave
Dishonored that to which the gods give honor!

ISMENE I don't dishonor them! But to defy
The citizens is beyond what I can do.

ANTIGONE Offer that excuse. But I will go heap earth
In a grave-mound for my beloved brother.

ANTIGONE begins to leave.

ISMENE Oh poor Antigone—I'm frightened for you.

ANTIGONE Don't fear for me! It's your life you should put right. 100

ISMENE At least don't tell a soul what you will do,
But keep it secret, and with you, I'll do the same!

ANTIGONE Oh—denounce me! I'll hate you even more if you
Keep quiet and don't proclaim all this to
everyone.

ISMENE You have a heart that's hot for what is chilling.

ANTIGONE But I know I'm pleasing those I must please most.

ISMENE   If you succeed! But you're in love with what's
                impossible.

ANTIGONE   Then when I'm out of strength—but only then—I will
                be stopped.

ISMENE   But it's wrong to go hunting for what's impossible.

ANTIGONE   If you say that, you will be hated by me.   110
                And justly to the dead man you'll remain
                A hated enemy. So let me and
                This ill-considered plan of mine endure
                This terrible thing—for I will suffer nothing
                So bad as to deny me a death with honor.

                        ANTIGONE *leaves, on the side leading out beyond*
                                                the city walls.

ISMENE   If you think so, then go. But know you're foolish
                To go, yet rightly dear to your dear ones.

                        ISMENE *goes into the royal house. The* CHORUS *of fifteen*
                        elderly Theban men, Kreon's counselors, enters from the
                                side that leads in from the city, while performing
                                                a choreographed song.

                                                First ode/Parados

CHORUS   Flashing ray of   *strophe a*

                                Sun, most beautiful
                        Light ever to
                                        Appear at seven-
                        Gated Thebes, at
                                        Last you, the   120
                        Eye of golden
                                        Day, appeared—
                        You came
                                        Slanting over
                        The River Dirkê,
                                        You made that

59

Argive warrior
   With silver-
White shield run
   Headlong in
Frightened flight,
   His armor heavy
And a sharp bit
   Stabbing him!

           Chanting.

Urged on by
   Furious two-sided
Quarrels of divisive
   Polyneikes,
He had risen and
   Flown to our land, he had 130
Come against us
   Shrieking like
An eagle that
   Spreads out its snow-
White wings, its
   Weapons, over
Us, and with all his
   Horse-tailed helmets.

           Singing.

Over our rooftops he   *antistrophe a*
   Loomed, with blood-
Thirsty gaping he
   Surrounded us, his
Murderous spear-
   Talons at our seven
Gates, but then he was
   Gone before he could
Glut his jaws with
   Our streaming blood and
Before pine-fed flames
   Of the fire-god could 140

Seize our city's crown
        Of towers. The loud
Clashing of war was
        Stretched taut at
His back, for this wrestling
        Was too hard
For one who matched himself
        Against the Theban serpent!

                          Chanting.

For Zeus utterly
        Hates the noise
Of an arrogant bragging
        Tongue, and as He
Watched those men
        Come like a flood at us
In their brazenness of
        Clanging gold, He
Struck with His
        Hurled fire one
Man who already had
        Raced to his goal   150
Atop our walls to
        Shout of victory.

                          Singing.

This man was tumbled   *strophe b*
        Crashing to the hard ground—
He who panting with
        Bakkhic fury had leapt
At us bearing torch-
        Fire and blew his breath
Of hatred on us like
        Hot winds. But finally
These things went
        Otherwise: Instead,
Ares the great war god,

> Strong as a charioteer's
> Lead horse, struck men
> > Hard and gave to some
> Men one fate and
> > To others, another.

Chanting.

> Seven captains attacking
> > Seven gates abandoned   160
> Their bronze weapons
> > That now become
> A tribute to battle-turning
> > Zeus, the god of trophies—
> Except for those two
> > Doomed, cursed men who
> Though born from one father
> > And one mother thrust
> Their two mutually
> > Victorious spears into
> Each other and shared one death in common.

Singing.

> But—since Nike, the goddess of victory,   *antistrophe b*
> > With great name and glory
> Has come, and her
> > Joy answers the
> Joy of Thebes,
> > City of many
> Chariots, let us
> > Forget this war   170
> That is over and
> > Let us go
> To the temples of all
> > The gods to celebrate
> In whirling dance
> > All night and may

Dionysos, Earth-shaker
> Of Thebes, lead us!

The CHORUS *notices the unannounced approach of*
KREON, with attendants, from the side that leads
in from the city.

Chanting.

But now comes the
> King of the land,
The son of Menoikeus,
> Kreon,
Newly crowned in these
> New circumstances
That the gods have given us.
> What course
Does he plan to steer, that
> He would convene
This special conclave
> Of elders,   180
Having sent us all a summons in common?

FIRST EPISODE / SCENE II

KREON Men, the gods have tossed our ship of state
On rolling seas and set it upright again.
I sent my messengers to summon you,
Away from everyone else, because I know
That you always honored the power of the throne
Of Laios, and also that you did the same
When Oidipous set this city right, and also
That when he died, you held his children steadfast
In your own thoughts. And since both of his sons,   190
Doubly destined, have died on the same day,
With their own hands both striking and struck down
In their own polluting murder of one another,
Now I hold all the power and the throne,

Because of my close kinship to the dead.
     It is impossible to know completely
The soul, the mind, the judgment of a man
Until we see his mettle tested against
His duties and his way with the laws. In my view,
A helmsman of the city as a whole   200
Who fails to lay his hand on the best advice
Yet is afraid of speaking and locks up
His tongue seems now and always the worst of men.
And any man who feels that someone close
To him is more important than his own
Fatherland—him I count as belonging nowhere.
May great all-seeing Zeus now be my witness:
If I saw doom instead of deliverance
Marching against my fellow citizens,
I would not be silent, nor would I love   210
An enemy of my land as a close friend—
Knowing that this ship keeps us safe, and only
When it sails upright can we choose friends for
          ourselves.
     These are the laws with which I make our city
Grow strong. And like a brother to these is the one
I have proclaimed to the citizens concerning
The sons of Oidipous: that Eteokles,
Greatest in glory with his spear, who died
In battle for this city, we will bury,
We will perform all pure and proper rites   220
And we will make the offerings to be sent
Down to the noblest of the dead, below;
But his brother by blood—I'm speaking now
Of Polyneikes—an exile who came back,
Who wanted to set fire to his fatherland
And to the gods of his own people and burn
Everything down from high to low, who wanted
To devour the blood he shared with his own kin,
And to enslave the others—this man!: for him
It has been proclaimed throughout the city   230
That no one is permitted to honor him
With burial or funeral gifts, or to wail

For him with grief, that he must lie unburied,
A corpse eaten by birds and dogs and torn
To pieces, shameful for anyone to see.
That's my intention. Never from my hand
Will come a greater honor for the evil
Than that which goes to the just. But him who bears
Good will toward this city—I honor him
Equally whether he is dead or living.   240

CHORUS Son of Menoikeus, it pleases you
To do as you wish to him who bears ill will
Toward the city and him who's friendly. No doubt
You have the power to use any law
In dealing with the dead or us the living.

KREON Make certain, then—watch over what I ordered!

CHORUS Appoint some younger man to take this task.

KREON Guards are on watch already near the corpse.

CHORUS Then what else are you commanding us to do?

KREON Not to join with those who disobey this.   250

CHORUS No one's such a fool as to be in love with dying.

KREON And that will be the price! But often, hope
For profit has destroyed men utterly.

*Approaching hesitantly from the side that leads in from
beyond the city walls, a* GUARD *speaks as he nears*
                                                    KREON.

GUARD My Lord, I cannot say that I'm arriving
Quite out of breath from running rapidly
And with light feet—I have had numerous
Worries along the way that made me halt,
And revolve myself, to go back whence I came.

My spirit spoke to me, quite often, saying
"Pathetic creature, why are you on the way   260
To where you'll have to pay the penalty?
And once more you cease your locomotion, fool?
And yet—if Kreon comes to know of this
From someone else, won't you be subject
            to pain?"
And as I cogitated this in my thoughts
I quickly kept on going, slowly, and so
I turned a short path into a long road.
What won at last was coming here to you.
If what I say is nothing—still, I'll say it,
Because I'm holding to the hope that what   270
I'll suffer can't be more than what's my due.

KREON   Why then do you show such a lack of heart?

GUARD   First, I'd like to tell you about myself:
I didn't do this thing, or see who did,
Nor would it be just if I were harmed.

KREON   You take aim at me. Yet you fence the thing
Around. Yet clearly you have news you could reveal.

GUARD   What is terrible makes one hesitate.

KREON   Out with it! Then take yourself away.

GUARD   I'm telling you! That corpse—just now some person   280
Has buried it and gone, and he sprinkled it
With thirsty dust and performed the proper rites.

KREON   What are you saying? What man dares do this?

GUARD   I do not know! There's no mark of a pickax,
No dirt dug up with a mattock. No—the ground
Is hard and dry, unbroken, without wheel tracks.
Whoever did this left no sign at all.
And when the first man of the day-watch showed us,

We all were much alarmed and amazed. The corpse
Had disappeared—not covered with a mound   290
But with a little dust thrown over him,
As if by someone trying to avoid
Pollution. There was not a sign of beast
Or dog that might have dragged and torn the body.
    Then came an uproar of evil words among us,
With guard accusing guard; and we might have come
To blows, in the end, without someone to stop us—
It was as if each one of us had done it,
Yet none of us was clearly the one. But each
Of us pleaded that he knew nothing of it.   300
All of us were ready to pick up
A lump of red-hot iron in our own hands,
Ready to walk through fire, ready to swear
By all the gods we hadn't done this thing,
We didn't know who had conspired in it
Nor did we know who was the one who did it.
But after all our searching turned up nothing,
One of us said something that made us hang
Our heads toward the ground in fear. We had
No answer, and no matter what we did,   310
We saw no way to come out well, for what
He said was that we must report to you
What had been done, not hide it. And this gained
The day, and I, the unluckiest—I won
The grand prize when we shook lots from a helmet.
So here I am—most unwelcome, I know.
Against my own will, too, since no one loves
A messenger who brings with him bad news.

CHORUS LEADER My Lord, my own thoughts have advised me anxiously
For a while that this was all directed by the gods.   320

KREON   *To* CHORUS LEADER.

Stop!—before your words give me my fill
Of anger, or you'll all be taken for fools
As well as elders. What you say is not
To be tolerated, when you say the gods

Care about this corpse. So was it they
Who covered it, because they honored him
For his good deeds toward them?—he who came here
To burn their country and the temples with columns
Around them and the offerings inside,
He who came to shatter laws and customs?   330
Or in your eyes, do the gods give honor
To persons who are evil? That cannot be!
    Yet for a long time in this city, men
Who barely can put up with me have raised
A secret uproar, they've been tossing their heads,
They haven't kept their necks under the yoke—
As justly they should have done—and been content
With me. I know what this is all about.
Those are the ones who bribed the guards to do it.
For nothing current grows among us worse   340
For men than silver: money ravages
The cities, it forces men to leave their homes,
It teaches mortals with good thinking to turn
To shameful deeds, it shows men how to commit
All crimes, and know all kinds of irreverence.
But those who hired themselves out to do this thing
Have now made sure they'll pay the penalty.

                                              To GUARD.

    If Zeus gets any reverence from me,
Know this—I swear it on my oath!: if you guards
Don't find out who with his own hand has done   350
This burying, and bring him into my sight,
Then Hades won't be punishment enough,
And before you're dead you'll hang alive until
You throw some light on this outrage. And that
Will teach you in the future where to get
Your profit from when you steal, and teach you not
To love this profiting from anything
And everything. One sees more people ruined
Than rescued by such shameful earnings as yours.

GUARD Will you allow me to say a word, or should I turn
       and go?   360

KREON Do you still not know how much your words annoy
       me?

GUARD Would it be your ears or your spirit that they sting?

KREON Why are you trying to diagnose where I feel pain?

GUARD He who did it hurts your mind; I hurt your ears.

KREON Ugh! It's plain that you were born to talk and talk!

GUARD That may be so. But I never did this thing.

KREON Yes, you did! What's more, you sold your spirit for
       some silver.

GUARD Ah!
       It's terrible for him who believes to believe what's
       false.

KREON Be clever with the word "believe"—but if
       You don't reveal who did this, you'll confess ·   370
       That dirty profits make for suffering!

                KREON *goes into the royal house with his men.*

GUARD   *Speaking to the departing* KREON, *who does*
                             not hear him.

       May he definitely be caught! But whether
       He is or is not found—which chance will decide—
       You won't see me come here again! Beyond
       My hopes and calculation, I've been saved!
       And now I owe the gods great gratitude!

He leaves on the same side from which he entered,
heading out beyond the city walls again.

The CHORUS *performs a choreographed song.*

Second ode / first stasimon

CHORUS At many things—wonders,   *strophe a*
                    Terrors—we feel awe,
        But at nothing more
                    Than at man. This
        Being sails the gray-
                    White sea running before
        Winter storm-winds, he
                    Scuds beneath high   380
        Waves surging over him
                    On each side;
        And Gaia, the Earth,
                    Forever undestroyed and
        Unwearying, highest of
                    All the gods, he
        Wears away, year
                    After year as his plows
        Cross ceaselessly
                    Back and forth, turning
        Her soil with the
                    Offspring of horses.

        The clans of the birds,   *antistrophe a*
                    With minds light as air,
        And tribes of beasts of
                    The wilderness, and water-
        Dwelling sea creatures—
                    All these he
        Catches, in the close-
                    Woven nets he   390
        Throws around them,
                    And he carries them
        Off, this man, most

Cunning of all.
With devices he
        Masters the beast that
Beds in the wild and
        Roams mountains—he harnesses
The horse with shaggy
        Mane, he yokes
The never-wearied
        Mountain bull.

He has taught himself   *strophe b*
        Speech and thoughts
Swift as the wind;
        And a temperament for
The laws of towns;
        And how to escape
Frost-hardened bedding
        Under the open   400
Sky and the arrows
        Of harsh rain—inventive
In everything, this
        Man. Without invention he
Meets nothing that
        Might come. Only from
Hades will he not
        Procure some means of
Escape. Yet he has
        Cunningly escaped from
Sicknesses that had
        Seemed beyond his devices.

Full of skills and   *antistrophe b*
        Devising, even beyond
Hope, is the intelligent
        Art that leads him
Both to evil and
        To good. Honoring the
Laws of the earth
        And the justice of   410
The gods, to which

                    Men swear, he stands
          High in his city.
                    But outside any
          City is he who dares
                    To consort with
          What is wrong: let
                    Him who might do
          Such things not
                    Be the companion
          At my hearth nor have
                    The same thoughts as I!

SECOND EPISODE / SCENE III

          The CHORUS *notices the* GUARD *returning on the side*
              that leads in from beyond the city walls, as he
              brings ANTIGONE *with him as his prisoner.*

CHORUS LEADER   *Chanting.*
          What monstrous thing is this,
                    Sent by the gods?—
          My mind is divided—how can I
                    Say this girl is not
          Antigone, when I recognize
                    That she is?
          Oh unfortunate child of your
                    Unfortunate father,   420
          Oidipous, what does this mean?
                    Can it be you
          They are bringing here,
                    For having dis-
          Obeyed the laws of
                    The king—You,
          Seized at the height of your folly?

GUARD Here's who did the deed! We caught this girl
          In the act of burying. But where is Kreon?

CHORUS   *As they speak,* KREON *comes out of the royal house*
                                          with attendants.
              Just when we need him, here he comes from the
                   house.

KREON   What is it? What has chanced to make my coming
                   timely?

GUARD   My Lord, mortals should not swear anything's
              Impossible!—since later thoughts can prove   430
              One's judgment quite mistaken: after your threats
              Came coldly storming at me, I resolved
              That I would be reluctant to return,
              But due to the fact that the happiness for which
              One prays, beyond one's very hopes, exceeds
              All other pleasures, here I am again—
              Although I solemnly swore I never would be.
                 I bring this girl! We caught her at the grave
              Performing funeral rites. This time we cast
              No lots—this piece of luck belongs to me   440
              And no one else. So now, My Lord, you take her
              Yourself, question and convict her. By rights,
              I should be free to be let off this trouble.

KREON   This woman whom you bring, how did you catch her?
                   Where?

GUARD   She was burying the man herself. Now you know
                   everything.

KREON   Do you grasp—are you saying right—the things you
                   speak?

GUARD   Yes! I saw her burying the corpse against
              Your orders. Now is what I'm saying clear and plain?

KREON   How was she spotted and then seized while doing it?

GUARD   Well, what happened was, when we went back there—   450

After those awful threats you made—we brushed
Off all the dust that was on the corpse, we did
A good job of uncovering the body,
Which was slimy; and then upwind, on top
Of a hill, we sat, to keep ourselves away
From the stink, so that it wouldn't hit us. Each man
Helped by keeping another awake and warning
Him loudly if he seemed to shirk the task.
This lasted till the time when the blazing circle
Of the sun had put itself at the midpoint   460
Of the sky and we were melting in the heat.
Then suddenly a whirlwind raised a pillar
Of dust from the ground, a storm of trouble high
As heaven, it spread across the lowland, it tore
Away the leaves of the trees and it filled up
The whole huge sky. We shut our eyes and endured
This supernatural plague.
                                    After a long while
The thing died down and this wailing child is seen . . .
The way a bird will give sharp cries when she finds
That her nest and bed are empty and her young   470
Are gone—it was like that when this girl sees
The corpse all bare, she moaned with wailing grief,
She cursed those who had done this, and at once
She carries in her hands the thirsty dust
And holds up high a fine bronze pitcher and then
She pours libations three times round the corpse.
When we see this, we rush to hunt her down
But she was not afraid, and we accused her
Of what she'd done, before, and what she now
Was doing. She did not at all deny it—   480
Which to me brought both satisfaction and pain,
Because to flee bad things yourself feels good,
But it is painful to lead one of your own
To something bad.
                                    Of course, all of these things
Are less to me than safety for myself.

KREON   *To* ANTIGONE.

You! You turning your head away, to the ground—
Do you admit or deny that you did this?

ANTIGONE I admit I did it; I do not deny it.

KREON   *To* GUARD.

You can take yourself wherever you want
To go—you're freed from serious charges, now.   490

As *the* GUARD *leaves,* KREON *turns to* ANTIGONE.

You—answer briefly, not at length—did you know
It was proclaimed that no one should do this?

ANTIGONE I did. How could I not? It was very clear.

KREON And yet you dared to overstep the law?

ANTIGONE It was not Zeus who made that proclamation
To me; nor was it Justice, who resides
In the same house with the gods below the earth,
Who put in place for men such laws as yours.
Nor did I think your proclamation so strong
That you, a mortal, could overrule the laws   500
Of the gods, that are unwritten and unfailing.
For these laws live not now or yesterday
But always, and no one knows how long ago
They appeared. And therefore I did not intend
To pay the penalty among the gods
For being frightened of the will of a man.
I knew that I will die—how can I not?—
Even without your proclamation. But if
I die before my time, I count that as
My profit. For does not someone who, like me,   510
Lives on among so many evils, profit
By dying? So for me to happen on
This fate is in no way painful. But if
I let the son of my own mother lie
Dead and unburied, that would give me pain.

This gives me none. And now if you think my actions
Happen to be foolish, that's close enough
To being charged as foolish by a fool.

CHORUS LEADER   *To* KREON.

It's clear this fierce child is the offspring of her fierce
Father! She does not know to bend amidst her
    troubles.   520

    KREON   *To* CHORUS LEADER.

Understand that rigid wills are those
Most apt to fall, and that the hardest iron,
Forged in fire for greatest strength, you'll see
Is often broken, shattered. And with only
A small sharp bit, I've noticed, spirited
Horses are disciplined. For grand ideas
Are not allowed in someone who's the slave
Of others . . .
        First, this girl knew very well
How to be insolent and break the laws
That have been set. And then her second outrage   530
Was that she gloried in what she did and then
She laughed at having done it. I must be
No man at all, in fact, and she must be
The man, if power like this can rest in her
And go unpunished. But no matter if
She is my sister's child, or closer blood
Relation to me than my whole family
Along with our household shrine to Zeus himself,
She and her sister by blood will not escape
The worst of fates—yes, I accuse her sister   540
Of conspiring in this burial, as much
As she.

                         To his men.

Go get her!

Some of KREON'*s men go into the royal house
to find* ISMENE.
To CHORUS LEADER.

Earlier I saw her
Inside, raving, out of her wits. The mind
Of those who plan in the dark what is not right
Will often find itself caught as a thief.
But I hate even more those who when captured
In evil acts then want to make them noble.

ANTIGONE   Now you've caught me, do you want something more
than my death?

KREON   I don't. If I have that, then I have everything.

ANTIGONE   Then why delay? To me, your words are nothing   550
Pleasing, and may they never please me; likewise,
My nature displeases you. And yet, for glory,
What greater glory could I have gained than by
Properly burying my own true brother?
These men would say it pleases them—if fear
Did not lock up their tongues. But one-man rule
Brings with it many blessings—especially
That it can do and say whatever it wants.

KREON   You alone among the Thebans see it this way.

ANTIGONE   These men see it, but shut their craven mouths
for you.   560

KREON   You feel no shame that you don't think as they do?

ANTIGONE   No—no shame for revering those from the same
womb.

KREON   Wasn't he who died against him of the same blood?

ANTIGONE Of the same blood—the mother and the father,
                the same.

KREON Why do you grace with irreverent honor that other
            one?

ANTIGONE Eteokles' dead body won't testify to that.

KREON It will, if you honor him the same as the irreverent
            one.

ANTIGONE It was no slave—it was my brother who died!

KREON Attacking this land!—the other stood against him, in
            defense.

ANTIGONE And yet it's Hades who desires these laws.   570

KREON But the good should not get equal honor with the
            evil.

ANTIGONE Who knows if down there that is not considered holy?

KREON An enemy, even when he's dead, is not a friend.

ANTIGONE My nature's not to join in hate but to join in love.

KREON Then go down there and love those friends, if you
            must love them!
            But while I am alive, a woman will not rule!

> *The doors of the royal house open, and* ISMENE *is led
> on stage by the men who had gone in search of her
> inside the house.*

CHORUS   *Chanting.*

And here, outside the

                    Courtyard gates,
Ismene has come,
                    With tears of sister-
Love falling from her.
                    A storm-cloud over
Her brow mars
                    Her flushed face   580
And wets her lovely cheeks.

KREON   *To* ISMENE.

    And you—hiding unnoticed in the house
    Like a snake that drank my blood! I didn't know
    I raised a double ruin to bring down
    The throne! Come, tell me, do you admit your part
    In this burial, or swear that you know nothing?

ISMENE I did this deed—if she will allow me that—
        And, I too, take the blame for my part in it.

ANTIGONE But Justice won't let you, because you did not wish
          To act with me, nor did I share this with you.   590

ISMENE But amidst your troubles I am not ashamed
        To sail beside you through your suffering.

ANTIGONE Hades and those below know whose the deed is.
          I don't like a loved one who only loves with words.

ISMENE Sister, no! Do not dishonor me by not
        Letting me die with you and purify our dead!

ANTIGONE Do not share my death, do not take as your own
          That which you did not touch! My death will be
              enough!

ISMENE How can I want to live if I am left without you?

ANTIGONE Ask Kreon! He's the one whose side you take!   600

ISMENE   Why do you grieve me so, when it doesn't help you?

ANTIGONE   Yes, mocking you hurts me instead, if I *am* mocking.

ISMENE   Then how can I still try to help you now?

ANTIGONE   Save yourself! I won't resent your escaping.

ISMENE   Must I, in my misery, fall short of your fate?

ANTIGONE   Yes—because you chose to live, and I to die.

ISMENE   But I did not leave these words of mine unsaid!

ANTIGONE   To one side you seemed right; to the other, I did.

ISMENE   Yet we are both blamed equally for doing wrong!

ANTIGONE   Be brave! You are alive—but my life has died   610
Already, for the sake of helping the dead.

KREON   I'd say one of these girls now stands revealed as out
Of her senses, and the other one was born that way.

ISMENE   Yes, My Lord, good sense that is innate
In people deserts them in the midst of troubles.

KREON   Yours did, when you chose to do evil with evildoers.

ISMENE   How can I live my life alone without her?

KREON   Don't speak of her—for she does not exist.

ISMENE   But will you kill your own son's bride-to-be?

KREON   There are other furrows he can plant.   620

ISMENE   Not the way he and she were fitting for each other.

KREON Evil wives for my son are something I detest!

ISMENE Dearest Haimon, how your father dishonors you!

KREON You irritate me too much!—you and your marriage-
bed.

ISMENE And will you really rob your son of her?

KREON It's Hades who will stop this wedding for me.

ISMENE It seems decided then, that she will die—

KREON By you and by me! No more delays! You men!—
Take them inside. From now on they must be
Women—not to be let run loose, for even   630
Bold men will try to make their escape when they
See Death begin to come too near their lives.

Some of KREON's *men take* ISMENE *and* ANTIGONE *into
the royal house.* KREON *remains on stage with the rest
of his attendants.*

The CHORUS *performs a choreographed song.*

Third ode / second stasimon

CHORUS Fortunate are they whose   *strophe a*
                Lives do not
        Taste of woe; but among
                        Those whose house the gods
        Shake, no ruin is absent
                        As it creeps over a
        Multitude of generations like
                        A storm tide of the salt
        Sea driven by northern
                        Gales from Thrace—waves

That speed over the ocean
          Depths dark as the under-
World and churn
          Up black sand from the sea-
Bed and with harsh
          Winds hurl it beating   640
Against headlands
          That groan and roar.

From ancient times come   *antistrophe a*
          These afflictions of the
House of the Labdakids
          That I see falling one
After another on yet
          Earlier afflictions of the dead;
Nor does one generation
          Release another, but some
God batters them instead; nor
          Do they have any
Way to be set free.
          The last rootstock of the
House of Oidipous,
          In light that was spreading,
Is reaped by blood-
          Red dust of the gods
Under the earth, for foolishness
          Of speech and a Fury in the mind.   650

Zeus, what transgression   *strophe b*
          Of men could overcome
Your power? Neither
          Sleep that catches
Everyone in its nets
          Nor the weariless passing
Of the months named
          For gods can
Overcome it—You,
          The Generalissimo immune
To time, hold
          The gleaming marble heights

Of Mount Olympos.
              For what is now and
What comes after and
              What came
Before, only one
              Law can account,
Which is that into the life
              Of mortal beings comes   660
Nothing great that lies
              Beyond the reach of ruin.

It is wide-wandering   *antistrophe b*
              Hope that brings
Benefit to many
              Men, but it deceives
Many others with desires
              Light as air. When
It comes upon
              A man, he cannot
See clearly until already
              He has burnt his
Foot on live coals.
              Wisely someone has
Kept before us the
              Famous saying that
A moment will come
              When what is bad
Seems good to the
              Man whom some   670
God is driving toward
              Ruin. Only a short
Time does he stay
              Beyond the reach of ruin.

              HAIMON *enters from the side leading in from the city.*

CHORUS LEADER   *Chanting.*
Here is Haimon, your
              Last and youngest offspring.

Does he come here
                    Grieving over the fate
Of Antigone, whom he
                    Would wed, and to rage
At the great pain of
                    Being cheated of his
Royal marriage to the
                    Girl he had betrothed?

THIRD EPISODE / SCENE IV

KREON Soon we'll know, better than the seers. My son,
       Do you come to rage at your father, having heard
       My final vote on your bride-to-be? Or are we   690
       Still loved as your own, whatever we may do?

HAIMON Father, I'm yours. And as your judgments are
        Both good and upright, then I'll follow them.
        No marriage could be a greater prize for me
        To win than being guided well by you.

KREON Yes, what's best is for you to hold that, son,
       In your heart and stand behind your father's will
       In everything. For this is why men pray
       To bring up dutiful offspring and to keep them
       At home: so they'll pay back a hated foe   690
       With trouble, and giving honor, love the friends
       Of their father as he does. Of him who breeds
       Useless children, what else can you say but that
       He only begets more burdens for himself,
       And more mockery among his enemies?
       So do not, son, throw out your own good sense
       For the sake of pleasure in a woman—you
       Should know an evil wife in bed with you
       At home is something that soon enough grows cold
       Wrapped in your arms. What could fester deeper   700
       Than someone closely tied to you who's evil?
       So spit this girl out as an enemy!

And let her marry someone else—in Hades.
Now that I've caught her as the only one
In all the city who openly defied me,
I won't be seen as false to my own word
By all the city—I'll kill her.
                      In the face
Of that, let her sing her hymns in praise of Zeus,
The god of bonds of blood! If those I've raised
And kept become rebellious, then those outside   710
The family will become so, even more.
He who is a good man in his own house
Will also be seen to be just in public life.
A man like that—I'm confident he would
Rule well and wish to be well ruled; he'd stand
His ground where ordered, even in a storm
Of spears—a just and worthy fellow soldier.
But any criminal who violates
The laws or thinks he can give orders to those
Who rule, will not get any praise from me.   720
Whoever is put into power by
The city must be obeyed in everything—
In small things, and what's just, and the opposite.
There is no greater evil than lack of rule.
This is what brings cities to ruin, it's this
That tears the household from its roots, it's this
That routs the broken ranks of allied spears!
No—what does save the skins of most of those
Who act right is obedience! Therefore—
We must safeguard the orders of the rulers,   730
And we must never be defeated by
A woman—better to be overthrown,
If we must be, by a man; then we will not
Be said to have been beaten by the women.

CHORUS If age has not misled us, you seem to speak
         Sensibly about the things you speak of.

HAIMON Father, the gods endow men with good sense—
         Highest of all the things that we possess.

And I could not say in what way your words
Are wrong—and may I never be capable   740
Of knowing how to say that. But someone else
Might have a good thought, also. My natural role
Is to watch out for you—for the things that people
Might say or do, or what they might blame you for.
And to the common citizen, when you
Dislike some word he says, your eye becomes
A terror. But I hear what's in the shadows—
How the city mourns for this girl, and how
She of all women least deserves the worst
Of deaths for the most glorious of deeds—   750
Since she did not allow her own true brother,
Fallen in slaughter, still unburied, to be
Destroyed by flesh-eating dogs and birds of prey.
Isn't golden honor what she merits?
Such talk is spreading secretly in the dark.

   To me, Father, there's no possession more
To be sought than your well-being—for in what
Could children feel a greater pride than in
A father with a flourishing reputation?
Or what is greater for the father than   760
The sons of whom he's proud? So don't invest
Your being in one single way to feel—
That what you say, but nothing else, is right.
Whoever thinks that only he himself
Owns all good sense, that he and no one else
Has such a tongue and mind—when men like that
Show what's inside them, then we see they're empty.

   Even a man who's clever should feel no shame
In learning things—however many they are—
And in not keeping himself so tightly strung.   770
You see how all along a river swollen
By winter rain, the trees that bend with the current
Save themselves and even their twigs, but those
That stand straight are annihilated, root
And branch. And a man who pulls his rigging tight
And will not slacken it capsizes and then . . .
He simply has to sail on—upside down.

Let go of your anger, allow yourself to change.
 Now, if there's judgment in the young, like me,
Then I would say it's best by far if a man   780
Is completely filled with knowledge by his nature.
But since things aren't inclined to be that way,
It's also good to learn from what's well said.

CHORUS My Lord it's only fair, if he speaks to the point, that
          you learn
     From him—and Haimon, you likewise. Both sides
          speak well.

KREON Should men of my age be taught what to think
     By someone who has only reached as yet his age?

HAIMON In nothing that's not just. If I am young,
     Do not look at my age, but at what I do.

KREON Oh—is what you do revering rebels?   790

HAIMON I'd never tell you to revere an evildoer.

KREON Isn't that the sickness that infects this girl?

HAIMON That's not what people of Thebes, who share
          this city, say.

KREON Should this city tell me what commands to give?

HAIMON See how you say that like a young new lord?

KREON Must I rule this land for someone else, not myself?

HAIMON There is no city that belongs to one man only.

KREON Isn't the city held to be his who rules?

HAIMON You'd do well as the single ruler of some
          deserted place.

KREON   It seems this man is fighting on the woman's side!   800

HAIMON   If you're the woman—for it's you I'm looking after.

KREON   By unjust accusations of your father, you worst
of men?

HAIMON   Because I see you doing wrong to justice.

KREON   So I'm doing wrong to show some reverence for
my rule?

HAIMON   You show no reverence trampling on the honors the
gods deserve!

KREON   A filthy way to think—submitting to a woman!

HAIMON   At least you won't find me brought down by something shameful.

KREON   What you say is all on her behalf, though.

HAIMON   And yours! And mine! And that of the gods down
below!

KREON   You will never marry this girl while she's alive.   810

HAIMON   Then she will die. And dying, she'll destroy—
someone else.

KREON   Are you so insolent as to attack me with threats?

HAIMON   What threat is it to speak against such empty thinking?

KREON   You'll regret lecturing when your own thoughts
were empty.

HAIMON   If you were not my father, I'd say that you can't think.

KREON You slave of a woman—don't you prate at me!

HAIMON You want to speak, but never hear the one you
           speak to?

KREON What!? By high Olympos you won't keep on
        Abusing me so freely!

To his men.

Lead in the girl—
The hateful thing—so she may die at once!   820
Here, beside her bridegroom, in his sight!

Some of KREON's *men go into the royal house in search
of* ANTIGONE.

HAIMON   *As he leaves to the side leading out beyond
the city walls.*

No! Don't even think she'll die beside me!
And you will never see my face again
With your own eyes—so go rave on among
Whoever would still want to be your friend!

CHORUS My Lord, the man has gone off quickly in his anger!
      The mind, at his age, can become weighed down
        by grief.

KREON Let him do it! Let him go and have grand thoughts
      Too big for a man. He won't save those girls from
        their fate!

CHORUS Is it your thought, then, to kill both of them?   830

KREON Not the girl who did not touch the deed—well said!

CHORUS And with what sort of death do you plan to kill her?

KREON   I'll lead her out to some deserted place
        Where mortals do not go, and seal her up,
        Still living, in a tomb dug into rock,
        With just enough to eat—for our expiation,
        So that the city as a whole avoids
        Pollution. There, where she can pray to Hades,
        The only god whom she reveres, perhaps
        She will be spared from dying—or else she'll learn   840
        At last what pointless waste of effort it is
        To worship what is down below with Hades.

            KREON *goes into the royal house with the rest of his*
            men; the CHORUS *performs a choreographed song.*

                                Fourth ode / third stasimon

CHORUS Eros, unconquered in   *strophe a*
                Combat! Eros, that
        Leaps down upon
                The herds! You
        That pass the night-
                Watch on a girl's
        Soft cheeks, You
                That cross the
        Open sea and
                Roam from hut to
        Hut in the far
                High fields—neither
        The immortals nor
                Man, who lives only a day, can escape
        From you, and he
                Who has you   850
        Inside himself
                Goes mad.

        You that pull   *antistrophe a*
                The reins of just
        Minds toward in-
                Justice, disfiguring

Men's lives; You
          That stir up this
Strife between two
          Men of the same
Blood, while victory
          Goes to the force
Of love in the gaze: the
          Desiring eyes of
The bride shine with
          Wedding joy—this Power on its throne
                    rules
Equally with the great
          Laws, for the goddess
Aphrodite at her play
          Cannot be conquered.   860

>   ANTIGONE *is brought out of the royal house*
>   *by* KREON's *men.*

CHORUS   *Chanting.*

But I myself, at the sight
          Of this, swing wide off
The track, beyond the
          Limits of what the Laws allow.
Now I can no longer hold
          Back the streams of
My tears when I see Antigone
          Fulfilling this final journey—
To that bridal chamber where all must sleep, at last.

FOURTH EPISODE / SCENE V

ANTIGONE   *Singing.*

Look at me,   *strophe b*
          Citizens of my native land!—I
Am walking

                          The last road,
I am seeing for
                          The last time
The radiance
                          Of the sun and
Never again!
                          While I am   870
Still alive, Hades,
                          Who makes us all
Sleep, at last,
                          Is leading me to
The banks of the River
                          Akheron. I have
No share of marriage
                          Rites, nor did
Any hymn of marriage
                          Sing me to
My wedding.
                          Instead my marriage will be to Akheron.

CHORUS   *Chanting*.

Do you not go with glory and
                          Praise when you disappear
Into that place where the
                          Bodies of the dead are
Hidden? Not struck down by
                          Diseases that waste one
Away, not having earned
                          The deadly wages of   880
The sword, but answering only
                          To the law of yourself, you
Are the only mortal who
                          Will go down alive into Hades.

ANTIGONE   *Singing*.

I have heard it   *antistrophe b*
                          Told that the pitiable Phrygian stranger,
Daughter of Tantalus,

                              Died at the
             Peak of Mount
                              Sipylos—rock
             That grew like
                              Ivy wound
             Around her
                              Tightly till it
             Stilled her, and
                              Men say that
             She, melting in
                              Rain and snow
             That never cease,
                              Dissolves into   890
             Tears running
                              Down the mountain
             Ridges beneath
                              Her brow: divine
             Power takes
                              Me, who am most like her, to bed.

CHORUS   *Chanting.*

             But you know she is a goddess and
                              Was born of gods, and we
             Are mortals born of mortals.
                              Yet for a woman who
             Has died it is a great thing
                              Even to be spoken of as having
             The same fate as those
                              Who are like gods,
             Both when alive and
                              Then afterward, when dead.

ANTIGONE   *Singing.*

             Ah, I am laughed at!   *strophe c*
                              Why, by the gods of my fathers, do you
             Insult me not
                              After I have gone   900

But when you see
            Me still before you?
Oh city, Oh men
            Of the city, with
Your many possessions!
            Ah, springs of Dirkê
And sacred ground
            Of Thebes of the
Beautiful chariots—at least
            You will be
Witnesses to how I go, un-
            Lamented by any
Friends—and because of what
            Kinds of laws?—to the high-
Heaped prison of my
            Tomb, my strange and
Dreadful grave. Ah,
            Unfortunate that I am—
Neither living among those
            Who are alive, nor   910
Dwelling as a corpse
            Among corpses, having
No home with either
            The living or the dead.

CHORUS   *Singing.*

Stepping ahead to the very
            Limits of audacity,
You have struck your foot
            Against the throne
Of Justice and fallen,
            Oh child! And for
Some torment of your
            Father's, you are paying, still!

ANTIGONE   *Singing.*

Of all my cares, you   *antistrophe c*

                    Have touched the one most painful
                          to me:
My father's doom—recurring
                    Like the plowing
Of a field three
                    Times—and the ruin
Of us all—the famed
                    Family of the Labdakids!   920
Ah, my mother's disaster
                    Of a marriage bed,
And the self-incestuous
                    Coupling of my father
With my ill-fated
                    Mother! From such
As they, I—
                    Who have been made
Miserable in my mind—
                    Was begotten! Under a
Curse, unmarried, I
                    Go back to them, having
No other home but
                    Theirs. Ah, my brother!—
You who aimed at
                    And won a marriage
That brought doom,
                    You have died
And then killed
                    Me, who am still alive!   930

CHORUS   *Singing.*

To show reverence
                    Is indeed some reverence.
But power, in him
                    Who holds power,
Is absolutely
                    Not to be opposed—
Your self-willed temper
                    Has destroyed you.

As ANTIGONE *sings these last verses of her lament,*
KREON *comes out of the royal house with*
more of his men.

ANTIGONE   *Singing.*
    Without anyone's   *epode*
        Weeping, without friends,
    Without a marriage-
        Song, I in my
    Misery am
        Led to the road
    Prepared for me,
        No longer am
    I allowed to
        See this fiery
    Eye of heaven. For
        My fate, there are   940
    No tears or cries from any
        Beloved friend.

KREON Don't you know that no one would stop their singing
And moaning before death if they didn't have to?

To his men.

Take her off! Quickly! Let the close-walled tomb
Wrap arms around her, as I've ordered, leave
Her there alone, deserted, where she can choose
Either to die, or in that sort of house
To go on living, in the tomb—as for us,
We're pure as far as that girl is concerned.
But she'll be deprived of any house up here!   950

ANTIGONE Oh tomb! Oh bridal bedchamber! Oh deep
Cave of a dwelling-place, under guard forever,
Where I must go to be with my own dear ones,
Most of whom Persephone has received

Dead among the shades! And I, the last
Of them, will go in the worst way of all
Down there before my portion of this life
Comes to me.

              But as I go I hold strong hopes
That I will arrive as one loved by my father,
Loved by you, mother, loved by you, my own   960
Dear brother—for when you died I washed and
    laid out
Your bodies properly with my own hands
And poured libations at your graves.

                    And now!—
Polyneikes—for tending to your body,
This is my recompense! Yet those who have
Clear thoughts think I did well to honor them.

For I would never have assumed this burden,
Defying the citizens, if it had been
My children or my husband who had died
And had been left to rot away out there.   970
In deference to what law do I say this?—
Were my husband dead, there could be another,
And by that man, another child, if one
Were lost. But since my mother and my father
Are hidden now in Hades, no more brothers
Could ever be born—

             This was the law by which
I honored you above all others, Oh
My own dear brother, but Kreon thought that I
Did wrong, that things I dared were terrible.
And now by force of hands he's leading me   980
Away, without a nuptial bed, without
A wedding ceremony, and receiving
No share of marriage nor of rearing children.
Deserted by those close to me, and destined
For ill, I come while still alive to the cave
Of the dead dug deep underground.

                   And what
Justice of the gods have I transgressed? And why
Should I, in my misfortune, keep looking to
The gods for help? To whom should I call out

To fight as my ally, when my reverence   990
Has earned me charges of irreverence?
If all this does seem good to the gods, then I
Through suffering would know within myself
That I did wrong; but if these men do wrong,
May the evils that they suffer be no more
Than what they are unjustly doing to me!

CHORUS   *Chanting.*

The same storms of
                        Her spirit, hurling
The same blasts,
                        Still possess this girl.

KREON   *Chanting,* KREON's *men having been reluctant to lead*
                                                    ANTIGONE *out.*

And these men
                        Leading her will
Soon begin to wail,
                        Because of their slowness!   1000

ANTIGONE   *Chanting.*

Oh! That pronouncement
                        Comes very near
To death!

KREON   *Chanting.*

I cannot encourage
                        Anyone to be so bold as
To think that these
                        Orders are not final.

                        KREON *goes into the royal house.*

ANTIGONE   *Chanting.*

Oh city of Thebes, of
                    My fathers and my land!
Oh gods of my ancestors!
                    I'm not going
To be led away—I'm
                    Led away now!
        KREON's *men begin to take* ANTIGONE *toward the side*
                        leading out beyond the city walls.

Look!—you rulers of Thebes—
                    On the last, solitary
Member of the royal
                    House! What things,
From what men,
                    I must suffer   1010
For having been
                    Reverent toward reverence!

    The men and ANTIGONE *leave. The Chorus performs a*
    choreographed song, addressing ANTIGONE *even though*
                                she is absent.

                    Fifth ode / fourth stasimon

CHORUS Even Danae's lovely   *strophe a*
                    Form was made to
        Exchange the light of
                    The sky for a dark
        Room bolted with
                    Bronze. Yoked by
        Force, she suffered—Oh
                    Child, child!—imprisonment
        As in a chamber like
                    A tomb, although
        She was of much-
                    Honored descent and entrusted with the
                        raining gold

Of the seed of
              Zeus. But the power
Of fate—whatever that is—
              Fills us with terror and
Awe. Neither wealth nor
              Weapons nor high walls   1020
Nor dark sea-battered
              Ships can escape it.
Likewise tamed under   *antistrophe a*
              A yoke was
The king of the
              Edonians, the angry
Son of Dryas, for
              Mocking with quick temper
The god Dionysos, who
              Confined him in a
Prison of rock. What he
              Had done, the terrible
Blooming of his madness,
              Drained out of him there. Then he
                   recognized the god
Whom he had madly
              Assaulted with his
Mocking words. He had
              Tried to suppress the women
Quickened by the god,
              And their fire of Dionysos;   1030
That god's Muses, who
              Love the flute, he enraged.

Where indigo waters   *strophe b*
              Of two seas beat against shores of the
                   Bosporus
Is the Thracian
              Place called Salmydessos, and there,
From his neighboring
              Land, Ares saw
An accursèd
              Blinding wound

                    Fall on the
                              Two sons of
                    Phineus, their wide
                              Eyes—that would
                    Demand reprisals—
                              Beaten blind by
                    His savage wife
                              With her sharp
                    Shuttlepoints in her
                              Blood-stained hands.   1040

                    Wasting away in   *antistrophe b*
                              Sadness, they lamented their sad fate,
                                        these sons
                    Of a mother cast
                              Out of her marriage. And yet she
                    And her seed
                              Reached back to
                    The ancient family of
                              The Erekhtheids and in
                    Faraway caverns she had
                              Been raised among the
                    Storms and gales of Boreas,
                              Her father—she was a
                    Child of gods, flying as
                              Fast as horses over peaks
                    Too steep to be crossed
                              On foot. But on her, too,
                    The Fates, that live long ages,
                              Pressed hard, Oh child!

                    FIFTH EPISODE / SCENE VI

              As the blind seer TEIRESIAS, *an old man led by a boy,*
                    enters from the city, he calls out to the CHORUS
                                                        of elders.

TEIRESIAS Lords of Thebes!—we come here sharing the road,   1050
           Two persons seeing through the eyes of one. Thus go

The blind, with someone else to show the way.

KREON *enters abruptly from the royal house,*
with attendants.

KREON What news do you have, old Teiresias?

TEIRESIAS I will explain—and you will obey the seer!

KREON I never shunned your thinking, in the past.

TEIRESIAS That is why you captained this ship of a city rightly.

KREON I am a witness, from experience, to your services.

TEIRESIAS Know that your fortunes stand once more on
the razor's edge!

KREON What is it? What you say gives me a shudder!

TEIRESIAS You'll understand if you attend to the signs   1060
Of my craft. For as I sat at the ancient site
Of my bird-divining, where all sorts of hawks
Gather, I heard an unknown noise as they
Screeched their barbaric maddened gibber-jabber!
I knew that with their talons they were tearing
Murderously at each other—for the flurry
Of wings was not without significance.
At once, frightened, I tried to sacrifice
On an altar blazing properly. However,
Fire-god Hephaistos did not flare brightly up   1070
From the offerings—instead, the fatty thighbones
Oozed slime onto the embers, that smoked and
sputtered;
And gall exploded, spewing high in the air,
The thighbones dripped with grease and lay exposed,
Without the fat that had covered them.
These things—
Failed signs from rites that did not signify—
I learned from this boy who's leading me, as I
Lead others. And it's from your thinking that

The city is sick. Our altars and our hearths
Are filled with food brought by the birds and dogs   1080
From the dead ill-fated son of Oidipous!
And this is why the gods still won't accept
Our prayers at holy sacrifice or the flames
That burn on thighbones, nor are the clamorous
     shrieks
That birds cry out good omens, for they have eaten
The blood-streaked fat of a slaughtered man!
                          Know this,
My son: making bad choices is something shared
By all men, but when a man goes wrong, he's not
Still ill-advised and not ill-situated
If he tries to rectify the evil he   1090
Has fallen into and stops insisting that
He will not move. Stubbornness will earn
The charge of botching things! Give way to the dead.
Don't keep stabbing at him who is destroyed.
What prowess can there be in killing the dead
Yet again?
          I do regard you well, so I
Speak well to you. It's sweetest to learn from one
Who speaks well, if his speaking assures your profit.

KREON Old man—you all, like archers, shoot your arrows
At me as if I were some target! You work   1100
Against me even with your divinations.
By people like you I have been bought and sold
And shipped like merchandise. So take your profit!
Go trade in silver alloys and in gold
From India, if that is what you wish.
But you will not put that man in a grave.
And even if the eagles of Zeus want
To seize him and to carry him as food
Up to the throne of their god!—not even then,
From fear of pollution will I let this man   1110
Be given burial! For I know well
That no man has the power to stain the gods.
And even mortal men of striking, awe-

Some skill take shameful falls, Teiresias,
You old man, when they make a lovely speech
Of shameful language for the sake of profit.

TEIRESIAS Ah!
Does no man know, does no man understand—

KREON What is this great shared truth that you're
expounding?

TEIRESIAS —to what extent the best of all we own is prudence?

KREON Yes—to the same degree wrong thinking is the worst.   1120

TEIRESIAS But that's the very sickness that fills you!

KREON I do not wish to return the seer's insult.

TEIRESIAS But you do, when you say my oracles are false!

KREON Since the whole breed of seers is money-loving.

TEIRESIAS And that of tyrants loves its shameful profiting.

KREON Do you not know that your words blame your
sovereign?

TEIRESIAS I know. It was through me that you have saved this city.

KREON You are a skillful seer—but you love what's unjust.

TEIRESIAS You'll make me say what should stay deep within my
mind.

KREON Do it!—so long as you don't speak for the sake of
profit.   1130

TEIRESIAS Is that what you think I have done, so far?

104

KREON Know that you will never buy and sell my judgment!

TEIRESIAS Then know this well: that you will not complete
Many swift courses of the racing sun
Before you yourself, from your own gut, will give
One corpse for other corpses, in exchange,
Because you thrust down there someone from here
Above, dishonorably compelling her,
A human spirit, to live inside a tomb,
While here you're keeping someone who belongs   1140
Below—a body with no share of the gods,
No share of a tomb, no holiness—and this
Has nothing to do with you or the gods above,
And yet by you, violence is done to them!
And that is why the devastating late-
Destroying ones, the Furies, who avenge
Hades and the gods, now lie in wait for you,
So you will be caught up in these same horrors.
Ponder whether I would tell you this
Because I was given silver! Time will test   1150
My mettle and will soon reveal much wailing
For the men and women of your own household.
And all the cities are rioting with hatred
Because only dogs, beasts, and wingèd birds
Of prey have purified in burial
The torn and mangled bodies of their dead,
Carrying back to the city and its hearths
A stench of unholiness.
                    With anger, now,
And like an archer, I have let these arrows
Fly at your heart, since you torment me so—   1160
And you will not outrun their hot pain.
                    Boy!
Lead me home, so that this man may let fly
His anger at some younger men and learn
To keep his tongue more quiet and his mind
Much better at thinking than it is right now.

> TEIRESIAS *and the boy leave, on the side leading out of*
> *the city.*

CHORUS My Lord, he's gone—with terrible predictions.
And for as long as this hair—now white, once
        black—
Has covered my head, I know that never yet
Has he pronounced a thing untrue to this city.

KREON I myself know this; and my mind is confused: 1170
It's terrible to give way. But to resist
And strike my soul with ruin—is terrible.

CHORUS Son of Menoikeus, be well-advised!

KREON What must I do? Tell me! I will obey.

CHORUS Go send the girl up from her deep-dug house!
Build a tomb for the one who lies there, dead!

KREON Do you approve of this? You think I should give way?

CHORUS As fast as possible, My Lord! The gods' swift-footed
Bringers-of-Harm cut down the evil-minded.

KREON Oh! This is hard—but I change my heart. I'll do it!   1180
One cannot fight against necessity.

CHORUS Then go and do these things! Do not leave them
        to others!

KREON I'm going now, immediately! You men!
All of you here and all the others, too!
Go! Go! Take tools and hurry to the place
You see out there! And I, since my decision
Has taken this turn—I who have put her there
In prison will be there to set her free
Myself. I am afraid it's best to observe
The established laws through all one's life, to the end.   1190

        KREON *and his men rush out of the city.*

        The CHORUS *performs a choreographed song.*

Sixth ode / fifth stasimon

CHORUS God of many names!—   *strophe a*
                    Glory of the young wife from the clan
Of Kadmos, child
                    Of thundering Zeus,
Guardian of magnificent
                    Italy, ruling where
The folds of the
                    Hills pleat the lap
Of Eleusinian Demeter,
                    Shared by all,
You, Oh Bakkhos,
                    That live in
Thebes, mother-city
                    Of the Bakkhai,
By the flowing
                    Waters of Ismenos
And on the very
                    Ground where the
Savage serpent's teeth
                    Were planted;   1200

You, whom the sputtering   *antistrophe a*
                    Smoking flames of pine torches
                         have seen,
Up beyond the
                    Double peak of
Rock, where the
                    Korykian nymphs
Walk with Bakkhic
                    Step and Kastalia
Flows down;
                    You that the ivy
Slopes of Nysaian
                    Hills send forth
To lead them in
                    Procession, and the
Green coast rich with
                    Grapes, while immortal

Followers cry out
          The Bakkhic chant as
You watch over
          The Sacred Ways of Thebes—   1210

This place that   *strophe b*
          You and Your
Mother, she who
          Was struck by
Lightning, honor
          As highest of all
Cities: now, when
          The force of
Disease holds the
          City fast and all
Its people, come
          Cleanse us! Stride over
The slopes of Parnassos or
          Cross the moaning narrows to us,

Oh You that   *antistrophe b*
          Lead the dance
Of the stars that breathe
          Out fire, You that
Watch over the voices
          Sounding in the night,   1220
Child of Zeus, His
          Son, show us Your
Presence as a god, Oh
          Lord, with Your
Bakkhantic Nymphs who
          Whirl around You in worship
And celebrate You in frenzied dance
          All the long night, Iakkhos! Generous
          giver!

SIXTH EPISODE / SCENE VII

*Arriving from the side leading in from beyond the city
        walls, a* MESSENGER *addresses the* CHORUS.

MESSENGER   All you who live near the houses of both Kadmos
            And Amphion—there is no person's life
            That I would praise or blame, no matter what
            The circumstances of it now, because
            Fortune puts right and fortune topples down,
            Always, the fortunate and unfortunate.   1230
            Of things that stand established for us mortals,
            No seer can predict what is to come.
            Once, in my view, Kreon was enviable—
            Because he saved this land of Kadmos from
            Its enemies, and took sole, absolute
            Command of this domain and governed it,
            Having sown the seeds of noble children.
            All that has flown. For when a man's enjoyment
            Betrays him, I don't think of him as living
            But as a dead man who can still draw breath.   1240
            Pile up your wealth at home, if you so wish,
            And live in the style of a king—but if enjoyment
            Of things like these is absent, I wouldn't pay
            The shadow of thin smoke to anyone
            For what's left afterward, compared to joy.

CHORUS   But what new grief of the royal house do you bring
                with you?

MESSENGER   They're dead. And for their dying, the living are
                to blame.

CHORUS   Who is the murderer? And who lies dead? Tell us!

MESSENGER   Haimon is killed—bloodied by a hand close to him.

CHORUS   By his father's hand? Or was it by his own?   1250

MESSENGER   His own, against himself, in fury at his father for
                murder.

CHORUS   Oh seer! How rightly you fulfilled your prophecy!

MESSENGER   Since things are so, you must prepare for what's to
come.

> *Unexpectedly,* EURYDIKE—HAIMON'S *mother—comes out*
> *the door of the royal house, alone.*

CHORUS   Yes, I see poor Eurydike nearby—
The wife of Kreon. She comes here, perhaps,
Because she heard about her son—or by chance.

EURYDIKE   Men of the city!—as I was at the door,
To go in supplication and in prayer
To the goddess Pallas, I overheard some talk,
And when I chanced to loosen and pull back   1260
The bolts of the outer door to open it,
Word of dire harm to this house struck my ears,
And I fell against my women slaves, afraid,
And fainted. But no matter what report
Has come, tell it again! And I will listen
As one who has lived through adversity.

MESSENGER   I myself was nearby, my dear mistress,
And will tell you, and won't hold back a word
Of the truth—for why should I soften for you
What would show me to be a liar, later?   1270
Always, the truth is the right thing.
                                             I went
As guide with your husband to the highest place
On the plain, where the body of Polyneikes
Still lay, unpitied and torn apart by dogs.
We prayed to the goddess of crossroads and Pluto
To restrain their anger and to be benign,
Then we washed the body with pure water,
And what was left of him we put with young,
Freshly broken branches and burned, and then
With earth of his own land we built a mound   1280
For burial, straight and true, and afterward
We went toward the young girl's hollowed-out

Bridal crypt of Hades with its floor of rock.
And near that chamber without funeral rites,
One man hears a shrill wailing that sounds
Far off, and he comes rushing up to tell
My master Kreon—who, as he creeps nearer,
Hears all around him pitiful shouts that cannot
Be understood, and he groans aloud and cries
These anguished words of grief: "Oh miserable me,   1290
Am I a seer? Am I traveling along
A path that's more unfortunate than all
The roads I've taken? What greets me is the voice
Of my son. You men! Come here quickly! Closer!
Go to the tomb! Go look inside the mound,
There where those fitted stones have been torn out,
Go right up to the mouth of it to find
If what I'm hearing is the voice of my son
Haimon—or if the gods are tricking me!"

    At these commands from our despairing master,   1300
We looked. And at the back of the tomb we saw
The girl there, hanging by her neck in a noose
Tied of fine-woven linen, and the boy
Pressing against her, falling with his arms
Around her waist and moaning because the bed
Of his bride had been despoiled, down below,
And because of his father's actions and his own
Ill-fated marriage. When Kreon sees them, he goes
Inside toward him, moaning sadly, then
With wailing cries he shouts, "You desperate boy—   1310
What a thing you've done! What was in your mind?
What happened that spoiled your reason? Come out,
    son!
I beg you, like a supplicant!" But the boy
Looks wildly at him with fierce eyes and spits
In his face and without giving him an answer
Draws his sharp, two-edged sword, but as his father
Fled rushing out, the blow missed. Instantly
The boy, ill-fated and furious at himself,
Leaned over his sword, pushing it half its length
Into his side, and still in his senses, he wraps   1320

The girl in the weak crook of his arm, pulling
Her close, and gasping he spurts a quick stream,
Blood-red drops on her white cheek.
                                    One corpse
Atop another corpse, he lies there now,
Desolate boy, who in the end has had
His wedding ceremony—but in the house
Of Hades, having shown to all men that
Sheer folly is much the worst of all man's evils.

                        EURYDIKE *turns and goes into the royal house.*

CHORUS   What do you think this means? The lady has gone
             back
             Inside again, without a word, either good or bad.   1330

MESSENGER I, too, am amazed. I cherish, though, the hope
              That having heard of her son's pain, she will
              Not wail her cries in public in the city,
              But in the shelter of her own house she
              Will lead the private grieving among her servants.
              She's not without good judgment, and won't do
                 wrong.

CHORUS LEADER I do not know. But too much silence seems
                  To me as weighty as loud pointless weeping.

MESSENGER But I will learn, once I am in the house,
              If she is keeping hidden some close secret   1340
              In her raging heart. You speak well—too much
                 silence
              Also can point to what weighs heavily.

               FINAL EPISODE / SCENE VIII

             The MESSENGER *goes into the house, while from the
             side that leads in from beyond the city,* KREON *and
                 some of his attendants arrive with the body
                                     of* HAIMON.

CHORUS   *Chanting.*

And here is our Lord
                    Himself, arriving
With a conspicuous sign
                    In his arms, a memorial,
His own ruin—
                    No one else's (if it is
Lawful for us to say so),
                    Having himself done wrong.

KREON   *Singing.*

Oh!   *strophe a*
The stubborn wrong-
                    Doing and death-
Dealing of mistaken
                    Thinking!
Here you see
                    Kindred who have   1350
Killed and been
                    Killed! Oh my
Foolish heedlessness!
                    Oh my young
Son, dead
                    So young,
Aiee!
                    Aiee!
You died, you were
                    Torn away from us
Because of my
                    Foolishness, not yours!

CHORUS   *Speaking.*

Ah, you seem to recognize what justice is, too late!

KREON   *Singing.*

Oh!   *strophe b*
In my desolation, I have
           Learned! Then, then, some god
Leapt with all his heavy
           Weight and struck me in the   1360
Head and sent me spinning
           Down savage roads, over-
Turning my joy, to be trampled
           On! Oh no! No!
The burden of being mortal—
           The sad, exhausting burden!

                    The MESSENGER *returns from within the house*
                                    and sees KREON.

MESSENGER   *Speaking.*

Master, the woes that you come bearing in
Your arms belong to you, and yet I think
You will see even more inside the house.

    KREON   *Speaking.*

What worse woe is there, following on these woes?

MESSENGER   *Speaking.*

Your wife, poor woman—the mother absolute
Of this corpse—is dead of knife wounds just inflicted.

    KREON   *Singing.*

Ah!   *antistrophe a*   1370
Ah, Harbor of Hades
           Never to be purified!
Why, why do
           You destroy me?

To MESSENGER.

You bringer of bad
        Tidings for me—what
Words are you saying?
        Aiee! You have killed
A destroyed man
        Twice over! Speak,
Boy! Of what new
        Killing do you tell me?
Aiee!
        Aiee!—
A woman's
        Sacrificial
Death piled on
        Top of death?

SERVANTS *open the palace door,*
revealing the body of EURYDIKE.

CHORUS   *Speaking.*

See her! She is no longer hidden deep within.   1380

KREON   *Singing.*

Ah!   *antistrophe b*
Miserable me, I see this
        Second horror! What fate,
What fate, is waiting for me still?
        Only now I held my
Son in my arms,
        Miserable me, and now
I see her body before me.
        Ah! Ah!
Pitiful mother!
        Ah! My son!

MESSENGER   *Speaking.*

At the altar, with a sharp-edged, pointed blade
She stabbed herself with sudden force and allowed
Her eyes to close on darkness—after she wailed
For the empty bed of dead Megareus   1390
And for this son, too; and last, she chanted hymns
Of evil curses on you, killer of sons.

KREON   *Singing.*

Aiee! Aiee!   *strophe c*
I shake with dread!
        Why has no one
Stabbed straight
        Into my chest with a two-
Edged sword?
        Desolate me, aiee!
Desolate the anguish
        That is now mixed into me!

MESSENGER   *Speaking.*

Yes—you were charged by the dead woman here
With blame for this death and the other one.

KREON   *Speaking.*

How was she torn away from us so bloodily?   1400

MESSENGER   *Speaking.*

With her own hand, she struck herself below her liver,
When she learned of her son's bleak end, that brought
        sharp wailing.

KREON   *Singing.*

Ah me! Because of my   *strophe d*
      Guilt, these things will
Never be fitted to
      Any other man. It was
I, I who killed you,
      In my useless misery!
I speak the truth.
      You servants! Lead
Me quickly, lead me
      Away from everything,
I who am no more
      Than nothing!

CHORUS   *Speaking.*

If woes bring profit, then you advise what's profitable.
When woes are in our path, the briefest are the best.   1410

KREON   *Singing.*

Let it come! Let it come!   *antistrophe c*
May it appear to me—
      That best of fates
That brings my
      Final day,
The most perfect!
      Let it come! Let it come!
So that I will not
      See another day!

CHORUS   *Speaking.*

That's in the future. We must do what lies before us.
Those who take care of these things will take their
      care.

KREON   *Speaking.*

But I have prayed for everything I long for.

CHORUS   *Speaking.*

Don't pray for anything—for from whatever good
Or ill is destined for mortals, there's no deliverance.   1420

KREON   *Singing, as he looks from* HAIMON's *body*
                                         to EURYDIKE's.

Lead me away   *antistrophe d*
          From everything, a useless
Man, who killed you,
          My child!—although not
By my intent. And I killed
          You, also. Ah, my helpless misery!
I do not know which one
          To look at or where to
Lean now to find support.
          Everything is twisted in
My hands, while onto my head
          Unbearable fate has leapt down!

                              KREON'S MEN *lead him away.*

CHORUS   *Chanting.*
          Good sense is the
                    First principle
Of happiness. We
                    Must not act
Disrespectfully
                    Toward the gods.
Grand words of arrogant
                    Men, paid back with   1430
Great blows, in old age
                    Teach good sense.

NOTES

I [Charles Segal] have profited from the commentaries of Andrew Brown, *Sophocles: Antigone* (Warminster, 1987), Mark Griffith, *Sophocles: Antigone* (Cambridge, 1999), and Richard Jebb, *Sophocles, The Plays and Fragments*, III (Cambridge, 1900); and also from R. D. Dawe, ed., Sophokles, *Tragoediae*, vol. 2 (Leipzig, 1985); from J. C. Kamerbeek, *The Plays of Sophocles, Commentaries, Part III, The Antigone* (Leiden, 1978); and from H. Lloyd-Jones and N. G. Wilson, *Sophoclea* (Oxford, 1990).

Line numbers are given in this order: translation (bold type) / Greek text. Quotations from the translation are in italics; paraphrases or other renderings are in quotation marks.

CHARACTERS

ISMENE: probably a little younger than Antigone, as the latter is to be married first, but the play gives no clear indication.

THE CHORUS: Sophokles has chosen a Chorus of elderly citizens, men of stature and importance, to emphasize the civic and political aspects of his theme. One should keep in mind that classical Athens also contains a large population of resident aliens ("metics") and slaves, and that neither are citizens. Freeborn Athenian women, though they have many rights, do not have the right to vote, hold public office, or own property in their own names. They are expected to remain primarily in the house and to be concerned with the rearing of children and the management of domestic affairs. They do, however, have important religious functions (many cults had priestesses), particularly in the area of funerary ritual.

MESSENGER, and VARIOUS MALE ATTENDANTS; SERVANTS; SLAVES: Though the Guard is probably a lower-class citizen, the other minor figures on the stage are probably slaves. Slavery was an accepted part of Athenian life and an essential part of the ancient economy. Slaves did much of the menial work in the household and were often the manual workers in agriculture, the various trades, and mining. Slavery is not particularly an issue in the play, except in those cases in which it appears as an insult in angry exchanges between characters (e.g., 527–28 / 479, 568 / 517, 816 / 756).

1-117 / 1–99 *Prologue*

1–2 / 1 *Ismene, my own true sister . . . sharing our common bond of birth* Antigone's dense opening first line addressing Ismene suggests both her intense involvement in kin ties and the disastrously involuted nature of these ties within the house of Oidipous. The English can only approximate the effect of what in the Greek is, literally, "common self-sistered head of Ismene," i.e., my very own sister. This formulation, "head of" someone, is fairly common in tragedy and is a somewhat more emotional, loftier, and more dignified form of address than the ordinary. The phrasing is significant, for the words "common" and "self-" (in various compounds, or sometimes translated in such form as "with their own hands," 192 / 172) recur throughout the play to describe the incest and self-blinding of Oidipous and the mutual fratricide of the two brothers; see note on 61–71 / 49–57.

3 / 2 *one evil left to us by Oidipous* The play at once reminds us of the sufferings of the house of Oidipous, which include King Oidipous' murder of his father, Laios, and his incestuous marriage with his mother, Queen Iokaste, from which have been born Ismene and Antigone and their brothers Polyneikes and Eteokles. In many versions of the myth, the death of the two brothers at one another's hands results from Oidipous' curse on them. In *Antigone*, Oidipous has presumably died at Thebes; in *Oidipous at Kolonos*, composed some thirty-five years after *Antigone*, Oidipous wanders for many years in exile, blind and impoverished, attended by a devoted Antigone, until he arrives at Athens, where he curses the brothers shortly before his death. The curse is to be fulfilled soon afterwards at Thebes, and the play ends with Ismene and Antigone returning to Thebes, the point where *Antigone* begins. In Euripides' *Phoinikian Women* (409 BCE) Oidipous is still alive at the time of the brothers' quarrel and death. Also see Appendix 2.

7–8 / 4 *nothing that's not weighed down by ruin* The reading of the manuscripts here is uncertain. We adopt a widely accepted nineteenth-century emendation.

10 / 8 *the general* Throughout the play Antigone avoids calling Kreon, "the new ruler of Thebes," "king," or "lord." For an Athenian audience, the term "general" could also suggest one of the ten generals elected each year, who had broad powers in the field. Most Greek tragedies are set in the remote time of Mycenaean kingdoms, with their mythical atmosphere, but allow anachronistic references to Athenian political institutions. See note on 680 / 632.

13–14 / 10 *evils of our enemies... against our friends and dear ones* Antigone ends her speech with the two terms whose definition becomes a central issue in the play. "Friends," *philoi* (which we translate as "dear ones," also), is a particularly important term. It can include loved ones in the intimacy of the family, or "friends" in our broader and looser sense, or those on one's side in politics, one's "allies." The play exploits this range of meanings very fully. The connotations of intimacy are especially strong, as the underlying meaning of *philos* is what lies in the realm of one's own, in contrast to the other or the outsider. "Evils of our enemies" here can mean either the evil that Kreon intends for one of Antigone's "friends" or "dear ones," i.e., her brother Polyneikes, or the sufferings appropriate to her family's enemies, including perhaps the Argive attackers.

18–19 / 13–14 *two brothers... twin blows* The repeated numerals emphasize both the pathos and the horror of the mutual fratricide and recall the dark background of the kin ties in this accursed house. Similar collocations recur later: 62–72 / 49–57, 190–91 / 170–71.

21 / 16 *This very night* It is presumably just before dawn, after the night battle. See note on 118–81 / 100–61.

28–29 / 23–24 The manuscript text of these lines is probably corrupt; we have followed a widely accepted emendation.

33–38 / 27–30 *proclamation... left unmourned, unburied... their greedy joy* Here and elsewhere in the play Sophokles echoes Homeric language for the exposure of a warrior's corpse. Whether Kreon is legally justified so to maltreat the body is left open, and this gray area enables the tragic conflict to develop. Homeric warriors often threaten to maltreat an enemy's body (as Achilles, notably, does to that of Hector at the end of the *Iliad*), but in fact do not often do so. In the fifth century each side was generally allowed to gather and bury their dead, but in Athens the bodies of traitors could be denied burial within its borders. We learn of Kreon's treatment of the body first from this description by Antigone, which of course puts his behavior in the worst light. She stresses the two major components of proper burial, the keening or lament over the body and covering it in a tomb or grave (see notes on 472–76 / 427–31, 962–65 / 900–903, and 1275–81 / 1199–1204). Her vivid language depicting its violation by birds of prey, the most horrible fate a Greek can imagine for a corpse, conveys at once her intense emotional involvement. Kreon's announcement of his decree in 230–35 / 203–6 echoes the language of Antigone here, but adds *dogs* to her *birds* and omits her vivid image of the *sweet-tasting treasure*. See note on 1080–81 / 1016–18.

40 / 31 *The noble Kreon* Antigone's irony, following immediately on her description of the exposed body of Polyneikes, intimates her hatred of Kreon that will emerge increasingly in the course of the action.

46–47 / 35–36 *by public stoning murdered* This is the punishment for traitors in Athens. Kreon's decree later, however, refers only to Antigone's underground burial, with its many thematic and poetic advantages for the play. Although our sources for the myth of Antigone are very scanty, it is possible that her underground burial is Sophokles' invention. See note on 944–50 / 885–90.

48–49 / 37–38 *whether you are noble ... cowardly* Antigone espouses what are traditionally male heroic values of nobility or honor: see notes on 87–90 / 72–74 and 114–15 / 96–97.

52 / 41 *joining in my action and my burden* Antigone's repetition, in the Greek, of two verbs beginning with the prefix *sun-* (or *syn-*), "together with," expresses her sense of family solidarity (which, however, will soon fracture). "Burden," *ponos*, means "suffering" as well as "work," "toil," or "effort." That meaning recurs emphatically at the end of the play in Kreon's outcry at the magnitude of his "burden," 1363 / 1276. The burden/suffering that Ismene here refuses but later will attempt to share proves greater than either sister can anticipate in this opening scene.

53–60 / 42–48 *What sort of dangerous act ... not for him to keep me from my own* This exchange at once depicts the contrast between Ismene's timidity and Antigone's defiance of authority.

61 / 49 *Oh!* These exclamations recur throughout the play and are part of the conventionalized language of emotional expression here and in all of Greek tragedy. The Greek interjection, as here, is often *oimoi*, which has no easy English equivalent. It is often rendered "alas" but may express a wide range of emotions, including sorrow, annoyance, impatience, or anger. It is possible that these words in our text may have been merely a shorthand indication to the actor of the need for an emotional cry of some sort whose exact tone he would indicate by gesture and inflection of voice. We have rendered these terms differently as the various contexts seem to require.

61–71 / 49–57 *But sister...shared a doom in common* See note on 1–2 / 1. The vocabulary of "self," "each other," "common," etc. recalls the crimes and pollutions that mark the misfortunes of Oidipous' family. The phrase "self-striking hand" is echoed several times later in the play for violence directed against the self (192 / 172, 350/ 306, 1249 / 1175, 1401 / 1315, and compare also 62–65 / 51–52 here), thus suggesting the continuation of the sufferings of the accursed family into the next generation. This turning of the family against itself is also the subject of the second stasimon (633–77 / 582–630). The language here, recalling Antigone's opening lines, associates the suffering of the two living sisters with the too closely intertwined dooms of the dead incestuous parents and the fratricidal brothers.

62–68 / 49–54 *Our father, after beating out his eyes...mother and wife...violently disfigured her own life* Sophokles is referring to the familiar story of Oidipous and Iokaste, the subject of his *Oidipous Turannos* (written at least a decade later). Oidipous discovers that he has unwittingly killed his father, Laios, and married his mother, Iokaste. After this discovery, he blinds himself and Iokaste hangs herself. Sophokles will repeat some of his language for the hanging and blinding in the *Oidipous Turannos* (1266–78).

74–75 / 59–60 *rulers' vote and power* The Greek word for "vote" suggests analogies with fifth-century BCE Athenian political institutions; see note on 680 / 632. The word for "rulers" is *turannoi*, which does not mean "tyrant" in our sense but nevertheless may carry a pejorative association of autocratic and illegitimate power; see note on 556 / 506.

76–77 / 61–62 *born as women...war with men* Ismene introduces the conflict of genders that is developed further in Kreon's obsession with being defeated by a woman.

87–90 / 72–74 *For me it's noble...tied by love...holy crime* Noble (*kalos*) is an important value term in classical culture. It includes physical beauty, but also denotes what is beautiful, admirable, or (in an earlier idiom) fine. Antigone here reveals some of the principal springs of her actions. She combines her concern with the heroic values implicit in *kalos*, beautiful or noble, with her commitment to the bonds of family love (*philia*) and her paradoxical situation of committing what she regards as a justifiable crime. As a woman who espouses masculine heroic values and defies male authority to commit *a holy crime*, she at once defines herself as a paradoxical figure, and hence as tragic. See notes on **53–60 / 42–48** and on **114–15 / 96–97** and **345 / 301.**

91–92 / 75–76 *those down below...those up here...forever* This is the play's first statement of the contrast between upper and lower worlds, and it comes appropriately in the context of Antigone's devotion to the dead. This contrast recurs in her important speech of defiance to Kreon in **495–518 / 450–70**, in her lament in **910–12 / 850–53**, and in Teiresias' warning in **1135–43 / 1066–73**.

105 / 88 *heart that's hot for what is chilling* Ismene's reproach implies Antigone's eagerness for actions that should make one "chilled" with fear. In *Oidipous at Kolonos* 621–22 the aged Oidipous predicts that his "chill corpse" will drink the "warm blood" of Athens' enemies. The association of "chilling" with death reinforces Ismene's repugnance to Antigone's plan.

110–12 / 93–94 *hated by me...to the dead man...a hated enemy* These words indicate the harsher side of Antigone, in sharp contrast to her devotion to the ties of family love or *philia*.

113 / 95 *ill-considered plan* The contrast of supposed good sense and Antigone's "foolish" sacrifice of her life to bury her brother becomes a major motif in the conflict between Antigone and Kreon and a major component of her tragedy. Compare also Ismene's objection in **83 / 68**, that Antigone's intended act *makes no sense.* When Ismene exits, the scene ends, in fact, with the contrast between Antigone's "foolishness" and love or *philia* within the family (**116–17 / 99**).

114–15 / 96–97 *suffer nothing so bad as to deny me a death with honor* The accumulation of three negatives in a single line in the Greek syntax perhaps expresses Antigone's passionate determination to overcome the obstacles on which Ismene has insisted. *Death with honor*, Antigone's last words in the prologue, reaffirm the heroic ethos of the male warrior that she has espoused. See note on 53–60 / 42–48.

117 / 99 *rightly dear to your dear ones* The motif of family love (*philia*) ends the scene, along with a contrast of "love" and "death" (115 / 97). See note on 113 / 95.

118–81 / 100–161 *Parodos* (first ode) The Chorus of elderly Theban citizens enters the orchestra singing what is essentially a hymn of celebration for the victory over Polyneikes and his Argive army. It begins with the Sun and ends with Dionysos, one of Thebes' major divinities. In between it mentions Zeus, whose fiery lightning wards off the fire of the attackers (148–49 / 131; compare 140 / 122–23, 154 / 135), Ares, god of war, and Victory. Choruses of citizens regularly sang and danced in such civic rituals, and the ritual character of the ode is clearly indicated by the exhortation in 171–72 / 152–54 to visit all the temples of the gods in thanksgiving. The Chorus' opening words mark the new dawn (see note on 21 / 16), and the sun's radiance symbolically expresses the joy of the city's new lease on life. The Chorus depicts the attackers both as bloodthirsty birds of prey and as furious madmen, seething with the wildness of the followers of Dionysos (153–54 / 135–36). By contrast, the ode ends with the city's celebration of Dionysos, born in Thebes and a major protective divinity (174 / 154). The ode introduces a perspective very different from Antigone's in the opening scene, revealing the terror of the threatened city and the anxiety of the citizens about their very survival. It thus helps frame the play's fundamental conflict between loyalty to family and loyalty to the city. Appropriately, the ode introduces Kreon, the new ruler of the city (175–81 / 155–61). The ode contains a number of verbal echoes of Aiskhylos' *Seven against Thebes* (467 BCE), probably Sophokles' most influential predecessor in dramatizing the myth. That play became famous for its depiction of martial valor in defense of the city.

119–20 / 101–2 *seven-gated Thebes* The struggle over the city focuses on the defense of its seven gates. See note on 160 / 141.

124 / 106 *Argive warrior* The reading is not completely certain. If it is correct, it is probably to be understood collectively as the Argive army that Polyneikes is leading against his native city. In 148ff. / 131ff. the enemy is individualized in the ferocious attacker, Kapaneus.

127 / 108–9 *sharp bit stabbing him* The metaphor of the bit is common in Greek tragedy and recurs later in the play. Although riders today use the bit to restrain the horse, the metaphor here seems to imply its use to drive the animal forward with greater urgency, as the Argive warrior is rushing in headlong flight.

128–34 / 110–16 *Chanting* After the highly lyrical meters of the preceding lines, the Chorus changes to anapests, the marching meter that often accompanies their entrance. They continue this alternation of anapests and lyrical meters throughout the ode. Here and elsewhere we have used the term "chanting" to indicate the anapests.

129 / 110 *Quarrels of divisive Polyneikes* The phrase in Greek plays on the second part of Polyneikes' name, *neikos*, "quarrel." The reading of the manuscripts presents problems, and we here adopt a widely accepted emendation.

140 / 123 *fire-god* Hephaistos is the god of fire, here mentioned metonymically.

144 / 126 *the Theban Serpent* Kadmos founded Thebes by slaying the serpent or dragon that guarded its spring, Dirke. He then sowed the creature's teeth in the ground, and from these sprung the original warrior-race of Thebes, the Spartoi (Sown Men or Planted Men). They immediately fought one another, anticipating the internal conflicts of Thebes' royal house, and only five survived to become the first citizens and founding race of Thebes. In the background may be the Homeric image of an eagle fighting a serpent, but a metaphorical wrestling is also implied. The text is not entirely certain. Variant readings would give the sense "a hard-won victory of his (the Argive's) snake antagonist" (Griffith) or "the attack of the Serpent antagonist against which the Argive could not prevail" (see Jebb).

152 / 134 *tumbled crashing to the hard ground* This attacker is probably to be identified with the fiercest of the attackers, the boastful Kapaneus, who, however, stands for the fury and savagery of the enemy army as a whole.

153 / 136 *Bakkhic fury* Though not referring specifically to Dionysos, the phrase draws on the image of the ecstatic wildness and madness of the devotees of this god in their dances and processes. The language recurs in the last ode with much more specific Dionysiac associations: see notes on 1196/ 1121 and 1221–24 / 1149–52.

157–58 / 139–40 *the great war god...lead horse* Ares, god of war, is compared to the horse on the right-hand side of a team of horses, the position given to the strongest horse.

160 / 141 *Seven captains* One opponent is matched to each of the seven gates of Thebes. Sophokles here (as elsewhere in the ode) may have in mind the celebrated description of the attack in Aiskhylos' *Seven against Thebes*, 375–676, where Eteokles, in a long speech, appoints one captain to guard each gate against his adversary, keeping the seventh post, tragically, for himself against his brother, Polyneikes. See note on **118–81 / 100–161.**

162 / 143 *battle-turning Zeus* Zeus *Tropaios* receives the dedication of the "trophies," the enemies' armor or weapons that the victors set up on the field, at the place where the enemy made their "turning" (*tropê*) in flight.

163–66 / 144–47 *two doomed, cursed men...one father...one mother...one death in common* Sophokles again uses the contrast of one and two and the language of mutuality to interweave the death of brother by brother with the incestuous union of Oidipous and Iokaste. The density of the language itself in Greek represents the disastrously introverted nature of the kin ties in this family. See note on **18–19 / 13–14.**

170 / 150–51 *Forget this war* Sophokles may be alluding here to the ancient motif of song as bringing forgetfulness of grief: e.g., Hesiod, *Theogony*, 54–55, 99–103.

174 / 154 *Dionysos, Earth-shaker of Thebes* Dionysos, one of the major divinities of Thebes, often manifests himself by earthquakes. His appearance as a savior here contrasts with the Dionysiac madness of the attackers in **153–54 / 135–36.**

175–376 / 155–331 *First episode*

182–240 / 162–210 Kreon's first speech reveals the basic lines of his character, his concern with the state, authority, and power. His emphasis on the safety of the city in a time of danger would probably win him the sympathy of the audience of Athenian citizens. At the same time, his vehement insistence on his own authority (conveyed by his repeated use of the first person) and his reference to *all the power and the throne* (194/ 173) are disquieting hints of the authoritarian mood that will become increasingly visible later and so cast at least a shadow of doubt on the full justice of exposing Polyneikes' corpse. His sententious language, though appropriate to a political figure, contains more than a hint of self-righteousness.

193 / 172 *own polluting murder of one another* Pollution, an important theme in the play, is often caused, as here, by the shedding of blood between kin. Sophokles again uses the language of "self-" for this intra-familial bloodshed: see notes on 1–2 / 1, 61–71 / 49–57, 944–50 / 885–90, 1078–79 / 1015, 1107–12 / 1040–43, 1153–58 / 1080–83, and 1371 / 1284.

204–5 / 182–83 *any man who feels that someone close to him* Kreon's word here is *philos*, which can mean "loved one," "personal friend," or political ally. For the multiple meanings of *philos*, see note on 13–14 / 10. Here, as a few lines later in 210–11 / 187, Kreon defines *philos* wholly in terms of loyalty to the city. The strong contrast to Antigone's definition in the prologue sets up the conflict between them in the next scene.

214–15 / 191 *These are the laws ... make our city grow strong* It turns out that Kreon's view of the "laws" has just the opposite effect on his city. See note on 495–518 / 450–70.

230–35 / 203–6 *It has been proclaimed ... for anyone to see* See note on 33–38 / 27–30. Whereas Antigone in the prologue is emotionally involved in the proper burial of a brother's body, Kreon is concerned with the assertion of his authority.

244–45 / 213–14 *use any law in dealing with the dead* This proposition is exactly what Antigone challenges in the name of a different law, particularly about the dead. See note on 495–518 / 450–70.

246–47 / 215–16 *Make certain ... some younger man* The Chorus initially understands Kreon's "watch over" literally, as if they were to guard Polyneikes' corpse.

252–53 / 221–22 *And that will be the price ... hope for profit* Kreon characteristically reasserts his power to inflict the death penalty. This statement about *profit* is the first of many such remarks and indicates his obsession with plots against him and the material gain that allegedly motivates them.

254ff. / 223ff. *Guard* Greek tragedy occasionally gives a vivid personality to minor figures—for example, the Nurse in Aiskhylos' *Libation Bearers*. The Guard's breathless entrance prepares us for something unusual. He might be a slave, but his freedom of expression suggests rather that he is a free citizen, perhaps an example of the independent Athenian of the lower classes. A practical man, he is wary of Kreon's authority but is not completely intimidated. In any case, his elaborate garrulousness, in counterpoint to Kreon's self-important urgency, injects an element of humor into the scene, while his earthy and canny frankness about saving his own skin contrasts with Antigone's idealistic readiness to die.

276 / 241 *You take aim at me* Some take this line to mean "aiming at me," in the sense of "trying to figure me out" or "trying to confuse me." Others take the word to be a metaphor from hunting.

290 / 255 *not covered with a mound* The phrase can also mean "buried in a tomb," but so elaborate an interment cannot be in question here. The same root can denote a tomb. Kreon uses it for Antigone's underground *tomb* in 944 / 886, and she soon after begins her last iambic speech by addressing her *tomb* (951 / 891). When Kreon does finally bury Polyneikes at 1280 / 1203, the messenger uses this word to mean *mound*.

292–93 / 256 *as if by someone trying to avoid pollution* Anyone who passed an unburied corpse without covering it with dust was considered polluted and so could bring a curse on himself, his family, and his city. Pollution will prove to be a major concern of the play: see notes on 193 / 172 and 467 / 421. The guard, of course, has no idea that the actual perpetrator had motives rather different from what he here supposes.

319–20 / 278–79 *my own thoughts . . . directed by the gods* The Chorus' mild suggestion raises the question of possible divine intervention in the first burial of Polyneikes, the problem of the so-called double burial. The absence of marks on the ground, according to the Guard's description (284ff. / 249ff.), might lend credence to the Chorus' suggestion. It has also been suggested that the reference to *the first man of the day-watch* (288 / 253) points to the gods, for Antigone is still speaking to Ismene before dawn (*this very night*, 21 / 16) and so presumably cannot yet have buried the body. The gods' burial of Niobe's slain children in *Iliad*, 24.610–12 is a famous example of divine intervention of this kind. If Antigone did bury the body the first time, she has returned to cover it up again, as the next scene shows, and one must ask why she returns a second time, for the previous sprinkling of dust (as the Guard implies) would presumably have sufficed for the ritual. But it is easy enough to supply Antigone's motives for returning to the body a second time, although there is no explicit evidence for these in the text: she may have felt that the guards' uncovering of the body was an indignity to the corpse that she would not tolerate, or, as some have suggested, she actually wants to get caught. Some have objected that the questions suggested by the mention of the two burials would not have been noticed by an audience in live performance. The controversy remains open. The Chorus' remark here, however, indicates how a spectator might feel: at the very least, the gods *might have* buried the body the first time. Perhaps it suffices for the play that the possibility is raised, if not decided. Kreon's angry reply to the Chorus' suggestion is the first of many indications of his arrogant assumption that the gods are entirely on his side and that his will coincides with theirs; see **321ff.** / 280ff.

321ff. / 280ff. Kreon's somewhat grandiose language stresses the enormity of the attack and so of Polyneikes' crime. Kreon's gods are the visible, public gods of the city, who are worshiped in *temples with columns around them*, in contrast to the less visible gods of the underworld and of family cult, to whom Antigone primarily looks. And he increasingly identifies these civic gods with his own authority.

333–38 / 289–92 *Yet for a long time . . . raised a secret uproar . . . been content with me* Kreon expresses his obsession with plots against his authority in terms of the imagery of subduing animals characteristic of his concern with hierarchy and control. The recurrence of this theme in the first stasimon (**393–96** / 347–51) links that ode with issues of human authority, power, and autonomy in the play as a whole. Sophokles is rather vague about the time it took for this dissatisfaction to develop and find expression in the city, as the edict has only recently been proclaimed (see **28–49** / 23–38). For dramatic effect, Sophokles obviously has to condense the sense of time, as he does later in Haimon's remarks about popular sentiment in favor of Antigone (**747–55** / 692–700). What exactly Kreon has in mind is also somewhat vague. Some interpreters think that the Thebans' dissatisfaction is at Kreon's recent edict about the exposure of Polyneikes' body; others suppose the reference is to his regency in general, about which the play is also vague. Kreon's assumption that there are supporters of Polyneikes within the city who may still cause trouble is in keeping with the internal politics of Greek city-states in the fifth century.

340–45 / 295–301 *For nothing current . . . silver . . . all kinds of irreverence* Kreon characteristically focuses on material gain as the main motive for wrongdoing. His words would resonate with an audience accustomed to accusations of bribery in civic affairs, but they also indicate the narrow rationalism and materialism with which he views the world. He will be stymied by the very different motivations of Antigone's actions.

345 / 301 *All crimes... all kinds of irreverence* The Greek word *panourgia* (from *pan*, "every," and *ergon*, "act" or "deed") means an unscrupulous disregard for the laws and for the rights of others that would lead one to do "any and every act." The word carries unsavory associations of the meanness of a common criminal: see Bernard Knox, *The Heroic Temper* (Berkeley, Calif., 1964), 93. Kreon further emphasizes his law-and-order point of view by repeating the constituent parts of the word in "every act" (*pantos ergou*) in the next line. The verbal form of *panourgia* is also Antigone's word for her *holy crime* or "holy villainy" in 90 / 74 (*hosia panourgêsasa*), combining the verb with its opposite, *hosia*, "holy."

348 / 304 *If Zeus gets any reverence* Kreon appeals self-righteously to Zeus. This elaborate periodic sentence expresses the vehemence of his anger. *Reverence* for the gods becomes a major motif in the play, along with the accusations of *irreverence* (see note on 345 / 301). Kreon's reverence is entirely for the Olympian gods of the public religion; Antigone has her own *reverence* for the gods of the lower world.

355–59 / 310–14 *where to get your profit from... profiting... shameful earnings* Kreon ends his tirade with more generalizations about the dangers of profit, greed, and money.

362–65 / 317–20 *Would it be your ears... diagnose where I feel pain... born to talk* There is a touch of humor here that both points up and undercuts Kreon's passionate assertions of his authority.

372–76 / 327–31 *May he definitely be caught... owe the gods great gratitude* The Guard's remarks are addressed to himself (and the Chorus) and not intended for Kreon's hearing. In any case, the Guard's practical concern with his own safety contrasts with Antigone's total disregard for hers in the next scene (when, contrary to his expectations, he will return). There are no stage directions in the manuscripts. It is probable, though not absolutely certain, that Kreon exits immediately after 371 / 326.

377–416 / 332–75 *First stasimon* (second ode), one of the most celebrated choral odes of Greek tragedy, known as the Ode on Man. See the Introduction, pp. 28–30. Sophokles here draws on contemporary theories of the origins of civilization associated with Sophists like Protagoras and Presocratic philosophers like Democritus. But he also models the opening of the poem on the central ode of Aiskhylos' *Libation Bearers* (458/457 BCE), substituting a praise of human intelligence for Aiskhylos' accusations of the deadly lust of women. The ode has multiple levels of meaning. The conservative elders of the city chorus speak in pious generalities, separating themselves from any criminal who would be *outside any city*; but their words, like almost everything in the ode, carry meanings that reach beyond what they can know at this moment. Three words of the opening phrase in the translation (*At many things— wonders, terrors—we feel awe*), awe, terror, and wonder, translate the ambiguity of the single Greek word *deinon,* which may refer to both Kreon and Antigone and, more broadly, to the ambiguous capacities of human beings generally, who, as the ode says (and as the play shows), may move *both to evil and to good* (409 / 367). The echo of Aiskhylos can evoke the dangerous and destructive passions of women and so point to Antigone. Yet the praise of mankind's control of nature also points to Kreon, particularly because the ode's language of taming, trapping, and hunting resonates with the authoritarian language of Kreon and his will to power and domination. The warnings about mankind's impotence before Hades, or Death (403–5 / 361–62), also evoke the area of conflict between Kreon and Antigone that will, in fact, reveal Kreon's inability totally to control and dominate his world. The pointed rhetorical juxtaposition of *inventive in everything* and *without invention* (401–2 / 360) in these lines encapsulates the play's tragic ambiguity of human power. It is echoed in the similar syntactical pattern of *high in his city . . . outside any city* (412–13 / 370).

382–83 / 338 *Earth . . . highest of all the gods* Here *highest* has the sense of "supreme," "most revered," because, as the foundation of all being, Earth is the oldest: see Hesiod, *Theogony,* 117–18, 126–33. Nevertheless, the adjective may have a certain paradoxical ring, which may suggest the interplay between upper and lower realms that is so important to the play: see note on 737–38 / 683–84.

394–95 / 350 *harnesses the horse* The manuscript reading for *harnesses* is corrupt, and this is a plausible emendation. Other editors emend to "fetters" or "hobbles."

409–11 / 368–69 *Honoring the laws of the earth and the justice of the gods* We are reminded of Kreon's and Antigone's very different views of which laws and gods to obey and also of their very different ways of understanding "earth": for Kreon "earth" is the political territory of Thebes, defined by human laws; for Antigone it is the realm of the gods below, who protect the rites of the dead: compare her speech in the next scene, **495–518** / 450–70. The manuscripts here read "weaving" or "threading in the laws," which is barely possible but unlikely, and so we have adopted the widely accepted emendation, "honoring".

413 / 371 *he who dares to consort* This "dares" recurs to describe Antigone's transgression, in Kreon's view: **494** / 449, **979** / 915.

417–632 *Second episode*

420 / 379–80 *Oh unfortunate child of your unfortunate father* The Chorus' address to Antigone again recalls the family misfortunes, which will also be the subject of the next ode.

422–23 / 382 *disobeyed the laws of the king* Antigone, of course, looks toward a different kind of law: see note on **495–518** / 450–70.

425–632 / 384–581 The direct, on-stage conflict between Antigone and Kreon is the only scene in the play that requires the use of all three actors permitted by the conventions of Greek tragedy. The actor who plays the Guard exits at **490** / 445 and returns at **577** / 526 in the role of Ismene.

425–26 / 384–85 *Here's who did the deed* The Guard's clipped phrasing expresses his eagerness to exculpate himself, which he expresses again at the opening of his speech to Kreon (**429–43** / 388–400).

434–35 / 392 *Happiness . . . beyond one's very hopes* The manuscripts read "happiness outside and beyond one's hopes," but syntactical difficulties are in favor of the emendation, *for which one prays*, which is also in keeping with the Guard's elation at escaping blame.

450ff. / 407ff. *Well, what happened was* As the Guard recounts the capture of Antigone, he becomes expansive. His narrative gives a vivid picture of the remote place, outside the city walls, where Polyneikes' corpse has been left to rot. The details of the *whirlwind* that *raised a pillar of dust . . . high as heaven* (**462ff.** / 417ff.) and *this supernatural plague* (**467** / 421) suggest the mysterious powers of nature and the gods that are not as controllable as the previous ode has implied. The motif of dust thrown into the sky also continues a pattern of interaction between upper and lower worlds that runs throughout the play. The hints of supernatural intervention remain consistent with the possibility (never more than that) that the gods have had a role in the burial; see note on **319–20** / 278–79. The dust storm, in any case, has helped Antigone to achieve her aim and casts an aura of mystery about this event.

463–64 / 418 *trouble high as heaven* Literally, "a woe, or grief, in the sky." The phrase can also mean "a trouble rising to the sky" or "a trouble sent from the sky." Sophokles has probably left some deliberate openness to other meanings to suggest the possibility of divine intervention: see the previous note.

467 / 421 *this supernatural plague* The phrase can mean both "sent by the gods" or merely "supernatural," "marvelous." "Plague" or "disease," which the Guard here uses in a general sense, becomes much more specific later in the dangerous "plague" of pollution from the exposed corpse. The Guard's description here, along with the *storm of trouble high as heaven*, foreshadows that pollution carried into the sky by the carrion-eating birds in Teiresias' prophecy in 1079–86 / 1015–22. See notes on 1078–79 / 1015 and 1107–11 / 1040–43.

472–76 / 427–31 *she moaned . . . pours libations* Antigone fulfills two of the offices to the dead that Kreon has forbidden, the ritual lamentation and the covering of dust; see notes on 961–62 / 901, 1275–85 / 1199–1204. The language of lamentation here is echoed later in the laments of Haimon in 1305 / 1224 and of Eurydike in 1389–92 / 1302–5, which, like Antigone's lament here, are offstage events reported by a narrator. The simile comparing Antigone's lament to the cries of a bird whose fledglings have been taken conveys her emotional intensity and also underlines her involvement in the traditional female role of lamenting the dead. It may also suggest some sympathy for her on the part of the narrator, the Guard, in contrast to Kreon's harshness; see note on 481 / 436. The comparison to the bird also suggests her identification with the subdued natural world of the Ode of Man, whose first antistrophe begins with the netting of birds (387ff. / 342ff.). Note, too, the Guard's metaphor of "hunting her down" in 477 / 433. His use of the passive *this wailing child is seen* in 468 / 423 also adds to the pathos of Antigone's helplessness. In his eagerness to re-create as vividly as possible an event that is so important to him (and to us), the Guard switches from past to present tense and back again.

479–80 / 434–35 *what she'd done, before, and what she now was doing* While the Guard emphasizes the two separate acts of defiant burial, he does not explicitly say that Antigone performed both acts, only that she made no denial. The careful phrasing still leaves open the possibility of divine agency for the first burial.

481 / 436 *both satisfaction and pain* Despite his joy for himself, the Guard still pities Antigone—the first expression of sympathy for her, and from an unexpected quarter.

484–85 / 439–40 *all of these things are less to me than safety for myself* The Guard's attitude contrasts with Antigone's defiant lack of concern for her personal safety.

486 / 441 *turning your head away, to the ground* Here Sophokles implies a stage direction to the actor playing Antigone. Antigone's gesture expresses defiance: she refuses to look at Kreon.

495–518 / 450–70 *It was not Zeus . . . to being charged as foolish by a fool* In contrast to her silent entrance and clipped answers to Kreon just before, Antigone now bursts forth in a torrent of high idealism. In this important speech she frames her motives in the largest and most general terms, expressing her defense of principles of justice and behavior. She identifies these both *with the gods below the earth* and with *laws of the gods, that are unwritten and unfailing,* in contrast to the man-made *proclamation* of Kreon. She thus raises the question of whether a "good" citizen has the right to disobey what she or he perceives as unjust authority, in the name of higher, more universal laws. She has in mind both the universally recognized right of the dead to burial (her "unwritten laws") and the particular rights of the gods beneath the earth, the chthonic divinities, like Hades and Persephone, who are concerned with the proper burial of the dead.

508–10 / 461–62 *But if I die before my time, I count that as my profit* Antigone's defiance of death and her notion of *profit* contrast with and undercut Kreon's views of the power of both.

513–15 / 466–67 *But if I let the son of my own mother lie dead and unburied* Here Antigone cites her intimate family ties as part of her motivation, parallel to the more abstract statement of principle at the opening of her speech. The former reasoning will dominate her last speech (**967ff.** / 905ff.).

517–18 / 469–70 *foolish . . . to being charged as foolish by a fool* Antigone ends her speech with the recurrent motif of sensible behavior, but her notion of good sense again contrasts with Kreon's narrowly materialistic and rationalistic view of human behavior.

519–20 / 471–72 *fierce child is the offspring of her fierce father* The Chorus returns to
Antigone's heredity from Oidipous to account for her behavior, harking
back to their same point earlier (see note on 420 / 379–80). Despite the
Chorus' repetition of this idea in the next ode, it would be an oversim-
plification to regard family heredity or the family curse as the sole key to
the meaning of the tragedy. It is a contributing factor, to be sure, but one
must keep in mind that the Chorus functions as an actor among actors;
their hypotheses are on the same level as those of the other characters'
attempts to account for the suffering. *Offspring* here is the reading of
most of the manuscripts. It is also the word that the Chorus uses to
introduce Haimon at 673 / 627. Here some editors amend to a word for
"spirit" or "temper": Antigone shows "the fierce temper of a fierce
father."

521–28 / 473–79 *rigid wills . . . hardest iron . . . a small sharp bit . . . someone who's the
slave of others* Kreon characteristically responds to the challenge to his
authority with harsh images of technological mastery and taming animals, both of which hark back to the Ode on Man. His references to
slavery and, sarcastically, to Antigone as *the man* (534 / 484) are also
typically vehement assertions of hierarchy and increasing indications of
his authoritarian views.

535–38 / 486–87 *no matter if she is my sister's child . . . our household shrine to Zeus*
Kreon's dismissal of family ties takes the form of rejecting *Zeus Herkeios*,
"Zeus of the courtyard," one of the gods who preside over and protect
the family. The defiance of Zeus is part of a pattern in Kreon's speeches
(see notes on 348 / 304 and 1107–12 / 1040–43), and in this case verges on
a dangerous impiety. In fact, Kreon's statement sounds even more
blasphemous than the translation can convey, for *Zeus Herkeios* stands
as a metonym for the family that Zeus' altar sanctifies and protects.
Literally, he says, "not even if she is a closer relation than *Zeus Herkeios*
entire."

544–45 / 493–94 *plan in the dark . . . as a thief* Kreon returns to his favorite idea of
secret plotting and wrongful gain.

550–54 / 499–504 *Then why delay . . . what greater glory . . . my own true brother* Antigone defies Kreon's greatest token of power, the ability to put
her to death. She again claims the traditionally masculine heroism,
or glory, that she had looked to in the prologue (see note on 48–49 /
37–38).

136

555–56 / 505 *if fear did not lock up their tongues* Compare Kreon's denunciation of anyone who *is afraid of speaking and locks up his tongue* in his opening speech, **202–3** / 180. Antigone's point is just the reverse of Kreon's— she accuses him of silencing, rather than encouraging, the citizens to speak out.

556 / 506 *one-man rule* Antigone's word, *turannis*, though it does not carry the fully pejorative notions of "tyranny" that develop with Plato, nevertheless associates Kreon with "tyrannical" behavior, that is, with the arbitrary exercise of power that lacks the full, legitimate authority of endorsement by all the people. "Tyrannies" developed in many Greek cities in the course of the sixth century, as influential men allied themselves with the people and took over power from the dominant aristocratic families. They often promoted large building programs and expanded religious and cultural institutions, such as festivals and public cults, to ingratiate themselves with the people, and were not necessarily seen as "tyrannical" in the modern sense. Peisistratos in Athens and Polykrates of Samos were particularly successful and noteworthy examples. Kreon has succeeded to his rule through the ties of kinship, as he says (**194–95** / 173–74), but as a new ruler he is still insecure and afraid of conspiracies, a common concern of "tyrants." See note on **74–75** / 59–60.

559–74 / 508–23 The line-by-line exchange, or stichomythia, sharply sets out the diametrically opposed viewpoints of Kreon and Antigone, particularly with regard to their valuing of family ties (*philia*) versus the demands of the city. In connection with the former, Antigone also asserts the importance of the laws of Hades (**570** / 519), that is, the rights of burial that belong to the gods of the lower world (see note on **495–518** / 450–70).

559 / 508 *alone among the Thebans* Kreon emphasizes Antigone's isolation, but his view will be challenged later by Haimon, who suggests that Kreon's position is the isolated one: **793–99** / 733–39.

563 / 512 *he who died against him* Kreon is referring to Eteokles.

567 / 516 *honor him the same as the irreverent one* Here, as throughout this debate, Kreon insists on *differentiating* the two brothers on the basis of their opposite loyalties to the city, whereas Antigone insists on their *equality* in terms of the bonds of family and the rights due to the dead.

568 / 517 *my brother who died* Antigone means Polyneikes, although, of course, both brothers have died.

570 / 519 *these laws* A variant reading has "Hades wishes equal laws," which some editors accept, although it has weaker manuscript authority.

574 / 523 *not to join in hate but to join in love* Sophokles gives Antigone's response great rhetorical force by apparently coining two new words for her, *sunekthein* and *sumphilein*. Antigone reasserts her commitment to family ties, her "friends" or "dear ones," *philoi*, but she does so with a particular emphasis on "sharing" or "joining in" the relationship of kin ties (*sum-philein*), in contrast to Kreon's sharp differentiation of "friends" and "enemies." For her, the supreme value is her bond of "joining with" those she regards as her "friends" or "loved ones," and she rejects Kreon's concern with separating her loved ones (*philoi*) as political "enemies" (*ekhthroi*). Knox, *Heroic Temper*, 82, catches this point well in his paraphrase, "I was born to join not in their political hatred for each other but in their love for each other as blood brothers"—to which one must add also her own bond of family love (*philia*) to both brothers. Karl Reinhardt, *Sophokles* (1947), trans. H. and D. Harvey (Oxford, 1979), 78–79, paraphrases, "I was not born into the circle which believes 'Hate your enemy,' but into the one where love between blood relations knows itself to be in harmony with its like." And he comments, "Not that Antigone is the personification of love, but her hate and love spring from a different level from that which produces Kreon's friendships and enmities." Lloyd-Jones, in his Loeb edition, also calls attention to the importance of birth, rather than "inborn nature," in Antigone's verb, *ephun*, and translates, "I have no enemies by birth, but I have friends by birth." While it is important to keep in mind the specific reference of *philein* to the ties of family and so not make Antigone indulge in a saccharine declaration of a universally loving nature, Lloyd-Jones' interpretation seems to give insufficient force to the repeated *sun-*, "sharing in" love or hate.

575–76 / 524–25 *Then go down there ... a woman will not rule!* Kreon impatiently and sarcastically dismisses Antigone's concern with the gods of the lower world. He treats her with increasing cruelty and callousness, which probably contribute to our declining sympathy for him in the middle third of the play.

584–85 / 533 *I raised a double ruin to bring down the throne* Kreon again focuses on maintaining his power, which may, in turn, reflect his insecurities about his new position.

587ff. / 536ff. The exchange between the two sisters, which has many echoes of their dialogue in the prologue, exhibits the fierceness of Antigone's commitment to her independence of action and her devotion to the dead and the realm of the dead (e.g., **610f. /** [559f.)]

600 / 549 *Ask Kreon . . . whose side you take* The last phrase uses a word that means both "kin" and "mourner" of the dead, implying perhaps Antigone's view of herself as the only one entitled to mourn Polyneikes, but also harshly insulting Ismene, as if Ismene regarded only Kreon as her "kinsman." So devoted to the bonds of kinship, Antigone is cruel and ungenerous to the last of her living kin.

602 / 551 This dense line has a number of possible meanings, as the verb can mean both "laugh" and "mock," and Antigone may be referring to "mocking" Ismene or "mocking" (laughing at) Kreon. Some have assumed that a line or two has dropped out.

619 / 568 *kill your own son's bride-to-be* This is the first allusion in the play to Haimon, and it comes from Ismene, not Antigone. The latter never speaks directly of Haimon, although, in her last scene on the stage, she laments the loss of marriage. See note on **623 / 572.**

620 / 569 *other furrows he can plant* The crude agricultural metaphor may allude to the Athenian marriage formula, which stipulates "the sowing of legitimate children." In *Oidipous Turannos*, Sophokles makes heavy use of such agricultural metaphors for the incestuous union of Oidipous and Iokaste. At the same time, the metaphor reveals Kreon's tendency to depersonalize and devalue intimate emotional ties by objectification, generalization, or cliché.

621 / 570 *Not the way he and she were fitting for each other* The word "fitting" belongs to the language of betrothal and so may imply the "appropriateness" of this marriage between first cousins, which considered highly desirable when the girl's father has died without male heirs and so leaves only daughters to inherit the property. Her marriage to her uncle's son (or even to the uncle himself, if he is unmarried) keeps the property in the family. "Fitting" can also mean that Haimon and Antigone are

623 / 572 *Dearest Haimon* This line has provoked considerable controversy. The manuscripts attribute it to Ismene, which we believe to be correct, as Ismene is the first to introduce the subject of Haimon. Having failed to soften Antigone, she now brings up the marriage in the hope of softening Kreon. Antigone, resolved to die for her devotion to her family of origin, shows no interest in Haimon and, as we have noted, never mentions him. By *your marriage-bed* in the following line, Kreon then means, "the marriage that you, Ismene, speak of," referring to her words immediately preceding. Attributions of speakers in the manuscripts, however, are not always reliable, and the first printed edition of Sophokles, the Aldine text of 1502, attributes the line to Antigone, and some editors have accepted this.

627–28 / 576–77 *Ismene: It seems decided, then, that she will die—Kreon: By you and by me!* The Greek word for "decided," which can also mean "decreed," has the sense of a political decision. Some interpreters take Kreon's reply to be in an ironic tone, which also reflects his tyrannical nature. Others think that Kreon understands Ismene's verb in an alternative sense, "it seems good," and, again, replies in an ironic tone of voice, but this meaning seems less probable, given the perfective verb form that Ismene uses. Some manuscripts attribute **627 / 576** to the Chorus leader, and some editors accept this. If this is so, then Kreon would be including them in his decision ("Yes, it has been decided by you [Chorus leader] and by me"), which seems less likely. Kreon's remarks in the rest of the scene are also sarcastic and callous. He adopts the same tone later in **942–43 / 883–84**.

633–77 / 582–630 *Second stasimon* (third ode) Coming directly after the condemnation of Antigone to death, the mood of this ode is darker, in every sense, than that of the previous two odes. This mood, along with the emphasis on the gods of the lower world and the remote power of Olympian Zeus, leads into the next phase of the action, where the tragic catastrophe begins to unfold. The Chorus here develops its earlier explanation of Antigone's imminent death in terms of the accursed house of her ancestors, the Labdakids. Labdakos is the father of Laios and so the great-grandfather of Antigone and Ismene.

635–36 / 585 *creeps over a multitude of generations* The Chorus' allusion to the family curse working over many generations recalls Antigone's opening lines of the play, about the sufferings of Oidipous that have now afflicted his daughters.

636–41 / 586–92 The image of the stormy, turbulent northern sea contrasts with the tamed sea of the first stasimon, the Ode on Man; this difference is indicative of the growing sense of disaster.

642–44 / 594–95 *afflictions . . . yet earlier afflictions of the dead* The Chorus means that the woes of the living Labdakids, i.e., Antigone and Ismene, are being added to those of the already dead members of the family, from Laios through Eteokles and Polyneikes. It is also possible to construe these dense lines to mean that the woes of the dead Labdakids are being added to those of their living kin, but this is rather less likely.

647–50 / 598–603 *rootstock of the House of Oidipous . . . reaped by blood-red dust of the gods under the earth . . . a Fury in the mind* These are among the most difficult and controversial lines of the play. The image of the bloody dust "reaping" or "mowing down" the root of Oidipous' house is bold, too bold for many editors, who emend the word "dust" (*konis*, the reading of all the manuscripts) to "knife" (*kopis*). But the manuscript reading is in keeping with the play's emphasis on the powers of the lower world; and the bloody dust evokes the death of the two brothers, the continuing doom of the house in Antigone's sprinkling of dust over Polyneikes' body, and perhaps also the dust storm in which she performs that burial (see **291 / 256, 451–52 / 409, 474 / 429**). The emendation *kopis*, moreover, would refer to a "chopper," or sacrificial knife, which does not seem particularly appropriate here. Further support for the manuscript reading comes from Aiskhylos' *Seven against Thebes*, which focuses on the death of the two brothers and is almost certainly in the background here. Aiskhylos' chorus describes how, at the mutual slaughter of the two brothers, "the earth's dust drinks the red clotted blood" (*Seven*, 734–37). In the next strophe Aiskhylos' chorus goes on to describe Oidipous' patricide and incestuous marriage, in which he "endured the bloody *root*" (referring to the incest and its consequences). That strophe ends with "the madness of *mind*" that "brought together" Oidipous and Iokaste as bride and bridegroom (*Seven*, 756–57), and Sophokles may also be referring to that passage in Aiskhylos' antistrophe here, *foolishness of speech and a Fury in the mind* (**650 / 603**). The Furies, or Erinyes, are the avenging deities of the lower world who typically punish the crime of bloodshed within the family. In this function they are also often the instruments that fulfill a family curse. They typically bring madness upon their victims. Thus, Antigone's *Fury in the mind* here seems to refer to her ritual burial of Polyneikes and its aftermath where (as the Chorus sees it) reason and good sense give way to the destructive madness and folly that persist in the house of Oidipous as the result of the inherited curse (e.g., **420** / 379–80, **612–13** / 561–62, **913ff.** / 853ff.). The reference to a Fury also picks up the motif of the dangerous power of the gods of the netherworld who will eventually punish Kreon; see note on **1145–46** / 1074. Sophokles' moralizing use of the agricultural imagery here also recalls Aiskhylos, *Persians*, 821–22, where King Dareios accounts for Xerxes' fall in similar terms: the latter's "outrage" (*hubris*) against Greece "mows down (*ex-amâi*) the much-lamenting harvest" that sprang up from the excessive overgrowth of his destructive folly (*atê*).

651ff. / 604ff. The second strophe contrasts the remote, eternal power of the gods with the sufferings of human beings and the mortal generations of the family and its sufferings. The Chorus gives particular prominence to Zeus, and we may recall Kreon's dangerous dismissal of Zeus' power at various points in the play; see notes on **495–518** / 450–70 and **708–9** / 658–59.

652–53 / 606 *sleep that catches everyone in its nets* This epithet of "sleep" is an emendation of the manuscript reading, "sleep the all-aging," which makes little sense here and is regarded as corrupt by most editors.

659–661 / 613–14 *only one law . . . beyond the reach of ruin* This divine law contrasts with Kreon's insistence on the human law of the city that he sees himself as representing. The text of this passage has some uncertainties, and we adopt a plausible and widely accepted emendation.

664 / 617 *desires light as air* Sophokles also uses this adjective of the birds trapped by human cleverness in the Ode on Man (**387** / 342), perhaps signaling here two opposite possibilities of human behavior. *Desires* also points ahead to the next ode, in which the force of erotic desire will emerge as one of the ingredients of the tragedy.

665–67 / 618–19 *he cannot see clearly until already he has burnt his foot* Sophokles seems to be adapting two traditional sayings—knowing one's disastrous situation only when it is too late, and walking on ashes as a metaphor for dangerous and foolish behavior.

668 / 622 *famous saying* The Chorus refers to a sentiment that occurs in various forms in early Greek literature and tragedy, that the gods destroy the judgment of the person bent on evil and destruction. As we might phrase it in our more psychologizing terms, the gods collaborate with the evil tendencies of the prospective criminal to lead him to his ruin. We would probably understand "god" as standing for all the invisible forces that twist a person's mind to destructive and self-destructive crimes.

671–72 / 624–25 The ode ends with a strong repetition of the word *ruin, atê*, which can also mean the folly or infatuation that leads to ruin. The same word also ends the previous strophe (**661 / 614**). See also notes on **1344–45 / 1258–60** and **1345 / 1260**.

673 / 626–27 *last and youngest offspring* The phrase hints at the dark motif of family ties in the background and also at the death of Kreon's other son, Megareus, mentioned in **1390 / 1303** (see note on **1387–92 / 1301–5**). The ominous associations of the phrase are also suggested by the use of *last* for the doomed race of Antigone's family in **647 / 599** and her *last road* in **867 / 807**.

678–842 / 631–780 *Third episode* The scene between Haimon and his father comes at roughly the midpoint of the play and marks a major shift of emphasis. It confirms the autocratic side of Kreon, introduces a new perspective on Antigone, and exposes the vulnerable area of Kreon's life, his own family ties. It also reflects his insensitivity in this area of family ties, for Kreon misunderstands his son's genuine concern for him and gradually allows his suspicion of Haimon's devotion to Antigone to overshadow his son's filial loyalty. Hence the brutal ending of the scene, with Kreon's further misunderstanding of Haimon's threat at his exit; see note on **811–12 / 751–52**, and also Introduction, pp. 12, 18–20.

678 / 631 *better than the seers* Sophokles is adapting a proverbial phrase indicating direct and immediate knowledge, but he may also be foreshadowing the importance of seers in the ensuing action.

680 / 632 *final vote* This is another term, like *general* in **10 / 8**, that would resonate with the contemporary Athenian audience, for whom voting is an important part of the democracy. See note on **74–75 / 59–60**.

682 / 635 *Father, I'm yours* Haimon, knowing his father's temperament, wisely begins with an affirmation of total allegiance, which he will totally reverse by the end of the scene. Here he encourages Kreon to expatiate, characteristically, on some of his favorite themes: obedience, hierarchy, the analogy between authority in the family and in the city, the dangers of subjection to women, and total commitment to the city.

699–700 / 650 *that soon enough grows cold wrapped in your arms* This striking phrase consists of only two words in the Greek, literally, "a cold embracing." The tragic irony in the phrase is that Kreon unwittingly foresees the way in which Haimon will, finally, wrap his arms about Antigone's corpse in **1320–21 / 1237**; and this irony is made more pointed by Kreon's having expressed an expectation of knowing *better than seers* what his son would do (**678 / 631**).

707 / 658 *I'll kill her* Kreon's phrase, as brutal in the Greek as it is in English, is not only tactless, addressed as it is to Antigone's betrothed, but also shows his cruelty and his tendency to associate the rule of law in the city with his personal authority; compare his similar first-person statement in **833 / 773**, *I'll lead her out.* (But see note on **833–34 / 773–74.**) We may contrast the emphasis elsewhere on her execution as the action of the entire city; compare **46–47 / 36, 837–38 / 776**. Haimon's restraint in the light of this brutal announcement is remarkable. Only at the end of the scene does he lose patience.

708–9 / 658–59 *let her sing her hymns in praise of Zeus the god of bonds of blood!* Kreon's dismissal of family bonds in favor of absolute obedience to the city once more takes the form of a dangerous defiance of Zeus; see notes on **348 / 304, 535–38 / 486–87, 651ff. / 604ff.** We are reminded particularly of his scorn of *Zeus Herkeios* in **535–38 / 486–87**. His scorn of women's lament recurs in his taunts to Antigone later; compare **942–43 / 883–84**. It is perhaps part of the tragic irony that the Greek word for "sing her hymns" recurs in Eurydike's "hymn" of curses against Kreon at the end (**1391–92 / 1305**)—a lament that he cannot dismiss this time; see note on **1387–92 / 1301–5**.

714–23 / 663–71 *A man like that* ... With many editors since the nineteenth century, we accept the transposition of some of these lines (especially **718–23 / 663–67**) to a later place in the speech. The problem, however, may lie more with Kreon than with the manuscripts. After his peremptory resolution to kill Antigone in **707 / 658**, he can still go on with his gnomic generalizations, oblivious to the devastating effect that it must have on Haimon.

722–23 / 666–67 *must be obeyed in everything...what's just, and the opposite* Some editors have suspected that these lines are spurious and deleted them. Yet they are in character, and they come at the point when Kreon, warming to his favorite subject, is carried away to excess. If they are authentic, they are revealing of Kreon's absolutist notion of "law," which for him is to be identified with obedience to authority, not justice. Contrast Antigone at **495–518** / 450–70.

731–34 / 679–80 Kreon ends with a restatement of another of his favorite themes: not being subject to women (compare **696ff.** / 648ff., also Ismene at **76–77** / 61–62). His last three lines contain a word play hard to render into English, for to be "defeated by" and "weaker than" are both from the same root (*hêttôn*, worse than, inferior to), so that to be "defeated by a woman" is also to be "weaker than a woman" or "inferior to a woman." On this note he ends his speech. See also **806** / 746.

737–83 / 683–723 Haimon again begins moderately, with neutral generalizations, but is soon on more delicate ground with his report of the city's secret praise of Antigone (**747ff.** / 691ff.), which, for the first time, offers a public perspective on Antigone contrary to Kreon's. Haimon is careful to phrase these views as the city's, not his own; but his remarks here endorse what Antigone herself, in her defiance of Kreon at **555–56** / 504–5, had said about other, hidden voices in the city and what Kreon had himself said about voices of dissatisfaction among the citizens (see note on **333–38** / 289–92). Haimon also indirectly validates Antigone's claims to "glory" or "honor" in the prologue (compare **87ff.** / 72ff., **114–15** / 96–97, **552–54** / 502–4, and see note on **550–54** / 499–504).

737–38 / 683–84 *good sense—highest of all the things that we possess* Haimon's *highest* echoes the epithet of Earth in the Ode on Man (**383** / 338). May there be some tragic irony in this exaltation of the two things that Kreon, as it proves, scorns?

742–44 / 688–89 A variant reading, which has weaker manuscript support, would make Kreon the subject and give the sense, "You are not naturally disposed to foresee everything that people say or do or have (as reasons) for blame." But, aside from the stronger manuscript support for the first reading, it seems more appropriate for Haimon at this point to speak of his own limitations rather than those of his father, whom he still hopes to win over by persuasion.

745–47 / 690–91 *to the common citizen . . . your eye becomes a terror* The syntax of the Greek is slightly harsh, and some editors have supposed that at least one line has dropped out. But the syntax, though awkward, is within the realm of possibility.

766–67 / 708–9 *when men like that show what's inside them . . . empty* The metaphor here refers to a folded writing tablet that would be read on being unfolded or *opened up*. The figure of "opening" the interior of a person so as to reveal the hidden truth of character recurs frequently in classical Greek literature and tragedy.

771–83 / 712–23 The metaphors of pliancy and yielding to nature recall Kreon's warnings to Antigone in terms of the hardness of metals, **521–24 / 473–76**. The sailing metaphor recalls Kreon's very different use of the same figure in his opening speech (**212–13 / 189–90**). But the son's plea for a hearing from the father despite his youth upsets Kreon's emphasis on hierarchy and obedience. Nor is Kreon, who prides himself on his "good sense," likely to welcome Haimon's closing suggestion that wisdom might reside in someone other than his father.

784–842 / 724–80 The Chorus, as often in such debates, attempts a compromise position, but the division between father and son is now out in the open, and the set speeches give way to the tense line-by-line conflict (stichomythia), like that between Ismene and Antigone in the prologue and in **599–609 / 548–58**, or between Antigone and Kreon in **559–74 / 508–23**.

810 / 750 *never marry this girl while she's alive* Another instance of Sophoklean tragic irony: Haimon will in fact "marry" Antigone when she is no longer alive (**1322–28 / 1234–41**). See note on **699–700 / 650**.

811–12 / 751–52 *destroy—someone else . . . attack me with threats* Kreon understands Haimon's words as a threat against his own life, whereas what follows indicates that here Haimon (despite his later attack on his father) is probably thinking already of his own suicide.

824 / 765 *rave on* The motif of "raving" or madness becomes prominent in the next two odes (**851 / 790, 1027–28 / 960**), but it has already appeared in the rage of the attackers in the parodos and in the *Fury in the mind* in the second stasimon (**650 / 603**).

827 / 767 *weighed down by grief* An echo (in English, *weighty*) will sound for Eurydike at her silent exit near the end (**1338 / 1251**).

828–29 / 768 *grand thoughts too big for a man* A similar warning about mortal presumption recurs in the Chorus' final lines, but with reference to Kreon—another of the reversals in his situation.

831 / 771 *did not touch* Although the Greek verb for "touch" is used in a general sense and has no expressed direct object in the original, it might imply actual contact with the forbidden corpse, as in **598 / 546–47**.

833–34 / 773–74 *I'll lead her out ... and seal her up* Although Kreon says that he himself will lead Antigone to her cave, he later delegates this task to his attendants at **944 / 885**.

838–42 / 777–80 *where she can pray to Hades ... pointless waste ... to worship what is down below with Hades* Kreon's repetition of Hades reflects his scorn of Antigone's involvement with the gods of the lower world (compare her *Justice, who resides in the same house with the gods below the earth* in **496ff. / 451ff.**). Teiresias' prophecy in the next scene ominously answers Kreon's taunt (**1133–48 / 1064–76**).

843–65 / 781–805 *Third stasimon (fourth ode)* This ode on the invincible power of passion or desire (*eros*, here personified as the god Eros), following directly on the conflict between father and son, marks the rising tide of emotional violence in the play. It suggests Haimon's erotic motivations, even though he only hinted at these in his previous exchange with his father. His anger there offers a glimpse of a passion that (in retrospect) the Chorus seems to see as fueled by *eros*. Nevertheless, *eros* is kept in the background of the play. Antigone's love for Haimon is never made explicit, although Ismene's remarks on the betrothal might be construed as implying it. It is probable, though not certain, that Kreon exits just before the ode, at **842 / 780**, which sounds like an exit line. It is easier to envisage Antigone's lyrical lament with the Chorus at **861–941 / 801–82**, following the Eros ode, without Kreon's presence on the stage. Kreon then reenters no later than **942 / 883** for his last scene with Antigone, and gives the final command to have her led away to her death (**999–1004 / 931–36**). There is, however, considerable disagreement about Kreon's presence during the odes, especially the third and fourth stasima: for discussion see R. P. Winnington-Ingram, *Sophocles: An Interpretation* (Cambridge, 1980), **136–37**, with n. 58; H. D. F. Kitto, *Form and Meaning in Drama* (London, 1956), 146–47.

843–44 / 782 *that leaps down upon the herds* We have adopted the widely accepted emendation *herds* for the manuscript's "possessions." The destruction of "possessions" or wealth by Eros seems less plausible here than its universal power over beasts, human, and gods.

147

848–50 / 787–88 *neither the immortals nor man, who lives only a day, can escape from you* The language here recalls the inescapable power of death in the Ode on Man (403–5 / 361–62) and so reminds us of forces in human life that intelligence and technology cannot overcome. In contrast to death in the Ode on Man, in this ode it is desire that rules both gods and mortals. Sophokles here alludes to the numerous myths of gods and goddesses mating with mortals, familiar from the poetry of Homer, Hesiod, Pindar, and others.

857–58 / 795–97 *love in the gaze . . . wedding joy* The dense language of this passage permits several different interpretations. It can refer to the Greeks' belief that desire is an active force that emanates from the eyes of the loved one, in this case the new bride, and inspires desire in the beholder. Or it can refer to the lover's desire for the bride's beauty, or to the eyes' desire for the bride. It is possible that aspects of all three meanings are present simultaneously. In any case, these lines emphasize the erotic side of marriage, over which Aphrodite presides (860 / 800), preparing for the eroticized death of Haimon in his *Liebestod* later.

858–59 / 797–98 *rules equally with the great laws* Editors have suspected a corruption because the claims for Eros seem exaggerated and because there is not a full metrical correspondence with the relevant line in the strophe. A more serious problem is that one would expect Eros to be the destroyer or transgressor of these "laws." Yet such grandiose claims are appropriate to the hymnic style, and no satisfactory emendation has been suggested. We keep the manuscript text. The word for "laws" here, *thesmoi*, is different from the "laws" of the city (*nomoi*) that the play uses elsewhere. It has a more solemn ring and suggests the existence of a divine power that cannot be controlled or legislated by human structures. The play uses it only here and at 862 / 801.

860 / 799–800 *Aphrodite at her play* "Play," which one perhaps does not expect at this moment of approaching crisis, is frequently associated with the lighter side of love, the "game" of seduction and persuasion over which Aphrodite, as goddess of love, presides. In this sense, it is common in lyric poets like Anakreon (middle of the sixth century BCE) and contrasts with the more dangerous aspect of the "invincible" power of desire that is the ode's main subject.

861–65 / 801–5 The Chorus' brief description of Antigone, in the marching meter of anapests, marks the transition from the formal ode on Eros to the lyrical exchange with Antigone that follows.

861–62 / 801–2 *I myself . . . swing wide off the track . . . what the Laws allow* The reference to the *Laws* harks back to the power of desire a few lines before (**858–59** / 797–98). Although the men of the Chorus for the most part identify with the city and are, besides, intimidated by Kreon, they are moved by sympathy for Antigone, whom they see now led in for immuring in the cave, and so emotionally they veer beyond what they consider permitted by the laws. In describing the cave where she will be walled up to die as her *bridal chamber*, the Chorus harks back to previous odes on the power of desire and the bride and also prepares for its lyrical exchange with Antigone, which is much concerned with her figurative "marriage" to Hades, god of the underworld.

866–1011 / 806–943 *Fourth episode*

866–941 / 806–82 This long lyrical exchange between Antigone and the Chorus, technically known as a *kommos*, is one of the most emotionally intense passages of the play. Antigone sings in lyric meters, and the Chorus replies in anapests and then changes to the more emotionally expressive lyric meters at **913–16** / 853–56 and **931–34** / 872–75. Antigone, hitherto firm and courageous in her resolve to die for her loyalty to family, now expresses her grief at the prospect of death in her rocky tomb, which she describes as a negated bridal chamber. The contrast with the preceding ode on the power of desire, with its fleeting allusion to the "playful" side of love at the end, enhances the pathos of her situation. We are here reminded of the youth and vulnerability of Antigone as an orphaned young girl on the verge of marriage. Even the stern, civic-minded elders of the Chorus are moved to pity (see note on **861–62** / 801–2).

866 / 806 *Look at me, citizens of my native land* Characters in Greek tragedy often call attention to the way they are viewed by others, in part because of a self-consciousness of the play itself as spectacle, in part because of a sensitivity to being exposed to public humiliation in a "shame culture" in which one's appearance in society defines one's rank and the respect one has (compare our "saving or losing face," or the Italian "bella/bruta figura"). Close parallels occur at the beginning of Aiskhylos' *Prometheus Bound* and Sophokles' *Aias*. Antigone turns to the Chorus as members of the city (*polis*), from which she now feels totally isolated. Here, as in her cry to the *polis* and its powerful citizens in **902–3** / 842–43 and in her final address to the Chorus in **1005–8** / 937–40, Antigone can still regard herself as belonging to and having legal rights in the *polis*—another indication that the absolute dichotomy of individual and "state" does not completely fit her situation. It enhances the pathos that, despite this appeal to the citizens, she has not heard Haimon's report of their sympathy (747–55 / 692–700).

873–76 / 813–16 *I have no share...hymn of marriage...Akheron* Throughout her lyrical lament Antigone contrasts her "marriage to Death" with the marriage of which she is being deprived. Her present song of lamentation makes a poignant contrast with the songs that would have been sung at her wedding. Girls who died before marriage were said to be "brides of Hades," and Akheron, the river that leads to the underworld, here stands for Hades' realm in general. In fact, Greek tragedy often exploits an association between marriage and death, in part because of the pathetic contrast, in part because the young girl's removal from her house of origin to the house of her husband in this virilocal marriage system was perceived as separation and loss both to the girl and her family and so could be the occasion for lament. For extensive discussion of this motif, see Gail Holst-Wahrhaft, *Dangerous Voices: Women's Laments and Greek Literature* (London and New York, 1992), and Rush Rehm, *Marriage to Death* (Princeton, 1994). *Hymn of marriage sing me to my wedding* in 875–76 / 815–16 emphasizes the ritual songs of marriage that Antigone will never hear. In this play hymns of marriage are replaced by funeral "hymns" and by the chanting of curses, the latter in Eurydike's "hymns" of imprecation against Kreon as she dies in 1391–92 / 1305. See notes on 708–9 / 658–59, 1309–10 / 1226–27, and 1387–92 / 1301–5.

877–79 / 817–18 *Do you not go with glory...hidden?* The Chorus harks back to Antigone's own earlier reasons for burying Polyneikes, but the glory she had hoped to win in the opening scene (see notes on 48–49 / 37–38, 87–90 / 72–74, and 114–15 / 96–97) seems less satisfying to her when she is on the point of death. Instead of looking to masculine, heroic values, she will reply with the example of a pitiable, maternal women. The shift to this more vulnerable and feminine mood increases the pathos and sense of tragic loss surrounding her. The Chorus itself here vacillates between sympathy and disapproval. Hence, while it recognizes her claim to honor, it also criticizes her as *answering only to the law of [herself]*, *autonomos* (the first occurrence of this word in extant Greek literature), that is, disobeying the laws (*nomoi*) of the city, to which the Chorus feels primary allegiance. But in her speech of 495–518 / 450–70, Antigone regards herself as the champion not of her "own laws" but of laws of the gods higher than those of the city. Note also her complaint about the "laws" under which she dies in her lament at 907 / 847.

883 / 824 *pitiable Phrygian stranger* Antigone here compares herself to Niobe, daughter of Phrygian Tantalos and wife of Amphion, an earlier king of Thebes. Comparing her numerous children boastfully to the two children of Leto, Niobe is punished by Leto's children, the gods Apollo and Artemis, who kill all of hers, whereupon in her grief she is transformed into the stony form of Mt. Sipylos in Phrygia (now western Turkey). This stony sleep of death harks bark to the epithet of Hades as making *us all sleep* in the previous strophe (871–72 / 810–11, and compare 865 / 804). There are numerous points of contact with Antigone's story—the lament and particularly the comparison of Niobe's petrification and her own enclosure in the stone prison of her cave—but Antigone, childless and unmarried, dies in a contrast of tragic irony with Niobe's fate. Homer has Achilles tell the myth of Niobe in *Iliad*, 24.602–17, and there is a more detailed version in Ovid, *Metamorphoses*, 6.148–312.

899 / 839 *Ah, I am laughed at* With her sensitivity to insult at this vulnerable moment, Antigone interprets pejoratively the Chorus' qualification of her comparison of herself to Niobe, although the Chorus also recognizes, again, the special honor that she gains by her death (895–98 / 836–38). The Greek word for *laughed at* is also used at 602 / 551 (see note) when Antigone acknowledges her own mocking of Ismene.

903 / 844 *springs of Dirke* Dirke is the fountain of Thebes closely associated with the origins and life of the city; it is mentioned first by the Chorus in the parodos (123 / 104).

906–7 / 847 *unlamented by any friends* This absence of friends (which, as often, here translates the word *philoi*, the intimate relations of the family) is exactly what Antigone tried to avoid for Polyneikes, at the cost of her life. The tragic irony enhances the pathos of her lament.

907–9 / 848–49 *the high-heaped prison . . . dreadful grave* There is some uncertainty about the text of these intricate lines, but the sense is clear. The accumulating words for piling up the earth and rocks for a grave all suggest various forms of imprisonment and burial and reinforce Antigone's growing horror of being entombed alive. See also 1175–76 / 1100–1101.

913–16 / 853–56 *Stepping ahead . . . the throne of Justice . . . some torment of your father's* Despite their previous sympathy, the Chorus continues to interpret Antigone's suffering as both a crime against the laws of the city and as the result of an inherited curse. Their lines reflect again the different views of "justice" in the play (compare Antigone in **495–518** / 450–70 and see note on **1357** / 1270). As before, the elders may still be intimidated by Kreon. Antigone never accepts these accusations of wrongdoing or moral failure or weakens in her initial resolve (see **114–15** / 96–97). In fact, she responds with another defense of her actions in her last speech (**967–91** / 905–24). Here, as in their final response at **931–34** / 872–75, the Chorus moves from anapests to more intense iambic meters, indicating a heightening of emotion parallel to the increasing intensity of Antigone's lament.

918–19 / 858–59 *My father's doom—recurring like the ploughing of a field three times* The text here is uncertain. We have adopted the plausible emendation of Lloyd-Jones and Wilson's Oxford Classical Text, reading *oitou*, doom, for *oikton*, the reading of the manuscripts. The latter would mean something like "the pity" or "pitiful situation" of the Labdakids (or, possibly, "the much repeated lamentation for Oidipous and the Labdakids"). Many editors accept the manuscript reading, but the emendation gives more natural syntax and a more plausible Sophoklean diction. Dawe prints the manuscript reading but adds in a note, "The construction of the words is not easily understood." Antigone here harks back to the much repeated theme of the accursed past of her family, developed at length in the second stasimon. *Like the plowing of a field three times* (literally, "thrice plowed") is a common metaphor for something gone over again and again; here the agricultural metaphor may imply the incest and other intra-familial crimes of the three generations of Labdakids: Laios, Oidipous, and the children of Oidipous. See notes on **61–71** / 49–57 and **633–77** / 582–630.

926–27 / 868 *having no other home but theirs* Antigone here echoes her phrasing at the end of the previous strophe (**911–12** / 852), *having no home with either the living or the dead*. The repetition, almost a refrain, evokes her emotional suffering as she recognizes, more and more fully, her isolation. The word used by Antigone for *having no home* (literally, "changing her home") here, as in **911–12** / 852 and used later by Kreon in **950** / 890, is *metoikos*, whose primary meaning for most Athenians would be "metic," that is, a resident alien. This daughter of the ancient royal house of Thebes has been so completely cast out by Kreon that she is now a "metic." Her language in **925–26** / 867 also points up her anomalous position as a "bride of Hades": instead of leaving her ancestral house as the bride of Haimon, who would, in the normal practice of virilocal marriage, take her from her house to his, she remains bound to the house of her parents, with its incestuous marriage and its accursed past. See Introduction, p. 31.

928–29 / 869–70 *marriage that brought doom* This refers to the marriage of the exiled Polyneikes to Argeia, daughter of the Argive king, Adrastos, who then supplied the army that attacked Thebes.

931–34 / 872–75 *To show reverence...power, in him who holds power...self-willed temper* The Chorus again qualifies its sympathy for Antigone. They acknowledge her *reverence* for the dead, but they are mindful of the overriding fact of Kreon's *power* or control, and they end with an accusation of Antigone's willfulness, echoing their earlier criticism of her as answering only to her own laws (881 / 821). "Self-willed" takes up the negative associations of "self-" in sufferings of the house of Oidipous (see notes on 1–2 / 1, 61–71 / 49–57, etc.). *Temper* echoes the first stasimon, 398–99 / 355–56, *temperament for the laws of the town.* If we are meant to recall that ode, we may be reminded of the contrasts between the achievements of intelligence that it celebrates and the passions that may destroy or threaten those achievements.

935–41 / 876–82 Antigone returns to her grief at her isolation from the "friends" or "dear ones" (*philoi*) who have been the chief concern of her life. The repetition of the word *philos*, "friend" or "dear one," in her first and last lines creates the effect of a refrain, like that on *metoikos* in lines 911–12 / 852 and 926–27 / 868. The repetition of themes and language throughout Antigone's lyrics in this section of the play not only emphasizes her intense emotions of loss and suffering but is also a characteristic feature of the kind of ritual lament that she is performing.

939–40 / 879 *see this fiery eye of heaven* Seeing the light of the sun is a frequent metaphor in Greek poetry for being alive, and bidding it farewell is also taking leave of the life-giving natural world that we share with all living creatures. The metaphor has special poignancy here because the mode of Antigone's death will be a literal enclosure in a dark place where she will never again see the sun. Contrast the Chorus' joyful invocation to the rays of the sun on behalf of the city to open their first ode (118–19 / 100–101).

942 / 883 *Don't you know...stop singing* The text has some uncertainties, but the general sense is clear. Kreon presumably returns to the stage as Antigone sings the last part of her lament (935–41 / 876–82), which he overhears.

His callousness will return bitterly on his own head at the end, when he is the one to sing a lengthy lament.

944–50 / 885–90 *Take her off! ... We're pure ... house up here* The contrast between Kreon's harshness and the pathos of Antigone's preceding lament is heightened by the fact that he echoes some of her words about burial underground, isolation, deprivation of her dwelling "above," and her house in the underworld. Kreon supposes that he can maintain his and the city's ritual purity by not actually shedding her blood (see **836–38 / 775–76**). Hence the change from the initial punishment by public stoning (see note on **46–47 / 35–36**). Teiresias, however, will soon warn him about just this pollution for the city (**1079ff. / 1016ff.** and compare **1215–16 / 1141**), and at the end Kreon will experience the terrible blood pollutions in his own house. See note on **1078–79 / 1015** and **1371 / 1284**.

945 / 886 *wrap arms around her* Continuing the inversion of marriage and death, Kreon metaphorically makes the cave of doom "embrace" the bride of Hades. That figurative embrace, however, will be answered by Haimon's literal embrace of Antigone in death (see note on **1320–21 / 1237**) and will give a deep irony to Kreon's claim of "purity." See the previous note and also note on **699–700 / 650**.

954 / 894 *Persephone* Goddess of the underworld and bride of its ruler, Hades, Persephone is carried off as a maiden to the realm of the dead to wed Hades; she is a mythical model for Antigone. See Introduction, pp. 30–32, and note on **926–27 / 868**.

955–56 / 895 *the last of them* Here, as elsewhere, Antigone forgets about Ismene.

959–61 / 898–99 *loved by my father, loved by you, mother, loved by you, my own dear brother* Repeating the word of family affection, *philos*, three times in the Greek, Antigone calls attention to the values to which she has sacrificed her life. At the same time, the direct address to mother and brother conveys her intense involvement in these emotions.

961–62 / 901 *washed and laid out your bodies* In describing the funerals of her family members, Antigone refers here to the full rituals of preparing the body for burial: the washing and dressing of the corpse (which was generally done by the women of the family) preliminary to its lying in the house, after which it was carried in a funeral procession to the grave, where libations were poured. In the case of her own burial of Polyneikes, however, she was not able to wash the body, but could only pour out libations and sprinkle a covering of dust. See **281–82 / 245–47** and **290–91 / 255–56** and the notes on **472–76 / 427–31** and **1275–81 / 1199–1204**.

962–65 / 900–903 *with my own hands and poured libations ... recompense* Listing the dead members of her family, Antigone here defines her family love, or *philia*, in terms of her performance of the funeral rites for them. Her address to Polyneikes by name (**964 / 902**) is the rhetorical climax of this statement of her devotion to family; see the previous note. Her statement that she has buried her father, Oidipous, implies the version that he has died at Thebes, not in exile; see note on line **3 / 2**. The phrase *with my own hands* is the single word *autokheir* in Greek, another compound of "self." Earlier in the play this word describes the double fratricide (see note on **1–2 / 1, 61–71 / 49–57, 193 / 172**, etc.), which was the subject of Antigone's opening speech; and it is Kreon's accusatory term for the perpetrator of Polyneikes' burial (**350 / 306**). It recurs later for the suicides of Haimon and Eurydike (**1249 / 1175, 1401 / 1315**), thereby connecting Antigone's action with these disasters and linking the sufferings of the house of Oidipous to the house of Kreon.

965–66 / 904 *those who have clear thoughts*. Antigone returns to her view of "good sense" or "right thinking," so different from Kreon's.

967–79 / 905–15 These have been among the most discussed verses in the play. Many editors regard them as a later interpolation, perhaps by an actor's company for later performance, and so delete them. Strongly in favor of genuineness, however, is the fact that the passage was known to Aristotle, who quotes some of the lines (*Rhetoric*, 3.1417a), although the quotation does not eliminate the possibility that the lines were added sometime in the late fifth or early fourth century BCE. Among the internal reasons alleged for viewing the lines as spurious are the apparent illogic of Antigone's argument and particularly her change of motivation for the burial from a defense of principles in **495–518 / 450–70** to a highly personal and intimate connection with the family. But to these objections it may be answered that Antigone has her own very emotional sort of logic, which now, at the point of her being led to her death, comes forth in the most personal terms. Of the external objections, the most important is Sophokles' echo of a story in Herodotos' *Histories*, 3.119. Here the wife of a Persian nobleman named Intaphernes, who has been caught in a conspiracy against King Dareios, uses a similar argument for choosing to save her brother rather than a son or husband. Those who delete the passage argue that an interpolator modeled it on this passage.

But Herodotos, who was a friend of Sophokles, was writing and giving readings of his work as early as the 440s. Stephanie West, "Sophocles' *Antigone* and Herodotus Book Three," in *Sophokles Revisited* (Oxford, 1999), 109–36, has recently pointed out additional evidence for the priority of Sophokles (see note on 1104–5 / 1038–39). Sophokles, moreover, has adapted the Herodotean material to Antigone's situation and character in significant ways. Intaphernes' wife would save a living brother; Antigone is going to die to bury a dead brother. Whereas the Persian wife (whose name is never given) in Herodotos has the approved female role of throwing herself on the king's mercy in her mourning and lamentation, Antigone is not only facing death, but is in the role of the transgressive and defiant tragic figure. And of course her own life is at stake, as that of Intaphernes' wife is not. Finally, it should be observed that Antigone does hark back to her initial rationalization of her motives in her emphasis on a "law" that she is following (971 / 908, 976 / 914), in the issue of the "Justice of gods" that she is accused of "transgressing" (987 / 921; compare 495–501 / 450–55, 913–15 / 853–55), in her "daring to do terrible things" (979 / 914–15; compare 283 / 248, 494 / 449; also 413 / 371) and in her *defying the citizens* (968 / 907; compare 74 / 59). This last phrase, in fact, exactly echoes Ismene's refusal in the prologue (95–96 / 79) and so at this point is the measure of how far Antigone's transgressive piety has taken her.

978 / 915 *my own dear brother* Antigone directly addresses Polyneikes for the second time (compare 960–61 / 899) and uses the same expression (literally, "head of my brother") that she had used to address Ismene in her opening line (1–2 / 1). Now the address is entirely to the dead, and the living sister is forgotten: see note on 955–56 / 895.

985–86 / 920 *still alive to the cave of the dead* Antigone repeats her lament about being between living and dead from her previous lyrics (910–12 / 850–52); see note on 926–27 / 868.

987 / 921 *Justice of the gods* Antigone harks back to her speech of 495–518 / 450–70 (see note) and her view of a Justice opposed to that of Kreon. See note on 995–96 / 927–28.

991 / 924 *charges of irreverence* Antigone reiterates the motif of her paradoxical *holy crime* or "holy wrongdoing" in 87–90 / 72–74 (see note); see also 931 / 872.

993 / 926 *through suffering would know* Sophokles is alluding to the familiar tragic motif (in Greek, *pathei mathos*), made famous by Aiskhylos' *Agamemnon*, 176–78.

995–96 / 927–28 *May the evils that they suffer be no more than what they are unjustly doing to me* Antigone means, of course, that they should suffer at least equal justice, and there is a bitter irony in this understatement. "She can imagine no worse fate," remarks Jebb. In Greek, "justice" is her last word in the speech (in the form of an adverb, *ekdikôs*, literally "in a way outside of justice"), but we should recall that "justice" in Greek (*dikê*) also implies the law of retribution. She has been "outside of justice" (compare **913–15 / 853–55**) in the eyes of the authorities, but she hopes they will find themselves in the same position, as in fact proves to be the case. In her last lines of iambic trimeter, like the hero of Sophokles' *Aias*, 835–42, Antigone thinks of vengeance. For all that she describes herself as sharing in loving rather than in hating (**574 / 523**), hers is no sweet and gentle nature. Greek popular morality (at least before Plato), in contrast to Christian, strongly endorses vengeance against those who have done one wrong.

997–1011 / 929–43 The Chorus, Antigone, and Kreon have a short, three-way exchange chanted in the marching meter of anapests as Antigone, escorted by Kreon's guards, exits to her underground cave in a slow, solemn procession. Kreon continues to speak with brutal, unpitying harshness. Antigone is alone and aware of her imminent death (**1001–2 / 933–34**). Kreon himself probably begins to exit into the palace after his final commands at **1003–4 / 935–36**, while Antigone sings her final lament (**1005–11 / 937–43**). Some have argued that Kreon remains on stage during the following ode, the fourth stasimon, but this seems to us less likely; see note on **1050–1165 / 988–1090**.

997 / 929–30 *The same storms of her spirit* The metaphor of the storm for Antigone's passion associates her, in the Chorus' mind, with what is wild, savage, and outside the city. The Chorus used the same metaphor for the fury of Kapaneus' attack on Thebes (**155 / 137**). Compare also *the storms and gales* of the North Wind, Boreas, in the following ode (**1046 / 984–85**).

1004 / 936 *are not final* Kreon's language here shows his rigid legalism and insistence on his authority.

1005–11 / 937–43 *Oh city of Thebes . . . last, solitary member . . . reverent toward reverence* Antigone makes her final appeal not to Kreon but to the land, gods, and lords of Thebes, which again emphasizes the pathos of the isolation of one who belongs to the royal house and has sacrificed her life to what she regards as part of the justice that the polis should recognize (**495–518** / 450–70). See notes on **866–941** / 806–82 and **866** / 806. She reiterates that she is the last of her house (compare **955–56** / 895), once more forgetting Ismene and harking back to the motif of the destruction of the entire family. Her last words, however, look to the gods, rather than men, and to the *reverence* for them that has brought her death. See note on **991** / 924.

1012–49 / 944–87 *Fourth stasimon* (fifth ode) The problems of this dense, difficult ode are exacerbated by some uncertainties about the text. The Chorus, in highly poetic language, tells three myths, which seem meant as some sort of consolation for Antigone but may also have some relevance to Kreon. Once more, the Chorus may say or imply more than it knows. The first myth is that of Danae, daughter of King Akrisios of Argos, who imprisons her in a tower of bronze to prevent her from conceiving a child who is prophesied to kill him. Zeus, however, visits her in a shower of gold and sires Perseus, who eventually fulfills the prophecy. The second myth is that of Lykourgos, son of Dryas, king of Thrace, who, like Pentheus in Euripides' *Bakkhai*, opposes Dionysos when the god arrives with his new cult. In a fit of madness sent by the god, Lykourgos thinks his son, Dryas (named after his grandfather, as is customary), is the god's hated vine and cuts him into pieces with an axe. Lykourgos is then imprisoned in a cave. The third myth, told in a particularly dense and allusive style, is also set in Thrace, at Salmydessos, on the Bosporos. King Phineus has two sons by his first wife, Kleopatra, daughter of Boreas, god of the North Wind, and Oreithyia, daughter of Erekhtheus, one of the early kings of Athens. Phineus divorces, kills, or otherwise maltreats Kleopatra and marries a second wife, who, like Kleopatra, is unnamed in this ode but is generally called Eidothea or Idaia. She blinds her two stepsons with her shuttle, and the ode ends by commiserating with the unhappy fate of Kleopatra, which befalls her despite her lofty ancestry.

How these myths relate to one another and to the play is a subject of considerable controversy. Both the Danae and Kleopatra myths mention the power of fate, or Moira (**1019** / 951 and **1049** / 987), and some commentators have taken this as the link among the three myths. Fate does not, however, play a role in Sophokles' account of Lykourgos here. Both the Danae and Lykourgos myths involve divine punishment, but it is not particularly prominent in the third. Imprisonment is also an obvious link between the Danae and Lykourgos myths, but it is not explicit in the Kleopatra myth, although in one version the children and perhaps Kleopatra, too, are imprisoned. Sophokles does refer to a cave, but it is the cave of Boreas where Kleopatra was raised. While the Danae myth best fits the situation of Antigone, the tale of Lykourgos, angrily opposing the gods, seems more appropriate to Kreon, particularly in light of the warnings by Teiresias that soon follow. Kreon also, like Danae's father, Akrisios, tries to interfere with sexual union. Moreover, both the Danae and Lykourgos myths result in disaster for the father-figure. The two bloodily wounded children of the Kleopatra myth may also foreshadow Kreon's loss of his two sons and the bloody suicide of his wife, Eurydike, at the end of the play. All three myths, like that of Niobe in 883–93 / 823–33, emphasize the high birth of the sufferer and so are appropriate to Antigone: Danae is *of much-honored descent* (1017 / 948), Lykourgos is *King of the Edonians* (1023 / 956), and Kleopatra is descended from the royal line of Athens (1044 / 982) and is also a *child of gods* (1047 / 986). Thus, the ode takes up and answers Antigone's final lament that she is *the last, solitary member of the royal house* (1008–9 / 941).

All three myths also involve violent deaths within the family (particularly if the Lykourgos myth is taken to imply his insane killing of his son) and so would be relevant to the houses of both Antigone and Kreon. Conceivably, all three myths may also reflect different views that the Chorus has of Antigone: she is cruelly imprisoned, like Danae; she is carried to violent excess, like Lykourgos; and she is a victim of human cruelty, like Kleopatra and her sons. But, more generally, the myths, taken together, exemplify the cruelty that family members can inflict on one another. Also, the agents and the victims include both men and women. In their concern with sexuality, anger, passion, and vengeance, moreover, all three myths are reminders of the violent and irrational forces in life that will soon break apart Kreon's apparently rational control of his world. The ode thus continues an undercurrent that runs through the previous two odes, on the curse on the house of Oidipous and on the power of Eros, respectively, and again contrasts sharply with the optimistic humanism of the Ode on Man.

1015 / 949 *Oh child, child* The Chorus again expresses sympathy for Antigone but, as before, is careful to qualify this in their subsequent reference to *the power of fate*.

1019–20 / 951 *fills us with terror and awe* The Chorus uses the same word, *deinon* (meaning both *terror* and *awe*), that described the ambiguous capacities of humankind in the first stasimon (**377 / 332**).

1029–31 / 962–65 *women quickened by the god... fire of Dionysos; that god's Muses* This refers to the maenads (literally "mad women") who are inspired by Dionysos and dance in torch-light processions in his honor. See note on **1221–24 / 1149–52**. The Muses, nine daughters of Zeus and Mnemosyne (Memory), are goddesses of song, dance, and poetry, often closely associated with Dionysos.

1032–34 / 966–71 *indigo waters of two seas... neighboring land, Ares* The region described is the Thracian Bosporos, the narrow channel separating what is now European from Asian Turkey, connecting the Sea of Marmara (the ancient Propontis) with the Black Sea, which are the "two seas" here mentioned. Salmydessos is a Thracian city on the Black Sea, on the European side of the Bosporos and slightly to its northwest. The area is Ares' *neighboring land* because Ares, god of war, is often associated with Thrace and the warlike Thracians. There are some textual corruptions in the opening lines here. The manuscripts contain the problematical word "rocks," which, with many editors, we delete. Editors who retain "rocks" in some form take it to refer to the so-called Dark Rocks in this area, mentioned by Herodotos. They are traditionally identified with the "Clashing Rocks," or Symplegades, guarding the entrance to the Black Sea, through which Jason and the Argonauts had to pass.

1038 / 975 *Beaten blind* The Chorus here uses the same verb that described Oidipous' self-blinding in the prologue (**62 / 52**) and in the self-blinding of Oidipous himself in the *Oidipous Turannos*.

1044 / 982 *Erekhtheids* This ancient family of the kings of Athens is named after their ancestor, Erekhtheus, who is the father of Kleopatra's mother, Oreithyia.

1046 / 985 *Boreas* As the god of the north wind, Boreas is associated with Thrace. He sweeps Kleopatra's mother, Oreithyia, off to Thrace, where Kleopatra is then raised in his cave dwelling.

1048–49 / 986–87 *on her, too, the Fates... pressed hard, Oh child* As in the case of the Danae, above, the Chorus expresses sympathy and consolation to Antigone by invoking the inevitability of fate and by calling her "child."

1050–1190 / 988–1114 *Fifth episode*

1050–1165 / 988–1090 The scene between Kreon and Teiresias, the old prophet of
Thebes, brings into the foreground the gods and the forces of nature
through which the gods act on the human world. Gods and forces of
nature have hovered in the background, but now move more threaten-
ingly into the foreground. Kreon presumably reenters abruptly from the
palace at the news of Teiresias' arrival, although (as with all the details of
staging) this is not completely certain. He says nothing about having
come out from the palace at 1053 / 991, but this first, sharp question,
What news do you have?, can also indicate his arrival just when the seer's
sudden presence makes the new situation seem urgent. This scene
closely parallels the three previous scenes. Each one contains a test or
trial that challenges Kreon's authority. After the obsequiousness of the
Chorus at his entrance, Kreon first confronts the Guard, with the first
news of the burial; then Antigone, who immediately defies him, and,
third, Haimon, who starts out by professing obedience but ends in bitter
hostility. Teiresias' entrance marks the first time that Kreon confronts
an older man and one who can claim an authority equal to or greater
than his.

1054 / 992 *and you will obey the seer* Like other old men in Sophokles, notably the
Teiresias of the *Oidipous Turannos*, the aged Oidipous of the *Oidipous
at Kolonos*, and Telamon, father of Aias, in the background of *Aias*,
Teiresias is accustomed to being obeyed and does not easily brook
opposition. Teiresias' early statement here of his authority prepares us
for the outcome of his conflict with Kreon.

1056 / 994 *captained this ship of a city rightly* Teiresias echoes the nautical imagery
with which Kreon described his rule in his first speech (182–83 / 162–63,
212–13 / 189–90), but in a very different tone that suggests the limits of
Kreon's initial confidence and egotism.

1057 / 995 Literally, "By my own experience [or, suffering] I have cause [am able] to
bear witness to (your) useful (things)." The Greek grammar suggests that
Kreon means he himself has experienced Teiresias' "useful things/bene-
fits" and can testify to them. If there is an allusion here to Teiresias'
having prophesied the need for Kreon's other son to die for Thebes (as
in Euripides' *Phoinikian Women*), the phrase "by my own experience,"
peponthôs, perfect participle of the Greek verb *paschein*, could have
its other meaning of "suffer" and not just the neutral "experience."

Sophokles, however, may be alluding to a somewhat different version of the myth. See notes on **1127** / 1058 and **1387–92** / 1301–5.

1058 / 996 *fortunes stand once more on the razor's edge* A common expression in Greek literature for being at the edge of extreme danger. The word "fortunes" here translates the Greek *tukhê*, "chance," often an important term in Greek tragedy, indicating the uncertainties of mortal life. Teiresias' prophecy is fulfilled in the Messenger's heavy emphasis on just these vicissitudes of "fortune" when he begins his account of the catastrophe, **1229–30** / 1158–59. Compare also Eurydike's "chance" exit from the house at **1256** / 1182 (see note on **1255–61** / 1182–86).

1060–62 / 998–1000 *signs of my craft...bird-divining* The ancient Greeks, like the ancient Romans, practiced divination through the movements and cries of birds in the sky.

1063–64 / 1001–2 Literally, something along the lines of "noise as they screamed a barbarous cry, stung by some awful madness." Teiresias, as befits a prophet, speaks in grandiose language. His expression *barbaric maddened gibber-jabber* refers to the unintelligible speech of non-Greeks, whom the Greeks called *barbaroi*. The word suggests that in the present crisis the communication between gods and mortals through the language of bird signs has become ominous and dangerous. The whole phrase conveys the utter strangeness and horror in the cries of these birds that Teiresias has been listening to all his life.

1071–75 / 1006–11 *instead, the fatty thighbones...lay exposed...covered them* Teiresias' description shows the disorder in the natural world through the motif, common in tragedy, of corrupted sacrifice. The thighbones of the sacrificial animal (in this case, presumably an ox) were wrapped in fat and placed on the altar and burnt with incense. Teiresias' language also echoes a word used to describe the rotting corpse of Polyneikes in **454** / 410 and so suggests a causal connection between the body that should have been put beneath the earth in reverence for the gods below and these offerings whose fragrant smoke should have mounted to the heavens in prayer to the gods above. Instead, the fire smolders, the fat fails to burn and runs downward, and what reaches the heavens is the bitter gall as it explodes upward. The Greek syntax in the description of the dripping thighbones might evoke a macabre image of the fat of the bones turning into a wet slime.

1078–79 / 1015 *from your thinking ... the city is sick* Kreon's legalistic attempt to avoid pollution in the bloodless killing of Antigone rebounds on the city in a much larger and more dangerous form. Such a pollution (*miasma*) is felt to be a kind of infectious disease that can bring plague, sterility, and death to the city and its environment. See notes on **467 / 421, 944–50 / 885–90,** and **1371 / 1284.**

1080–81 / 1016–18 *food brought by the birds and dogs ... son of Oidipous* Teiresias recalls the descriptions of the exposed corpse of Polyneikes in both Antigone's and Kreon's early speeches in the play (**31–38 / 26–30, 233–35 / 204–6**). Now, however, the fearful results of that exposure are becoming visible on the plane of divine action. By referring to Polyneikes by his patronymic, he also evokes the curse on the house of Oidipous.

1085–86 / 1022 *eaten the blood-streaked fat* The language recalls the Chorus' description of the bloodthirsty attack on Thebes by Polyneikes and his army in **139 / 121–22** and Kreon's description in **227–28 / 201–2.** Now, however, the tasting of Theban blood has taken on a different meaning as the threat to the city has shifted from outside to within, from the attackers to the ostensible defender.

1086–89 / 1023–26 *Know this ... ill-advised ...* Teiresias takes up the "good sense" or "wise counsel" that Kreon has claimed for himself against the folly of Antigone.

1092–93 / 1027–28 *He will not move. Stubbornness ... botching things* Teiresias' advice about the dangers of inflexibility recalls the warnings of Haimon in **768–77 / 710–17.** *Stubbornness* implies a self-will that resembles that of Antigone. The accusation of ineptitude or stupidity must be particularly infuriating to Kreon, who prides himself on his logic and intelligence.

1098 / 1032 *your profit* Teiresias reiterates this dominating preoccupation of Kreon, but takes it in a direction that will soon enrage the ruler; see note on **1102–5 / 1035–39.**

1099 / 1033 *you all, like archers* Kreon may be thinking of the previous mutterings against him. See **747–55 / 693–700** and note on **333–38 / 289–92.**

1102–5 / 1035–39 Kreon's language of profit, trade, and mercantilism repeats his suspicions of bribery and conspiracy; see **252–53 / 221–22, 354–59 / 310–14, 508–10 / 461–62, 1098 / 1032, 1130 / 1061, 1132 / 1063,** and notes on

1116 / 1047 and **1409** / 1326. However, Kreon will soon be put on the defensive.

1104–5 / 1038–39 *gold from India* Stephanie West (see note on **967–79** / 905–15), 113–14, has plausibly suggested that this reference to Indic gold is indebted to Herodotos' *Histories* (3.94.2), as India is not generally mentioned as a source of gold.

1107–12 / 1040–44 *eagles of Zeus . . . fear of pollution . . . power to stain the gods* Kreon's hyperbole puts him on dangerous ground, particularly as he touches so scornfully on the serious matter of pollution. With characteristic confidence, he presupposes a clear separation between human and divine realms and identifies the gods with his own policies. In what follows, however, his confidence about limiting and controlling pollution—like his confidence about controlling Hades and Eros—proves ill-founded; see Introduction, pp. 33–34. For his cavalier way of dismissing Zeus, see notes on **348** / 304 and **535–38** / 486–87.

1116 / 1047 Kreon ends his tirade by repeating his accusations of profit from **1103** / 1037 and his recurrent suspicions of monetary gain and bribery. See note on **1102–5** / 1035–39. Oidipous' accusations in *Oidipous Turannos*, 532–42, mine this theme for similar effects.

1125 / 1056 Teiresias takes up the criticism of Kreon's autocratic behavior raised by Antigone and Haimon earlier and turns the charge of greed back on the king.

1126 / 1057 *your sovereign* In Greek, this is the rare and archaic-sounding *tagos* (found only here in Sophokles' extant plays). Kreon perhaps uses it to emphasize his power and perhaps also to neutralize the pejorative associations of Teiresias' "tyrants" just before (both words are generalized by being in the plural).

1127 / 1058 *It was through me that you have saved this city* This assertion may allude to Teiresias' prophecy that only the blood of one descended from the original Theban Planted Men could save Thebes; see notes on **1057** / 995 and **1387–92** / 1301–5.

1133–34 / 1064–65 *complete many swift courses of the racing sun* The prophecy of tragic doom coming in terms of days, or a single day, is a recurrent motif in Sophokles (e.g., *Aias*, *Trakhinian Women*, *Oidipous Turannos*); see note on **1189–90** / 1113–14. Kreon's doom will come within a few hours.

1135 / 1066 *your own gut* The Greek word is used more commonly of the mother's "womb" rather than the father's "loins." Antigone uses a form of it to describe her brother as born *from the same womb*, in **562 / 511**. Kreon has hitherto treated the realm of marriage and generation with scorn. Now, rather than producing a living child, Kreon's male "womb"—his male way of being—will figuratively produce the death of his living child.

1138–39 / 1069 *dishonorably compelling her, a human spirit* The Greek for *human spirit* is *psukhe*, which may also suggest "shade" and so points to the ambiguity of Antigone's present position between living and dead at this point, as she lamented in her last lyrics. It is part of Kreon's violation of the order of things that he has made her a "shade" when she is still alive and in the upper world. The word "dishonorably," Greek *atimôs*, has a wide range of associations. It implies Kreon's harshness to a member of the royal family (and his own family), his "dishonoring" of the gods, and probably also, as Griffith suggests, his "disenfranchisement" of Antigone, that is, her loss of civic rights. But it can also include her loss of the rites and honor of a proper burial.

1141 / 1070 *body with no share of the gods* The text is uncertain here and has often been emended to something like "no share of offerings" or "of rites." Alternatively, *of the gods* may be construed with "those below" in the previous line ("one of those who belong to the gods below"), though this disturbs the parallelism with "someone from here above" just before. In that case, "rites" or some such word would be understood with the phrase "with no share."

1142–44 / 1072–73 Another difficult and much discussed passage: the meaning seems to be that the burial of the dead belongs neither to Kreon nor to the gods of the upper world, but that the latter have nevertheless suffered "violence" or outrage from the pollutions of the human carrion that the birds and dogs have carried to their altars (**1079–86 / 1016–22**). Hence the Furies mentioned in the subsequent lines (**1145–47 / 1075–76**) avenge the gods of both the lower and upper worlds.

1145–46 / 1074 *late-destroying* Teiresias uses a grandiose compound of which the first part evokes the old, archaic (and tragic) idea that the gods may be slow to punish but are inexorable. The suggestion that Hades has its "avengers" (here identified with the Furies) gives a darker meaning to Kreon's scornful references to Hades earlier (see note on **495–518 / 450–70** and **838–42 / 777–80**; compare also **352 / 308**) and points toward the peripeteia, or reversal, in his circumstances. The Furies are dread goddesses of the underworld and always evoke horror, particularly here, where their epithet suggests their inexorable pursuit and punishment of their victims.

1146–47 / 1075 *who avenge Hades* Hades stands here collectively for the gods of the lower world, whose Justice Antigone had invoked in her defiant speech of 495–518 / 450–70. Teiresias, however, says nothing specific of Antigone, though she seems to be clearly implied in 1136–38 / 1068–69. The silence about her name has the effect of making Kreon's punishment appear as part of a broad reaction of Sophokles' characteristically remote gods to a disturbance in the balance of nature rather than as revenge for a human crime against a particular individual.

1150–51 / 1078 *Time will test my mettle* We try to keep a wordplay in the Greek, as the word for "time" here can mean "delay" and also "rubbing" to test true metal and distinguish it from false. Thus it continues the motif of *given silver* in the previous line, which literally means "covered over with silver," as if the bribery of Teiresias were analogous to making false coinage, that is, false prophecy. With slightly different punctuation and consequently different syntax, the lines can also mean, "much wailing of men and women—and there will be no long delay of time—will reveal (these things) to your household."

1153–58 / 1080–83 Some editors place these lines after Teiresias' earlier description of the pollutions of the cities ending at 1086 / 1022, and others delete them as spurious or suggest that a line or two has dropped out before them. The lines, however, are in keeping with the widening scope and mounting authority of Teiresias' prophecy. Sophokles here seems to be alluding to a version of the story told in Euripides' *Suppliants*, in which Kreon refuses to bury the fallen Argive attackers and is then forced to do so by the armed intervention of the Athenian king, Theseus. As part of Athenian patriotic lore, the allusion would be easily recognized by Sophokles' audience. This "burial" by *dogs, beasts, and wingèd birds of prey* is to be understood ironically: the only "burial" of the corpses has been in the bellies of these scavengers. Gorgias of Leontini, a contemporary sophist and rhetorician, called vultures "living tombs." The Greek has a single verb for *have purified in burial* in 1155 / 1081, for which the manuscripts offer two variants, *kathêgnisan* or *kathêgisan*. The former contains the root of the word for "pure," *hagnos*, in the sense of "make pure by (proper) burial" or "sanctify," and so would continue the motif of "purity" and pollution in the play. This reading is supported by the fact that Sophokles uses other forms of this verb in 220 / 196 and

596 / 545. With the majority of editors, therefore, we read *kathêgnisan*. The verb *kathêgisan* means "consecrate by offerings" or "dedicate," and is explicitly associated with burial only in later writers. On the other hand, this latter reading finds some support in the fact that the same root occurs in 282 / 247, *kathagisteuein*, literally "avoiding pollution," in the context of burial.

1159 / 1084 *like an archer* Teiresias throws back at Kreon his own metaphor accusing prophets at 1099–1100 / 1033–34.

1170ff. / 1095ff. For the issue of "giving way" or "yielding" in Kreon's character see 521ff. / 473ff., 729–34 / 677–80, 771–77 / 712–17, 1093–94 / 1029–30, 1177 / 1102. Teiresias describes Kreon's "unyielding" temperament as *stubbornness* in his warning at 1092 / 1028. "Giving way" in general is a major test of the Sophoklean hero, and the true hero, like Aias or Elektra or Antigone here, does not give way. See in general Knox, *Heroic Temper*, chapters 1 and 2.

1174 / 1099 *I will obey* Kreon's assent recalls Teiresias' insistence that he obey, at the beginning of the scene (1054ff. / 992ff.), but now Kreon is in a very different mood. This is the first time that he eagerly asks for advice, and also the first time that the Chorus takes a forceful initiative in suggesting it in the following lines.

1175 / 1100–1101 *Go send the girl up* The word *anes* here may recall the Eleusinian myth of Persephone and her *an-hodos*, or road upward, when her mother, Demeter, secures her temporary liberation from Hades. The hope of restoring Antigone to the upper world, however, is to prove futile. See note below on 1195 / 1120 and Introduction, pp.30–31. The Chorus' description of Antigone's underground tomb echoes earlier language, of Kreon himself at 834–35 / 774 and of Antigone at 907–9 / 848–49.

1179 / 1103–4 *Bringers-of-Harm.* This is another allusion to the Furies. See notes on 647–50 / 598–603 and 1145–46 / 1074.

1183–90 / 1108–14 Kreon's instructions imply that he will send his attendants to bury Polyneikes while he simultaneously will go to set Antigone free. In the Messenger's subsequent narrative, however, it appears that Kreon first accompanied his attendants to Polyneikes and only afterwards went to liberate Antigone (1271–83 / 1196–1205)—a delay that may have been fatal for all concerned. His emphatic *I . . . myself* in 1186–89 / 1111 implies his acceptance of responsibility for his punishment of Antigone, but at the end of the play he will also have to accept the more agonizing responsibility for his *foolish heedlessness* and *foolishness* (**1347–56** / 1261–69) when his intended rescue of Antigone fails and recoils back on himself.

1189–90 / 1113–14 *I am afraid it's best to observe the established laws through all one's life, to the end* At this point of reversal, Kreon seems to recognize, too late, an area of "law" apart from his authority in the city. The phrase could suggest those "unwritten laws" that Antigone invoked at **495–518** / 450–70 and that Kreon dismissed. *Through all one's life, to the end* carries an ominous ring in tragedy, which often emphasizes how uncertain is the final end of a human life. Kreon here looks to the completion of a more or less normal life, whereas Teiresias framed his prophetic warning in terms of a cycle of days (**1133–34** / 1064–65), and this is in fact fulfilled at the end as Kreon experiences the tragic reversal of his life in a single day (**1412–15** / 1329–32), as often happens in Sophoklean and other tragedy (e.g., *Aias*, 753–57, *Oidipous Turannos*, 438, 1283). We may recall also the "one day" of the fratricidal deaths of Polyneikes and Eteokles (**19** / 14, **69–71** / 55–57, **190–91** / 170–71). The contrast between the respective exits of Kreon and Antigone is striking: he leaves the stage yielding, as she does not, and his final words are about his fear, whereas hers were about her *reverence*.

1191–224 / 1115–54 *Fifth stasimon* (sixth ode) This ode of supplication, the last ode of the play, summons Dionysos, patron god of Thebes, to come to his birthplace and save his city by warding off the *disease* of pollution about which Teiresias has just warned (compare **1215–16** / 1140–41). The ode is an important part of the structural design of the play, for it answers the parodos, the first ode, which ends with Dionysos and nocturnal ritual (**171–74** / 152–54). Now, however, joyous thanksgiving gives way to anxious prayer, civic choruses in the temples within the city change to a figurative chorus of fiery stars in the heavens, and citizens are replaced by the frenzied female worshipers of Dionysos (**1218–24** / 1146–52).

1191 / 1115 *God of many names* Greek gods typically have many epithets to denote their different functions or different local cults, and it is important to address the deity by the appropriate name. So here the Chorus invokes Dionysos, in hymnic fashion, by referring to several of his places of worship.

1191 / 1116 *Glory of the young wife* Semele, daughter of Kadmos, is the mother of Dionysos by Zeus and gives birth to him prematurely when Hera, Zeus' Olympian wife, tricks her into asking Zeus to show himself to her in his full divine glory. She is killed by his lightning, but Zeus saves the infant. The myth, told at length in Euripides' *Bakkhai*, is the basis of Thebes' special claim on Dionysos.

1192 / 1115 *Kadmos* The founder of Thebes, Kadmos is the father of Semele, Dionysos' mother. See note on **144 / 126**.

1193 / 1119 *Italy* The worship of Dionysos was especially popular in the Greek colonies of Sicily and southern Italy (Magna Graecia, or Great Greece, as it came to be called), which was also noted for its wine production. Some have seen here a possible indication of particular Athenian interest in the area with the founding of its colony, Thurioi, in **443 / 442**. The suggested emendation to "Ikaria," a village northeast of Athens famous for its worship of Dionysos, is unnecessary.

1195 / 1120 *Eleusinian Demeter, shared by all* Dionysos, in the cult form of Iakkhos (the last word of the ode in Greek at **1224 / 1152**), has an important place in the rites of Demeter at the panhellenic sanctuary of Eleusis, on the southern outskirts of Athens. The rites are open to all who undertake initiation (hence *shared by all*) and promise to the initiates a blessed life in the hereafter. Demeter is here paired with her daughter, Persephone, and in fact the rites (which were kept secret) gave a prominent place to the myth of the latter's rescue from Hades by her mother. Both the promise of return from Hades and of some kind of personal salvation that mitigates the pain of death stand in ironic counterpoint to the events of the play. See note on **954 / 894** and **1175 / 1100–1101**, and also Introduction, pp. 30–31.

1196 / 1121 *Bakkhos* This epithet of Dionysos is used especially in connection with his role as wine god and with his ecstatic cult of frenzied processions and dances.

1197 / 1122 *Thebes, mother-city of the Bakkhai* Thebes is the birthplace of Dionysos (see note on **1191–1224 / 1115–54**) and therefore is a place where the *Bakkhai*, the female worshipers of the god in his dances and processions, have special prominence.

1198 / 1124 *Ismenos* This river flows through Thebes.

1200 / 1124–25 *Savage serpent's teeth were planted* See note on **144 / 126**.

1201–5 / 1126–30 *pine torches … double peak of rock … Korykian nymphs … Kastalia flows down* Sophokles here refers to an important aspect of the Theban cult of Dionysos. His *Bakkhai*, or female worshipers, honor the god in a nocturnal procession every other year on the heights of Mt. Parnassos, above Delphi, accompanied by torches, ecstatic dances, and the tearing apart of wild animals. The *double peak* refers to the twin crags prominent above Delphi, known as the Phaidriades, which these processions pass. In these upland plateaus of Parnassos is also the cave sacred to the Korykian Nymphs, who are closely associated with the god and are here imagined as accompanying these nocturnal processions. The spring of Kastalia flows down from these heights to Delphi below. Its water is sacred and was thought to bring poetic inspiration.

1205–8 / 1131–33 *ivy slopes of Nysaian hills send forth … coast rich with grapes* More cultic details of Dionysos: Nysaian hills refer to Nysa, a mountain sacred to Dionysos located variously in Egypt, Italy, Asia Minor, and Thrace. The ivy, because of its deep green, curling vine, is associated with the god's vital energies and vegetative power, and the grape (with its vines) belongs to Dionysos as god of wine. The Greek verb for *send forth* (*pempei*) connotes an escort or ritual procession (*pompê*), and Dionysos is often depicted on contemporary vases as arriving in such processions, escorted by nymphs and satyrs. The figurative use here makes it seem as if the god leads his own Dionysiac landscape in such a procession.

1208–9 / 1134–36 *immortal followers cry out the Bakkhic chant* Sophokles is using a verb that means to "utter *euoi*," the cry of the Bakkhants in their excited worship of Dionysos. Dionysos is himself sometimes referred to as "the Euian one," the god worshiped by the shouts of *euoi*! The word *followers* is a widely accepted emendation for a Greek word meaning "songs," "verses," "chants" in the manuscripts, which some editors accept. To have "songs cry out the Bakkhic chant," however, seems redundant; and *followers* suits the idea of a Bakkhic procession here; see the previous note.

1211–13 / 1139 *Your mother, she who was struck by lightning* Semele gives birth to Dionysos amid the lightning flashes of Zeus' majesty; see note on **1191 / 1116**.

1215–16 / 1140–41 *Disease … the city … and all its people, come cleanse us* The Chorus calls on Dionysos to bring an end to the pollution caused by the unburied corpse of Polyneikes, which both is a "disease" and also may be the fearful cause of diseases; see notes on **467 / 421** and **1078–79 / 1015**.

The pollution, or *miasma*, is feared as a kind of infectious stain or filth that needs "cleansing." The present anxiety undercuts Kreon's earlier confidence about avoiding pollution; see note on **944–50** / 885–90. Note, too, the contrast with the confidence in the human power to overcome disease in the Ode on Man (**405–6** / 363–64). Scattered references to Dionysos as healer occur in the ancient sources; this is the earliest. In the Greek, our wording *come cleanse us! Stride*...is literally "come with cleansing foot," which may be a reference to the cathartic effect of ecstatic Dionysiac dance, given the emphasis on ecstatic dancing throughout the ode; see Scott Scullion, "Dionysos and Katharsis in *Antigone*," *Classical Antiquity* 17 (1998), 96–122. As Griffith notes re: Greek lines **1140–45**, "*katharsis* can be painful." Kreon discovers this for himself: see note on **1371** / 1284.

1217 / 1144–45 *slopes of Parnassos...moaning narrows* Dionysos would come to Thebes either from the west via Parnassos and Delphi, where he is worshiped, or from the northeast across the narrow channel of the Euripos, which lies between the mainland of Boeotia and the island of Euboea.

1218–20 / 1146–48 *Lead the dance of the stars...the voices sounding in the night* This beautiful and remarkable image projects into the night sky the dances of Dionysos and his worshipers in their nocturnal processions on earth. The Dionysos who watches *over the Sacred Ways of Thebes* at the end of the previous antistrophe (**1210** / 1135–36) now extends his presence to vast cosmic distances. This shift from the city to the heavens parallels the shift from the nocturnal processions of joy in the parodos to these more remote, figurative choruses of fiery stars at a time of anxiety; see note on **1191–1224** / 1115–54.

1221–24 / 1149–52 *show us Your Presence...Bakkhantic Nymphs...frenzied dance* Dionysos often makes his appearance in sudden, unexpected, spectacular ways, and the Greek verb here, *pro-phanêthi*, implies a request for such a Dionysiac "epiphany." These female worshipers and attendants of Dionysos accompany the god in his processions and share the madness or "frenzy" of his ecstatic dances; see notes on **1196** / 1121 and **1201–5** / 1126–30 The word translated as "Bakkhantic Nymphs" is the Greek *Thyiades*, women or nymphs caught up in the ecstatic worship of Dionysos, from a verb meaning to "rush or leap furiously." Sophokles offers his own implicit gloss in the following phrase, "frenzied dance," where "frenzied," or "maddened," *mainomenai*, evokes the more familiar term, *mainades*, maenads, literally "maddened women," although the Thyiades here are probably to be thought of as nymphs rather than mortal women. Though Dionysos is here invoked as a savior god of the city, the reference to the Dionysiac madness continues the mood of mounting emotional violence that begins with the second stasimon and continues in the erotic subject of the third. It also resumes the theme of Dionysiac madness in the story of Lykourgos, who attacked the god's female followers in the fourth stasimon (1022–31 / 955–65).

1225–1342 / 1155–1256 *Sixth episode* constitutes the reversal or peripeteia of the play. The Chorus' hopeful prayer for help and release from pollution in the preceding ode is immediately answered by the wrenching events of the Messenger's speech and by the accumulating pollutions in the house of Kreon. Sophokles often exploits this sharp contrast, notably in *Aias*, *Oidipous Turannos*, and *Elektra*. The following scene has been carefully arranged so that the Messenger reports the events not merely to the elders of the Chorus, whom he addresses in his opening line, but also to Eurydike, wife of Kreon and mother of Haimon, who enters at 1254 / 1180. She has not previously been mentioned and may well be Sophokles' invention (see note on 1255–61 / 1182–86). Her response then leads directly into the final catastrophe and the final blow to Kreon's life.

1225–26 / 1155 *live near...both Kadmos and Amphion* The Messenger addresses the citizens of Thebes (and particularly the Theban elders of the Chorus) in terms of the founders of the city—Kadmos who slew the dragon that guarded Thebes' sacred spring (see note on 144 / 126), and Amphion, who built the walls of Thebes by causing the stones to leap into place through the magical power of his lyre, thereby resembling Orpheus in the power of his music over the natural world.

1229–30 / 1158–59 *Fortune...the fortunate and unfortunate* Such generalizations on the precariousness of human fortunes are common in messenger speeches and indeed in tragedy generally. The fourfold repetition on the root of the word for "fortune" or "chance" here, *tukhê*, reinforces the point. See notes on 1058 / 996, 1255–61 / 1182–86, and 1292 / 1213.

1231 / 1160 *things that stand established* The sense seems to be that no one can foresee how long the present circumstances can last for mortals. The phrase harks back to Kreon's obedience, too late, to the *established laws* in 1190 / 1114.

1235–36 / 1163 *absolute command* The Messenger means this as a compliment, but it also recalls Kreon's too absolute view of his authority; compare 194 / 173 and 796–99 / 736–39.

1237 / 1164 *seeds of noble children* The phrase echoes Haimon's still gentle attempt to persuade his father in **760–61 / 703**, and so reinforces the Messenger's contrast here between Kreon's previous prosperity and his present precarious situation.

1238–39 / 1165–66 *when a man's enjoyment betrays him* The text is somewhat uncertain, but the general sense is clear. A variant reading, with weaker manuscript authority, would give the sense "When men betray (i.e., abandon or lose) their pleasures"; another would give "When pleasures betray (abandon) men." We follow the majority of the manuscripts in reading *a man's enjoyment* (literally, "pleasing"), with the singular *man's*, which is supported by the scholia and better fits the specific application to Kreon. This hedonistic statement is revealing for the degree to which the Greeks view human life in terms of enjoyment or pleasure, in contrast to mere biological existence. The Messenger's generalization (which should not necessarily be identified with Sophokles' own philosophy) doubtless reflects popular sentiment. Brown aptly cites a fragment of Simonides, "Without pleasure what life of mortals or what absolute rule is desirable?"

1242 / 1169 *live in the style of a king* The tyrant, who rules by his own authority and without being responsible to other authorities, is the model of the happy life. Yet "tyranny" may also carry ominous associations of absolute power.

1249 / 1175 *bloodied by a hand close to him* The second half of this line, *autokheir haimassetai*, literally, "self-handed he was bloodied," plays on the two Greek words of which it consists. *Autokheir* can refer either to killing by one's own hand (so later in **1401 / 1315**, of Eurydike's suicide) or by a kindred hand. In the latter case, Haimon's death is assimilated to the fratricidal deaths in Antigone's house (e.g., **71 / 56**), an association reinforced by the "self-" language of the Messenger's reply in **1251 / 1177**. The verb "spilled the blood," *haimassetai*, also plays on the name of Haimon, as if his destiny is foreshadowed in his name. Greek literature is fond of this kind of false etymology, e.g., Pentheus and *penthos*, "grief," in Euripides' *Bakkhai*.

1255–61 / 1182–86 *She comes . . . by chance . . . I chanced to loosen . . . the bolts* By calling attention to Eurydike's "chance" arrival, Sophokles perhaps indicates that her presence as the recipient of the Messenger's narrative is not part of the traditional tale but is his own invention. She does not occur in any earlier extant version of the myth. "Chanced" in **1260 / 1186** repeats the

same root as the word "chance" in **1256** / 1182 (*tukhê . . . tungkhanô*). See
notes on **1058** / 996 and **1229–30** / 1158–59.

1259 / 1184 *Pallas* Pallas Athena, major Olympian goddess, daughter of Zeus, is an
appropriate divinity for a woman to supplicate. Offering such prayers of
supplication would be one of the reasons for women to leave the house.
Compare Iokaste's emergence from the house in *Oidipous Turannos*
(911–23) to pray to Apollo.

1266 / 1191 *as one who has lived through adversity* This may hint at the death of Kreon's
elder son; see notes on **673** / 626–27 and **1387–92** / 1301–5.

1267–70 / 1192–95 The Messenger's promise of an accurate account assures the
veracity of what follows but also proves to be fatal for Eurydike.

1271–1328 / 1196–1243 The Messenger relates the deaths of Haimon and Antigone.
Greek tragedy rarely shows scenes of violence on stage but prefers to
narrate them through a messenger's speech, as here. The ancient audience was accustomed to the oral performances of the Homeric poems
and of choral song and so, one imagines, would enter fully into the story.
This is one of the most powerful such speeches in Greek tragedy. It
completes the motif of Antigone's "marriage in Hades" and marks the
reversal in Kreon's fortunes, from power and prosperity to helplessness
and misery. Four narrative devices contribute to its effectiveness: (1) the
tenses shift back and forth between past and present as the Messenger
begins the account of the encounter between father and son at **1285ff.** /
1206ff.; (2) the quotations in direct discourse make this encounter very
vivid; (3) the sequence of events is clear and rapid; (4) Sophokles keeps
the emphasis on the interaction between father and son but does so in a
way that reveals its fully tragic character. Though the Messenger reports
Kreon's words to his son, all verbal communication fails. Haimon
refuses to answer and instead replies only with silent, violent gestures,
culminating in his bloody embrace of Antigone's corpse as he dies. (See
also note on **1401** / 1315.)

1271–83 / 1196–1205 On Kreon's change from his earlier intention first to rescue
Antigone and then to bury Polyneikes, see note on **1183–90** / 1108–14.

1275–81 / 1199–1204 This account of the formal burial of Polyneikes not only gives
closure to the motif of the unburied corpse; it also gives him the full rites
of burial that Antigone could perform only in part. The culminating
detail is that the tomb is formed by a *mound for burial straight and true.*

Compare the first account of the burial in 290–91 / 255–56, where the Guard specifically states that the body was *not covered with a mound*. See note on 472–76 / 427–31. At the same time both the completed ritual and the visible mound contrast with the perverted "funeral" ritual of Antigone, buried out of sight in an underground chamber. See note on 962–65 / 900–903.

1283 / 1205 *bridal crypt of Hades...floor of rock* In the fusion of marriage and funeral Antigone's bed is in a stony cave/tomb instead of bridal chamber.

1291 / 1212 *Am I a seer?* Kreon's reference to prophecy here fulfills his earlier unknowing foreshadowing of the tragic events in the play, notably his description of Antigone as a "cold embrace" for Haimon, 699–700 / 650.

1292 / 1213 *A path that's more unfortunate* This echo of the word for "fortune" or "chance" puts into Kreon's own words the Messenger's initial generalization about the reversal of his situation; see note on 1229–30 / 1158–1159.

1296 / 1216 *fitted stones* We keep the manuscript reading, *harmon* (lit. "joint," "fitting"). The passage is difficult. Lloyd-Jones and Wilson emend to *agmon*, with the sense "the gap made by tearing away the stones." Dawe supposes that some lines have dropped out after this verse. The cave presumably has a mound of earth and stones at its entrance, perhaps blocking the passageway into a Mycenaean chamber tomb or *tholos*, as Griffith plausibly suggests, which has been reused for this purpose. In any case, the entrance, or mouth, would have been sealed with piled-up earth and a loose "fitting" of stones, which (as we subsequently learn) Haimon has "torn away" to open his access.

1298–99 / 1217–18 *hearing...the gods are tricking me* Kreon's fear introduces the important motif of communication (see note on 1271–1328 / 1196–1243) and also admits the possibility that the gods may not be entirely on his side and that he may not understand their actions.

1302–3 / 1222 *noose tied of fine-woven linen* Wedding and funeral again come together, as the description suggests a veil, used in both marriage and burial ceremonies.

1305–8 / 1224–25 *bed...marriage* Both of these words in the Greek mean both *bed* and by metonymy *marriage*. Some editors have therefore suspected that the second line is an interpolation. Although Haimon does not mention

Antigone by name, the *bed* can also stand by further metonymy for the bride. The *spoiling* or "corruption" of the bed (and bride) is soon answered by the spoiling or ruin of Haimon himself (i.e., of his sanity, as Kreon fears in 1310–12 / 1228–30), and then by Haimon's suicide.

1309–10 / 1226–27 *moaning...wailing cries* Lamentation engulfs this family, as it had Antigone's, and it will continue in Eurydike's lament later.

1310–11 / 1228–29 *You desperate boy...in your mind?* Kreon's exclamation here can indicate both disapproval (of Haimon's "reckless" or "desperate" behavior) and compassion. Though Kreon's cry might at first be understood as possibly addressed to the dead Antigone, the context makes it clear that he is thinking entirely of his son.

1314–15 / 1232 *spits in his face* Perhaps this is an ironic reversal of Kreon's paternalistic urging of Haimon to "spit out" Antigone as an enemy in 702 / 653.

1316 / 1233 *two-edged* The adjective can also mean "double-hilted," which some interpreters prefer.

1318 / 1235 *furious at himself* Combined with the silence, the spitting, and the drawn sword, the phrase indicates the total breakdown of communication between father and son, as well as Haimon's wild passion.

1320–21 / 1237 *wraps the girl in the weak crook of his arm* See notes on 699–700 / 650 and 945 / 886. The figurative "embrace" of Antigone by her tomb has now become an actual embrace, but both acts fuse marriage and death.

1327–28 / 1242–43 Messengers in tragedy often end their narratives with similar generalizations on the human condition.

1330 / 1245 *without a word* Eurydike's silent exit, which resembles that of Iokaste in *Oidipous Turannos* and of Deianeira in *Trakhinian Women* at analogous crises, continues the motif of silence and failed communication in the Messenger's narrative. The Messenger and Chorus immediately reflect on the meaning of this silence (1337–42 / 1251–56).

1334–35 / 1247–49 *But in the shelter...among her servants* Literally, "will not utter forth/cry forth her cries (*goous*) into the city, but rather beneath (the shelter of) her house will bring forth her private (literally, belonging to the house, *oikeion*) grief to her servants." Women in fifth-century Athens were not expected to lament in public, and the mourning for warriors killed in battle was taken over by a public ceremony at which the chief magistrate pronounced a funeral oration. In the most famous extant example of such funeral orations, Perikles' speech in Thucydides' *History of the Peloponnesian War*, 2.34–46, Perikles says that a woman's reputation consists in being least talked about among men "either concerning excellence or blame" (2.45.2). Sophokles heavily overdetermines the contrast between house and city by the repetition "under her own roof / in private," as the latter word, *oikeion*, means, literally, "belonging to the house," *oikos*.

1343–431 / 1257–353 *Exodos* The final scene of the play begins with another *kommos* (see note on **866–941 / 806–82**), an emotional exchange largely in lyric meters, between Kreon and the Chorus. Kreon enters in what is essentially a funeral procession, either carrying (or more probably supporting with attendants) the body of Haimon. If the body is represented by a dummy of some sort, it is possible to understand *in his arms* (**1344 / 1258**) literally, but it is perhaps more likely that the corpse is carried or wheeled in on a bier by his attendants. This arrangement is perhaps suggested also by the Chorus' words at **1365 / 1279** (literally, "These things you hold before your hands") and would make the actor's task easier. But there would obviously be a more graphic pathos if Kreon is actually carrying the body in his arms. Conceivably, he enters carrying the body and is then relieved of it by attendants, as **1383–84 / 1297** implies. The carefully balanced antiphonal responsions between single mourner and Chorus throughout this scene evoke the ritual of burial that often concludes Greek tragedies. The finales of Euripides' *Andromakhe* and *Women of Troy* offer close parallels. Comparable, too, are the funeral procession at the end of Sophokles' *Aias* and the entrance of Kadmos with the mutilated body of his grandson, Pentheus, at the end of *Bakkhai*.

The shift to song and song meters here marks a strong shift of tone after the long Messenger's speech. This last entrance of Kreon contrasts with the energy he displays earlier when confronting Teiresias, at **1050ff. / 988ff.** So forceful and confident before, Kreon is now a broken man, and this radical change is indicated in part by his singing for the first time in lyric meters, the emotional rhythms of dochmiacs (essentially syncopated iambics). His only previous utterances outside of the dialogue meter of iambic trimeter were his short anapestic exchanges with Antigone at **999–1000 / 931–32, 1003–4 / 935–36**. The lyrical *kommos* not only shows his changed relation to those around him but also harks back to the lyrical laments of Antigone with the Chorus just before she is led off to the cave.

1344–45 / 1258–60 *conspicuous sign . . . a memorial, his own ruin* This now answers the previously absent or "unclear" or "unintelligible" signs, e.g., the marks of burial at **287 / 252**, the cries of the birds of omen at **1060–67 / 998–1004**, and the shout from the cave in **1288–89 / 1209–10**. Haimon's body, on the stage, is now both the visible "sign" of Kreon's "ruin" and its concrete, physical embodiment.

The word translated as "ruin," *atê* (**1345 / 1260**), also means the "infatuation" or "madness" that leads up to the ruin. That is, it refers both to the subjective mental disposition that caused the disaster and to the objective result, the disaster itself; see note on **671–72 / 624–25**. In the former sense, Haimon's body now makes tangible Kreon's inner disposition, which has led him to this terrible moment. So understood, these lines can also be seen as a kind of metatheatrical discourse, calling attention to the drama's ability to reveal, in visual "signs" on stage, the invisible causes of the tragic events in the emotional and moral behavior of the characters.

Kreon's vocabulary here also seems to echo that of the Athenian funeral speech or *epitaphios logos*, a public discourse pronounced over fallen warriors at a state funeral in the fifth century (see note on **1334–35 / 1247–49**). If so, there is a deep irony because Kreon is lamenting a private, not a public, loss, and his son did not die heroically for the city, like his brother Megareus (see note on **1387–92 / 1301–5**), but because of a wild, individual passion for a girl condemned by the city. This "illustrious memorial" would also suggest both a parallel and a contrast to the "glorious bier" of the dead Megareus (if that is the correct reading) in **1387–92 / 1301–5**.

1345 / 1260 *His own ruin—no one else's* The Chorus, which previously has mentioned "ruin," *atê*, in general terms (**661 / 614, 671–72 / 624–25**), now attributes it specifically to Kreon. This does not mean that Antigone has not contributed to the disaster, but not through the kind of "infatuation" that *atê* here implies.

1357 / 1270 *recognize what justice is, too late* The Chorus implicitly validates Antigone's claim to justice in her defiant speech to Kreon in **495ff. / 450ff.** and reverses its view of Antigone's "stumbling against the throne of Justice" in **914–15 / 854–55**. The Chorus also acknowledges the retributive justice for which Antigone prayed in what were almost her last words, **995–96 / 927–28**.

1363 / 1276 *burden . . . exhausting burden* The Greek word *ponos* means "pain," "suffering," "effort," "toil," etc., and has earlier been used for Antigone's acceptance of the "burden" of burying Polyneikes (52 / 41, 967 / 907) and for the guards' "task" of enduring the stench of Polyneikes' rotting corpse (458 / 414). The phrasing here, with its bleak repetition of "burdens," expresses Kreon's utter despair. His language uses the same lyricism of the dirge that had characterized Antigone's final laments.

1364ff. / 1277ff. The final blow to Kreon comes from the news of Eurydike's death, brought by the Messenger. The staging probably made use of the *ekkyklêma*, a low platform wheeled out from the central door of the scene building, which represents the royal house of Kreon. Thus we are reminded both of the play's opening scene, when Antigone and Ismene stand before that door, and of the increasingly domestic and personal nature of a catastrophe for one who had placed city over house.

1368 / 1282 *mother absolute* For *pammêtor*, literally, "the all-mother" (a single word in the Greek), there is no easy English equivalent. It conveys the sense of the wholly devoted mother, the mother in the very fullest sense of the word, the one who defined herself as totally mother and so feels most keenly the loss of a son, whose death she does not survive. The juxta-position with *nekrou*, corpse, adds pathos. She is now mother only of a dead son and so has gone from all-mother to no-mother. This highly poetical word recurs elsewhere as an epithet of Earth or of the venerable Rhea (mother of Zeus and Hera) as the "mother of all." In its evocations of a universal maternity, both divine and human, the epithet may also recall the female goddesses of death and rebirth, Persephone and Demeter, in the background, or the ever-grieving Niobe of Antigone's lament after the second stasimon, or the mourning mothers of the fourth stasimon. See Introduction, pp. 31–32.

1371 / 1284 *Harbor of Hades, never to be purified* In contrast to his earlier confidence about avoiding pollution for the city (**944ff. / 885ff.**), Kreon finds a pollution in his own case that he cannot "cleanse" or "purify." See notes on **1078–79 / 1015** and **1215–16 / 1140–41.** The metaphor of his own house as a "harbor of Hades" also contrasts with his previous nautical imagery (**182–83 / 162–63, 212–13 / 189–90**) and with his use of Hades (death) as an instrument of his own power (e.g., **352 / 308, 838–42 / 777–80**). See notes on **495–518 / 450–70** and **559–74 / 508–23.** Antigone, meanwhile, has invoked Hades as the divine authority for her insistence on burying Polyneikes (e.g., **570 / 519**).

1376–79 / 1289–92 *Of what new killing . . . piled on top of death* The Greek is very dense here. The last element of the total collapse of Kreon's ordered world is that this death at an altar (*bômia*, 1387 / 1301) is a kind of perverted ritual of sacrifice, as *sphagion* literally means "sacrificial victim." The altar here, moreover, is presumably that of Zeus Herkeios—the household shrine of Zeus who protects the family—which Kreon had so confidently scorned in his condemnation of Antigone; see note on 535–38 / 486–87. That a woman should kill herself in so agonizing a way adds to the horror (see note on 1401 / 1315).

1380 / 1293 *See her* For the probable use of the *ekkyklêma* here to display Eurydike's body, see note on 1364ff. / 1277ff.

1383–84 / 1297 *Only now I held my son in my arms* If Kreon did enter actually carrying the body, he has now put it down or it has been taken by his attendants. See note on 1343–1431 / 1257–1353.

1387–92 / 1301–5 These lines present a number of textual and interpretative problems. The manuscripts are divided between assigning the speech to the Chorus or the Messenger, but the latter is far more likely. At least one line has dropped out after 1387 / 1301, which does not make a complete sentence and in any case is corrupt. We have adopted a plausible emendation for 1387 / 1301 and have added a possible version of one missing line. The lost verse or verses presumably described Eurydike's approach to the altar and gestures preliminary to stabbing herself. In 1390 / 1303 the manuscripts read "dead Megareus' glorious bed," or perhaps "glorious bier," which most editors emend either to "glorious lot" or to "empty bed," both readings involving the change of a single letter of the Greek. Sophokles seems to be referring to a version of a story found in Euripides' *Phoinikian Women*, in which Teiresias tells Kreon that only the willing sacrifice of a descendant of the original Theban Planted Men can save Thebes from the Argive attack (see note on 1057 / 995). In that play, Kreon's son, there called Menoikeus (after Kreon's father), hurls himself off the wall into the Serpent's den and so saves Thebes. In the version that Sophokles seems to be following, Eurydike (rightly or not) seems to blame Kreon for Megareus' suicide, so that he is the killer of both his sons—Haimon in the immediate present ("this son") and Megareus. (In Euripides' version, Kreon, a much more sympathetic character, puts family ahead of city and tries to forestall his son's possible death.) But if Sophokles is following this version of the Theban legend, Megareus' death presumably must have been fresh, i.e., during the Argive attack, and so Sophokles has carefully kept it in the background. There are a few passing hints earlier; see notes on 673 / 626–27, 1127 / 1058, 1266 / 1191. If we keep the manuscript reading, "glorious bier" could refer to the honor of Megareus' patriotic self-sacrifice. We have, however, accepted the emendation "empty bed" for a number of reasons. Syntactically, it suits the following reference to Haimon's equally "empty bed" (although the possessive genitive of the manuscripts is also sometimes emended to the accusative, "looks to the bed and to this [other] one, Haimon"). "Empty bed" would also reflect Eurydike's grief at the loss of both of her sons' future marriages and so reinforce the parallel with Antigone. This interpretation is supported by the way it echoes Antigone's lament over Polyneikes like a mother bird *when she finds that her nest and bed are empty* (*orphanon lekhos*, 469–70 / 425) and by the fact that Antigone, like Eurydike, "curses" the perpetrator (473 / 427). We are reminded, too, of "the unfortunate bed" of Antigone over which Haimon groans and wails in 1305–8 / 1224–25. Yet both the reading and the exact sense of 1390–92 / 1303–5 remain obscure.

1395–96 / 1309 *two-edged sword* Literally, a "double-whetted sword," this is sharp on both edges. Kreon now takes up and applies to himself the Messenger's description of Eurydike's *sharp-edged blade* at 1387 / 1301.

1398 / 1312 *charged by the dead woman* The language is that of Athenian legal terminology and may be an ironical reflection on Kreon's legalistic frame of mind earlier in the play.

1400 / 1314 *torn away from us* Kreon repeats the verb he used for the death of Haimon at 1355 / 1268, thereby linking the two deaths.

1401 / 1315 *With her own hand...below her liver* The liver may be used here in a general sense for the abdominal region, but it may also be intended as the specific organ, as the liver is considered the seat of the passionate emotions. This particularly bloody and painful death bears out the Messenger's language of a murderous sacrificial slaughter at 1387ff. / 1301ff. and 1368–69 / 1282–83. Like Antigone herself, women in Greek tragedy usually commit suicide by hanging (e.g., "Iokaste" in *Oidipous Turannos*). Deianeira's suicide in Sophokles' *Trakhinian Women*, who stabs herself through her side "downward toward her liver and chest," is another exception. Seneca's Jocasta, in his *Oedipus*, stabs herself in the womb, a gruesome variant characteristic of that author. *With her own hand*, in Greek *autokheir*, is the last occurrence of these "self-" compounds in the play, and it marks the climax of the destruction and passion turned against oneself or one's family. The word was last used of Haimon in 1249 / 1175. The whole passage has echoes of Haimon's lament and suicide in 1305–8 / 1224–25 as well as of Antigone's lament and curses over Polyneikes' body at 467–73 / 422–28. In the destruction of Kreon's house, father and son and husband and wife communicate in terms of murderous gestures rather than intimate communication. Haimon does not answer his father's words (1313–15 / 1231–32), and Eurydike exits from the stage in silence. Haimon spits in his father's face before killing himself, and Eurydike calls down curses on her husband at her death (1391–92 / 1305). Sophokles thus links the death of Eurydike with the deaths of Antigone and Haimon as the steps that, in retrospect, form the sequence leading to Kreon's destruction.

1402 / 1316 *sharp wailing* Literally, "when she learned this (present) sharp-bewailed suffering of her son." The *sharp wailing* leads to the *sharp-edged* knife of her suicide (1387 / 1301). There is a lot of "sharpness" here at the end (also 1395–96 / 1309), which adds to the atmosphere of violence and suffering. Is there tragic irony in the contrast between this sharpness and the Chorus' exultation in the metaphorical *sharp bit* that saved Thebes in the parodos (127 / 108–9)?

1408 / 1325 *no more than nothing* These words represent the climax of Kreon's utter spiritual and literal annihilation. The phrase takes up and fulfills, on stage, the Messenger's introduction to Kreon's disaster in 1240–45 / 1167–71: *a dead man who can still draw breath . . . the shadow of thin smoke*. Sophokles is fond of this figure of the tragic life as reduced to "nothing": e.g., *Oidipous Turannos*, 1186–88, *Elektra*, 1165–67, *Philoktetes*, 1018, 1217.

1409 / 1326 *profit* This is the last and most devastating iteration of what had been Kreon's obsessive preoccupation. See note on 1102–5 / 1035–39.

1420 / 1337–38 *destined for mortals . . . no deliverance* Greek tragedies often end with such moralizing generalizations by the Chorus (as also in its final lines below on "teaching good sense"), but they constitute only one attempt to grasp the meaning of these devastating events, and not necessarily the most profound. See note on 1427–31 / 1349–53.

1421 / 1339 *Lead me away* This small touch subtly marks once more the total inversion of power and weakness at the end of the play, for such was Kreon's command regarding Antigone in 833 / 773 and 944 / 885.

1424 / 1342–43 *I do not know which one to look at* Like Eurydike in 1389–91 / 1303–4, he is divided between two sources of agony.

1425 / 1344–45 *everything is twisted* This completely overturns Kreon's earlier confidence in his ability to "direct" and keep his city "upright" or "right" (*orthos*, literally "straight") in his first speech (e.g., **182ff.** / 162ff., **686ff.** / 639ff.).

1427–31 / 1348–53 As the Chorus chants its final moralizing song, Kreon leaves the stage, led away by his attendants, as he has twice requested (**1406–8** / 1321–25, **1421** / 1339). In the Greek performance, we do not know what was done with the bodies of Haimon and Eurydike. They might have been left on the stage as the visible evidence of the tragic waste and loss, or they might have been carried back into the palace, or carried with the Chorus as they exit after their final song, or possibly carried off with Kreon as he exits, as members of the house that he has destroyed. The final lines mention a number of important themes in the play: good sense, disrespectful actions toward the gods, excessive or boastful speech, and the contrast between the old and the young. As often in Greek tragedy, such gnomic closure offers a measure of continuity and communal solidarity after disorienting, chaotic violence. At the same time, the tendentious moral only points up the discrepancy between the tragic events and the construction of a rational, coherent world order. *Happiness*, in **1428** / 1348 here, seems very far away; none of the major characters has shown good sense; Antigone has died for her reverence; and the young victims will have no chance to learn in old age. Whatever Kreon may yet learn as he grows old seems beside the point amidst the completeness of his destruction now.

APPENDIX 1:
THE DATE OF *ANTIGONE*

The only external evidence for the dating of *Antigone* is a statement in the ancient Argument attributed to the Hellenistic scholar Aristophanes of Byzantium and prefixed to the play in the manuscripts. Thanks to the success of *Antigone*, the Argument reports, Sophokles was elected one of the ten generals to serve in the Athenian war against the revolt of the island of Samos, an important member of the Athenian naval empire. The Samian revolt took place in 441–439 BCE, and the connection of the play with it, even allowing for exaggeration, would suggest a date in 442 or 441. As the elections took place in late spring, *Antigone* would have been first performed at the great festival of Dionysos in March 442 or 441. The connection between the generalship and the play, however, may be the invention of the often unreliable biographical tradition and may mean only that the play was performed sometime around 440, plus or minus a few years. Some scholars, therefore, for various reasons, have preferred a slightly later date. There is no absolute certainty, but a date in this period would suit the play's style and dramaturgy, and it is widely accepted. In any case, the play seems to belong to Sophokles' full maturity. Born in 496/97, he would have written it in his mid-fifties, after he had been presenting plays at the dramatic festivals for some thirty years, since his first victory in the dramatic competitions in 468. The play would be about a decade earlier than the *Oidipous Turannos* (429–425), with which it shares certain features (e.g., an angry encounter between a king and a prophet and the silent exit of a queen to commit suicide).

APPENDIX 2:
THE MYTH OF ANTIGONE, TO THE END OF THE FIFTH CENTURY BCE

The story of Oidipous and his children is referred to in Homer and was told in a number of epic and probably lyric poems of the seventh and sixth centuries BCE, of which only sparse fragments survive. We know very little of the story of Antigone herself prior to Sophokles. The ancient sources report various versions, many of uncertain date, no one of which exactly tallies with Sophokles' version.* It is uncertain whether Sophokles is the first to have Antigone sacrifice her life to bury her brother. It is probable (but by no means certain) that the framing of the conflict between Kreon and Antigone, her and Haimon's deaths in the cave, and the figure of Eurydike are Sophokles' inventions. The dramatists always felt free to add new details and to interpret the story in their own way. Euripides' lost *Antigone* of 431, for example, probably ended with Dionysos as deus ex machina rescuing the heroine from death.

Sophokles' most important predecessor is Aiskhylos, whose *Seven against Thebes* was performed in 467, and is the only surviving play of a trilogy that included *Laios* and *Oidipous*. Echoes of Aiskyhlos' language suggest that Sophokles has *Seven against Thebes* in mind at several points.

Seven against Thebes dramatizes the events that immediately precede the action of Antigone—that is, the conflict between the two sons of Oidopous, Eteokles, and Polyneikes, for the throne of Thebes. Eteokles, the defender of the city against his brother's army from Argos, puts a Theban warrior in command at six of the seven gates to defend them

---

* For a brief survey of the ancient evidence, see J. C. Kamerbeek's "Introduction" to his commentary, 1–5; Griffith's introduction, 7–12 (full bibliographic citations are at the beginning of the Notes, p. 119); also my *Tragedy and Civilization*, 190, with notes 111–14 on 449 (see For Further Reading).

against seven captains of the Argive attackers, and he places himself at the seventh gate, where the two brothers kill each other in battle. *Seven against Thebes* ends with a lament over the two fallen brothers, which editors variously attribute to the Chorus, divided into two halves, or to Antigone and Ismene. At this point a herald enters and announces the decree to the leaders of the city not to permit the burial of Polyneikes. Antigone states her determination to bury him, and the manuscript ends with the two half Choruses divided in allegiance between Antigone and the city's leaders, respectively. In contrast to Sophokles' play, *Seven against Thebes* does not mention Kreon, nor does it isolate Antigone.

Unfortunately, there is considerable controversy about how much of this ending is due to Aiskhylos and how much may have been a later addition under the influence of Sophokles' own play. The issue remains unresolved. If the ending of *Seven against Thebes* is in fact by Aiskhylos, Sophokles has shifted the emphasis from Aiskhylos' central themes of inherited guilt and the family curse to the conflict between Antigone and Kreon and her heroic defiance of the latter's authority.

Some fifteen or twenty years after *Antigone*, Euripides' *Suppliants*, dated to the late 420s, uses a doubtless early version of the story, in which Kreon refuses burial to all of the Argive dead and not just to Polyneikes. This Athens-centered version has no place in it for Antigone. Here the Athenian king, Theseus, heeding the supplications of the mothers of the fallen warriors, finally compels Kreon to bury them. Sophokles seems to be alluding to this version in lines 1153–56 / 1080–83 of *Antigone*.

By the end of the fifth century BCE, Sophokles' version of the myth, with Antigone at its center, is familiar. In the *Phoinikian Women* of 409, Euripides tells the story of the two brothers' deaths at Thebes differently, but he ends with Antigone, who leads the old Oidipous into exile. The last scene includes her dialogue with Kreon, in which she defies his decree of exposing Polyneikes' corpse in a stichomythia that obviously echoes Sophokles' (1646–68); and she tells Oidipous of her determination to bury her brother even if it means her death (1745–46).

Sophokles himself returns to Antigone at the very end of his life in his *Oidopous at Kolonos*, composed some thirty-five years after *Antigone* and produced posthumously. This play, set at Athens in the last days of the aged Oidopous' life, is a "prequel" to *Antigone*. The father curses both his sons, predicting their death. After failing to dissuade. Polyneikes from what will prove to be his fatal expedition against Thebes, Antigone at the end decides to go back to the doomed city and try to prevent the two brothers from killing one another. Although the ending says nothing about the burial of Polyneikes or Antigone's death, Sophokles clearly has his earlier play in mind.

APPENDIX 3:
THE TRANSMISSION
OF THE TEXT

Antigone, along with the six other extant plays of Sophokles (out of over a hundred that he wrote), survives primarily in numerous Byzantine manuscripts, ranging in date from the tenth to the fifteenth centuries CE. There is, therefore, a period of some 1,500 years between Sophokles' original text and our earliest manuscripts. In some cases the manuscripts can be supplemented by quotations or comments in other classical authors (themselves transmitted in medieval manuscripts) or occasionally by papyrus fragments preserved from Hellenistic and Greco-Roman Egypt, generally dating from the third century BCE to the fifth century CE. In the case of Sophokles, however, we are dependent mostly on the Byzantine manuscripts. The first printed edition appeared from the celebrated Venetian printing house of Aldo Manuzio (Aldus Manutius) in 1502.

Before reaching the medieval manuscripts, these texts (like those of most classical Greek authors) were copied, edited, and recopied numerous times. This process resulted in numerous errors or corruptions. Later scribes often made mechanical errors or misunderstood and hence miscopied the text because an earlier script was unfamiliar or because they did not fully grasp Sophokles' dense poetic vocabulary and syntax, especially in the choral odes. It used to be assumed that the earliest manuscripts were the most reliable (especial the tenth-century manuscript designated as L and now in the Laurentian library in Florence), but even these have many errors, and recent research has shown that good readings are to be found in a much wider range of manuscripts.

Since the Renaissance, classical scholars have worked intensively to restore the text to something like its original form through comparative study of the manuscripts and through close critical examination of Sophokles' language and meaning. The process still continues. In numerous passages, and not only in the odes, editors and translators have to choose among variant readings in the manuscripts or among the conjectures and emendations of modern scholars for passages that are clearly wrong in the manuscripts. Although no two modern editors agree on all parts of the text, there is a wide consensus on much of it, embodied in the editions of Jebb, Dawe, Lloyd-Jones and Wilson, and (most recently) Griffith (see beginning of Notes, 117). We have not followed any single edition and have indicated our choices for some of the most controversial passages in the Notes.

OEDIPUS THE KING

Translated by

STEPHEN BERG

and

DISKIN CLAY

INTRODUCTION

The first thing we know about Oedipus is what we see. Fixed, kinglike, powerful, his features do not change. His face is a mask. Oedipus' first words, and the very fact that he has appeared in person to meet a delegation of Thebans, show that he is a man of compassion. Thebes is not at three removes from its king. When Kreon arrives with news from Delphi, he asks Oedipus if he does not prefer to go inside the palace to hear Apollo's response. Oedipus would rather hear the response "with all these people listening." The action of the *Oedipus* begins in the open, and Oedipus is onstage throughout the play. Even when he is in the palace and out of sight, he remains within the range of the choral song and at the center of the speech of the palace servant who comes out to report Jocasta's death and Oedipus' self-blinding. When Oedipus last appears before the Chorus and the audience in the theater of Dionysos, his mask and its great hollow eyes are bloodstained.

"Children, why are you here?" Oedipus asks this question, but he already knows its answer, and he has been quick to act on what he knows. While the people of Thebes crowd the temples and shrines of the city's gods and look into embers for signs of their disposition (27–28 / 21), Oedipus has not been asleep. Confronted with the plague that is wasting his city, he has already attempted to work from effect to cause, and has sent to Delphi and the oracle of Apollo for a response to his question: "What must I say or do to save Thebes?" At the beginning of the *Oedipus*, Oedipus is both ahead of the action of the play and behind it.

The *Oedipus* begins with a question, and in no other Greek tragedy are more questions asked. As Oedipus attempts to discern the unknown in the physiognomy of the known, one question inevitably leads to another. Oedipus has experience. This is why the delegation of Thebans turn to him in their quest for a better future. They hope that the past will be a guide to this future and know that Oedipus' intelligence has already been tested in his encounter with the Sphinx (53–58 / 35–39). When Kreon arrives on stage, Oedipus prays for good luck and the safety Kreon's face seems to promise (98–99 / 80–81). At first, the world of appearance and experience seems to guarantee a future that is still dark and unknown.

The new riddle that now confronts Oedipus is the discovery of the source of the plague in the underlying pollution which is its cause. With Apollo's response, the hunt for Laios' murderer and the source of this pollution begins, and the language of the play comes to be controlled by the metaphors of the hunt: discovery, paths and wandering, inference, conjecture, and revelation. What is dark will be brought to light. The murder of Laios is ancient history, but Oedipus' wit searches for the one clue that could teach him the rest (145 / 120–21). What he is looking for are signs or tokens (*semeia, symbola*). These are at the heart of Oedipus' quest (295 / 221). A *symbolon* (or *semeion*) is the half of a whole that has been broken—a joint or a tally.[1] Oedipus attempts to fit pieces together to gain a picture of the whole, and he is looking for the tallies that brought together strangers and the members of broken families. It is characteristic of Oedipus' intelligence that it makes of the world of appearance the half that will fit into a larger whole. He believes that the obscure and unknown can be seen in the face of appearances.

It is Oedipus' confidence that the invisible can be read in the physiognomy of the visible that controls his language and actions. In his flight from Corinth and the man and woman he considered his father and mother, Oedipus takes his bearings on the distant and invisible when he measures his distance from Corinth by the stars (1035 / 795). When the shepherd who saved him from death on Mt. Kithairon appears as Oedipus' last hope and the last piece in the puzzle of his life (cf. 1334 / 1058–59), Oedipus does not recognize him. But he can guess who he must be. There is a harmony and measure between the unknown shepherd and the man he sees before him (1408–9 / 1112–16). When the Corinthian arrives to announce the death of Polybos, Oedipus asks him to "convey" or "signify" to him news of his father's death. "Convey" rather than "tell" because Oedipus has no immediate knowledge of

---

1. For the range and sense of the word *symbolon*, consider the word as it describes the two sexes as broken halves of a primordial whole in Plato, *Symposium* 191 D, and compare Empedocles, *Fragment* B 63. *Semeia*, the tokens that led to the recognition of blood ties in Greek tragedy, are discussed by Aristotle in the *Poetics*, Chapter 16; cf., in their contexts, Euripides' *Electra* 577; *Ion* 1386; and in comedy, Menander, *The Arbitration* (*Epitrepontes* 331–333), and *Rape of the Locks* (*Perikeiromene* 135).

Polybos' death or what is happening in Corinth. And when he has heard the Messenger's oblique account, he attempts to make the news of Polybos' death join with the oracle that he was fated to kill his father. If he died "from wanting me to be with him," then you could say that I killed him.

The very actions and conjectures which distract Oedipus in his search for the truth speak eloquently for his character. He is intelligent, quick to act and react, political, suspicious. He is quick to spot a plot in the murder of Laios, for he is not satisfied that the man who was king before him could have been killed by bandits acting alone. They must be part of a plot hatched in Thebes (148–50 / 124–25). Oedipus is also a man who sees himself as acting and reacting alone at the center of things. Kreon and the one survivor of the attack on Laios both speak of "bandits," but Oedipus strangely speaks of the bandit. His language is surely governed by the plot of Sophocles' play, but it must be determined, too, by Oedipus' sense of himself as an individual at the center of his actions—one man in control of things, and not part of a group. He is affected by the plague as no one else. He places himself at the heart of his city's sufferings, for he suffers for his city, for himself, and for the priest and the others he sees before him (85 / 64).

The question he asks of Delphi is what can I do or say to save my city (93 / 72). Apollo's response requires action: drive out the man who is polluting Thebes with the stain of Laios' blood upon him. What makes Oedipus impervious to Teiresias' accusation that he, Oedipus, is the killer of Laios, and worse, is his interpretation of these words as the face of a plot Kreon has constructed against him. Oedipus' political instinct and his sense of himself are so strong that he can tell Jocasta that Kreon is plotting against his "person" and shift the curse he had laid on the murderer of Laios onto Kreon (842–44 / 642–43). Voltaire complained in his *Lettre III* on Sophocles' *Oedipus* (1719) that Oedipus absurdly went about consulting oracles and pronouncing curses rather than discovering the one witness to the murderer of Laios. It seemed implausible (*invraisemblable*) that a king who wanted to get to the bottom of things would act as Oedipus does.[2] But in truth, Oedipus' estimate of human nature is plausible. What is absurd in Sophocles' *Oedipus* is the fact that the events of Oedipus' own life were not subject to the control of human intelligence. At the end, Kreon says as much.

---

2. *Oeuvres Complètes de Voltaire: 2 Théatre I* (1877) *Lettre III* (on Sophocles' Oedipus), pp. 18–28. Voltaire's long list of Sophocles' violations of the "rules of common sense" shows an unparalleled acuteness to the surface contradictions and "unrealistic" details of the plot of the *Oedipus* and a resolute and confident obtuseness to the genius of Sophoclean irony.

Oedipus first appears strikingly both as what he is and seems. He tells the world that he is Oedipus—"Everybody everywhere knows who I am: Oedipus. King." Oedipus is already known to the group of Thebans who sit at the altars of his palace. And he is known to Sophocles' audience.[3] Behind Oedipus' words, which seem so incongruous to a modern sense of realism, is a requirement of full disclosure. What is known must be brought out into the open for all to see. Kreon is obliged to tell Oedipus and Sophocles' audience (127–28 / 103–4):

> My lord, before you came to Thebes, before you came to power,
> Laios was our king.

Oedipus must tell Jocasta, his wife of many years: "My father was Polybos, of Corinth. My mother, (cf. p. 250) Merope, was Dorian." The requirement for illumination of the obvious, the imperious need to bring the background into the foreground, might seem Homeric. What Oedipus tells his wife about his family is as incongruous to a standard of realism as it is true to a demand for full disclosure. In the *Iliad*, Homer responds to this demand when he has Helen identify to Priam the Greeks who have been waging war against him for ten years (3.162–242). Homer and his audience want to contemplate the world, no matter how familiar it might seem, set out clearly before them. But in Sophocles the statement of the obvious has still another motive. What is obvious is brought out into the open to reveal the dark background and shadowy past the audience could see behind the stage building of the palace and the apparent sense of the words of the actors. This background is revealed in Oedipus' response to Kreon's description of Laios: "I know. But I never saw Laios." Oedipus had seen Laios, once, at or near a place where three roads meet.

A part of this background are the memories that gradually come to threaten Oedipus and his sense of control and security. At first, he seems secure and nearly a god. The Thebans who have come to his palace gather before *his* altars. He is master of Thebes (52 / 33). Yet even his first words, when they have become a matter for reflection, betray an insecurity. He calls the group of suppliants "children" and so associates himself with his people and their history. Oedipus seems stable, the pilot of the ship of state, but he is a man without roots. He has come to Thebes and Jocasta as a harbor (582 / 420, 1548 / 1208). He looks for security and

3. Before the presentation of his play itself, Sophocles had mounted a platform and announced to his audience the title of his play and its theme—a practice discussed by Pickard-Cambridge, *The Dramatic Festivals of Athens* (Oxford 1968), 67–68.

roots in Thebes, in kingship and marriage to the wife of the murdered king. His search for the murderer is something he does for Laios "as for my own murdered father" and "for every royal generation of Thebes" (361–66 / 264–68). His thought of all that binds him to Laios—the kingship of Thebes, the same bed and the same wife, and even the possibility of common children by this wife—speaks for the same thing. His doubts and uneasiness about his origin seem to spring from an episode in Corinth when a drunken companion told him that he was not his father's son. The word that injured Oedipus was *plastos*— bastard, a fabrication (1023 / 780). What Oedipus wants to discover is not art or artifice but nature: his origins, his seed, his nature, the truth. He is not sure that he knows the truth about himself. Apollo would not give him an answer when he went from Corinth to Delphi to discover the truth about his origins (1025 / 787–88). None of Teiresias' prophecies strike home to Oedipus, but one word touches him (597–601 / 435–37):

> TEIRESIAS Call me fool, if you like, but your parents,
> who gave you life, they respected my judgment.
>
> OEDIPUS Parents?
> What do you mean?
> Who are my mother and father?

Oedipus' doubts about his origins break out in this startled reaction. There is another moment like this in the play. It comes when Jocasta confidently tries to show Oedipus how little trust can be placed in oracles. She will bring to light (*phanō*) decisive indications (*semeia*) of what she says. There was an oracle that Laios would be killed by his son, but robbers killed him—at the three ways. These words stun Oedipus. His memory of what happened near the three ways moves him to wander over old and new paths of fear and memory (953 / 727; cf. 90 / 67). He is so lost in thought that he does not register what Jocasta goes on to tell him about how her son died, with his ankles pierced and strung together, on a mountain where there are no roads or people. One join in the puzzle of his life prevents him from making another that could connect his old wound and his name (Oedipus, Swollenfoot) with Jocasta's son. For Oedipus, the phrase "at the three ways" is the first path he encounters, and this is the path he takes.

When Oedipus takes over the search for the murderer of Laios, he speaks as a god and prophet:

> I will begin the search again, I
> will reveal the truth, expose everything

He will bring the truth to light (*phanō*, **162** / 132). Both Oedipus and Jocasta use the language of prophecy, and unwittingly they become prophets. Jocasta's revelation comes at the turning point of the play, for with her proofs the action turns from the public to the private, from the search for the murderer of Laios to Oedipus and his past which is haunted by oracles. Just as it seems that the oracles concerning Laios have lost their life, and the Chorus is shaken in its confidence in the gods, the Messenger from Corinth arrives. Jocasta's prayer to Apollo to "help us purify ourselves of this disease" (**1170** / 921) is answered. Moments before the Chorus had put a condition on its worship of the gods (**1144–51** / 897–902):

> no
> I will never go to the holy untouchable stone
> navel of the earth at Delphi
> never again
> go to the temples at Olympia at Abai
> if all these things are not joined
> if past present future are not made one
> made clear to mortal eyes

They will no longer dance. But in their dance to honor the god Dionysos, all the pieces of the oracles of the gods fit together. *Symbola* join. And Oedipus, whose intelligence and passion have driven him to seek his origins and to seek in the world around him equalities and commensurability, succeeds in bringing to light his life "from its very beginning." He has discovered his nature (*physis*).

At the end of the play, all of the pieces of the puzzle of Oedipus' life fit together, beautifully, into a tale of sound and fury, told by a dramatic artist of supreme genius. In Sophocles' *Oedipus* art and nature come together. But they are incommensurable. Sophocles' art can reveal the darkness of Oedipus' life and origins. It cannot imitate it or explain it. The artistry of the *Oedipus* bespeaks a world of purpose and design. The underlying tale of Oedipus' life has no purpose or design. The servant who tells what went on within the palace speaks of "wailing, madness, shame and death, every evil men have given a name" (**1657–58** / 1284–85). The tale of Oedipus' life makes no sense. Of all the questions asked in the *Oedipus*, one is not asked: Why did Oedipus suffer what he suffered?

II

Apollo and Zeus comprehend. They know and understand how human affairs stand. As for mortal men, no human can be called a better prophet than another (675–84 / 498–507). In its response to the accusations and prophecies of Teiresias, the Chorus establishes a boundary between gods and men. The gods "grasp everything." The word means that they can put things together. They are *xunetoí*, they comprehend (cf. 1149–50 / 901–2). In the *Oedipus*, only two mortals know how the pieces of Oedipus' life fit together: Teiresias and the old shepherd who saved Oedipus' life. The Chorus says of Teiresias that he is the only man in whom truth is inborn (411 / 299). Oedipus says of him that he knows what can be taught and what must be locked in silence: the things of the heavens and the things that move upon the earth (413–14 / 301). The very syntax of this sentence crosses the human and the divine. On the higher level are things that must be locked in silence (*arrheta*) and the things of the heavens. On the lower level are the things that can be taught and the things that move upon the earth. Teiresias' knowledge comprehends heaven and earth. Despite his reluctance, he is compelled to say the unspeakable. In the *Oedipus* heaven and earth come together. What is revealed about the life of one man is unspeakable.

At the beginning of the play the gods appear as closer to men than they do at the end. The smoke and prayers rising up from plague-stricken Thebes appear to join gods and men. The city and its king look to the gods for the beginning and end of their grief. It is the priest of Zeus who speaks for Thebes. And when Kreon returns from Delphi, his face is bright and flushed, and still seems to reflect the brilliance of the place (100–101 / 82–83). He is wearing a garland of laurel, heavy with berry clusters. In their entrance song the Chorus sings of Delphi where the voice of the god is music (*aduepes*). The Chorus calls Thebes "bright." Its song puts a beautiful and radiant face on all of the gods but Ares and Hades. It is full of light. Hope is the bright seed of the future. Apollo's bowstring is twisted with gold thread. The daughter of Zeus is golden. The Chorus asks her to send it the "warm bright face of peace of help of our salvation" Artemis dances on the mountains "sowing light where your feet brush the ground." The faces of the gods are bright; Dionysos' "blazing like the sea when the sun falls on it." The Chorus asks him to roar with the face of fire on the murderer of

Laios, and it calls upon Zeus to destroy the fire of plague with the fire of his lightning.

At the beginning of the *Oedipus*, the things of heaven are bright, immortal, radiant. They seem near to Thebes. But as the divine help the city prays for draws nearer, Parnassos, Olympos, and the "huge clear fields of heaven" of the second *stasimon* retreat into the distance. The gods are referred to less and less frequently. Yet the brilliance of the entrance song of the Chorus is not a façade disguising the darkness of the world Oedipus penetrates at the end of the play. It casts its light on what happens in the play. It is the language that first describes Ares, the god the gods would drive from heaven (*apotimon*, 283 / 215), that comes to describe Oedipus. And the striking image of the murderer of Laios as a lonely bull, wandering "among caves and grey rocks cut from the herd" (655–57 / 476–78), comes to describe Oedipus who will be driven from Thebes.

In the bloody, mutilated face of Oedipus, the Chorus can see the warm, bright face of the peace it had prayed for (243 / 188). But it is not Apollo with a wall of arrows, or Zeus with his lightning, or Dionysos with his blazing pine torch, that destroys "Ares" and the source of the plague. It is Oedipus who sinks the brooches he tore from the body of his wife and mother into eyes that have seen and failed to see too much. These brooches were of beaten gold (1634 / 168). This is the last reference to gold in the play. In Oedipus' face we seem to see for a moment the face of things human and the last and faint reflection of things divine.

A modern audience asks why Oedipus blinded himself. But this is not the question the Chorus asks (1728–38 / 1327–32):

> CHORUS What you did was horrible,
> but how could you quench the fire of your eyes,
> what demon lifted your hands?

> OEDIPUS Apollo Apollo
> it was Apollo, always Apollo,
> who brought each of my agonies to birth,
> but I,
> nobody else, *I*,
> I raised these two hands of mine, held them
> above my head,
> and plunged them down,
> I stabbed out these eyes.

The question the Chorus asks springs from a common belief, and a common need to find the sources of human action outside the self. For the Chorus, the demonic is the explanation for the violent, inexplicable, more than human shifts in men's actions. Some *outside* force, some god or devil, must have stirred Oedipus to do what he did. But if "Apollo" were Oedipus' full answer to the question of the Chorus, he would lose his last illusion of responsibility for his actions. Oedipus reveals his character in its deepest places when he says "I, I raised these two hands...I stabbed out these eyes." A man's inner character is his *daimon*.[4] In his unalienable conviction that he can control his life, Oedipus stands apart from and above those who surround him. The Chorus attributes Oedipus' success with the Sphinx to some god who gave him what he needed to free Thebes (58 / 38). Oedipus attributes it to himself (536 / 396). When Oedipus is at the point of discovering the answer to the riddle of his own life, his agitation frightens Jocasta so much that she comes out to the altar of Apollo to pray for some solution. Despite her proclaimed skepticism about oracles, she believes that Oedipus' strange behavior, his agitation and his passion to know the truth, must be brought on by some god. So she prays to Apollo who is "close to my life" (1168 / 919). This, too, is the belief of the household servant who witnessed Oedipus' rage and self-mutilation. Oedipus was taken over by "some god, some demon" (1619 / 1258). Some devil showed him the way to his wife. In the last choral song, human happiness (*eudaimonia*) is just that—"hap"—luck with the hidden and incomprehensible powers of the gods. Oedipus had none of this luck. He and his destiny are *dysdaimon*. His very life, which is the perfect expression of the dark abyss beneath human life, is a *daimon* (1518–19 / 1194). Some demon leapt on him (1684 / 1303), as bad luck had leapt on his father (359 / 262), and cleared the gap between appearance and reality.

But in the tale of Oedipus' life, of his *daimon*, there is one action that did not come from the outside and that was not a passion, but something he willed and did knowingly. He put out his eyes. Except for this, the action of the *Oedipus* could be called a "passion." The Chorus does not get an answer it could be content with. Oedipus' life belonged to Apollo,

---

4. This is Heraclitus' reply to the Homeric and common Greek conception of a *daimon* external to a man's character as controlling and explaining the strange and exceptional in his actions and behavior. In Homer, the clearest expression of this notion is the word *daimonie*. When Paris is strangely moved to stay in bed with Helen rather than fighting the Greeks on the plain of Troy, Hector tries to call him to his senses: *daimonie* (*Iliad* 6.521; cf. 326)—which is best translated "What's got into you?" Heraclitus' response to this mode of thought is "a man's character is his 'daimon,' " Fragment B 119 (Diels-Kranz).

but his blindness he claims for himself. When he has seen what was hidden behind the visible façade of his life, he can no longer look upon the new reality that has come to the surface. Without moving an inch, Oedipus fulfills his curse and drives himself from Thebes and the bright, shining statues of the gods (*agalmata*, 1792 / 1379). Or rather he banishes them, since for the Chorus and the audience in the theater of Dionysos, it is Oedipus who remains at the center of things.

The outline of his life was drawn by Apollo. Oedipus' only free action is to blot out this outline. For him, the visible does not wear the face of things unseen. The sight (*opsis*) of his parents is no longer "the sweetest thing on earth" (1780–82 / 1375). Blind, he can put from him, or attempt to, the unspeakable things of the heavens. He has seen enough of what can be told by men—of the things that "move upon the ground." The significance of his action can be stated simply, in terms that are Greek and taken from a language in which knowledge is the memory of things seen: *Oida*, "I have seen," "I know," is a part of Oedipus' name:

> By nature all men have a craving for knowledge. One sign of this is the love they have for their senses, for apart from their usefulness they are loved for themselves, and more than any other, the sense of sight. For men prefer sight to practically anything else, not only as a means to doing something but even when they intend to do nothing at all. The reason for this love is that more than the other senses, sight makes it possible to discern reality and reveals many distinctions.
>
> (Aristotle, *Metaphysics* A 1.980a; translated by Diskin Clay)

III

The world of the actors in Greek tragedy does not have the same integrity as that of the audience seated in the theater of Dionysos. The audience have a godlike vantage on the action of the play. They comprehend in its outline the story of Oedipus' life. But their knowledge of what is fated to happen to Oedipus is not exactly that of the gods, for what the human spectators know is the past, and this knowledge is expressed in their myths. The gods know past, present, and future. Their knowledge is expressed not in myth, but in prophecy. Their oracles are alive (660 / 481–82). In time, their prophecies "come out," like Apollo and like the sun (1274–77 / 1011, 1492 / 1182–83). If the vantage of the gods and Sophocles' audience is similar in that they both contemplate the fate of a man who does not know his fate, men and gods react differently to what they see. The gods of the *Oedipus* are not the gods of the *Iliad* and *Odyssey* who occasionally, in the case of some men at least, are moved to look down on human sufferings and human fate with interest, compassion, and involvement. In Sophocles' *Oedipus*, the "gazing gods" do not "lean forward from the sky" (Pope's brilliant rendition of *Iliad* 22.218). Only men feel pity. It is the pity felt by a slave that made the horrors of Oedipus' life possible (1486 / 1178), and these horrors inspire pity (1576–77 / 1224–26). But the gods remain distant, radiant, and clear. They are constantly called upon by humans. But as their workings become more visible in the play, the gods themselves seem to grow more remote. After Jocasta has caught sight of the truth and rushed into the palace, the Chorus sings of the gods for the last time. The Chorus asks if its king, who thinks that he is the son of Luck, is not part divine—the son of some god who walks the mountains: of Pan and a mountain nymph, or Apollo, or Hermes. The last words of the Chorus' song conjure up a vision of Dionysos *at play* with the nymphs of Helicon (1404 / 1109). A final illusion drifts cloudlike, brightly, insubstantially over the darkness of the truth. And when the Chorus gives articulation to its thought and feeling for the last time in the play, the gods have nearly disappeared. The Chorus can only speak of Oedipus' life as a *daimon* and cry out "o Zeus" (1527 / 1198). Oedipus is *atheos*—godless (1774 / 1360). But the only emotion attributed to the gods of the *Oedipus* is anger and their hatred for Oedipus (1967 / 1519). There is nothing in Sophocles' treatment of his life and family that could explain that hatred.

The dramatic irony of Sophocles' *Oedipus* is not an isolated, surface phenomenon. It comes from the gap that opens up between gods and men, appearance and reality. In the agony of his discoveries, Oedipus finds the perfect expression for this gap: "how beautiful I was when you sheltered me as a child and oh what disease festered beneath that beauty" (1812–13 / 1395–96). There are moments when this disease breaks through the surface of the play; when the illusory world of the drama on stage is disrupted by the demonic forces at work in Sophocles' plot. Early on, Oedipus says that he will do all he can to find the murderer of Laios "as I would fight for my own murdered father" (361 / 264). Sophocles' audience is in the divine position of knowing the truth and knowing that Oedipus is blind to the truth of what he says. But Sophoclean irony is more complex than this textbook example.

The language of the play is under the control of a force larger than its human actors. This is the demonic force of the plot. Kreon speaks of the bandits who killed Laios; but Oedipus speaks of *the* bandit (148 / 124). He asks Kreon, "*Who is* the man? *Who* is Apollo's victim?" (126 / 102), and is uneasy that the same man who killed Laios might want to take his revenge on Oedipus with the same violent hand (169 / 140). *Revenge.* Oedipus' choice of this strange word *is* explained only at the end of the play when he takes his revenge on the murderer with the same violent hand that killed Laios. The killer is called the man whose hand did the deed (*autocheir*, 367 / 267). When he has blinded himself, Oedipus stands before the Chorus and says: "I raised these two hands of mine (*autocheir*) . . . I stabbed out these eyes."

Teiresias knows the unspeakable. His inner vision opens up to him past, present, and future. He *was* not on stage to hear the curse Oedipus lays on the murderer of Laios (339–41 / 246–48). But when he repeats this curse in the prophecy of the grim future he sees for Oedipus (591 / 428), some demonic presence is felt on stage. This same presence makes itself felt as the memory of Oedipus' past begins to come to the surface of the play. In her futile attempt to reassure Oedipus, Jocasta speaks of the place where Laios was killed by robbers as *at* the meeting of three ways. But Oedipus' memory is more precise. Laios was not murdered. He was *cut down—near* a crossroads (cf. 956 / 730 and 1040 / 800–801).

The gods' vision of the future and the audience's knowledge of the outlines of Oedipus' past are concentrated on the stage of the theater of Dionysos. Prophecy and myth have the same point of focus. Jocasta speaks of the voices of prophecy which "gave shape" (*diorisan*) to a future in which Laios would be killed by his son (948 / 723). Oedipus speaks of the same thing when he looks back on his past. He thinks of himself as the son of a benevolent Luck (*tyche*, 1368–73 / 1080–83):

> I am like the months, my brothers the months—they shaped me
> when I was a baby in the cold hills of Kithairon,
> they guided me, carved out my times of greatness,
> and they still move their hands over my life.

The months "shaped" Oedipus (*diorisan*, 1370 / 1083). But when he finally sees the shape of his life, he blots it out.

When Oedipus is led out from his palace to face, without seeing, the Chorus and Thebes, Sophocles seems to be asking a question of his audience. It can be put in the form of a riddle: "There is a creature which moves upon the earth on two feet, on four, and on three. He has one name." At the end of the *Oedipus*, this riddle seems not so much a question as a prophecy. And indeed in their last song the Chorus calls the Sphinx the singer of a "song of the future" (1530 / 1200). The song of the Sphinx is still another version of the story of Oedipus. As the play opens, Oedipus stands upright and securely, at the height of his power. He has helped Thebes stand up straight again. But he began life as a maimed and helpless infant on Kithairon. He could barely crawl. At the end of his life he will need a staff to feel his way to another country. The answer to the riddle of the Sphinx is man, but Oedipus is not *Everyman*. He has suffered and done too much. The power of his life and the darkness he has penetrated as he sees the light bring him to the country of Teiresias' prophecy, to Athens and the awful groves of the Furies. It is this power (*menos*) that is felt and commemorated in Sophocles' last play, which he set in his own *deme* of Kolonos.

When they left the theater of Dionysos, Sophocles' godlike Athenians returned to the life of their city and the plague that was ravaging Athens. Outside the theater of Dionysos, they lost their divinity and had to face the demonic forces that break into human life and disrupt human calculation (cf. the *daimonia* of Thucydides II 64). This is the ultimate Sophoclean irony.

IV

Oedipus is the source of the plague that wastes Thebes. He is the end of the inquest into the murder of Laios. But the revulsion of nature expressed in the plague, and the reaction of the Chorus to "crimes unnameable things" (636 / 464), seem out of proportion to what first appears to be the crime of a stranger or strangers in a foreign country. It is only in the speech of the palace servant at the end of the play that words are found for the unspeakable. Raging within the palace Oedipus proclaims what he is. He wants to reveal to Thebes the man who murdered his father, the man—but the servant cannot bring himself to repeat what Oedipus said of his mother (1666 / 1289). It is unspeakable. The horror and fascination of the unspeakable are at the heart of the final scene of the *Oedipus*. When Oedipus emerges from his palace he is blind; his mask is bloodstained. He has the stain of his father's blood upon him. He has committed incest. His children are his brothers and sisters. He stands in the light of the sun, and the very elements recoil before him. He is no longer king of Thebes. He is no longer a man. He is a thing—"this cursed, naked, holy thing, hide him from the earth and the sacred rain and the light" (1852–53 / 1426–28). Oedipus has become an *agos*, something both sacred and cursed, and by the end of the play his curse has extended in its range from Thebes to the natural world.

The unspeakable holds much of the wisdom of the dramatic festivals which Athens held to honor the god Dionysos. The Athenians who came to witness the dramatic contests witnessed and heard named the most terrible things that could occur in the workaday life of their *polis*. During the rest of the year the words for the things represented on stage were dangerous. Except perhaps in Greece, there is no way of conveying to a modern audience, who live a world apart from the intense, close, public, curious, jealous, and family-centered world of Athens, the horror and fascination of the words for those who beat or killed their fathers or mothers, or the citizen soldier who abandoned his shield in battle. *Patrophonos*—father killer. These words were sticks and stones. They stirred up feelings that came from a deep sense of family and of civic identity. The repressed feelings created by tight family and civic bonds were expressed in the festivals of Dionysos. On the tragic stage the Athenian spectator could see parents who kill and devour their children; children who strike and murder their parents; wives who kill their husbands. And on this stage incest, a thing for which there is no proper name in Greek, was spoken of. But in their everyday lives, and in the Athenian courts of law, men spoke of "the kind of marriages that happen in tragedies."

The dramatic festivals were a time of freedom that made life in Athens livable. In the fourth century, prisoners were released from jail and no debts could be contracted. It was a time of freedom of speech (*parrhesia*) when Athenians could hear, if not repeat, words of terrible fascination. This begins to reveal the significance of Aristotle's observations that the plots of Greek tragedy were taken mainly from the stories of great families and that the kind of learning peculiar to tragedy was the recognition of blood ties.[5]

In the larger context of the social function of Greek tragedy, Oedipus can be seen as an everyman—the sleeping man in every city who cannot live in political society. This everyman resembles the tyrant who makes his brief appearance at the very center of the *Oedipus*. The great antistrophe beginning (1115 / 873)

> arrogance insatiable pride
> breed the tyrant

---

5. *Poetics* 13.1453a19, and 9.1452a31.

is a part of the Chorus' reaction to the implications of Jocasta's words of comfort to Oedipus. A disbelief in the oracles of the gods, however qualified and hedged, threatens to destroy the fabric of the city and raise in its place the grim and ancient figure of the *tyrannos*. One commentary to the reflections of the Chorus on piety, arrogance, and tyranny comes from Socrates' description of the *tyrannos* who sleeps in the soul of waking men. When the higher parts of the soul sleep, it wakes:

> The beastly and wild part, gorged with food or drink, is skittish and, pushing sleep away, seeks to satisfy its dispositions... in such a state it dares to do everything as though it were released from, and rid of, all shame and prudence. And it doesn't shrink from attempting intercourse, as it supposes, with a mother... or attempting any foul murder at all. (*Republic* IX 571 c, trans. Allan Bloom)

The Chorus seems to take Oedipus into the net of its allusion. The words of caution they offered Oedipus are words for a man careful not to *stumble* (807 / 617), and Oedipus has told Thebes that with god's help he and his city will be revealed as lucky or *fallen* (cf. 178 / 146). The words of the Chorus now seem to hit home. They call up a familiar vision of the tyrant's climb and plunge from a place where he can't put his feet anywhere (1120–23 / 876–79). *Feet.* The word hobbles behind Oedipus throughout the play (cf. 642 / 468). *Breeds,* too, seems to reflect Oedipus' attempt to know himself by discovering who his parents were.

But just as the net of allusion seems to tighten about the king of Thebes, Oedipus slips out (1125–27 / 880–82):

> but let men compete let self-perfection grow
> let men sharpen their skills
> soldiers citizens building the good city

This struggle is Oedipus' struggle. The movement of the antistrophe of this *stasimon* repeats the movement of the last antistrophe of the first *stasimon*. Then the Chorus frees Oedipus from the heavy and obscure charges Teiresias brings against him by reflecting back on his struggle for Thebes (685–90 / 508–12). If the *tyrannos* the Chorus calls up comes from "the cursed thoughts that Nature gives way to in repose" (*Macbeth* II i 8), he also comes from another age. He haunts Sophocles' stage for a moment, touching untouchable things, fed on thing after thing, endlessly, giving no reverence to the shrines of the gods. He has a major but mute part to play in Sophocles' *Oedipus*. At the end of the play there is no talk of Oedipus' *fall*. Rather the Chorus speaks of the storm of disaster that has overwhelmed him (1983 / 1527), and the god or devil that leapt on him (1684 / 1303).

The moment the Chorus finishes its song about the tyrant who "does not fear justice fear the gods bow to their shining presences," Jocasta appears before the altar of Apollo with offerings. The role of the *tyrannos* of the second *stasimon* is like that of the family quarrel (*neikos*) of the first. In looking to the past, to a family cursed by a quarrel and, for a moment, to the figure the *tyrannos*, Sophocles is opening and closing the doors of his stage to one explanation of the story of Oedipus. In Sophocles, the fate of Oedipus does not have the familiar and intelligible shape of the fate of a *tyrannos* or a character caught up in a family curse. His Oedipus is not an Agamemnon, caught up in the second generation of an inherited curse and acting like a *tyrannos*, or an Eteokles, whose fate was sealed by the acts of his grandfather and the curses of his father.[6]

At the end of his discoveries, Oedipus is the object of horrible curiosity. Kreon calls him "this cursed, naked, holy thing" (1852 / 1426). He is an *agos*—both cursed and sacred. And all of Kreon's safe and prudent maxims do not support him in the moment of his terrible isolation. All things are not good in their proper time (1962 / 1516). Natures such as his are hardest to bear (894 / 674–75), and the heavy burden he has to bear, once it has been made clear, brings him neither luck nor peace (105–6 / 87–88). One day has shown Oedipus to be as "evil" and as unhappy in his parents as a man can be (803 / 615). The earlier and haunting images of the god the gods would drive from them and the solitary bull who has been cut from its herd (657 / 478) have come to gather around the solitary figure of Oedipus. This object of universal revulsion is still a man. He has banished from him the world in which the unknown joined beautifully with what he thought he knew. It made no sense. He still calls upon the gods, but he can no longer see their bright stone statues. Yet he still wants to be the master of his own life. His one free act was to put out his eyes. And his last act is to reach out to his daughters, to the things that remain dearest to him, and clasp them to him.

---

6. Within the space I have, I develop my reasons for this interpretation of Sophocles' treatment of the Oedipus myth in the notes to 196 / 156, 669 / 487, and 1115 / 873.

V

What Oedipus discovers is the story repeated in handbooks of Greek mythology. It goes something like this:

> Laios and Jocasta are told by an oracle that Laios will be killed by a son. Jocasta has a son. She gives him to a shepherd to expose on Mt. Kithairon, but the shepherd pities the baby and gives him to another shepherd, who gives him to Polybos, king of Corinth. Polybos and his wife Merope bring him up as their son. One day a drunken companion tells Oedipus that he is not his father's son. Oedipus goes to Delphi to learn the truth of these words, but can learn nothing except that he is fated to kill his father, marry his mother, and have children by her. To frustrate this prophecy he decides to keep away from Corinth, and on his way down from Delphi he meets Laios, who is on his way there to consult the oracle, is provoked, kills Laios and all of his companions but one. He then goes to Thebes and frees the town from the Sphinx by solving her riddle, marries the widowed queen, has four children by her. A plague breaks out in Thebes, and in his search for the cause of the plague, Oedipus discovers the story of his life and blinds himself.

In the *Iliad* we hear of the funeral of the "fallen" Oedipus (23.679), but learn nothing about how he fell. In the *Odyssey*, Odysseus catches sight of Epikaste in Hades and tells the Phaeacians a part of her story (11.271–80). In her ignorance she did a "great deed" and married her son who had killed his father. Odysseus says that the gods made this known, but he does not say how. Oedipus continues to be king of Thebes "through the baneful designs of the gods," but Epikaste hangs herself and leaves her son the Furies that avenge a dead mother.

We have no ancient date for the *Oedipus*, but Bernard Knox must be right in seeing in the association of Ares with the plague in Thebes a reflection of the plague that erupted in Athens in the second year of the Peloponnesian war and flared up again in 425. On the internal evidence of the play, taken with Thucydides' description of the plague, 425 is as close as we can come to a date for its first production.[7] Oedipus' name means Swollenfoot but it can also be translated Witfoot—the man who knows or is known by his foot. The conventional title of the play is *Oedipus Tyrannos*, or *Oedipus the King*. But the original title was probably *Oedipus*, and *tyrannos* later served to distinguish it from the *Oedipus at Kolonos*. We have yielded to tradition and given it the title *Oedipus the King*.

---

7. "The Date of the Oedipus Tyrannus," *American Journal of Philology* 77 (1956), 133–47.

VI

The text of this translation is the Greek text printed by Jebb, *Sophocles: I The Oedipus Tyrannus*, Cambridge 1887. Our translation attempts a solution to the problems of the Greek text at 622–27, which Jebb attempted to solve by a necessary transposition of lines and an unnecessary lacuna (see the note to **814–16** / 624–26). We have been helped by his commentary to the play and that of J. C. Kamerbeek, *The Plays of Sophocles: IV The Oedipus Tyrannus*, Leiden 1967. An even more valuable commentary was Bernard Knox's *Oedipus at Thebes*, New Haven 1957. I learned much about the play from J. B. McDiarmid when I studied it with him in the fall of 1961. Joseph Russo has read my Introduction, and I thank him for being Oedipus to some of the oracles I pronounced in an earlier version.

DISKIN CLAY

A NOTE ON THE CHORUSES

I have not punctuated the choruses because they fluctuate somewhere between talk and song and lack many of the usual bridges of logic found in prose syntax. Also, I wanted to distinguish them from the rest of the play, musically, since they are a consciousness separate from the action and thought of the characters, though deeply involved with events as they occur. Perhaps terms like "broken song" or "chant"—speech free to range from the conversational to the lyrical through exclamation, narration, exposition, description—are definitions which help us to grasp the structural attitude of the choruses. Without Greek, I had to imagine something in English bred by the original as I found it described by Diskin Clay, Jebb, and other experts, something which today's reader and audience would find both strange, immediate, and convincing, something fifteen people could say as if they were one. I can think of no corresponding voice in our society, no single expression of authority which, when we hear it, we feel we must believe. I shaped the choruses to catch that power, and to establish the fluidity of contact with and response to each action, each wave of consciousness which the choral voice must reflect.

STEPHEN BERG

OEDIPUS THE KING

Translated by

STEPHEN BERG

and

DISKIN CLAY

CHARACTERS

OEDIPUS	king of Thebes
PRIEST	of Zeus
KREON	Oedipus' brother-in-law
CHORUS	of Theban elders
LEADER	of the chorus
TEIRESIAS	prophet, servant to Apollo
JOCASTA	wife of Oedipus
MESSENGER	from Corinth
SHEPHERD	member of Laios' household
SERVANT	household slave of Oedipus

Delegation of Thebans, servants to lead Teiresias and Oedipus; attendants to Oedipus, Kreon, Jocasta; and Antigone and Ismene, the daughters of Oedipus.

Line numbers in the right-hand margin of the text refer to the English translation only, and the Notes beginning at p. 287 are keyed to these lines. The bracketed line numbers in the running heads refer to the Greek text.

Dawn. Silence. The royal palace of Thebes. The altar of Apollo to the left of the central palace. A delegation of Thebans—old men, boys, young children—enters the orchestra by the steps below the altar, assembles, and waits. They carry suppliant boughs—olive branches tied with strips of wool. Some climb the steps between the orchestra and the altar, place their branches on the altar, and return to the orchestra. A PRIEST stands apart from the suppliants at the foot of one of the two stairs. Silence. Waiting. The central doors open. From inside the palace, limping, OEDIPUS comes through the palace doors and stands at the top of the steps leading down into the orchestra. He is dressed in gold and wears a golden crown.

OEDIPUS   Why, children,
why are you here, why
are you holding those branches tied with wool,
begging me for help? Children,
the whole city smolders with incense.
Wherever I go I hear sobbing, praying. Groans fill the air.
Rumors, news from messengers, they are not enough for me.
Others cannot tell me what you need.
I am king, I had to come. As king,
I had to know. Know for myself, know for me.   10
Everybody everywhere knows who I am: Oedipus. King.
Priest of Zeus, we respect your age, your high office.
Speak.
Why are you kneeling? Are you afraid, old man?
What can I give you?
How can I help? Ask.
Ask me anything. Anything at all.
My heart would be a stone
if I felt no pity for these poor shattered people of mine
kneeling here, at my feet.   20

215

PRIEST Oedipus, lord of Thebes, you see us, the people of Thebes,
       your people,
crowding in prayer around your altar,
these small children here, old men bent with age, priests,
       and I, the priest of Zeus,
and our noblest young men, the pride and strength of
       Thebes.
And there are more of us, lord Oedipus, more—gathered in
       the city, stunned,
kneeling, offering their branches, praying before the two
       great temples of Athena
or staring into the ashes of burnt offerings, staring,
waiting, waiting for the god to speak.
Look,
look at it,   30
lord Oedipus—right there,
in front of your eyes—this city—
it reels under a wild storm of blood, wave after wave
       battering Thebes.
We cannot breathe or stand.
We hunger, our world shivers with hunger. A disease
       hungers,
nothing grows, wheat, fruit, nothing grows bigger than a
       seed.
Our women bear
dead things,
all they can do is grieve,
our cattle wither, stumble, drop to the ground,   40
flies simmer on their bloated tongues,
the plague spreads everywhere, a stain seeping through our
       streets, our fields, our houses,
look—god's fire eating everyone, everything,
stroke after stroke of lightning, the god stabbing it alive—
it can't be put out, it can't be stopped,
its heat thickens the air, it glows like smoking metal,
this god of plague guts our city and fills the black world
       under us where the dead go
with the shrieks of women,

living women, wailing.
You are a man, not a god—I know.   50
We all know this, the young kneeling here before you
    know it, too,
but we know how great you are, Oedipus, greater than any
    man.
When crisis struck, you saved us here in Thebes,
you faced the mysterious, strange disasters hammered
    against us by the gods.
This is our history—
we paid our own flesh to the Sphinx until you set us free.
You knew no more than anyone, but you knew.
There was a god in it, a god in you.

                              The PRIEST *kneels.*

Help us. Oedipus, we beg you, we all turn to you,
    kneeling to your greatness.
Advice from the gods or advice from human beings—you   60
    will know which is needed.
But help us. Power and experience are yours, all yours.
Between thought and action, between
our plans and their results a distance opens.
Only a man like you, Oedipus, tested by experience,
can make them one. That much I know.
Oedipus, more like a god than any man alive,
deliver us, raise us to our feet. Remember who you are.
Remember your love for Thebes. Your skill was our
    salvation once before.
For this Thebes calls you savior.
Don't let us remember you as the king—godlike in power—   70
who gave us back our life, then let us die.
Steady us forever. You broke the riddle for us then.
It was a sign. A god was in it. Be the man you were—
rule now as you ruled before.
Oh Oedipus,
how much better to rule a city of men than be king of
    empty earth.
A city is nothing, a ship is nothing
where no men live together, where no men work together.

OEDIPUS Children, poor helpless children,
I know what brings you here, I know.   80
You suffer, this plague is agony for each of you,
but none of you, not one suffers as I do.
Each of you suffers for himself, only himself.
My whole being wails and breaks
for this city, for myself, for all of you,
old man, all of you.
Everything ends here, with me. I am the man.
You have not wakened me from some kind of sleep.
I have wept, struggled, wandered in this maze of thought,
tried every road, searched hard—   90
finally I found one cure, only one:
I sent my wife's brother, Kreon, to great Apollo's shrine at
     Delphi;
I sent him to learn what I must say or do to save Thebes.
But his long absence troubles me. Why isn't he here?
     Where is he?
When he returns, what kind of man would I be
if I failed to do everything the god reveals?

*Some of the suppliants by the steps to the orchestra stand
to announce* KREON's *arrival to the* PRIEST. KREON *comes
in by the entrance to the audience's left with a garland
                                                    on his head.*

PRIEST You speak of Kreon, and Kreon is here.

OEDIPUS (*turning to the altar of Apollo, then to* KREON)
Lord Apollo, look at him—his head is crowned with laurel, his
     eyes glitter.
Let his words blaze, blaze like his eyes, and save us.

PRIEST He looks calm, radiant, like a god. If he brought bad news,   100
would he be wearing that crown of sparkling leaves?

OEDIPUS At last we will know.
Lord Kreon, what did the god Apollo say?

KREON   His words are hopeful.
              Once everything is clear, exposed to the light,
              we will see our suffering is blessing. All we need is luck.

OEDIPUS   What do you mean? What did Apollo say? What should
                    we do?
                Speak.

KREON   Here? Now? In front of all these people?
              Or inside, privately?   110

                              KREON *moves toward the palace.*

OEDIPUS   Stop. Say it. Say it to the whole city.
                I grieve for them, for their sorrow and loss, far more than I
                    grieve for myself.

KREON   This is what I heard—there was no mistaking the god's
                    meaning—
              Apollo commands us:
              Cleanse the city of Thebes, cleanse the plague from that city,
              destroy the black stain spreading everywhere, spreading,
              poisoning the earth, touching each house, each citizen,
              sickening the hearts of the people of Thebes!
              Cure this disease that wastes all of you, spreading, spreading,
              before it grows so vast nothing can cure it.   120

OEDIPUS   What is this plague?
                How can we purify the city?

KREON   A man must be banished. Banished or killed.
              Blood for blood. The plague is blood,
              blood, breaking over Thebes.

OEDIPUS   Who is the man? Who is Apollo's victim?

KREON   My lord, before you came to Thebes, before you came to
                    power,
              Laios was our king.

OEDIPUS I know. But I never saw Laios.

KREON Laios was murdered. Apollo's command was very clear: 130
Avenge the murderers of Laios. Whoever they are.

OEDIPUS But where are his murderers?
The crime is old. How will we find their tracks?
The killers could be anywhere.

KREON Apollo said the killers are still here, here in Thebes.
Pursue a thing, and you may catch it;
ignored, it slips away.

OEDIPUS And Laios—where was he murdered?
At home? Or was he away from Thebes?

KREON He told us before he left—he was on a mission to Delphi,   140
his last trip away from Thebes. He never returned.

OEDIPUS Wasn't there a witness, someone with Laios who saw what
happened?

KREON They were all killed, except for one man. He escaped.
But he was so terrified he remembered only one thing.

OEDIPUS What was it? One small clue might lead to others.

KREON This is what he said: bandits ambushed Laios, not one man.
They attacked him like hail crushing a stalk of wheat.

OEDIPUS How could a single bandit dare attack a king
unless he had supporters, people with money, here,
here in Thebes?   150

KREON There were suspicions. But after Laios died we had no
leader, no king.
Our life was turmoil, uncertainty.

OEDIPUS But once the throne was empty,
   what threw you off the track, what kept you from searching
   until you uncovered everything, knew every detail?

KREON The intricate, hard song of the Sphinx
   persuaded us the crime was not important, not then.
   It seemed to say we should focus on what lay at our feet, in
    front of us,
   ignore what we could not see.

OEDIPUS Now *I* am here.   160
   I will begin the search again, I
   will reveal the truth, expose everything, let it all be seen.
   Apollo and you were right to make us wonder about the
    dead man.
   Like Apollo, I am your ally.
   Justice and vengeance are what I want,
   for Thebes, for the god.
   Family, friends—I won't rid myself of this stain, this disease,
    for them—
   they're far from here. I'll do it for myself, for me.
   The man who killed Laios might take revenge on me
   just as violently.   170
   So by avenging Laios' death, I protect myself.
   (*turning to the suppliants*) Rise, children,
   pick up your branches,
   let someone announce my decision to the whole city of
    Thebes.
   (*to the Priest*) I will do everything. Everything.
   And, with the god's help, we will be saved.
   Bright Apollo, let your light help us see.
   Our happiness is yours to give, our failure and ruin yours.

PRIEST Rise. We have the help we came for, children.
   The king himself has promised.   180
   May Apollo, who gave these oracles, come as our savior now.
   Apollo, heal us, save us from this plague!

OEDIPUS *enters the palace. Its doors close.* KREON *leaves*
by a door to the right on the wing of the stage. The PRIEST
and suppliants go down into the orchestra and leave by
the entrance to the left as a Chorus of fifteen Theban
elders files into the orchestra by the entrance on the right,
preceded by a flute player.

CHORUS voice   voice   voice
voice who knows everything o god
glorious voice of Zeus
how have you come from Delphi bathed in gold
what are you telling our bright city Thebes
what are you bringing me
health death fear
I know nothing   190
so frightened rooted here
awed by you.
healer what have you sent
is it the sudden doom of grief
or the old curse the darkness
looming in the turning season

o holy immortal voice
hope golden seed of the future
listen be with me speak
these cries of mine rise   200
tell me
I call to you reach out to you first
holy Athena god's daughter who lives forever
and your sister Artemis
who cradles the earth our earth
who sits on her great throne at the hub of the market place
and I call to Apollo who hurls light
from deep in the sky
o gods be with us now
shine on us your three shields   210
blazing against the darkness
come in our suffering as you came once before
to Thebes o bright divinities

and threw your saving light against the god of grief
o gods
be with us now

pain pain my sorrows have no sound
no name no word no pain like this
plague sears my people everywhere
everyone army citizens no one escapes   220
no spear of strong anxious thought protects us
great Thebes grows nothing
seeds rot in the ground
our women when they labor
cry Apollo Apollo but their children die
and lives one after another split the air
birds taking off
wingrush hungrier than fire
souls leaping away they fly
to the shore   230
of the cold god of evening
west

the death stain spreads
so many corpses lie in the streets everywhere
nobody grieves for them
the city dies and young wives
and mothers gray-haired mothers wail
sob on the altar steps
they come from the city everywhere mourning their
        bitter days
prayers blaze to the Healer   240
grief cries a flute mingling
daughter of Zeus o shining daughter show us
the warm bright face of peace of help
of our salvation

                The doors of the palace open. OEDIPUS *enters.*

and turn back the huge raging jaws of the death god Ares
drive him back drive him away

his flames lash at me
this is his war these are his shields
shouts pierce us on all sides
turn him back lift him on a strong wind   250
rush him away
to the two seas at the world's edge
the sea where the waters boil
the sea where no traveler can land
because if night leaves anything alive
day destroys it
o Zeus
god beyond all other gods
handler of the fire
father   260
make the god of our sickness
ashes

Apollo
great bowman of light draw back your bow
fire arrow after arrow
make them a wall circling us
shoot into our enemy's eyes
draw the string twined with gold
come goddess
who dances on the mountains   270
sowing light where your feet brush the ground
blind our enemy come
god of golden hair
piled under your golden cap Bacchus
your face blazing like the sea when the sun falls on it
like sunlight on wine
god whose name is our name Bacchus
god of joy god of terror
be with us now your bright face
like a pine torch roaring   280
thrust into the face of the slaughtering war god
blind him
drive him down from Olympos

drive him away from Thebes
forever

OEDIPUS Every word of your prayers has touched me.
   Listen. Follow me. Join me in fighting this sickness, this
     plague,
   and all your sufferings may end, like a dark sky,
   clear suddenly, blue, after a week of storms,
   soothing the torn face of the sea,   290
   soothing our fears.
   Your fate looms in my words—
   I heard nothing about Laios' death,
   I know nothing about the murder,
   I was alone, how could I have tracked the killer, without a
     clue,
   I came to Thebes after the crime was done,
   I was made a Theban after Laios' death. Listen carefully—
   these words come from an innocent man.

          Addressing the CHORUS.

   One of you knows who killed Laios.
   Where is that man?   300
   Speak.
   I command it. Fear is no excuse.
   He must clear himself of the dangerous charge.
   Who did this thing?
   Was it a stranger?
   Speak.
   I will not harm him. The worst he will suffer is exile.
   I will pay him well. He will have a king's thanks.
   But if he will not speak because he fears me,
   if he fears what I will do to him or to those he loves, 310
   if he will not obey me,
   I say to him:
   My power is absolute in Thebes, my rule reaches everywhere,
   my words will drive the guilty man, the man who *knows*,
   out of this city, away from Thebes, forever.

Nothing.
My word for him is nothing.
Let him *be* nothing.
Give him nothing.
Let him touch nothing of yours, he is nothing to you.   320
Lock your doors when he approaches.
Say nothing to him, do not speak.
No prayers with him, no offerings with him.
No purifying water.
Nothing.
Drive him from your homes. Let him have no home,
        nothing.
No words, no food, shelter, warmth of hand, shared worship.
Let him have nothing. Drive him out, let him die.
He is our disease.
                    I know.   330
                        Apollo has made it clear.
Nothing can stop me, nothing can change my words.
I fight for Apollo, I fight for the dead man.
You see me, you hear me, moving against the killer.
My words are his doom.
Whether he did it alone, and escaped unseen,
whether others helped him kill, it makes no difference—
let my hatred burn out his life, hatred, always.
Make him an ember of suffering.
Make all his happiness   340
ashes.
If he eats at my side, sits at my sacred hearth, and I know
        these things,
let every curse I spit out against him find *me*,
come home to *me*.
Carry out my orders. You must,
for me, for Apollo, and for Thebes, Thebes,
this poor wasted city,
deserted by its gods.
I know—the gods have given us this disease.   350
That makes no difference. You should have acted,
you should have done something long ago to purge our guilt.

The victim was noble, a king—
you should have done everything to track his murderer down.
And so,
because I rule now where he ruled;
because I share his bed, his wife;
because the same woman who mothered my children might
   have mothered his;
because fate swooped out of nowhere and cut him down;
because of all these things   360
I will fight for him as I would fight for my own murdered
   father.
Nothing will stop me.
No man, no place, nothing will escape my gaze. I will not
   stop
until I know it all, all, until everything is clear.
For every king, every king's son and his sons,
for every royal generation of Thebes, *my* Thebes,
I will expose the killer, I will reveal him
to the light.
Oh gods, gods,
destroy all those who will not listen, will not obey.   370
Freeze the ground until they starve.
Make their wives barren as stone.
Let this disease that shakes Thebes to its roots—
or any worse disease, if there is any worse than this—waste
   them,
crush everything they have, everything they are.
But you men of Thebes—
you, who know my words are right, who obey me—
may justice and the gods defend you, bless you,
graciously, forever.

LEADER Your curse forces me to speak, Master.   380
     I cannot escape it.
     I did not murder the king, I cannot show you the man who
       did.
     Apollo told us to search for the killer.
     Apollo must name him.

OEDIPUS No man can force the gods to speak.

LEADER Then I will say the next best thing.

OEDIPUS If there's a third best thing, say that, too.

LEADER Teiresias sees what the god Apollo sees.
Truth, truth.
If you heard the god speaking, heard his voice,   390
you might see more, more, and more.

OEDIPUS Teiresias? I have seen to that already.
Kreon spoke of Teiresias, and I sent for him. Twice.
I find it strange he still hasn't come.

LEADER And there's an old story, almost forgotten,
a dark, faded rumor.

OEDIPUS What rumor? I must sift each story,
see it, understand it.

LEADER Laios was killed by bandits.

OEDIPUS I have heard that story: but who can show me the man who 400
saw the murderer?
Has anyone seen him?

LEADER If he knows the meaning of fear,
if he heard those curses you spoke against him,
those words still scorching the air,
you won't find him now, not in Thebes.

OEDIPUS The man *murdered*. Why would words frighten him?

> TEIRESIAS *has appeared from the stage entrance to the*
> *right of the audience. He walks with a staff and is helped*
> *by a slave boy and attendants. He stops at some distance*
> *   from center stage.*

228

LEADER   Here is the man who can catch the criminal.
         They're bringing him now—
         the godlike prophet who speaks with the voice of god.
         He, only he, knows truth.   410
         The truth is rooted in his soul.

OEDIPUS Teiresias, you understand all things,
         what can be taught, what is locked in silence,
         the distant things of heaven, and things that crawl the earth.
         You cannot see, yet you know the nature of this plague
               infesting our city.
         Only you, my lord, can save us, only you can defend us.
         Apollo told our messenger—did you hear?—
         that we could be saved only by tracking down Laios' killers,
         only by killing them, or sending them into exile.
         Help us, Teiresias.   420
         Study the cries of birds, study their wild paths,
         ponder the signs of fire, use all your skills of prophecy.
         Rescue us, preserve us.
         Rescue yourself, rescue Thebes, rescue me.
         Cleanse every trace of the growing stain left by the dead
               man's blood.
         We are in your hands, Teiresias.
         No work is more nobly human than helping others,
         helping with all the strength and skill we possess.

TEIRESIAS Wisdom is a curse
         when wisdom does nothing for the man who has it.   430
         Once I knew this well, but I forgot.
         I never should have come.

OEDIPUS Never should have come? Why this reluctance, prophet?

TEIRESIAS Let me go home.
         That way is best, for you, for me.
         Let me live my life, and you live yours.

OEDIPUS Strange words, Teiresias, cruel to the city that gave you life.

Your holy knowledge could save Thebes. How can you keep
    silent?

TEIRESIAS What have you said that helps Thebes? Your words are
      wasted.
    I would rather be silent than waste my words.   440

OEDIPUS Look at us,   (OEDIPUS *stands, the* CHORUS *kneels*)
    kneeling to you, Teiresias, imploring you.
    In the name of the gods, if you know—
    help us, tell us what you know.

TEIRESIAS You kneel because you do not understand.
    But I will never let you see my grief. Never.
    My grief is yours.

OEDIPUS What? You know and won't speak?
    You'd betray us all, you'd destroy the city of Thebes?

TEIRESIAS I will do nothing to hurt myself, or you. Why insist?   450
    I will not speak.

OEDIPUS Stubborn old fool, you'd make a rock angry!
    Tell me what you know! Say it!
    Where are your feelings? Won't you ever speak?

TEIRESIAS You call me cold, stubborn, unfeeling, you insult me. But
    you,
    Oedipus, what do you know about yourself,
    about your real feelings?
    You don't see how much alike we are.

OEDIPUS How can *I* restrain my anger when I see how little you care
      for Thebes.

TEIRESIAS The truth will come, by itself,   460
    the truth will come
    no matter how I shroud it in silence.

OEDIPUS   All the more reason why you should speak.

TEJRESIAS   Not another word.
                     Rage away. You will never make me speak.

OEDIPUS   I'll rage, prophet, I'll give you all my anger.
                     I'll say it all—
                     Listen: I think you were involved in the murder of Laios,
                     you helped plan it, I think you
                     did everything in your power to kill Laios,   470
                     everything but strike him with your own hands,
                     and if you weren't blind, if you still had eyes to see with,
                     I'd say you, and you alone, did it all.

TEIRESIAS   Do you think so? Then obey your own words, obey
                     the curse everyone heard break from your own lips:
                     Never speak again to these men of Thebes,
                     never speak again to me.
                                               You, it's
                     you.   480
                     What plagues the city is *you*.
                     The plague is *you*.

OEDIPUS   Do you know what you're saying?
                     Do you think I'll let you get away with these vile accusations?

TEIRESIAS   I am safe.
                     Truth lives in me, and the truth is strong.

OEDIPUS   Who taught you this truth of yours? Not your prophet's
                     craft.

TEIRESIAS   *You* taught me. You forced me to speak.

OEDIPUS   Speak what? Explain. Teach me.

TEIRESIAS   Didn't you understand?
                     Are you trying to make me say the word?   490

OEDIPUS What word? Say it. Spit it out.

TEIRESIAS Murderer.
I say *you*,
you are the killer you're searching for.

OEDIPUS You won't say *that* again to me and get away with it.

TEIRESIAS Do you want more? Shall I make you really angry?

OEDIPUS Say anything you like. Your words are wasted.

TEIRESIAS I say you live in shame, and you do not know it,
do not know that you
and those you love most   500
wallow in shame,
you do not know
in what shame you live.

OEDIPUS You'll pay for these insults, I swear it.

TEIRESIAS Not if the truth is strong.

OEDIPUS The truth *is* strong, but not your truth.
You have no truth. You're blind.
Blind in your eyes. Blind in your ears. Blind in your mind.

TEIRESIAS And I pity you for mocking my blindness.
Soon everyone in Thebes will mock you, Oedipus.   510
They'll mock you
as you have mocked me.

OEDIPUS One endless night swaddles you in its unbroken black sky.
You can't hurt me, you can't hurt anyone who sees the light
of day.

TEIRESIAS True. Nothing I do will harm you. You, you
and your fate belong to Apollo.
Apollo will see to you.

OEDIPUS Are these your own lies, prophet—or Kreon's?

TEIRESIAS Kreon? Your plague is *you*, not Kreon.

OEDIPUS Money, power, one great skill surpassing another,
if a man has these things, other men's envy grows and grows,   520
their greed and hunger are insatiable.
Most men would lust for a life like mine—but I did not
      demand my life,
Thebes gave me my life, and from the beginning, my good
      friend Kreon,
loyal, trusted Kreon,
was reaching for my power, wanted to ambush me, get rid of
      me by hiring this cheap wizard,
this crass, conniving priest, who sees nothing but profit,
whose prophecy is simple profit. *You*,
what did *you* ever do that proves you a real seer? What did
      you ever see, prophet?
And when the Sphinx who sang mysteriously   530
imprisoned us
why didn't you speak and set us free?
No ordinary man could have solved her riddle,
it took prophecy, prophecy and skill you clearly never had.
Even the paths of birds, even the gods' voices were useless.
But I showed up, I, Oedipus,
stupid, untutored Oedipus,
I silenced her, I destroyed her, I used my wits, not omens,
to sift the meaning of her song.
And this is the man you want to kill so you can get close   540
      to King Kreon,
weigh his affairs for him, advise him, influence him.
No, I think you and your master, Kreon, who contrived this
      plot,
will be whipped out of Thebes.
Look at you.
If you weren't so old, and weak, oh
I'd make you pay
for this conspiracy of yours.

LEADER   Oedipus, both of you spoke in anger.
         Anger is not what we need.
         We need all our wits, all our energy to interpret Apollo's   550
             words.
         Then we will know what to do.

TEIRESIAS Oedipus, you are king, but you must hear my reply.
           My right to speak is just as valid as yours.
           I am not your slave. Kreon is not my patron.
           My master is Apollo. I can say what I please.
           You insulted me. You mocked me. You called me blind.
           Now hear *me* speak, Oedipus.
           You have eyes to see with,
           but you do not see yourself, you do not see
           the horror shadowing every step of your life,   560
           the blind shame in which you live,
           you do not see where you live and who lives with you,
           lives always at your side.
           Tell me, Oedipus, who are your parents?
           Do you know?
           You do not even know
           the shame and grief you have brought your family,
           those still alive, those buried beneath the earth.
           But the curse of your mother, the curse of your father
           will whip you, whip you again and again, wherever you   570
               turn,
           it will whip you out of Thebes forever,
           your clear eyes flooded with darkness.
           That day will come.
           And then what scoured, homeless plain, what leafless tree,
           what place on Kithairon,
           where no other humans are or ever will be,
           where the wind is the only thing that moves,
           what raw track of thorns and stones, what rock, gulley,
           or blind hill won't echo your screams, your howls of anguish
           when you find out that the marriage song,   580
           sung when you came to Thebes, heard in your house,
           guided you to *this* shore, this wilderness
           you thought was home, *your* home?

And you do not see
all the other awful things
that will show you who you really are, show you
to your children, face to face.
Go ahead! Call me quack, abuse Kreon, insult Apollo, the god
who speaks through me, whose words move on my lips.
No man will ever know worse suffering than you,   590
your life, your flesh, your happiness an ember of pain. Ashes.

OEDIPUS (*to the* CHORUS) Must I stand here and listen to these
            attacks?

TEIRESIAS (*beginning to move away*) I am here, Oedipus, because you
            sent for me.

OEDIPUS You old fool,
            I'd have thought twice before asking you to come
            if I had known you'd spew out such idiocy.

TEIRESIAS Call me fool, if you like, but your parents,
            who gave you life, they respected my judgment.

OEDIPUS Parents?
                    What do you mean?   600
                            Who are my mother and father?

TEIRESIAS This day is your mother and father—this day will give you
            your birth,
            it will destroy you, too.

OEDIPUS How you love mysterious, twisted words.

TEIRESIAS Aren't you the great solver of riddles?
            Aren't you Oedipus?

OEDIPUS Taunt me for the gift of my brilliant mind.
            That gift is what makes me great.

TEIRESIAS   That gift is your destiny. It made you everything you are,
            and it has ruined you.   610

OEDIPUS   But if this gift of mine saved Thebes, who cares what
            happens to me?

TEIRESIAS   I'm leaving. Boy, take me home.

OEDIPUS   Good. Take him home. Here
            I keep stumbling over you, here you're in my way.
            Scuttle home, and leave us in peace!

TEIRESIAS   I'm going. I said what I came to say,
            and that scowl, darkening your face, doesn't frighten me.
                How can you hurt me?
            I tell you again:
            the man you've been trying to expose—
            with all your threats, with your inquest into Laios' murder—   620
            that man is here, in Thebes.
            Now people think he comes from Corinth, but later
            they will see he was born in Thebes.
            When they know, he'll have no pleasure in that news.
            Now he has eyes to see with, but they will be slashed out;
            rich and powerful now, he will be a beggar,
            poking his way with a stick, feeling his way to a strange
                country.
            And his children—the children he lives with—
            will see him at last, see what he is, see who he really is:
            their brother and their father; his wife's son, his mother's   630
                husband;
            the lover who slept with his father's wife; the man who
                murdered his father—
            the man whose hands still drip with his father's blood.
            These truths will be revealed.

            Go inside and ponder *that* riddle, and if you find I've lied,
            then call me a prophet who cannot see.

OEDIPUS *turns and enters the palace.* TEIRESIAS *is led out
through the stage entrance on the right.*

CHORUS who did crimes unnameable things
       things words cringe at
       which man did the rock of prophecy at Delphi say
       did these things
       his hands dripping with blood   640
       he should run now flee
       his strong feet swallowing the air
       stronger than the horses of storm winds
       their hooves slicing the air
       now in his armor
       Apollo lunges at him
       his infinite branching fire reaches out
       and the steady dread death-hungry Fates follow and never
          stop
       their quick scissors seeking the cloth of his life

       just now   650
       from high snowy Parnassus
       the god's voice exploded its blazing message
       follow his track find the man
       no one knows
       a bull loose under wild bushes and trees
       among caves and gray rocks
       cut from the herd he runs and runs but runs nowhere
       zigzagging desperate to get away
       birds of prophecy birds of death circling his head
       forever   660
       voices forged at the white stone core of the earth
       they go where he goes always

       terror's in me flooding me
       how can I judge
       what the god Apollo says
       trapped hoping confused
       I do not see what is here now

when I look to the past I see nothing
I know nothing about a feud
wounding the families of Laios or Oedipus   670
no clue to the truth then or now
nothing to blacken his golden fame in Thebes
and help Laios' family
solve the mystery of his death

Zeus and Apollo know
they understand
only they see
the dark threads crossing beneath our life
but no man can say a prophet sees more than I
one man surpasses another   680
wisdom against wisdom skill against skill
but I will not blame Oedipus
whatever anyone says
until words are as real as things

one thing is clear
years back the Sphinx tested him
his answer was true
he was wise and sweet to the city
so he can never be evil
not to me   690

> KREON *enters through the stage entrance at right, and*
> *addresses the* CHORUS.

KREON Men of Thebes, I hear Oedipus, our king and master,
has brought terrible charges against me.
I have come to face those charges. I resent them bitterly.
If he imagines I have hurt him, spoken or acted against him
while our city dies, believe me—I have nothing left to live for.
His accusations pierce me, wound me mortally—
nothing they touch is trivial, private—
if you, my family and friends,
think I'm a traitor, if all Thebes believes it, says it.

LEADER   Perhaps he spoke in anger, without thinking,   700
         perhaps his anger made him accuse you.

KREON   Did he really say I persuaded Teiresias to lie?

LEADER   I heard him say these things,
         but I don't know what they mean.

KREON   Did he look you in the eyes when he accused me?
         Was he in his right mind?

LEADER   I do not know or see what great men do.

         (*turning to* OEDIPUS, *who has emerged from the palace*)

         But here he is—Oedipus.

OEDIPUS What? *You* here? Murderer!
         You dare come here, to my palace, when it's clear   710
         you've been plotting to murder me and seize the throne of
              Thebes?
         You're the bandit, *you're* the killer.
                                        Answer me—
         Did you think I was cowardly or stupid?
         Is that why you betrayed me?
         Did you really think I wouldn't see what you were plotting,
         how you crept up on me like a cloud inching across the sun?
         Did you think I wouldn't defend myself against you?
         You thought I was a fool, but the fool was *you*, Kreon.
         Thrones are won with money and men, you fool!   720

KREON   You have said enough, Oedipus. Now let me reply.
         Weigh my words against your charges, then judge for
              yourself.

OEDIPUS Eloquent, Kreon. But you won't convince me now.
         Now that I know your hatred, your malice.

KREON Let me explain.

OEDIPUS Explain?
What could explain your treachery?

KREON If you think this stubborn anger of yours, this perversity,
is something to be proud of, you're mad.

OEDIPUS And if you think you can injure your sister's husband,   730
and not pay for it, *you're* mad.

KREON I would be mad to hurt you. How have I hurt you?

OEDIPUS Was it you who advised me to send for that great holy
prophet?

KREON Yes, and I'd do it again.

OEDIPUS How long has it been since Laios disappeared?

KREON Disappeared?

OEDIPUS Died. Was murdered. . . .

KREON Many, many years.

OEDIPUS And this prophet of yours—was he practicing his trade at the
time?

KREON With as much skill, wisdom and honor as ever.   740

OEDIPUS Did he ever mention my name?

KREON Not in my presence.

OEDIPUS Was there an inquest? A formal inquiry?

KREON Of course. Nothing was ever discovered.

OEDIPUS Then why didn't our wonderful prophet, our Theban wizard,
        denounce me as the murderer then?

KREON I don't know. And when I don't know, I don't speak.

OEDIPUS But you know this. You know it with perfect certainty.

KREON What do you mean?

OEDIPUS This: if you and Teiresias were not conspiring against me,   750
        Teiresias would never have charged *me* with Laios' murder.

KREON If he said that, you should know.
       But now, Oedipus, it's my right, my turn to question you.

OEDIPUS Ask anything. You'll never prove I killed Laios.

KREON Did you marry my sister, Jocasta?

OEDIPUS I married Jocasta.

KREON And you gave her an equal share of the power in Thebes?

OEDIPUS Whatever she wants is hers.

KREON And I share that power equally with you and her?

OEDIPUS Equally.   760
        And that's precisely why it's clear you're false, treacherous.

KREON No, Oedipus.
      Consider it rationally, as I have. Reflect:
      What man, what sane man, would prefer a king's power
      with all its dangers and anxieties,
      when he could enjoy that same power, without its cares,
      and sleep in peace each night? Power?
      I have no instinct for power, no hunger for it either.

It isn't royal power I want, but its advantages.
And any sensible man would want the same.   770
Look at the life I lead. Whatever I want, I get from you,
with your goodwill and blessing. I have nothing to fear.
If I were king, my life would be constant duty and constraint.
Why would I want your power or the throne of Thebes
more than what I enjoy now—the privilege of power
without its dangers? I would be a fool to want more
than what I have—the substance, not the show, of power.
As matters stand, no man envies me, I am courted
and admired by all. Men wear no smiling masks for Kreon.
And those who want something from you come to me   780
because the way to royal favor lies through me.
Tell me, Oedipus, why should I give these blessings up
to seize your throne and all the dangers it confers?
A man like me, who knows his mortal limits and accepts
        them,
cannot be vicious or treacherous by nature.
The love of power is not my nature, nor is treason
or the thoughts of treason that go with love of power.
I would never dare conspire against your life.

Do you want to test the truth of what I say?
Go to Delphi, put the question to the oracle,   790
ask if I have told you exactly what Apollo said.
Then if you find that Teiresias and I have plotted against
        you,
seize me and put me to death. Convict me
not by one vote alone, but two—yours and mine, Oedipus.
But don't convict me on the strength of your suspicions,
don't confuse friends with traitors, traitors with friends.
There's no justice in that.
To throw away a good and loyal friend
is to destroy what you love most—
your own life, and what makes life worth living.   800
Someday you will know the truth:
time, only time reveals the good man;
one day's light reveals the evil man.

LEADER Good words
        for someone careful, afraid he'll fall.
        But a mind like lightning
        stumbles.

OEDIPUS When a clever man plots against me and moves swiftly
         I must move just as swiftly, I must plan.
         But if I wait, if I do nothing, he will win, win everything,   810
         and I will lose.

KREON What do you want? My exile?

OEDIPUS No. Your death.

KREON You won't change your mind? You won't believe me?

OEDIPUS I'll believe you when you teach me the meaning of envy.

KREON Envy? You talk about envy. You don't even know what
       sense is.
       Can't you listen to me?

OEDIPUS I am listening. To my own good sense.

KREON Listen to *me*. I have sense on my side, too.

OEDIPUS You? You were born devious.   820

KREON And if you're wrong?

OEDIPUS I still must govern.

KREON Not if you govern badly.

OEDIPUS Oh Thebes, Thebes...

KREON Thebes is mine too.

LEADER   (*turning to* JOCASTA, *who has entered from the palace,*
          accompanied by a woman attendant)
          Stop. I see
          Jocasta coming from the palace
          just in time, my lords, to help you
          settle this deep, bitter feud raging between you.
          Listen to what she says.   830

JOCASTA   Oedipus! Kreon! Why this insane quarreling?
          You should be ashamed, both of you. Forget yourselves.
          This is no time for petty personal bickering.
          Thebes is sick, dying.
                              —Come inside, Oedipus
          —And you, Kreon, leave us.
          Must you create all this misery over nothing, nothing?

KREON   Jocasta,
          Oedipus has given me two impossible choices:
          Either I must be banished from Thebes, my city, my home,   840
          or be arrested and put to death.

OEDIPUS   That's right.
          I caught him plotting against me, Jocasta.
          Viciously, cunningly plotting against the king of Thebes.

KREON   Take every pleasure I have in life, curse me, let me die,
          if I've done what you accuse me of, let the gods
          destroy everything I have, let them do anything to me.
          I stand here, exposed to their infinite power.

JOCASTA   Oedipus, in the name of the gods, believe him.
          His prayer has made him holy, naked to the mysterious   850
          whims of the gods, has taken him beyond what is human.
          Respect his words, respect me, respect these men standing at
                  your side.

CHORUS   (*beginning a dirge-like appeal to* OEDIPUS)
          listen to her

        think yield
        we implore you

OEDIPUS What do you want?

CHORUS be generous to Kreon give him respect
        he was never foolish before
        now his prayer to the gods has made him great
        great and frightening   860

OEDIPUS Do you know what you're asking?

CHORUS I know

OEDIPUS Then say it.

CHORUS don't ever cut him off
        without rights or honor
        blood binds you both
        his prayer has made him sacred
        don't accuse him
        because some blind suspicion hounds you

OEDIPUS Understand me: 870
        when you ask for these things
        you ask for my death or exile.

CHORUS no
        by the sun
        the god who bathes us in his light
        who sees all
        I will die godless no family no friends
        if what I ask means that
        it is Thebes
        Thebes dying wasting away life by life   880
        this is the misery
        that breaks my heart

and now this quarrel raging between you and Kreon
is more more than I can bear

OEDIPUS Then let him go, even if it means I must die
or be forced out of Thebes forever, stripped of all my rights,
        all my honors.
Your grief, *your* words touch me. Not his.
I pity you. But him,
my hatred will reach him wherever he goes.

KREON It's clear you hate to yield, clear   890
you yield only under pressure, only
when you've worn out the fierceness of your anger.
Then all you can do is sit, and brood.
Natures like yours are a torment to themselves.

OEDIPUS Leave. Go!

KREON I'm going. Now I know
you do not know me.
But these men know I am the man I seem to be, a just man,
not devious, not a traitor.

                    KREON *leaves*.

CHORUS woman why are you waiting   900
lead him inside comfort him

JOCASTA Not before I know what has happened here.

CHORUS blind ignorant words suspicion without proof
the injustice of it
gnaws at us

JOCASTA From both men?

CHORUS yes

JOCASTA What caused it?

CHORUS enough enough
         no more words   910
         Thebes is so tormented now
         let it rest where it ended

OEDIPUS Look where cooling my rage,
         where all your decent, practical thoughts have led you.

CHORUS Oedipus I have said this many times
         I would be mad helpless to give advice
         if I turned against you now
         once
         you took our city in her storm of pain
         straightened her course found fair weather   920
         o lead her to safety now
         if you can

JOCASTA If you love the gods, tell me, too, Oedipus—I implore you—
         why are you still so angry, why can't you let it go?

OEDIPUS I will tell you, Jocasta.
         You mean more, far more to me than these men here.
         Jocasta, it is Kreon—Kreon and his plots against me.

JOCASTA What started your quarrel?

OEDIPUS He said I murdered Laios.

JOCASTA Does he know something? Or is it pure hearsay?   930

OEDIPUS He sent me a vicious, trouble-making prophet
         to avoid implicating himself. He did not say it to my face.

JOCASTA Oedipus, forget all this. Listen to me:
         no mortal can practice the art of prophecy, no man can see
              the future.
         One experience of mine will show you why.
         Long ago an oracle came to Laios.
         It came not from Apollo himself but from his priests.

It said Laios was doomed to be murdered by a son, his son
    and mine.
But Laios, from what we heard, was murdered by bandits
    from a foreign country,
cut down at a crossroads. My poor baby   940
was only three days old when Laios had his feet pierced
    together behind the ankles
and gave orders to abandon our child on a mountain, leave
    him alone to die
in a wilderness of rocks and bare gray trees
where there were no roads, no people.
So you see—Apollo didn't make that child his father's killer,
Laios wasn't murdered by his son. That dreadful act which
    so terrified Laios—
it never happened.

All those oracular voices meant was nothing, nothing.
Ignore them.
Apollo creates. Apollo reveals. He needs no help from men.   950

OEDIPUS (*who has been very still*)
    While you were speaking, Jocasta; it flashed through my
        mind
    like wind suddenly ruffling a stretch of calm sea.
    It stuns me. I can almost see it—some memory, some image.
    My heart races and swells—

JOCASTA Why are you so strangely excited, Oedipus?

OEDIPUS You said Laios was cut down *near* a crossroads?

JOCASTA That was the story. It hasn't changed.

OEDIPUS Where did it happen? Tell me. Where?

JOCASTA In Phokis. Where the roads from Delphi and Daulia meet.

OEDIPUS When?   960

JOCASTA Just before you came to Thebes and assumed power.
Just before you were proclaimed King.

OEDIPUS O Zeus, Zeus,
what are you doing with my life?

JOCASTA Why are you so disturbed, Oedipus?

OEDIPUS Don't ask me. Not yet.
Tell me about Laios.
How old was he? What did he look like?

JOCASTA Streaks of gray were beginning to show in his black hair.
He was tall, strong—built something like you.   970

OEDIPUS No! O gods, o
it seems each hard, arrogant curse
I spit out
was meant for me, and I
didn't
know it!

JOCASTA Oedipus, what do you mean? Your face is so strange.
You frighten me.

OEDIPUS It *is* frightening—can the blind prophet see, can he really see?
I would know if you told me . . .   980

JOCASTA I'm afraid to ask, Oedipus.
Told you what?

OEDIPUS Was Laios traveling with a small escort
or with many armed men, like a king?

JOCASTA There were five, including a herald.
Laios was riding in his chariot.

OEDIPUS Light, o light, light
now everything, everything is clear. All of it.
Who told you this? Who was it?

JOCASTA A household slave. The only survivor.   990

OEDIPUS Is he here, in Thebes?

JOCASTA No. When he returned and saw that you were king
         and learned Laios was dead, he came to me and clutched
               my hand,
         begged me to send him to the mountains
         where shepherds graze their flocks, far from the city,
         so he could never see Thebes again.
         I sent him, of course. He deserved that much, for a slave,
               and more.

OEDIPUS Can he be called back? Now?

JOCASTA Easily. But why?

OEDIPUS I am afraid I may have said too much—   1000
         I *must* see him.
         Now.

JOCASTA Then he will come.
         But surely I have a right to know what disturbs you, Oedipus.

OEDIPUS Now that I've come this far, Jocasta,
         hope torturing me, each step of mine heavy with fear,
         I won't keep anything from you.
         Wandering through the mazes of a fate like this,
         how could I confide in anyone but you?

         My father was Polybos, of Corinth.   1010
         My mother, Merope, was Dorian.
         Everyone in Corinth saw me as its first citizen,
         but one day something happened,
         something strange, puzzling. Puzzling, but nothing more.
         Still, it worried me.
         One night, I was at a banquet,

and a man—he was very drunk—said I wasn't my father's son,
called me "bastard." That stung me, I was shocked.
I could barely control my anger, I lay awake all night.
The next day I went to my father and mother,   1020
I questioned them about the man and what he said.
They were furious with him, outraged by his insult,
and I was reassured. But I kept hearing the word "bastard"
     "bastard"—
I couldn't get it out of my head.
Without my parents' knowledge, I went to Delphi: I
     wanted the truth,
but Apollo refused to answer me.
And yet he did reveal other things, he did show me
a future dark with torment, evil, horror,
he made me *see*—
see myself, doomed to sleep with my own mother, doomed 1030
to bring children into this world where the sun pours down,
children no one could bear to see, doomed
to murder the man who gave me life, whose blood is *my*
     blood. My father.
And after I heard all this, I fled Corinth,
measuring my progress by the stars, searching for a place
where I would never see those words, those dreadful
     predictions
come true. And on my way
I came to the place where you say King Laios was murdered.

Jocasta, the story I'm about to tell you is the truth:
I was on the road, near the crossroads you mentioned,   1040
when I met a herald, with an old man, just as you
     described him.
The man was riding in a chariot
and his driver tried to push me off the road
and when he shoved me I hit him. I hit him.
The old man stood quiet in the chariot until I passed under
     him,
then he leaned out and caught me on the head with an ugly
     goad—

its two teeth wounded me—and with this hand of mine,
this hand clenched around my staff,
I struck him back even harder—so hard, so quick he couldn't
     dodge it,
and he toppled out of the chariot and hit the ground, face   1050
     up.
I killed them. Every one of them. I still see them.

                                        (*to the* CHORUS)

If this stranger and Laios
are somehow linked by blood,
tell me what man's torment equals mine?

Citizens, hear my curse again—
Give this man nothing. Let him touch nothing of yours.
Lock your doors when he approaches.
Say nothing to him when he approaches.
                                And these, these curses,
with my own mouth I   1060
spoke these monstrous curses against myself.

                    OEDIPUS *turns back to* JOCASTA.

These hands, these bloodstained hands made love to you in
     your dead husband's bed,
these hands murdered him.

If I must be exiled, never to see my family,
never to walk the soil of my country
so I will not sleep with my mother
and kill Polybos, my father, who raised me—his son!—
wasn't I born evil—answer me!—isn't every part of me
unclean? Oh
some unknown god, some savage venomous demon must   1070
     have done this,
raging, swollen with hatred. Hatred
for me.

Holiness, pure, radiant powers, o gods
don't let me see that day,
don't let it come, take me away
from men, men with their eyes, hide me
before I see
the filthy black stain reaching down over me, into me.

The CHORUS *has moved away from the stage.*

LEADER Your words make us shudder, Oedipus,
    but hope, hope   1080
    until you hear more from the man who witnessed the
        murder.

OEDIPUS That is the only hope I have. Waiting.
    Waiting for that man to come from the pastures.

JOCASTA And when he finally comes, what do you hope to learn?

OEDIPUS If his story matches yours, I am saved.

JOCASTA What makes you say that?

OEDIPUS Bandits—you said he told you bandits killed Laios.
    So if he still talks about bandits,
    more than one, I couldn't have killed Laios.
    One man is not the same as many men.   1090
    But if he speaks of one man, traveling alone,
    then all the evidence points to me.

JOCASTA Believe me, Oedipus, those were his words.
    And he can't take them back: the whole city heard him,
        not only me.
    And if he changes only the smallest detail of his story,
    that still won't prove Laios was murdered as the oracle
        foretold.
    Apollo was clear—it was Laios' fate to be killed by my son,

but my poor child died before his father died.
The future has no shape. The shapes of prophecy lie.
I see nothing in them, they are all illusions.   1100

OEDIPUS   Even so, I want that shepherd summoned here.
Now. Do it now.

JOCASTA   I'll send for him immediately. But come inside.
My only wish is to please you.

                              JOCASTA *dispatches a servant.*

CHORUS   fate
          be here let what I say be pure
          let all my acts be pure
          laws forged in the huge clear fields of heaven
          rove the sky
          shaping my words limiting what I do   1110
          Ólympos made those laws not men who live and die
          nothing lulls those laws to sleep
          they cannot die
          and the infinite god in them never ages

          arrogance insatiable pride
          breed the tyrant
          feed him on thing after thing blindly
          at the wrong time uselessly
          and he grows reaches so high   1120
          nothing can stop his fall
          his feet thrashing the air standing on nothing
          and nowhere to stand he plunges down
          o god shatter the tyrant
          but let men compete let self-perfection grow
          let men sharpen their skills
          soldiers citizens building the good city
          Apollo
          protect me always
          always the god I will honor   1130

if a man walks through his life arrogant
strutting proud
says anything does anything
does not fear justice
fear the gods bow to their shining presences
let fate make him stumble in his tracks
for all his lecheries and headlong greed
if he takes whatever he wants right or wrong
if he touches forbidden things
what man who acts like this would boast   1140
he can escape the anger of the gods
why should I join these sacred public dances
if such acts are honored

no
I will never go to the holy untouchable stone
navel of the earth at Delphi
never again
go to the temples at Olympia at Abai
if all these things are not joined
if past present future are not made one   1150
made clear to mortal eyes
o Zeus if that is your name
power above all immortal king
see these things look
those great prophecies are fading
men say they're nothing
nobody prays to the god of light no one believes
nothing of the gods stays

> JOCASTA *enters from the palace, carrying a branch tied with*
> *strands of wool, and a jar of incense. She is accompanied*
> *by a servant woman. She addresses the* CHORUS.

JOCASTA Lords of Thebes, I come to the temples of the god
with offerings—this incense and this branch.   1160
So many thoughts torture Oedipus. He never rests.
He acts without reason. He is like a man

255

who has lost everything he knows—the past
is useless to him; strange, new things baffle him.
And if someone talks disaster, it stuns him: he listens, he is
    afraid.
I have tried to reassure him, but nothing helps.
So I have come to you—
Apollo, close to my life, close to this house,
listen to my prayers: (*she kneels*)
               help us purify ourselves of this disease, 1170
help us survive the long night of our suffering,
protect us. We are afraid when we see Oedipus confused
and frightened—Oedipus, the only man who can pilot
    Thebes
to safety.

A MESSENGER *from Corinth has arrived by the entrance
to the orchestra on the audience's left. He sees* JOCASTA
praying, then turns to address the CHORUS.

MESSENGER Friends,
can you tell me where King Oedipus lives
or better still, where I can find him?

LEADER Here, in this house.
This lady is his wife and mother
of his children. 1180

MESSENGER May you and your family prosper.
May you be happy always under this great roof.

JOCASTA Happiness and prosperity to you, too, for your kind words.
But why are you here? Do you bring news?

MESSENGER Good news for your house, good news for King Oedipus.

JOCASTA What is your news? Who sent you?

MESSENGER I come from Corinth, and what I have to say I know will
    bring you joy.
And pain perhaps. . . . I do not know.

JOCASTA Both joy and pain? What news could do that?

MESSENGER The people of Corinth want Oedipus as their king.   1190
That's what they're saying.

JOCASTA But isn't old Polybos still king of Corinth?

MESSENGER His kingdom is his grave.

JOCASTA Polybos is *dead*?

MESSENGER If I'm lying, my lady, let me die for it.

JOCASTA You. (*to a servant*) Go in and tell Oedipus.
O oracles of the gods, where are you now!
This man, the man Oedipus was afraid he would murder,
the man he feared, the man he fled from has died a natural
death.
Oedipus didn't kill him, it was luck, luck.   1200

She turns to greet OEDIPUS *as he comes out of the palace.*

OEDIPUS Jocasta, why did you send for me? (*taking her gently by the
arm*)

JOCASTA Oedipus,
listen to this man, see what those ominous, holy predictions
of Apollo mean now.

OEDIPUS Who is this man? What does he say?

JOCASTA He comes from Corinth.
Your father is dead. Polybos is dead!

OEDIPUS What?
Let me hear those words from your own mouth, stranger.
Tell me yourself, in your own words.   1210

MESSENGER If that's what you want to hear first, then I'll say it:
Polybos is dead.

OEDIPUS How did he die? Assassination? Illness? How?

MESSENGER An old man's life hangs by a fragile thread. Anything can
                  snap it.

OEDIPUS That poor old man. It was illness, then?

MESSENGER Illness and old age.

OEDIPUS Why, Jocasta,
              why should men look to the great hearth at Delphi
              or listen to birds shrieking and wheeling overhead—
              cries meaning I was doomed to kill my father?   1220
              He is dead, gone, covered by the earth.
              And here I am—my hands never even touched a spear—
              I did not kill him,
              unless he died from wanting me to come home.
              No. Polybos has bundled up all these oracles
              and taken them with him to the world below.
              They are only words now, lost in the air.

JOCASTA Isn't that what I predicted?

OEDIPUS You were right. My fears confused me.

JOCASTA You have nothing to fear. Not now. Not ever.   1230

OEDIPUS But the oracle said I am doomed to sleep with my mother.
              How can I live with that and not be afraid?

JOCASTA Why should men be afraid of anything? Fortune rules our
                  lives.
              Luck is everything. Things happen. The future is darkness.
              No human mind can know it.
              It's best to live in the moment, live for today, Oedipus.
              Why should the thought of marrying your mother make
                  you so afraid?
              Many men have slept with their mothers in their dreams.

Why worry? See your dreams for what they are—
　　nothing, nothing at all.
Be happy, Oedipus.   1240

OEDIPUS All that you say is right, Jocasta. I know it.
　　I should be happy,
　　but my mother is still living. As long as she's alive,
　　I live in fear. This fear is necessary.
　　I have no choice.

JOCASTA But Oedipus, your father's death is a sign, a great sign—
　　the sky has cleared, the sun's gaze holds us in its warm,
　　　　hopeful light.

OEDIPUS A great sign, I agree. But so long as my mother is alive,
　　my fear lives, too.

MESSENGER Who is this woman you fear so much?   1250

OEDIPUS Merope, King Polybos' wife.

MESSENGER Why does Merope frighten you so much?

OEDIPUS A harrowing oracle hurled down upon us by some great god.

MESSENGER Can you tell me? Or did the god seal your lips?

OEDIPUS I can.
　　Long ago, Apollo told me I was doomed to sleep with my
　　　　mother
　　and spill my father's blood, murder him
　　with these two hands of mine.
　　That's why I never returned to Corinth. Luckily, it would
　　　　seem.
　　Still, nothing on earth is sweeter to a man's eyes   1260
　　than the sight of his father and mother.

MESSENGER And you left Corinth because of this prophecy?

OEDIPUS Yes. And because of my father. To avoid killing my father.

MESSENGER But didn't my news prove you have nothing to fear?
I brought good news.

OEDIPUS And I will reward you for your kindness.

MESSENGER That's why I came, my lord. I knew you'd remember me
when you returned to Corinth.

OEDIPUS I will never return, never live with my parents again.

MESSENGER Son, it's clear you don't know what you're doing.   1270

OEDIPUS What do you mean? In the name of the gods, speak.

MESSENGER If you're afraid to go home because of your parents.

OEDIPUS I am afraid, afraid
Apollo's prediction will come true, all of it,
as god's sunlight grows brighter on a man's face at dawn
when he's in bed, still sleeping,
and reaches into his eyes and wakes him.

MESSENGER Afraid of murdering your father, of having his blood
on your hands?

OEDIPUS Yes. His blood. The stain of his blood. That terror never   1280
leaves me.

MESSENGER But Oedipus, then you have no reason to be afraid.

OEDIPUS I'm their son, they're my parents, aren't they?

MESSENGER Polybos is nothing to you.

OEDIPUS Polybos is not my father?

MESSENGER No more than I am.

OEDIPUS   But you are nothing to me. Nothing.

MESSENGER   And Polybos is nothing to you either.

OEDIPUS   Then why did he call me his son?

MESSENGER   Because I gave you to him. With these hands
I gave you to him.   1290

OEDIPUS   How could he have loved me like a father if I am not
his son?

MESSENGER   He had no children. That opened his heart.

OEDIPUS   And what about you?
Did you buy me from someone? Or did you find me?

MESSENGER   I found you squawling, left alone to die in the thickets of
Kithairon.

OEDIPUS   Kithairon? What were you doing on Kithairon?

MESSENGER   Herding sheep in the high summer pastures.

OEDIPUS   You were a shepherd, a drifter looking for work?

MESSENGER   A drifter, yes, but it was I who saved you.

OEDIPUS   Saved me? Was I hurt when you picked me up?   1300

MESSENGER   Ask your feet.

OEDIPUS   Why,
why did you bring up that childhood pain?

MESSENGER   I cut you free. Your feet were pierced, tied together at the ankles
with leather thongs strung between the tendons and the bone.

OEDIPUS   That mark of my shame—I've worn it from the cradle.

MESSENGER That mark is the meaning of your name:
Oedipus, Swollenfoot, Oedipus.

OEDIPUS Oh gods
who did this to me?   1310
My mother?
My father?

MESSENGER I don't know. The man I took you from—he would know.

OEDIPUS So you didn't find me? Somebody else gave me to you?

MESSENGER I got you from another shepherd.

OEDIPUS What shepherd? Who was he? Do you know?

MESSENGER As I recall, he worked for Laios.

OEDIPUS The same Laios who was king of Thebes?

MESSENGER The same Laios. The man was one of Laios' shepherds.

OEDIPUS Is he still alive? I want to see this man.   1320

MESSENGER (*pointing to the* CHORUS) These people would know that
better than I do.

OEDIPUS Do any of you know this shepherd he's talking about?
Have you ever noticed him in the fields or in the city?
Answer, if you have.
It is time everything came out, time everything was made clear.
Everything.

LEADER I think he's the shepherd you sent for.
But Jocasta, she would know.

OEDIPUS (*to* JOCASTA)
Jocasta, do you know this man?
Is he the man this shepherd here says worked for Laios?   1330

JOCASTA What man? Forget about him. Forget what was said.
It's not worth talking about.

OEDIPUS How can I forget
with clues like these in my hands?
With the secret of my birth staring me in the face?

JOCASTA No, Oedipus!
No more questions.
For god's sake, for the sake of your own life!
Isn't my anguish enough—more than enough?

OEDIPUS You have nothing to fear, Jocasta.   1340
Even if my mother
and her mother before her were both slaves,
that doesn't make you the daughter of slaves.

JOCASTA Oedipus, you *must* stop.
                                        I beg you—stop!

OEDIPUS Nothing can stop me now. I must know everything.
Everything!

JOCASTA I implore you, Oedipus. For your own good.

OEDIPUS Damn my own good!

JOCASTA Oh, Oedipus, Oedipus,   1350
I pray to god you never see who you are!

OEDIPUS (*to one of the attendants, who hurries off through the
        exit stage left*)
You there, go find that shepherd, bring him here.
Let that woman bask in the glory of her noble birth.

JOCASTA God help you, Oedipus—
you were born to suffer, born
to misery and grief.

These are the last last words I will ever speak, ever
Oedipus.

(JOCASTA *rushes offstage into the palace. Long silence.*)

LEADER Why did Jocasta rush away,
Oedipus, fleeing in such pain?   1360
I fear disaster, or worse,
will break from this silence of hers.

OEDIPUS Let it break! Let everything break!
I must discover who I am, know the secret of my birth,
no matter how humble, how vile.
Perhaps Jocasta is ashamed of my low birth, ashamed to be
      my wife.
Like all women she's proud.
But Luck, goddess who gives men all that is good, made *me*,
and I won't be cheated of what is mine, nothing can dishonor
      me, ever.
I am like the months, my brothers the months—they   1370
      shaped me
when I was a baby in the cold hills of Kithairon,
they guided me, carved out my times of greatness,
and they still move their hands over my life.
I am the man I am. I will not stop
until I discover who my parents are.

CHORUS if I know if I see
if the dark force of prophecy is mine
Kithairon
when the full moon
rides over us tomorrow   1380
listen listen to us sing to you
dance worship praise you
mountain where Oedipus was found
know Oedipus will praise you
praise his nurse country and mother
who blessed our king

I call on you Apollo
let these visions please you
god Apollo
healer   1390

Oedipus son
who was your mother
which of the deathless mountain nymphs who lay
with the great god Pan
on the high peaks he runs across
or with Apollo
who loves the high green pastures above
which one bore you
did the god of the bare windy peaks Hermes
or the wild, dervish Dionysos   1400
living in the cool air of the hills
take you
a foundling
from one of the nymphs he plays with
joyously lift you hold you in his arms

OEDIPUS Old men, I think the man coming toward us now
must be the shepherd we are looking for.
I have never seen him, but the years, chalking his face and
hair, tell me
he's the man. And my men are with him. But you probably
know him.

LEADER I do know him. If Laios ever had a man he trusted,   1410
this was the man.

OEDIPUS (*to the* MESSENGER)
You—is this the man you told me about?

MESSENGER That's him. You're looking at the man.

OEDIPUS (*to the* SHEPHERD *who has been waiting, hanging back*)
You there, come closer.

Answer me, old man.
Did you work for Laios?

SHEPHERD I was born his slave, and grew up in his household.

OEDIPUS What was your work?

SHEPHERD Herding sheep, all my life.

OEDIPUS Where?   1420

SHEPHERD Kithairon, mostly. And the country around Kithairon.

OEDIPUS Do you remember ever seeing this man?

MESSENGER Which man?

OEDIPUS (*pointing to the* MESSENGER)
This man standing here. Have you ever seen him before?

SHEPHERD Not that I remember.

MESSENGER No wonder, master. But I'll make him remember.
He knows who I am. We used to graze our flocks together
in the pastures around Kithairon.
Every year, for six whole months, three years running.
From March until September, when the Dipper rose,   1430
    signaling the harvest.
I had one flock, he had two.
And when the frost came, I drove my sheep back to their
    winter pens
and he drove his back to Laios' fold.
Remember, old man? Isn't that how it was?

SHEPHERD Yes. But it was all so long ago.

MESSENGER And do you remember giving me a baby boy at the time—
to raise as my own son?

SHEPHERD   What if I do? Why all these questions?

MESSENGER   That boy became King Oedipus, friend.

SHEPHERD   Damn you, can't you keep quiet.   1440

OEDIPUS   Don't scold him, old man.
It's you who deserve to be punished, not him.

SHEPHERD   What did I say, good master?

OEDIPUS   You haven't answered his question about the boy.

SHEPHERD   He's making trouble, master. He doesn't know a thing.

OEDIPUS *takes the* SHEPHERD *by the cloak.*

OEDIPUS   Tell me or you'll be sorry.

SHEPHERD   For god's sake, don't hurt me, I'm an old man.

OEDIPUS   *(to one of his men)* You there, hold him. We'll make him
talk.

The attendant pins the SHEPHERD's *arms behind his back.*

SHEPHERD   Oedipus, Oedipus,
god knows I pity you.
What more do you want to know?   1450

OEDIPUS   Did you give the child to this man?
Speak.   Yes or no?

SHEPHERD   Yes.
And I wish to god I'd died that day.

OEDIPUS   You *will* be dead unless you tell me the whole truth.

SHEPHERD   And worse than dead, if I do.

OEDIPUS   It seems our man won't answer.

SHEPHERD   No. I told you already. I gave him the boy.

OEDIPUS   Where did you get him? From Laios' household? Or where?

SHEPHERD   He wasn't *my* child. He was given to me.   1460

OEDIPUS   (*turning to the* CHORUS *and the audience*)
          By whom? Someone here in Thebes?

SHEPHERD   Master, please, in god's name, no more questions.

OEDIPUS   You're a dead man if I have to ask you once more.

SHEPHERD   He was one
          of the children
          from Laios'
          household.

OEDIPUS   A slave child? Or Laios' own?

SHEPHERD   I can't say it . . . it's
          awful, the words   1470
          are awful . . . awful.

OEDIPUS   And I,
          I am afraid to hear them . . .
          but I must.

SHEPHERD   He was Laios' own child.
          Your wife, inside the palace, she can explain it all.

OEDIPUS   *She* gave you the child?

SHEPHERD   My lord . . . yes.

OEDIPUS Why?

SHEPHERD She wanted me to abandon the child on a mountain.   1480

OEDIPUS His own mother?

SHEPHERD Yes. There were prophecies, horrible oracles. She was afraid.

OEDIPUS What oracles?

SHEPHERD Oracles predicting he would murder his own father.

OEDIPUS But why did you give the boy to this old man?

SHEPHERD Because I pitied him, master, because I
         thought the man would take the child away, take him to
              another country.
         Instead he saved him. Saved him for—oh gods,
         a fate so horrible, so awful, words can't describe it.
         If you were the baby that man took from me, Oedipus,   1490
         what misery, what grief is yours!

OEDIPUS (*looking up at the sun*)
         LIGHT   LIGHT   LIGHT
         never again flood these eyes with your white radiance, oh
              gods, my eyes. All, all
         the oracles have proven true. I, Oedipus, I
         am the child
         of parents who should never have been mine—doomed,
              doomed!
         Now everything is clear—I
         lived with a woman, she was my mother, I slept in my
              mother's bed, and I
         murdered, murdered my father,
         the man whose blood flows in these veins of mine,   1500
         whose blood stains these two hands red.

              OEDIPUS *raises his hands to the sun, then turns and walks*
                                        into the palace.

269

CHORUS man after man after man
        o mortal generations
        here once
        almost not here
        what are we
        dust ghosts images a rustling of air
        nothing nothing
        we breathe on the abyss
        we are the abyss   1510
        our happiness no more than traces of a dream
        the high noon sun sinking into the sea
        the red spume of its wake raining behind it
        we are you
        we are you Oedipus
        dragging your maimed foot
        in agony
        and now that I see your life finally revealed
        your life fused with the god
        blazing out of the black nothingness of all we know   1520
        I say
        no happiness lasts nothing human lasts

        wherever you aimed you hit
        no archer had your skill
        you grew rich powerful great
        everything came falling to your feet
        o Zeus
        after he killed the Sphinx
        whose claws curled under
        whose weird song of the future baffled and destroyed   1530
        he stood like a tower high above our country
        warding off death
        and from then on Oedipus we called you
        king our king
        draped you in gold
        our highest honors were yours
        and you ruled this shining city
        Thebes   Thebes

now
your story is pain pity no story is worse   1540
than yours Oedipus
ruined savage blind
as you struggle with your life
as your life changes
and breaks and shows you who you are
Oedipus   Oedipus
son father you harbored in the selfsame place
the same place sheltered you both
bridegroom
how could the furrow your father plowed   1550
not have cried out all this time
while you lay there unknowing
and saw the truth too late

time like the sun sees all things
and it sees you
you cannot hide from that light
your own life opening itself to you
to all
married unmarried father son
for so long   1560
justice comes like the dawn
always
and it shows the world your marriage now

I wish
o child of Laios
I wish I had never seen you
I grieve for you
wail after wail fills me and pours out
because of you my breath came flowing back
but now   1570
the darkness of your life
floods my eyes

The palace doors open. A SERVANT *enters and approaches*
                              the CHORUS *and audience.*

SERVANT Noble citizens, honored above all others in Thebes,
if you still care for the house of Laios,
if you still can feel the spirit of those who ruled before, now
the horrors you will hear, the horrors you will see, will shake
    your hearts and shatter you with grief beyond enduring.
Not even the waters of those great rivers Ister and Phasis
could wash away the blood
that now darkens every stone of this shining house,   1580
this house that will reveal, soon, soon
the misery and evil two mortals,
both masters of this house, have brought upon themselves.

The griefs we cause ourselves cut deepest of all.

LEADER What we already know
has hurt us enough,
has made us cry out in pain.
What more can you say?

SERVANT This:
Jocasta is dead. The queen is dead.   1590

LEADER Ah, poor
unhappy Jocasta,
how did she die?

SERVANT She killed herself. She did it.
But you did not see what happened there,
you were not there, in the palace. You did not see it.
I did.
I will tell you how Queen Jocasta died,
the whole story, all of it. All I can remember.
After her last words to Oedipus   1600
she rushed past us through the entrance hall, screaming,
raking her hair with both hands, and flew into the bedroom,
    their bedroom,
and slammed the doors shut as she lunged at her bridal bed,
crying "Laios" "Laios"—dead all these years—

remembering Laios—how his own son years ago
grew up and then killed him, leaving her to
sleep with her own son, to have his children, *their* children,
children—not sons, not daughters, something else,
      monsters. . . .
Then she collapsed, sobbing, cursing the bed where she held
      both men in her arms,
got husband from husband, children from her child.   1610
We heard it all, but suddenly, I couldn't tell what was
      happening.
Oedipus came crashing in, he was howling,
stalking up and down—we couldn't take our eyes off him—
and we stopped listening to her pitiful cries.
We stood there, watching him move like a bull, lurching,
      charging,
shouting at each of us to give him a sword, demanding we
      tell him
where his wife was, that woman whose womb carried him,
him and his children, that wife who gave him birth.
Some god, some demon, led him to her, and he knew—
none of us showed him—   1620
suddenly a mad, inhuman cry burst from his mouth
as if the wind rushed through his tortured body,
and he heaved against those bedroom doors so the hinges
      whined
and bent from their sockets and the bolts snapped,
and he stood in the room.
There she was—
we could see her—his wife
dangling by her neck from a noose of braided, silken cords
tied to a rafter, still swaying.
And when he saw her he bellowed and stretched up and 1630
      loosened the rope,
cradling her in one arm,
and slowly laid her body on the ground.

That's when it happened—he
ripped off the gold

brooches she was wearing—one on each shoulder of her
        gown—
and raised them over his head—you could see them flashing—
and tilted his face up and
brought them right down into his eyes
and the long pins sank deep, all the way back into the sockets,
and he shouted at his eyes: 1640
"Now you won't see me, you won't see
my agonies or my crimes,
but in endless darkness, always, there you'll see
those I never should have seen.
And those I should have known were my parents, father and
        mother—
these eyes will never see their faces in the light.
These eyes will never see the light again, never."
Cursing his two blind eyes over and over, he
lifted the brooches again and drove their pins through his
        eyeballs up
to the hilts until they were pulp, until the blood streamed out 1650
soaking his beard and cheeks,
a black storm splashing its hail across his face.

Two mortals acted. Now grief tears their lives apart
as if that pain sprang from a single, sorrowing root
to curse each one, man and wife. For all those years
their happiness was truly happiness, but now, now
wailing, madness, shame and death,
every evil men have given a name,
everything criminal and vile
that mankind suffers they suffer. Not one evil is missing.   1660

LEADER But now
        does this torn, anguished man
        have any rest from his pain?

SERVANT No, no—
        then he shouted at us to open the doors and show everyone
            in Thebes

his father's killer, his mother's—I cannot say it.
Once we have seen him as he is
he will leave Thebes, lift the curse from his city—
banish himself, cursed by his own curses.
But his strength is gone, his whole life is pain,   1670
more pain than any man can bear.
He needs help, someone to guide him.
He is alone, and blind. Look,
look—the palace doors are opening—now
a thing
so horrible will stand before you
you will shudder with disgust and try to turn away
while your hearts will swell with pity for what you see.

The central doors open. OEDIPUS *enters, led by his household*
servants. His mask is covered with blood. The CHORUS *begins*
                    a dirge to which OEDIPUS *responds antiphonally.*

CHORUS horror horror o what suffering
        men see   1680
        but none is worse than this
        Oedipus o
        how could you have slashed out your eyes
        what god leaped on you
        from beyond the last border of space
        what madness entered you
        clawing even more misery into you
        I cannot look at you

        but there are questions
        so much I would know   1690
        so much that I would see
        no   no
        the shape of your life makes me shudder

OEDIPUS I   I
         this voice of agony
         I am   what place am I
         where? Not here, nowhere I know!

What force, what tide breaks over my life?
Pain, demon stabbing into me
leaving nothing, nothing, no man I know, not human,   1700
fate howling out of nowhere what am I
fire   a voice   where   where
is it being taken?

LEADER   Beyond everything to a place
so terrible nothing is seen there, nothing is heard.

OEDIPUS   (*reaching out, groping*)
Thing   thing   darkness
spilling into me, my
black cloud smothering me forever,
nothing can stop you, nothing can escape,
I cannot push you away.   1710

I am
nothing but my own cries breaking
again and again
the agony of those gold pins
the memory of what I did
stab me
again
again.

LEADER   What can you feel but pain.
It all comes back, pain in remorse,   1720
remorse in pain, to tear you apart with grief.

OEDIPUS   Dear, loyal friend
you, only you, are still here with me, still care
for this blind, tortured man.
Oh,
I know you are there, I know you, friend,
even in this darkness, friend, touched by your voice.

LEADER   What you did was horrible,

but how could you quench the fire of your eyes,
what demon lifted your hands?   1730

OEDIPUS Apollo   Apollo
it was Apollo, always Apollo,
who brought each of my agonies to birth,
but I,
nobody else, I,
I raised these two hands of mine, held them above my head,
and plunged them down,
I stabbed out these eyes.
Why should I have eyes? Why,
when nothing I saw was worth seeing?   1740
Nothing.

LEADER Nothing. Nothing.

OEDIPUS Oh friends. Nothing.
No one to see, no one to love,
no one to speak to, no one to hear!
            Friends, friends, lead me away now.
Lead me away from Thebes—Oedipus,
destroyer and destroyed,
the man whose life is hell
for others and for himself, the man   1750
more hated by the gods than any other man, ever.

LEADER Oh I pity you,
I weep for your fate
and for your mind,
for what it is to be you, Oedipus.
I wish you had never seen the man you are.

OEDIPUS I hate
the man who found me, cut the thongs from my feet,
snatched me from death, cared for me—
I wish he were dead!   1760

I should have died up there on those wild, desolate slopes of
    Kithairon.
Then my pain and the pain
those I love suffer now
never would have been.

LEADER   These are my wishes, too.

OEDIPUS   Then I never would have murdered my father,
never heard men call me my mother's husband.

Now
I am
Oedipus!   1770
Oedipus, who lay in that loathsome bed, made love there
    in that bed,
his father's and mother's bed, the bed
where he was born.

No gods anywhere now, not for me, now,
unholy, broken man.
What man ever suffered grief like this?

LEADER   How can I say that what you did was right?
Better to be dead than live blind.

OEDIPUS   I did what I had to do. No more advice.
How could *my* eyes,   1780
when I went down into that black, sightless place beneath
    the earth,
the place where the dead go down, how,
how could I have looked at anything,
with what human eyes could I have gazed
on my father, on my mother—
oh gods, my mother!
What I did against those two
not even strangling could punish.

And my children, how would the sight of them, born as
    they were born,
be sweet? Not to these eyes of mine, never to these eyes.   1790
Nothing, nothing is left me now—no city with its high walls,
no shining statues of the gods. I stripped all these things
    from myself—
I, Oedipus, fallen lower than any man now, born nobler
    than the best,
born the king of Thebes! Cursed with my own curses, I
commanded Thebes to drive out the killer.
I banished the royal son of Laios, the man the gods revealed
is stained with the awful stain. The secret stain
that I myself revealed is *my* stain. And now, revealed at last,
how could I ever look men in the eyes?
Never. Never.   1800

If I could, I would have walled my ears so they heard nothing,
I would have made this body of mine a wall.
I would have heard nothing, tasted nothing, smelled
    nothing, seen
nothing.
      No thought. No feeling. Nothing. Nothing.
So pain would never reach me anymore.

O Kithairon,
why did you shelter me and take me in?
Why did you let me live? Better to have died on that bare
    slope of yours
where no man would ever have seen me or known the   1810
    secret of my birth!

Polybos, Corinth, that house I thought was my father's home,
how beautiful I was when you sheltered me as a child
and oh what disease festered beneath that beauty.
Now everyone knows the secret of my birth, knows
how vile I am.

O roads, secret valley, cluster of oaks,

O narrow place where two roads join a third,
roads that drank my blood as it streamed from my hands,
flowing from my dead father's body,
do you remember me now?   1820
Do you remember what I did with my own two hands, there
        in your presence,
and what I did after that, when I came here to Thebes?
O marriage, marriage, you gave me my life, and then
from the same seed, my seed, spewed out
fathers, brothers, sisters, children, brides, wives—
nothing, no words can express the shame.
No more words. Men should not name what men should
        never do.

                                        (*to the* CHORUS)

Gods, oh gods, gods,
hide me, hide me
now   1830
far away from Thebes,
kill me,
cast me into the sea,
drive me where you will never see me—never again.

        (*reaching out to the* CHORUS, *which backs away*)

Touch this poor man, touch me,
don't be afraid to touch me. Believe me, nobody,
nobody but me can bear
this fire of anguish.
It is mine. Mine.

LEADER Kreon has come.   1840
        Now he, not you, is the sole guardian of Thebes,
        and only he can grant you what you ask.

OEDIPUS (*turning toward the palace*)
        What can I say to him, how can anything I say

make him listen now?
I wronged him. I accused him, and now everything I said
proves I am vile.

KREON (*enters from the entrance to the right. He is accompanied
                        by men who gather around* OEDIPUS.)

I have not come to mock you, Oedipus; I have not come to
        blame you for the past.

                                (*To attendants*)

You men, standing there, if you have no respect for human
        dignity,
at least revere the master of life,
the all-seeing sun whose light nourishes   1850
every living thing on earth.
Come, cover this cursed, naked, holy thing, hide him
from the earth and the sacred rain and the light,
you powers who cringe from his touch.
Take him. Do it now. Be reverent.
Only his family should see and hear his grief.
Their grief.

OEDIPUS I beg you, Kreon, if you love the gods,
grant me what I ask.
I have been vile to you, worse than vile.   1860
I have hurt you, terribly, and yet
you have treated me with kindness, with nobility.
You have calmed my fear, you did not turn away from me.
Do what I ask. Do it for yourself, not for me.

KREON What do you want from me, Oedipus?

OEDIPUS Drive me out of Thebes, do it now, now—
drive me someplace where no man can speak to me,
where no man can see me anymore.

KREON   Believe me, Oedipus, I would have done it long ago.
        But I refuse to act until I know precisely what the god   1870
           desires.

OEDIPUS   Apollo has revealed what he desires. Everything is clear.
        I killed my father, I am polluted and unclean.
        I must die.

KREON   That is what the god commanded, Oedipus.
        But there are no precedents for what has happened.
        We need to *know* before we act.

OEDIPUS   Do you care so much for me, enough to ask Apollo?
        For *me*, Oedipus?

KREON   Now even you will trust the god, I think.

OEDIPUS   I will. And I turn to you, I implore you, Kreon—   1880
        the woman lying dead inside, your sister,
        give her whatever burial you think best.
                             As for me,
        never let this city of my fathers see me here in Thebes.
        Let me go and live on the mountain, on Kithairon—the
           mountain
        my parents intended for my grave.
        Let me die the way they wanted me to die: slowly, alone—
        die *their* way.
        And yet this much I know—
                         no sickness,   1890
        no ordinary, natural death is mine.
        I have been saved, preserved, kept alive
        for some strange fate, for something far more awful still.
        When that thing comes, let it take me
        where it will.

                OEDIPUS *turns, looking for something, waiting.*

        As for my sons, Kreon,
        they are grown men, they can look out for themselves.

But my daughters, those two poor girls of mine,
who have never left their home before, never left their
 father's side,
who ate at my side every day, who shared whatever was 1900
 mine,
I beg you, Kreon,
care for them, love them.
But more than anything, Kreon,
I want to touch them,

         He begins to lift his hands.

let me touch them with these hands of mine,
let them come to me so we can grieve together.
My noble lord, if only I could touch them with my hands,
they would still be mine just as they were
when I had eyes that could still see.

Oedipus' two small daughters are brought out of the palace.

O gods, gods, is it possible? Do I hear   1910
my two daughters crying? Has Kreon pitied me and brought
 me
what I love more than my life—
my daughters?

KREON I brought them to you, knowing how much you love them,
    Oedipus,
  knowing the joy you would feel if they were here.

OEDIPUS May the gods who watch over the path of your life, Kreon,
  prove kinder to you than they were to me.
  Where are you, children?
  Come, come to your brother's hands—

(taking his daughters into his arms)

his mother was your mother, too,   1920

283

come to these hands which made these eyes, bright clear
    eyes once,
sockets seeing nothing, the eyes
of the man who fathered you. Look . . . your father's eyes,
your father—
who knew nothing until now, saw nothing until now, and
    became
the husband of the woman who gave him birth.

                                            I weep for you
when I think how men will treat you, how bitter your lives
    will be.
What festivals will you attend, whose homes will you visit
and not be assailed by whispers, and people's stares?   1930
Where will you go and not leave in tears?
And when the time comes for you to marry,
what men will take you as their brides, and risk the shame
    of marrying
the daughters of Oedipus?
What sorrow will not be yours?
Your father killed his father, made love
to the woman who gave birth to him. And he fathered you
in the same place where he was fathered.
That is what you will hear; that is what they will say.
Who will marry you then? You will never marry,   1940
but grow hard and dry like wheat so far beyond harvest
that the wind blows its white flakes into the winter sky.
Oh Kreon,
now you are the only father my daughters have.
Jocasta and I, their parents, are lost to them forever.
These poor girls are yours. Your blood.
Don't let them wander all their lives,
begging, alone, unmarried, helpless.
Don't let them suffer as their father has. Pity them, Kreon,
pity these girls, so young and helpless except for you.   1950
Promise me this. Noble Kreon,
touch me with your hand, give me a sign.

                          KREON *takes his hands.*

                                        Daughters,
daughters, if you were older, if you could understand,
there is so much more I would say to you.
But for now, I give you this prayer—
                              Live,
live your lives, live each day as best you can,
may your lives be happier than your father's was.

KREON No more grief. Come in.   1960

OEDIPUS I must. But obedience comes hard.

KREON Everything has its time.

OEDIPUS First, promise me this.

KREON Name it.

OEDIPUS Banish me from Thebes.

KREON I cannot.   Ask the gods for that.

OEDIPUS The gods hate me.

KREON Then you will have your wish.

OEDIPUS You promise?

KREON I say only what I mean.   1970

OEDIPUS Then lead me in.

                OEDIPUS *reaches out and touches his daughters, trying to*
                                        take them with him.

KREON Oedipus, come with me. Let your daughters go. Come.

OEDIPUS No. You will not take my daughters. I forbid it.

KREON You *forbid* me?
You have no power anymore.
All the great power you once had is gone,
gone forever.

The CHORUS *turns to face the audience.* KREON *leads*
OEDIPUS *toward the palace. His daughters follow. He*
moves slowly, and disappears into the palace as the
CHORUS *ends.*

CHORUS O citizens of Thebes, this is Oedipus,
who solved the famous riddle, who held more power
    than any mortal.
See what he is: all men gazed on his fortunate life,   1980
all men envied him, but look at him, look.
All he had, all this man was,
pulled down and swallowed by the storm of his own life,
and by the god.
Keep your eyes on that last day, on your dying.
Happiness and peace, they were not yours
unless at death you can look back on your life and say
I lived, I did not suffer.

NOTES

Formally, the *Oedipus* has the articulations of every Greek tragedy. It is built out of a Prologue, or opening scene, a *Parodos*, or the entrance song of the Chorus, and song and speech alternate throughout the play. What follows the *Parodos* is the first of four "episodes" which alternate with *stasima*, or sections of choral song. The last episode was called the *Exodos*, or exit scene. Aristotle distinguished between the *Parodos* and *stasima* (*Poetics* 12.1452b22), but the most fundamental distinction between the "parts" of a Greek tragedy is between song and speech, dance and the stage. Like the choral songs, the *Parodos* was sung or chanted in a dialect and in rhythms that were distinct from the Attic dialect and mainly iambic rhythm of the spoken parts. Thus, the Prologue, episodes, and *exodos* are the spoken parts of the play. The sung or lyrical parts of the *Oedipus* are made up of the entrance song of the Chorus, four choral songs (*stasima*), and two *kommoi*, or dirges sung in an antiphonal recitative between Oedipus on stage and the Chorus in the orchestra (853–912 / 649–97, 1679–1776 / 1297–1368). The *stasimon* which follows Jocasta's discovery of the truth about her son and marriage is part of an excited dance form known as a *hypórchema* (1376–1405 / 1086–1109). Formally, and fundamentally, the middle of *Oedipus* is the song beginning "Fate be here let what I say be pure."

The lyrical parts of the *Oedipus* have a movement, language, rhythm, and logic of their own. Our manuscripts of the Greek text of Sophocles do not record the music that accompanied the choral song. They do not give us a choreography for how the dancers moved in the orchestra, and they give us only clues to what the audience in the theater of Dionysos saw before them. Fifteen dancers (*choreutai*) moved onto the dancing floor just below the low stage platform, led by a flute player. They move, sing together in a rectangular formation of five rows (facing the audience), three deep. At the center of the first row is the "head man" or Leader of the Chorus—the Koryphaios. The Chorus sings in unison, and speak, and is spoken to, as one man. The Chorus of the *Oedipus* is made up of Theban elders, summoned to the palace (and stage) by Oedipus who asked the people of Kadmos to assemble before his palace.

The particles and logic which control the thought and emotion of the language of the actors on stage do not carry over into the Chorus. In Greek dramatic lyric, as in the choral songs of Pindar and Bacchylides, verbs are rare and they control, with inevitable and deliberate ambiguities, large stretches of the song they inform. Because of a lyrical lack of subordination in the logic of the Chorus' song, the audience, who are closer to the Chorus than they are to the actors onstage, are compelled to become a part of the Chorus and to supply themselves the necessary and subtle ligatures that bind phrase to phrase. And as in the language of Greek cultic poetry, compound epithets are nets with which men attempt to snare and contain the power of their gods. Thought moves from *strophe* to *antistrophe:* turn and return. In the first movement of their entrance song, the Chorus invokes the voice of prophecy; in the *antistrophe,* they call upon Athena. Apollo occupies the same place in both *strophe* and *antistrophe.* We have attempted to reproduce in English, which has no tradition for this kind of song, the essential gaps and ambiguities of Greek choral song by a kind of Broken Poetry. We have also attempted to capture and reproduce the overarching thematic unities that make a whole of this Broken Poetry.

A part of the ancient lore which fills the margins of our manuscripts of Aristophanes' *Frogs* is an explanation and derivation of the word *stasimon:* "this is the part the dancers sing when they are stationary." What this means is not that the Chorus is rooted to the dancing floor; it is not. Rather the Chorus has taken positions on the dancing floor. The action of the *Oedipus* does not come to a standstill with the sections of lyrical song. What has been said and done on stage moves onto another plane of reaction and reflection, which often mirrors the action of the play as a whole rather than the facets of its development. Formal and conservative, in the sense that old men are conservative and wed to traditional values, and fundamentally *polis*-bound, the Chorus is physically and naturally the intermediaries between the audience and the remote hero who moves above them on the tragic stage.

Sophocles' Chorus was fifteen in number, his actors three. There were also a number of silent actors on stage. All Greek tragedies were contests (*agones*), and the actors in these contests were called *agonistai.* The most important of these, the Protagonist, played the part of Oedipus. There is no difficulty in assigning the parts taken by the second and third actors. It is sure that Sophocles would have given the same actor the parts of Teiresias and the old shepherd who saved Oedipus' life.

1–182 / 1–150 Prologue

3 / 3 those branches tied with wool A delegation of Thebans has come to the palace of Oedipus and taken up the position of suppliants before the stage and the altar of Apollo. They have placed branches twined with wool on the altar as an offering to Apollo, the god whose oracles shape the plot of the *Oedipus* and who was also a god of healing. In the *Iliad*, Apollo was the god of plague.

21 / 13 In his description of the three ages of the suppliants who have gathered before the palace of Thebes, the priest seems to give a faint hint of the human condition and the riddle of the Sphinx; cf. the note to **156 / 130**.

22 / 16 around your altar Immediately, the altar that belongs to the stage and the palace of Thebes. But the ambiguity of Sophocles' language takes in Oedipus in its suggestion that Oedipus is a god (cf. **58 / 38**, and **50 / 31**, where the suggestion is denied). Thebes calls Oedipus *soter*, saviour, and Oedipus appears (at **286 / 216**) in response to the prayers of the Chorus (cf. **244 / 188**).

26 / 20–21 the two great temples of Athena One of these must have been the temple of Athena Ongka. It is not clear which aspect of the goddess the second temple honored, but in Athens there were two temples to Athena on the Acropolis. These temples and the plague are two of the bonds uniting Thebes and Athens in the *Oedipus*. Cf. Introduction v and the note to **1978 / 1524**.

27 / 21 staring into the ashes At the oracular shrine of Apollo Ismenios, where the behavior of things such as incense or flour placed in the fire of the altar declared symbolically the configuration of the past, present, or future. His altar was made of ash, and he was called Ashen Apollo.

63 / 44 our plans and their results In Greek the outcome of the plans of men of experience is called *symphoras*—a word that usually means disaster. It describes the plague in **121 / 99** and Oedipus' fate in **1983 / 1528**. Here this (disastrous) outcome is said to *live*—like the oracles that wheel around the head of the doomed man in **659 / 481–82**.

92 / 70–71 *great Apollo's shrine at Delphi* To the temple of Apollo at Delphi where the god and his priestess, the Pythia, gave oracles revealing not only the future, but the hidden past and present. At the entrance to the temple was an inscription which read: "Know thyself," GNOTHI SAUTON.

115 / 96–97 *Cleanse the city of Thebes* The Greek word is *miasma*—pollution. What this pollution comes from is the stain of his father's blood on Oedipus' hands. For the Greek, *miasma* was something palpable and contagious. The verb "to pollute," "defile," also means to stain. The connection between these two notions is strikingly apparent in the Homeric simile which likens the blood spreading over the wounded Menelaos' thighs to the dye with which a woman stains ivory (*Iliad* 4.141–47). In Homer's Greek the word for the staining of dye and the staining of blood is the same (*miainein*). The product of staining is *miasma*. Oedipus uses a similar word (*kelis*) for his own defilement: "the filthy black stain reaching down over me" (1078 / 833); his hands bloody the bed of the man he killed (1062 / 821). Oedipus is unclean, and Apollo gives Thebes a choice of purifications: either fresh blood is needed to wash away the blood of the murdered man, or the source of taint and disease (*miasma*) must be driven from Thebes. Apollo's language—"you must drive the man out"—suggests the religious term for driving an *agos*, or source of defilement, from a city (cf. 543 / 402). In the course of the *Oedipus*, the doomed man of Apollo's prophecy becomes an *agos*—a thing both sacred and cursed (see the note to 1852 / 1426).

There is still another word for this pollution in the *Oedipus*—*mysos*, "this stain, this disease" (167 / 138); Oedipus pronounces it, and it is known in Sophocles only here. *Mysos* is a word with distinct and significant associations: in Aeschylus it described the defilement of a woman who had murdered her husband and a son who had shed his mother's blood (*Choephoroi*, 650; *Eumenides*, 838; cf. Empedocles, *Purifications*, fragments 137 and 115, translated in the note to 1852 / 1426). Here, in a discord between the appearances of the play and the hidden realities known to Sophocles' audience, we confront one of the most subtle ironies of the *Oedipus*. Appearance is that the source of the pollution and plague that infest Thebes is the blood on the hands of an unknown bandit who murdered the king of Thebes in another country. He was one among many. Just as the search for the murderer of Laios turns from a band of men to the quest for the one man who did "crimes unnameable things," the pollution that infects Thebes proves to be a more terrible thing than it appears at first: it comes from a man who murdered his father. Here a gap opens up between appearance and reality. The only connection between these distant worlds is the "demonic" or inexplicable appearance of words like *mysos* and the "unnameable things" in the first *stasimon*.

The revulsion of nature provoked by the murder of a father by his son is expressed in a plague in which the fundamental continuity between generations is aborted. Fruits and grains harden in their protective sheaths. Children come stillborn from their mothers' wombs. A tradition known to Pausanias gives us a measure of the real cause of the Theban plague. At Potniai (a small town near Thebes) the drunken votaries of the god Dionysos kill his priest at a sacrifice. The city is immediately infected by a plague. Apollo is consulted for a cure. His response gives one of the two possibilities of the *Oedipus*: the stain of the priest's blood is cleansed by the ritual murder of a young man (*Guide to Greece*, IX 8.1). The Athenians in Sophocles' audience had reason to remember the pollution and curse that came from the murder of suppliants at the altars of the Furies just below the acropolis (Thucydides, I 126).

146 / 122–23 *bandits . . . not one man* All that is known about the murder of Laios comes from the sole survivor who not only spoke of bandits but was emphatic that one man did not do the deed. His insistence is significant for the play. The sole survivor of Oedipus' attack on Laios and his party is the household slave who was to expose Oedipus on Kithairon, but took pity on the baby. In the play, he is the only mortal besides Teiresias to know the truth about Oedipus and his life. When he fled from the scene of the murder he did not know that Laios was dead. But on his return to Thebes he learned that Laios had been killed and that Oedipus had taken his place as king of Thebes (992 / 758–59). We are not told that he recognized Oedipus as the child he saved, but the fact that he insisted that Laios had been killed by bandits—not by one man alone—and his desire never to see Thebes again (996 / 762) speak for themselves. Sophocles gave his audience a sense of all that this shepherd knows well before his reluctant appearance.

156 / 130 *The intricate, hard song of the Sphinx* Her song, and oracle (cf. **1530 / 1200**), is this:

> There is a creature that moves upon the earth
> on two feet, on four, and on three.
> He has one name, and of all the creatures that move
> upon the land, and through the bright air and sea,
> only this changes his condition. But when he
> walks with the most limbs to support him,
> he moves slowest and his limbs are weakest.

The answer to her riddle is Man; in Sophocles' play Oedipus is revealed as an infant on Kithairon, a man standing steady at the height of his power, and a blind exile who must walk upon the earth with a staff to support him and direct his way.

183–285 / 151–215 Parodos

196 / 156 *the turning season* The Chorus envisages the possibility that the past is in control of the present—a possibility that is later rejected. See Introduction IV and the note to 669 / 487.

197–216 / 157–66 This prayer to three of the gods who protect or might protect Thebes bears a striking resemblance to the kind of cultic hymn that is a prayer based on precedent. The best example of this kind of appeal is Sappho's hymn to Aphrodite: "come to me now, if ever before you have heard and heeded my voice and prayer." "You saved me before" seems to lead nowhere, for the "black flame of suffering" (cf. 212 / 166) is very thin as a description of the tyranny of the Sphinx. Bernard Knox has argued that the only satisfactory way of grounding this reference is to see in it an allusion to the first of the plagues that wasted Athens (cf. Introduction V). The association of Ares and the plague in Sophocles is strange, and the best explanation of it seems to be historical, and to forge still another link between Thebes and Athens. The first outbreak of the plague in Athens occurred in the second year of Athens' war with Sparta (429 B.C.).

231 / 177 *the cold god of evening* is Hades, god of the dead, whose dwellings were thought to lie beyond the setting sun.

243 / 188 *the warm bright face of peace* At the end of this ode, Oedipus is on stage. There is no better cue in what the Chorus says than this for his appearance.

252 / 192–95 *the two seas at the world's edge* The Atlantic and the Black Sea or "Euxine" or sea "hospitable to strangers" by the Greek habit of euphemism which avoids provoking dangerous powers by naming them by their contraries.

277 / 210 *god whose name is our name* So Thebes, the site of the oriental Dionysos' vindication of his claim to power over Greece, is called "Bacchic" (cf. *Ajax* 574 and 430).

292

286–635 / 216–462 *First episode*

316 / 230 *the curse* Oedipus describes his curse on the murderer of Laios as an *epos*—
the word that describes the language that comes from Delphi (cf. 107 /
89). It is in fact prophetic, and it haunts the play (see the note to 591 /
428, and cf. 1055–61 / 817–20).

366 / 267–68 *for every royal generation of Thebes* In Sophocles' Greek, Oedipus gives
the lineage of the kings of Thebes. His interest in the history of his
adoptive city reveals his desire to sink down roots. When he has discovered his lineage, Oedipus no longer needs to qualify "as if he were
my father" (361 / 264). And he is no longer interested in a family whose
tree can be described as:

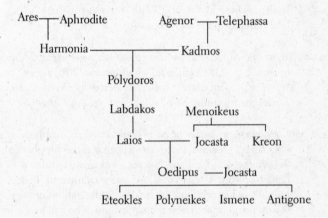

458 / 337–38 *You don't see how much alike we are* The play of words is extremely
subtle: Oedipus says of Teiresias that he is capable of provoking a rock.
Teiresias replies by saying that Oedipus' anger, temper, or temperament
is close to his own. *Orge* is the word on which all of this turns, and it is
associated here with *physis*, origin or nature, literally, the "nature" of a
rock. It would seem that Oedipus resembles Teiresias in a fixity of
disposition. Teiresias has no choice but to know what he knows, and
Oedipus has no choice, except for the decisive act of blinding himself,
but to suffer what he suffers.

490 / 360 *Are you trying to make me say the word?* The word that hangs on Teiresias'
lips is *phoneus*, murderer—the word Oedipus responds to by the strong

term "pain, hurt" (*pēmonaí*). In Greek, words were sticks and stones; see Introduction IV, and Lysias' speech *Against Theomnestos* (Speeches X and XL). The unspeakable words of Apollo's response to Oedipus, the language that describes the plot of the play itself, are *oneide*—bitter, hateful insults and the acts that provoke them (**1036** / **797**).

514–15 / **376–77** *You, you and your fate belong to Apollo* Just the reverse of what a long manuscript tradition preserves. This tradition has Teiresias say: "I am not doomed to be ruined by you." The reasons for abandoning this tradition and shifting the reference to Oedipus are first the context: Oedipus speaks of Teiresias as incapable of harming him or anyone who has the power of sight. Teiresias answers by saying that he cannot in fact do any harm to Oedipus, nor can Kreon himself (**518** / **379**). The second consideration is simply that the reference to the ruin of Teiresias leads nowhere in the play, but "you and your fate belong to Apollo" leads directly to **1731–38** / **1329–31**.

537 / **397** *stupid, untutored Oedipus (mēden eidōs Oidípous)* Here Oedipus associates his name with the verb *oida*, which means "I have seen" and therefore "I know"—a meaning Shelley rendered by Witfoot. The name also carries the meaning "Swollenfoot," cf. **1304–8** / **1034–36**.

591 / **428** *your happiness an ember of pain* Here Teiresias' words echo the precise language of Oedipus' curse (**316–41** / **230–48**), as they have already when the prophet tells Oedipus, "Never speak again to these men of Thebes" (**476** / **351–52**). These words are one guarantee of Teiresias' skill as a prophet and insight into the hidden configurations of the present, since he was not present to hear them. Oedipus, who had begun by addressing Teiresias as godlike and treating him as a man (cf. **412–14** / **300–301**), is slow to register the strange echoes of his own language in what Teiresias says; he is too absorbed in his concern for the human and the political. The realization of their meaning begins to come only later: "It is frightening—can the blind prophet see?" (**979** / **747**).

636–90 / **463–512** *First stasimon*

669 / **487** *I know nothing about a feud* The Chorus does not know how to react to the accusations Teiresias has made against Oedipus. Neither the present nor the future can give the Chorus the basis for understanding his words, and the past offers no help. Sophocles' Thebans know of no quarrel or feud (*neikos*) that involved *either* the sons of Labdakos *or* the son of

Polybos. Translators usually reduce the sense of this language to: "I know of no trouble between Laios and Oedipus." But the Greek is disjunctive, and Laios and Oedipus are referred to by their patronymics. I have suggested (Introduction IV) that in Aeschylus' treatment of the history of the house of Laios in his tragic trilogy *Laios, Oedipus, Seven*, Sophocles had an answer at hand to the question of his Chorus. The plot of the *Seven*, like the plot of the *Oresteia*, is under the control of the past. What happens to Oedipus' sons is brought about by a father's curse and the disobedience of Laios—"an old breach of law, long since begotten" (in the translation of Hecht and Bacon, 940–41). The consequences of this breach work through three generations (743), in three waves (758–60). The intelligibility of this Aeschylean past is not a part of Sophocles' *Oedipus*.

675 / 498 *Zeus and Apollo know* The gods who have shaped and guaranteed the plot of the *Oedipus* are *xunetoi* and *eidotes*, literally, capable of putting things together, seeing and knowing. Finally these gods will reveal to men how the pieces in the puzzle of Oedipus' life fit together (1149–51 / 901–2).

691–1104 / 513–862 *Second episode*

814–16 / 624–26 *You won't change your mind* In the manuscript this line is given to Oedipus and follows directly on "I'll believe you when you teach me the meaning of envy" (given to Kreon). The context demands that the order and attribution of the verses be reversed. It is Oedipus who must relent and believe what Kreon has said in his own defense (cf. 819 / 627, 849 / 646, 853 / 649 and *Ajax* 371). This rearrangement takes care of one problem in the text, but seems to create another by leaving a gap in the movement of thought between lines 814 / 624 and 816 / 626. Our translation reproduces in English what it is that Kreon responds to in Oedipus' threat. In the Greek it is Oedipus' use of the word envy (*phthonein*) which triggers Kreon's response: (Envy?) "Envy, you talk about envy. You don't even know what sense is" (*phronein*).

833 / 636 *petty personal bickering* Jocasta's entrance is the turning point of the *Oedipus*. From this moment on the action of the play turns from the public to the private, from the search for the murderer of Laios to Oedipus' search for his origins.

845–48 / 644–45 By his oath, which is nearly incomprehensible to a modern audience, Kreon has put himself outside the sphere of the human and exposed

himself to the terrible and ambiguous powers of the gods. He is *enágēs*.
For the meaning of *agos*, see the note to 1852 / 1426.

853–912 / 649–97 *Kommos* An antiphonal dirge between Oedipus on stage and the
Chorus in the orchestra.

1028 / 789–90 *a future dark with torment* What Apollo revealed to Oedipus in answer
to Oedipus' question about his birth involves one of the most terrible
words in the Greek language (*patróktonos*, cf. 1666 / 1288) and something so repellingly attractive that Greek had no generic word for it (it
fills the silence at 1666 / 1289). Apollo's predictions and the plot of the
Oedipus center on acts that are called *oneíde* (cf. the note to 490 / 360).
Oedipus' tormented thoughts about the life that awaits his daughters
(1927–42 / 1486–1502) give a modern audience some notion of how
stinging Apollo's words were for Greeks who lived in a "shame culture"
and spoke a language in which "to hear well or badly" meant to have a
good or bad reputation.

1040 / 800–801 *near the crossroads you mentioned* Jocasta spoke of the place where
roads join as the place of Laios' murder (940 / 716). Oedipus' memory is
more precise.

1105–58 / 863–910 *Second stasimon*

1106 / 864 *let what I say be pure* The Chorus reacts to what Jocasta has said about the
force of oracles (cf. 1145–51 / 897–902). Jocasta will have even more
shocking things to say just before Apollo's oracles are revealed as alive
and true: "oracles of the gods, where are you now!" (1197 / 946–47). And
so will Oedipus (1217–27 / 964–72). But Jocasta's deeds are those of a
pious woman who recognizes in Oedipus' agitation the work of some god
or demon (1159–74 / 911–23). "Let all my acts be pure" is the Chorus'
response to Oedipus' sudden fear that he has been polluted by the stain of
Laios' blood (1062–78 / 821–33).

1115 / 873 *arrogance insatiable pride* The Greek word for this is *hubris*—a going beyond
limits. These lines, and the rest of this *stasimon*, have been taken to refer
to Oedipus, to Jocasta, to Laios and his violent seduction of Chrysippos,
the son of Pelops, or to a concept of empire and man in which Oedipus
and the arrogance of imperial Athens come to be fused in one dramatic
symbol. The desperate ingenuity and discordant variety in the interpretations of the meaning of this *stasimon* might itself prove to be a part of

Sophocles' meaning, or point to it. Behind the image of the *tyrannos* the Chorus recalls in its familiar features, there is some of the substance of the *Oedipus*. Oedipus has touched untouchable things (1139 / 891), and on the level of verbal ripples, the language of the Chorus seems to spread to Oedipus in the word "breeds" and the pointed references to feet and a fall (cf. Introduction IV). But what of the other details—the insatiable desires for forbidden things, the greed, the high-headed and high-handed contempt for justice and the gods? These are the marks of the *tyrannos*. This tragic costume is too big for Oedipus, and it comes from another age. It fits the Xerxes of Aeschylus' *Persians* and the Agamemnon of the *Oresteia* better than it does Oedipus (cf. *Agamemnon*, 367–84; 456–74; 527–32; 750–81; 905–11; 944–57).

In this *stasimon*, which is at the center of the play, Sophocles seems to turn to one possible explanation of Oedipus' tragedy, not because it can explain why Oedipus suffered what he suffered, but precisely because it cannot. By opening and closing the doors of his stage on the traditional figure of the *tyrannos*, Sophocles seems to assert that the action of the *Oedipus* is both autonomous and radically conditioned by forces that are beyond human understanding and human control. Neither the offenses of Laios nor the "tyrannical" actions of Oedipus explain the fate of Sophocles' hero. In this central ode, the Chorus responds to a moment in the discovery of the truth of Oedipus' life and fate. They are old men, wed to the past and limited and defined by the restraints and sentiments of a democratic *polis*. A measure of the incommensurability of their world and that of the Sophoclean hero is their evocation of the *tyrannos*. At the end of the play, this same Chorus can turn to the audience and point to Oedipus and intone: "Count no man happy until he is dead."

1148 / 899–900 *the temples at Olympia at Abai* The importance of these places is that they were both sites of oracles; Abai had an oracular sanctuary of Apollo and Olympia had an oracle of Zeus—the two gods who know the plot of the *Oedipus* (cf. 675 / 498, 963–64 / 738, 1731 / 1329).

1159–1404 / 911–1085 *Third episode*

1168–69 / 919–20 *Apollo . . . listen to my prayers* This is the cue for the entrance into the orchestra of the Messenger from Corinth. Jocasta prays for a "solution" to Oedipus' state acceptable to men and the gods. Her word is *lysis*. It means both a cleansing and a dénouement to the action of play (cf. Aristotle, *Poetics* 18).

1307 / 1036 *That mark is the meaning of your name* Oedipus, Swollenfoot. For Oedipus, Witfoot, see the note to 537 / 397.

1376–1405 / 1086–1109 *Third stasimon* This short, buoyant song is not a full choral *stasimon*. It closely resembles a dance form known as a *hypórchema*. Similar in mood and function is the exultant song to Pan in *Ajax* 693–718, which comes just before the news of Ajax's suicide. A good example of the *hypórchema* or "dance-song" is the vigorous Dionysiac song Pratinas composed for a chorus of satyrs (translated by A. M. Dale in her *Collected Papers* [Cambridge 1969], p. 168.)

1406–1501 / 1110–85 *Fourth episode*

1502–72 / 1186–1222 *Fourth stasimon*

1502 / 1186 *man after man after man* Literally, "O generations of mortals"; the beginning of this last choral song recalls inevitably Glaukos' reply to Diomedes in *Iliad* 6.145:

> why ask of my generation?
> As is the generation of leaves, so is that of humanity.
> The wind scatters the leaves on the ground, but the
> live timber
> burgeons with leaves again in the season of spring returning.
> So one generation of men will grow while another dies.

(In the translation of Richmond Lattimore)

> But significantly, and characteristically, the Sophoclean metaphor is that of light and darkness, appearance and the dark background, that both qualifies and defines the illusion of human happiness.

1573–1988 / 1223–1530 *Exodos*

1679–80 / 1297 *horror horror o what suffering men see* It could be that what the Chorus sees is one of the "blind masks" that the lexicographer Pollux (early second century A.D.) treats briefly in his article on tragic masks (*Onomasticon* IV 141). But the mask Oedipus wears does not resemble that of Teiresias, or a Phineus or a Thamyris. The artisan who made it would have had his model in the language of the messenger from the palace who describes Oedipus' self-mutilation.

1679–1776 / 1297–1368 *Kommos*

1730 / 1328 *what demon lifted your hands* For the conception of character and responsibility behind this question, see Introduction II.

1852 / 1426 *this cursed, naked, holy thing* This *agos*. In its distance from the Greek conception of the sacred English must break the Greek word into its two, seemingly contradictory elements. For the Greek, the sacred is both holy and cursed, awful and dangerous, pure and polluted. By an oath earlier in the play Kreon had made himself *enágēs*—that is, he had placed himself outside the human and exposed himself to the ambivalent powers of the divine (845–48 / 644–45). Jocasta had prayed to Apollo for a solution to Oedipus' troubled state that would be acceptable to the gods (a *lysin euagē* 1170 / 921), and this is the answer to her prayer: Oedipus has become an *agos*.

The modern conception of the sacred does not possess the ambiguity of the ancient, and for a modern audience, the risks of Kreon's oath are impossible to appreciate. By penetrating the sphere of the sacred, Oedipus has acquired a power, a *menos*, that is fundamentally ambivalent. The Oedipus of the *Oedipus* at *Kolonos* represents a power that can work for either good or ill. In the grove of the Eumenides, the benevolent ones who are also Furies, Oedipus can become either benevolent (*eumenes*) or destructive (*dysmenes*), and his ambiguous and ambivalent power is at the center of the play. This same power is at the center of the last scene of the *Oedipus*.

Like the plague, the elemental recoil and revulsion provoked by Oedipus' crimes is an expression of a deep sympathy between man and nature. Oedipus' crimes, and the perversion of the natural order they represent, expel him from Thebes and the world of man. The earlier images of expulsion and isolation, of Ares the god the gods would drive from heaven and the solitary bull cut off from the herd, come to center on Oedipus at the end of the play (283–85 / 215, 655 / 478, 1828–34 / 1410–12). Oedipus is *atheos*, abandoned by the gods (1774 / 1358). He was driven from Corinth out of his fear that he would kill his father (*apoptolis*); and now he will be driven from Thebes.

The loathing felt for Oedipus goes beyond Thebes. As he stands blindly before the light of the sun, it becomes elemental. Like the Sinner Man the Holy Rollers sing of, Oedipus has no place in the natural world:

> Run to the sea,
> Sea'll be aboilin'—
> Run to the moon
> Moon'll be ableedin'.—

The theme is an old one. In Empedocles' *Purifications* (Diels-Kranz fragment B 115), the world of air, earth, fire, and water repels the godlike man who has polluted himself with bloodshed:

> The force of the bright clear air drives him to the sea,
> The sea spews him out onto land and earth,
> The earth into the brilliant rays of the burning sun,
> And the sun plunges him into the streams of bright, clear air.

1891 / 1456 *no ordinary, natural death is mine* This strange language points enigmatically to the events of Sophocles' last treatment of the Oedipus story in *Oedipus at Colonus*. In his final prophetic denunciation, Teiresias had revealed Oedipus' fate (**626–27 / 455–56**):

> rich and powerful now, he will be a beggar,
> poking his way with a stick, feeling his way to a strange country.

At the end of the play, Oedipus' fate remains unclear. Thebes still awaits some word from Delphi. In *Oedipus at Colonus*, Oedipus' fate becomes as clear as an oracle can be. The "strange country" of Teiresias' prophecy is Athens where Oedipus seeks refuge and the "resting place" revealed by Apollo is the grove of the Furies near the shrine to the local hero Colonus in Sophocles' own *deme* or township (cf. Euripides, *Phoenissae* 1705–7).

1978 / 1524 *O citizens of Thebes* These final lines are intoned, not sung, by the Chorus as a whole. When the Chorus of Theban elders turns to an Athenian audience, the gradual fusion of Thebes and Athens is complete. Chorus members point to the figure of Oedipus on stage who is slowly led back into the palace. What they say has caused great unhappiness among those who admire Sophocles and his *Oedipus*. It is difficult not to agree that they are bathetic, but it is equally difficult to reject them. Euripides' Oedipus looks back on them at the end of the *Phoenician Women* (1757–63). The judgment that these closing lines are "unworthy" of Sophocles is indisputable, if what this judgment means is that Sophocles would not have used them himself to sum up the meaning of his *Oedipus*. But the fact is that Sophocles does not speak through the Chorus; he speaks only through his *Oedipus* as a whole. What the final words of the *Oedipus* suggest is that there is an unbridgeable gap between the tragic hero on stage and the Chorus whose traditional wisdom cannot comprehend the fate of a hero like Oedipus (cf. *Women of Trachis*, 1–3, and *Ajax* 1428–30). The Athenians who found them profound would have gone from the theater of Dionysos down to the seashore.

OEDIPUS AT COLONUS

Translated by

EAMON GRENNAN

and

RACHEL KITZINGER

INTRODUCTION

The *Oedipus at Colonus*, written by Sophocles in the last years of his life (he died in 406 BCE) and not produced until after his death (perhaps in 401 BCE), is a powerful exploration of what survives endings—the ending of an individual life (Oedipus dies at the end of the play); the ending of a city (in 404 Sophocles' native city, Athens, came to the end of its role as the primary political presence in the Mediterranean world through its defeat by Sparta and its allies after a long and costly war); and the end of the poet's own life (Sophocles was probably ninety when he wrote the play). The play is composed out of this sense of familiar and known things coming to an end, as it looks back at the figure of Oedipus as a young man and at Sophocles' treatment of his story in his earlier plays, *Antigone* (442?) and *Oedipus Tyrannus* (430?). But the play also looks forward to a future that Sophocles offers his play as a way of facing and even welcoming—however unknowable and strange that future might be.

THE TWO EARLIER PLAYS

By 406 BCE Sophocles had written about 125 plays—tragedies and satyr plays—to be performed at the City Dionysia, the annual civic celebration in Athens of the god Dionysus. Seven of these 125 plays have survived, and three of these seven center on the myth of Oedipus. In 442?, Sophocles wrote the *Antigone*, whose story comes at the end of the myth of the Labdacids, the family of Laius and his son, Oedipus. Oedipus' male children (and brothers), Eteocles and Polyneices, are engaged in a dispute over succession to the kingship of Thebes. Polyneices makes an alliance with neighboring Argos and brings an army to attack Thebes. In the course of the battle the brothers kill each other, fulfilling their father/brother's curse on them. The *Antigone* begins on the day after the battle when Creon, the boys' uncle, has decreed that one, Eteocles, is to be buried with full honor, as he died defending Thebes, while Polyneices' corpse is to be left to rot, as Creon considers him a traitor to Thebes. Their sister, Antigone, refuses to acknowledge the political distinction between the brothers, buries Polyneices, and is condemned to death by Creon. Rather than waiting to die in the tomb in which Creon has buried her alive, Antigone kills herself, thus essentially ending the line of Oedipus and the story of Oedipus' tragic marriage to his mother, Jocasta (although Ismene, Oedipus' other daughter, survives, her story ends with Antigone's death).

Ten years later Sophocles writes the *Oedipus Tyrannus*, which dramatizes Oedipus' own discovery of the fact of that marriage and his earlier murder of his father, Laius. The setting of this play is again the unfortunate Thebes, this time being devastated by a plague. Oedipus, as Thebes' king, is determined to save the city and its inhabitants from this destruction. As he relentlessly follows the clues the god Apollo has given him about the cause of the plague, he uncovers the story of his own past: his chance meeting with his (unknown) father whom he kills in a dispute over a right of way, and his marriage to his (unknown) mother, Jocasta, as a result of his inspired answer to the Sphinx's riddle. Marriage to Jocasta was his reward from a grateful Thebes, which had been devastated by the attacks of the Sphinx. She could be stopped only by an answer to her riddle, "What walks on four legs in the morning, two legs at noon, and three legs in the evening and has a single voice?" Oedipus' answer—"man"—he will spend the rest of his life coming to understand. The reward the Cadmeians (another name for the Thebans) offer him for ridding them of the Sphinx is the throne of Thebes and marriage to the queen, Jocasta, Oedipus' mother. As Oedipus relentlessly pursues the truth about this past, Jocasta is the first to understand what has happened, and, anticipating her failure to stop Oedipus from discovering and revealing the whole story, she hangs herself. When Oedipus finally reconstructs the story and recognizes that he is both the destroyer and the savior of Thebes, he fulfills the curse he himself has placed on the person responsible for the plague by blinding himself—in essence exiling himself from human society. The play ends with his unsuccessful attempt to persuade Jocasta's brother Creon, who has become king in his place, to complete the exile by banishing him from Thebes.

In these two plays we see the richness of this story for Sophocles' exploration of what tragedy as a genre can offer its audience. Against the backdrop of an extreme threat to a city's well-being, individuals struggle with each other and themselves to understand the limits of human action and understanding in the light of the patterns of an order outside their control. Neither play offers answers. Rather, both dramatize, in radically different ways, the dynamic struggle to make sense of the world through the choices humans make, the values they uphold by those choices, the limits of language to articulate and to persuade others of the correctness of those choices, and the irresolvable conflicts that ensue. The structure of the plot in each play arises out of the tension created by the power and futility of human attempts, through language and action, to construct a meaningful world. In the *Antigone*, the conflict between Antigone's and Creon's understandings of what the death of Polyneices and Eteocles demands of them, and how to fulfill those demands, is viscerally represented in the pushing of each side to destructive extremes, out of which a restorative compromise can be imagined only as the product of extreme suffering. The action of the play is structured around a series of confrontations between two characters in which the opposition, which seems absolute and fixed, in fact moves Antigone and Creon, the two main opponents, to see the destructive results of their passionately held positions. In the *Oedipus Tyrannus* Oedipus' driving determination to keep asking questions gives the play a powerful sense of precipitous linear movement, which, as it takes the audience into the future, in fact takes us back into the past, until the two come together at the brink of a chasm of despair from which it is hard to imagine the possibility of recovery.

THE STRUCTURE OF THE *OEDIPUS AT COLONUS*

The structure of the *Oedipus at Colonus* is quite different. It moves forward neither by opposition nor by a driving, if complex, linear motion. Rather, the *Oedipus at Colonus* moves in waves of arrivals and departures in counterpoint with the single arc of Oedipus' faltering arrival at the beginning of the play, his seated presence at center stage throughout the action until the very end, and his dramatic departure at the end, without assistance and accompanied by lightning, thunder, and the voice of a god. At issue in these waves of coming and going are the laws, the patterns—in Greek, the *nomoi* (a word that means both law, custom, and melody)—by which we order our lives, in conjunction with a pattern we cannot know but which provides a kind of counterpoint, constantly transforming the meaning we think we are creating. Oedipus serves as the focal point of this conjunction, and in the paradoxes and judgments that arise from his presence the audience catches a glimpse of the ineffable harmony between what changes and what remains unchanging—between the human and divine, the knowable and the unknowable, the powerless and the powerful.

For the audience at the end of the fifth century this play is Sophocles' gift to the city-state in which he had lived and which he had served his entire life. Athens' attempt at a new form of government, democracy, seemed to be reaching a crisis in its final defeat by the oligarchic Spartans, with whom Athens had been at war, on and off, for twenty-five years. In this play the death of Oedipus in Colonus, Sophocles' own birthplace and a town within sight of the Acropolis, promises to the Athenians the protection of the hero forever, some kind of eternal life for the city. The city's survival is perhaps not to be imagined as the preservation of the laws that have ordered its existence or the continuity of its political hegemony but as the manifestation of a spirit that the play only suggests, adumbrates like a mystery, in the complex interplay of the rhythms of its plot.

In the opening scene two figures enter the theater: an old, blind man and a young woman. They are travelers, beggars without home or possessions, and their arrival in this place, as in every place they come to, poses the question: How will they find what they need to survive? Stripped of everything that defines a life, what does their existence mean? Oedipus' opening speech begins to explain the sense he has made of this stage of his life, one so different from the complex layers of his earlier history, as Sophocles portrays it in the *Oedipus Tyrannus*, where everything turned out to mean more than it seemed, and all understanding led only to more mystery. He says of himself: "who asks little and gets less, though even less / than little is enough—" (5–6 / 5–6). He goes on to explain the things that allow him to be content, to be at peace with this bare existence "... the long / companionship of time, and bitter trouble, / and beyond that the manner I was born to, teach me / to be easy with whatever happens" (6–9 / 7–8). While these things allow him inner ease, he explains in the last lines of the speech the means by which he interacts with others to get what he needs: "As strangers / we've learned how to listen to the natives of a place / and to act according to what we hear" (13–15 / 12–13). He has learned an openness to the laws and habits of the particular place he comes to and a willingness to comply with the circumstances of the moment. This opening speech gives us the world of the play, the backdrop against which all that will happen is to be understood. Oedipus has defined the rhythms that finally, after years of struggle, allow him to live in some kind of difficult but resolved accommodation to the world and his own history. It is a life stripped to its essentials: the character one is born with, the accumulated experience of acting and suffering, the rhythm of change that time brings and an openness to whatever happens.

Against this backdrop is played out a series of encounters between Oedipus and others, where others' actions, ambitions, and desires—their ways of being in the world—are tested and judged by the touchstone of Oedipus' achieved wisdom. In this way Oedipus turns out to be once again, as he was in the *Oedipus Tyrannus*, a riddle: the combination of his apparent destitution and his enormous hidden power serves as a test of others' humanity, as each newcomer responds to the presence of the old, blind beggar seated on a bare rock. The Greeks understood all suppliants, as Oedipus is, as a test: those who are in need of protection challenge those with power to take the correct measure of their power as provisional and limited. It is out of an understanding that any human, however secure, could easily become as helpless as the suppliant and that all human power pales in comparison with the divine and eternal power of the gods, and especially of Zeus, who protects suppliants, that one is moved to put oneself at risk in the service of those who are powerless. But Oedipus is a different kind of test because he is, in fact, not helpless, although he seems to be, and in this way the *Oedipus at Colonus* is not merely a "suppliant play." His interactions are based not on a vivid disparity of power between himself and others, but rather on others' ability to understand the discrepancy between his appearance and the power he embodies, the discontinuity between his past and his future, the coexistence of his dependence and autonomy.

Oedipus' power comes not only from the understanding he has struggled to achieve. The first indication that the pattern of Oedipus' life is also shaped by something beyond his own understanding and the laws and customs of those he encounters comes in the second half of the opening scene, when Oedipus learns from an unnamed citizen of Colonus that he has taken a seat in the grove of the dread goddesses (Furies, Erinyes, Eumenides—they have many names and yet often go unnamed, just referred to as the Dread Ones). For the citizen of Colonus his presence there is a violation: the Eumenides are divinities so powerful that one must not even speak out loud in the vicinity of their sacred grove, much less walk into it and sit down. They are ancient earth goddesses whose role is to bring punishment to humans who commit the most basic and intense of crimes: violation of the natural, unalienable bonds between members of a family, the very basis of our common humanity. They are fierce and implacable—accepting no excuse, no explanation to moderate their punishment of violations in their sphere. For Oedipus, this grove is the place that he has known, from Apollo's prediction, would be the end of his journey, the place where finally he can rest. Here again is the riddle, now not on the level of human interactions with Oedipus but on the level of the rhythms and patterns outside human control that order the world: why would Oedipus, the greatest violator of family ties that we can imagine, find peace at last in the grove of the Eumenides?

What about Oedipus can make sense of this disparity between his past and his destined future? We learn later, from Ismene his daughter, who is the first visitor to approach Oedipus, that there is even more to this riddle. For Apollo has now prophesied that wherever Oedipus dies will be a source of eternal protection for the surrounding country, for whoever has accepted him and not asked him to move on. Here again the riddle: why is the polluted Oedipus to become a source of protection and safety for those willing to embrace him? And—looking beyond the ending of the play—what kind of protection does he offer, since his burial place in Colonus—the "bulwark" at the outskirts of Athens—has not kept the Athens of 402 BCE (when the play is first being performed, after Sophocles' death in 406) from devastating defeat at the hands of the Spartans? How then is the audience to understand the power that, in alliance with the divine world, Oedipus offers, which is so incongruent with his past story, his present state, and the imminent future of the audience watching the play?

The substance of these riddles plays out in two interweaving strands of action in the play. One corresponds to the riddle of the larger order: the transformation of Oedipus from helpless and blind old man when he first enters the stage to guide and authority at the end of the play, one whose place of death will have power after his death, as the object of a hero cult. This transformation is the mirror of, and answer to, the change that Oedipus undergoes from king to polluted being in the *Oedipus Tyrannus*, but now Oedipus is a knowing participant, in harmony with the rhythm of the transformation, which he knows will happen in its own time. The other strand is played out in the interaction between Oedipus and all those who come into contact with him, as he sits on his rock in the middle of the stage. Through these encounters, unfolding in the uncertain immediacy of the moment, what becomes possible is an understanding of a human order that can take account of Oedipus' paradoxical power. For example, the citizen of Colonus, who approaches Oedipus and Antigone as soon as they have settled in the grove, is the first to be tested by his presence. His response to the violation of the grove shows the kind of order he lives by. Despite all appearance he understands he must consult with all the citizens of Colonus before deciding what to do with Oedipus: "Stay there, / there where you first appeared, while I / go to the citizens (who live *here*, not in the city) / and tell them what's happened. For they will decide / to take you in or send you away" (89–93 / 77–80). This citizen, despite his knowledge of the inviolability of the grove, knows the appropriate rhythm of judgment he must demonstrate in response to Oedipus' intrusion: as a citizen, he cannot act without the rest of the citizen body—no matter how obvious it is that Oedipus is where he should not be.

THE CHORUS

When that body of citizens arrive, in the form of the Chorus, they can claim with appropriate authority that Oedipus must move in order for them to talk to him, and Oedipus, on the basis of his openness to what is taught to him by the inhabitants of whatever place he comes to, can put in abeyance the knowledge that he belongs in the grove, to comply with their demand. Here, too, the different rhythms are in harmony, with Oedipus moving between his own understanding and that of the Chorus, but Sophocles dramatizes vividly the difficulty in that harmony by the excruciating slowness and effort with which Oedipus moves from the rock where he has placed himself within the grove to the rock at its edge, where the Chorus has insisted he sit to speak with them. It is only when, at their insistence, Oedipus reveals his identity that he becomes a test for the Chorus; having accepted the anonymous beggar as a suppliant, they now want to drive Oedipus away.

The Chorus is not, in Sophoclean tragedy, responsible for developing the action of the play, but rather reflects on that action from their perspective, as interpreters through the particular medium of song and dance of what they see. From their perspective, the story they have always heard of Oedipus' past makes his presence among them intolerable. Oedipus responds on their level, on the level of story and reputation, to question the validity of Athens' reputation as a city that accepts strangers, if the Chorus demands that he leave:

> Then what's become of reputation? What good is
> a good name if it fades like morning dew?
> What good is it if Athens stands alone, as they say,
> a god-fearing city—alone able to save
> the sick, afflicted stranger. Where is the good in this for me,
> seeing—since my name alone makes you tremble—
> you'll drag me from this sanctuary here
> and drive me away? (275–82 / 258–65)

Because of Oedipus' challenge to the Chorus to live up to the way their city is spoken of, to be consistent with the laws and customs it is known for, the Chorus agrees to summon Theseus—the legendary king of Athens—to make a decision about Oedipus. As the figure whose action will represent Athens, what he does will reveal how Athenian law can, through actions based on the judgments it allows, respond to the riddle of Oedipus.

But the Chorus throughout the play articulates another level of order, one that is abstracted from the mechanics of decision and action and creates in song and dance a kind of understanding that mediates between the human and divine worlds. As a body, the Chorus, though characterized as older citizens of Colonus, is separated from the actors not only by performing exclusively in the orchestra, the circular area between the stage and the seats of the audience, but also by their form of expression: dance and choral song. While the Chorus leader interacts with the characters in speech, when the Chorus performs as a whole it is always in the form of sung lyrics and movement that follows the rhythm of the song. Their mode of expression and their language, in both form and content, remove the play's events from the contingency of the moment. This way of responding to Oedipus is first illustrated in the instructions that the Chorus leader gives Oedipus so that he can perform a ritual of purification for his violation of the grove. In his detailed account of each step in the ritual, the Chorus leader describes a series of actions abstracted from human choice, feeling, and even understanding, but nonetheless meaningful in relation to the divine power of the Eumenides and Oedipus' violation, as the Chorus understands it, of their grove.

In their next four songs, when they lead Oedipus to tell the story of his past, or sing a hymn to Athens that represents the city in terms of its gods, their gifts to the city, and its natural beauty, or describe the battle between Theseus and Creon over the possession of Antigone and Ismene as a battle of right against wrong, or describe the misery that Oedipus' life represents as a headland beaten by waves from every direction, the Chorus transforms the ever-changing, continuous struggle of human action into language whose rhythms, sound, and descriptive power create an ordered, self-contained poetic narrative with a formal integrity that is the closest humans can come to an expression of a permanent order. This, then, is the way the Chorus responds to the challenge of Oedipus' presence. They leave the decision of what to do to Theseus, but they incorporate Oedipus' story and Athens' story into an order of their own, in the rhythms and movement of their song and dance. Within the context of the action and the choices the other characters are engaged in, the limit of the Chorus' order is apparent in their restriction to the space of the orchestra and the movements of dance. But what they express in their dance and song is an essential dimension of the way humans make sense of their world.

EPISODES

In between the Chorus' songs, the episodes dramatize the arrival of four visitors, each in his or her own way drawn to respond to Oedipus' presence in Athens. Very roughly, they fall into categories of friends and enemies. Ismene and Theseus give Oedipus what he needs to survive out of genuine feeling for him and a deep understanding of what the laws they live by demand of them. Polyneices and Creon come to gain control of Oedipus' power for their own ends, although they present themselves as acting out of pity for Oedipus' suffering and in his interest and argue on the basis of positive norms of behavior. In each case Oedipus both interprets and judges these characters' actions, culminating in the violent curse he places on his son—a curse that poses the deepest challenge to the audience's understanding of Oedipus' judgment. As we watch each encounter, we see the complexity of each character's response to Oedipus, in the incongruity between the way the laws of society order their behavior and the way that Oedipus, from the perspective he describes in the prologue, responds to them. This series of comings and goings, all centered on the question of where Oedipus belongs, creates a kind of dramatic fugue that plays out the various rhythms by which we live, rhythms created by the interplay of feeling, understanding, experience, and values.

At the center of these visitations is Creon's forceful removal of Antigone and Ismene and Theseus' return of them. This self-contained and unique action at the heart of the play has no apparent consequence: they are taken and returned within the course of two hundred lines or so, and there is no lasting effect of their departure. But it is another manifestation of the rhythms of loss and gain, strength and impotence, departure and return, violation and restoration, which represent Sophocles' understanding of what human experience must be. The rhythm of loss and restoration that Creon's abduction of the two women dramatizes mirrors on the level of human action the mysterious and divinely orchestrated transformation of Oedipus, from his entrance as a wandering beggar at the beginning of the play to his departure "home," summoned by a god, at the end.

In the first episode Ismene arrives to tell Oedipus of the oracles that make explicit the nature of the gift he offers to those who take him in and to bring him news of his two sons' struggle for the throne of Thebes. Her traveling alone through the countryside to find Oedipus is an absolute violation of the behavior appropriate to an unmarried woman, as is Antigone's wandering, which the care of her father requires. In fact, when Creon comes, he throws in Oedipus' face the debasement of the two women in the eyes of the world as an argument for Oedipus' return to Thebes. But Oedipus' judgment of his daughters and of his sons reveals the difficulty of basing one's choice of how to behave on social norms. He addresses his daughters about his sons:

> Ach, those two! In their nature, in their way of life,
> they mimic Egyptian habits. For the men of Egypt
> sit indoors weaving, while their wives
> go out every day in the world
> to provide what they need. So here you both are,
> while those fit for the task do housework
> like maids. The two of you do their work, this hard work—
> caring for my suffering self. (370–77 / 337–45)

Oedipus here claims that his children's behavior is uniquely counter to Greek social norms by evoking the "counter culture" of Egypt, which the Greeks viewed as a mirror image of their own society. By so doing he exposes the provisional nature of a judgment based solely on social norms, since in Egypt the children's behavior would be normal. Oedipus' comparison raises a further complication: from another perspective Antigone and Ismene are doing exactly what is expected of Greek women, caring for their male relation, while Eteocles and Polyneices are pursuing their political ambitions, exactly what would be expected of them as Greek men. By this comparison Oedipus wishes to condemn his sons for "staying at home" and pursuing their own interests and to praise his daughters for their courage in wandering the world to take care of him. If we understand his words simply on the level of social norms they fail to achieve his purpose, as they equate his sons and his daughters in the violation of those norms, and they also point to the ways in which his children are, in fact, meeting, not violating, expectations of behavior. It is clear, then, that when Oedipus uses Egypt to point to the "alien" behavior of his children, he is judging them not on the basis of a social order, the standards of which are relative and ambiguous, but on the basis of values that he does not or cannot at this point articulate but that become clear by the end of the play.

A similar complexity is involved in trying to understand and judge Theseus' and Creon's interactions with Oedipus. The two men can, from one perspective, be seen as examples of good and bad men in positions of power. Theseus' unquestioning acceptance of Oedipus and his offer of protection and a home amply fulfill Athens' reputation as an open society, able to find a place for whoever comes there. His controlled handling of Creon's abduction of Antigone and Ismene attests to his diplomacy and careful use of force, especially in contrast to Creon's provocative rhetoric and rash violence. Yet Theseus, by accepting

Oedipus into Athens, establishes Thebes as a future enemy, a chilling reminder, for the audience of the play, of the war that has ended in Athenian defeat. And Creon, who is, on the surface, a shameless seeker after his own advantage, is acting on behalf of his city and at their request to bring Oedipus back as Thebes' protector, a city that can legitimately lay claim to his loyalty as his mother city, a city that in the *Oedipus Tyrannus* he destroyed himself to save. Even Oedipus' fury at Thebes' intention to settle him only on the boundary of the city, not on Theban soil, is hard to understand from the perspective of one kind of order, since there is no denying the fact that he is guilty of incest and patricide and is therefore a polluted being whose presence on his native soil is forbidden by law.

In all of these conflicting perspectives, or ways of ordering action, Oedipus moves with a kind of moral certainty, even as he is engaged in the ebb and flow around him. First, he explains in detail the incorrectness of the Chorus', and later Creon's, understanding of his past actions. The self-blame that led him, at the time of his discovery of those crimes, to blind himself has been replaced by a clear-sighted understanding of his own essential innocence, grounded in his ignorance of what he was doing. This self-understanding does not make him any less aware that he is a polluted being—he does almost forget when he tries to take Theseus' hand, but he then stops himself, Sophocles' clever way of dramatizing his awareness. But it does allow Oedipus to draw a distinction between an internal state and an external one, the first dependent on his own sense of himself, the second determined by the laws and judgments of society.

When Creon tries to shame him into returning to Thebes by depicting him as one who can never escape his crimes, whose presence in the world is an affront to others, he tries to persuade not only Oedipus but the Chorus and the audience to see Oedipus as the sum of his actions and what people say about them. For a character in a play, and for the Greeks of this time, that definition of what constitutes a person is not obviously inadequate. Like characters in a play, who can be known only by what they do and say in front of an audience, Athenians thought of themselves as fully defined by the way others viewed their actions and received their words. Oedipus' insistence on something like a conscience, achieved over long years by learning to draw a distinction between who he is and what he has done, between the identity society gives him and his sheer physical existence in the world, is the center of his moral authority. The notion of an internal monitor, guided by the integration of thought, feeling, and action—a sense of a person's moral self separate from conformity to the laws and expectations established by society—is a new development in the Greeks' sense of the individual, one to be fully realized only in the next century by Socrates' student, Plato. But it is at the heart of Sophocles' intuition in this play about the gift that Oedipus has to offer Athens, and the *Oedipus at Colonus* has to offer its audience.

Even Theseus, whose immediate acceptance of Oedipus, based on his own experience as an exile, seems to reveal a man of deep understanding, shows the limit of his point of view in comparison to Oedipus. He concludes his acceptance of Oedipus with the words "For I know / I'm a man, and know / I've no greater claim on tomorrow than you" (627–29 / 567–68). Here he shows an understanding of the relative extent of his own power, an understanding that leads him immediately to want to protect the suppliant Oedipus. But later, when Oedipus warns him that this acceptance will bring his city into conflict with Thebes, at this time Athens' close ally, Theseus cannot understand how that could come about. His belief in the permanence of the laws of his city and the alliances it constructs with other cities prevents him from seeing the same limit to his city's power that he sees in himself. Yet for the audience, in their current political situation, that limit is all too distressingly apparent. This incomprehension evokes from Oedipus one of the great speeches of the play, in which he points out to Theseus the inevitable pattern of change and transformation that underlies all aspects of human life and that goes to the heart of the limit of human power:

> Dearest son of Aegeus, none but the gods
> escape old age and death; all else
> time in its relentless flood sweeps away.
> The strength of earth and of the body fades,
> trust dies and distrust flourishes,
> and the same spirit never endures
> between friend and friend, city and city.
> For some now, for others later,
> joy becomes bitter, then bitterness joy.   (671–79 / 607–15)

Essential, then, to the kind of understanding Oedipus has, giving him the ability to judge both himself and others, is an awareness of the fundamental impermanence of the natural and constructed world in which humans live. In the face of that impermanence, the challenge is to find the solid ground on which to base the choices we make and the actions we perform. Oedipus' understanding of change and loss does not make him *feel* the loss any less—when Antigone and Ismene are taken from him he is in despair—but it gives him an unerring sense of how actions conform to and violate the rhythms that constitute the fragile fabric of human order. A man who has wandered without a home for years, who has believed himself the son of two different sets of parents, who has been the savior and destroyer of his city, he makes manifest, in his unmoving position on his rock, the certainty that arises out of radical uncertainty, the capacity to know the continuity in flux, and the moral understanding that the endless years of living as an outcast in the eyes of the world with the knowledge of his own innocence has brought him.

His uncompromising moral sense emerges clearly and shockingly in his encounter with his son. In Oedipus' explanation to Theseus of the wrong Polyneices has done to him, he describes not only the way his sons did nothing to prevent his exile—a fate that the Greeks viewed as a living death—but argues that the timing of the exile was a particular affront because it violated the change in his own understanding of his guilt, which the passage of time had brought him. As he came to see that his guilt was only to have physically committed the acts of murder and incest, not to have worked knowingly for the destruction of his parents, the limit of his blame became clear to him, and he no longer felt the need to go into exile. He was content to remain isolated in his own home. The city's move to exile him, and his sons' passivity, took no account of his changed understanding. Oedipus' sense of the proper timing of things is another aspect of his understanding of the natural rhythm of change as a manifestation of an unchanging order, and it is through Oedipus that we understand something of what it means to be in tune with both.

When Ismene brings him word of the oracle's prediction of the value of his tomb, he says: "So when I am no longer, then I'm a man?" (428 / 393), pointing to the paradoxical disparity between what humans consider the "prime of life" and that other rhythm his life illustrates. His sense of urgency about Theseus' arrivals throughout the play is the product of his knowledge that the moment when he can reveal the precise facts of his gift to Theseus is not within his control, while Theseus is fully immersed in the self-created rhythms of his political life. At the end of the play the thunder and lightning and the voice of a god saying "Why / do we put off our departure like this? What / a long delay you're making!" (1800–1802 / 1627–28) are dramatic manifestations of that larger order at work in Oedipus' life. The human experience of that rhythm is the passage of time—"the long companionship of time," as Oedipus says in his opening speech—which for someone like Oedipus has brought a fuller sense of the meaning of his actions. He charges both

Creon and Polyneices with violating that rhythm, Creon when he offers to take him back to Thebes, long after his desire to do so has disappeared, and Polyneices when he allowed his exile, although Oedipus understood that it was no longer a necessity.

But Oedipus' cursing of Polyneices is based not only—not largely, even—on Polyneices' ignorance of the changes that time brings, although Polyneices himself points to his guilt here: "To my shame I've come too late / to see all this.... But since Compassion / shares the throne with Zeus in all he does, / let her stand beside you also, father— / for the wrongs that are done have some cure / and they're over now, there'll be no more of them" (1385–93 / 1264–70). His claim that the damage is reparable perhaps indicates the shallowness of his understanding of the rhythm of change, but Polyneices' real crime is his violation of the one unchanging, inalienable fact of human existence: the relationships of blood. They are the only thing that neither time nor circumstance nor human will can change, as Oedipus discovered to his enormous cost as a young man when his true parentage was revealed to him. What Oedipus sees is that Polyneices' knowing repudiation of his father to secure his own political future removes from Polyneices the only unchanging reality a human being has: the bond of children to those who gave them life. This violation is unforgivable in Oedipus' eyes because that unchanging relationship provides a stability that is the basis of human order and moral understanding.

The strongest challenge to Oedipus' point of view comes from his daughter Antigone: "he is your child; show him / some understanding. Other men have bad children / and feel deep anger; but rebuked / by the gentle appeals of those dear to them, / they soften their hearts" (1312–16 / 1192–1194). Although Antigone's plea for compassion is enough to persuade Oedipus to allow Polyneices into his presence, it has no power to stop Oedipus from cursing him. Here finally we understand why Oedipus belongs in the grove of the Eumenides, the unforgiving goddesses who punish violation of family bonds. Oedipus puts a human face on that absolute judgment, one that comes from his deepest understanding of the impermanence of human existence and the moral need for humans, living within the flux of things, to keep their bearings by paying attention to the one unchanging fact of our existence. Oedipus' earlier discovery, despite his lived experiences, of the ineluctable truth of his true parentage and the profound disorientation that resulted from his (unwilling) ignorance of that truth, makes him deeply aware of the way it must anchor people's experience; his years of wandering, living in the constant movement of exile, have taught him the enormous difficulty of being fully human in the world without that anchor. It is the combination of living through the two extremes of these experiences that makes him uniquely able to judge the way others deal with the tension between the stability and change of a human life. The episodes, which bring the Citizen of Colonus, Ismene, Antigone, Theseus, and Creon within the sphere of Oedipus' judgment, culminate in this encounter between father and son. Oedipus obliterates the kind of future for himself that men try to gain through their sons in order to secure for Athens his guiding spirit. He condemns his son to death for the failure to establish for himself the necessary moral framework in which to act—based on an understanding of what cannot change and what must change—and he bequeaths to Athens the protection of his own understanding.

SOPHOCLES' GIFT TO ATHENS

Oedipus' sense of the inviolability of the blood relationship of child to parent may give him the power of a Fury, but the protection that Oedipus will offer Athens after his death comes not from that power alone but from the combination of impotence and power that makes him so paradigmatically human. That impotence is manifest not only in his beggarly appearance, blindness, and dependence, but also in the moment of his greatest power, when he curses his son. Although Oedipus' language has the force to make believable that his curse will be fulfilled (as we know from myth and from Sophocles' *Antigone*, it is), he does not have control over all the consequences of that curse. After the curse, Antigone and Polyneices have a conversation in which Antigone tries to persuade Polyneices not to pursue the war against his brother. Polyneices, as if already bound by the curse, can see no alternative to walking straight into the disaster he knows awaits him at Thebes. In this moment he provides an interesting contrast to his father in the *Oedipus Tyrannus*, who, when he received an oracle saying he would kill his father and marry his mother, did everything he could to avoid what the oracle predicted and later pursued indefatigably the truth of what he had done. Polyneices' willingness knowingly to sacrifice his army and allies, while keeping them in ignorance, subtly offers evidence for the connection between his treatment of his father and his moral helplessness. He is unable to know the moment when he must act in keeping with, or in defiance of, the opportunities that present themselves. But he does ask Antigone to bury his body after he is killed, and Antigone promises to do so. She thus binds herself to the fate we see played out in the *Antigone*, which Sophocles deliberately evokes here. So Oedipus' curse on his son is the indirect but nonetheless effectual cause of Antigone's death; yet on the very grounds he curses his son he wishes absolutely to protect his daughter. This he cannot do. The combination of Polyneices' passivity in the face of his father's anger, Antigone's will to act out of her love for her family (the mirror image of Polyneices' weakness), and her move away from the protecting influence of Oedipus' cult at Athens back to Thebes, with which the play ends, are all part of the web of change and flux in human life that will continue after Oedipus' death and that he cannot stop or control.

But the most vibrant and constant evidence of Oedipus' extraordinary combination of weakness and strength, and of his awareness of the double rhythm of the human and divine order, comes from his language, as is only fitting in a form of theater that was as dependent on the spoken word as Greek theater was. Oedipus has an extraordinary range of expression: from inarticulate cry to authoritative argument, from song to speech, from command to pleading, from curse to blessing, from expressions of hatred to those of love, from anger to gratitude, from teaching to questioning. And beyond this he shows a clear understanding of a kind of speech that outlasts the moment of speaking (which perhaps is of particular importance for the effect that Sophocles hopes to create with the performance of the play itself). This kind of speech is embodied in the secret words that he passes on to Theseus, which he promises will teach "things / which age can never spoil" (1673–74 / 1519), words that are to be repeated only once in a lifetime, when Theseus, and then another in each generation, passes them on at the moment of death. It is embodied in the curse, which will work its power long after the words themselves have faded. And it is to be found in Oedipus' words that outlast his death, as the Messenger reproduces his final speech to his daughters as a direct quote rather than reported speech, thus re-creating Oedipus' voice after his death and perpetuating the power of his speech.

In Oedipus' mouth that most provisional and momentary act, the act of spoken communication (it is important to remember that this tragedy was composed to be viewed only once) has also a permanence that defies the fragility of sound. What is common to the whole range of Oedipus' expression is its authority, the sense that the language comes from the depth of his understanding and the integrity of his thought, feeling, and action. It is unlike the speech of all the other characters in the play, whose words inevitably reveal also their limits. Ismene, for example, will not tell of her experience in traveling to find Oedipus because she does not want to experience the pain of it again. Antigone speaks consistently and exclusively out of her feeling for her father and her brother and is persuasive and effective as far as that feeling goes, but her speech (and her action) expresses no other dimension of character. Theseus, too, is limited in the range of what he can express, as his speech always conforms to his political consciousness and the role he must play within the polis. Polyneices fears to speak at all without some indication of his father's goodwill. When Antigone persuades him to speak despite Oedipus' silence, he delivers a plea to Oedipus to become his ally in the form of a catalogue of the six other leaders who have joined him in his attack on Thebes. On many levels this catalogue betrays the poverty of Polyneices' language: although it is a standard part of the story of the "Seven against Thebes," it is strangely out of place here, when Poly-neices' appeal to Oedipus cannot be made on the basis of an "epic" portrayal of the battle he is about to fight; the audience knows that all six leaders die at Thebes, so it also sounds like an epitaph before the fact; and for Oedipus, so far removed for years from the context in which these names would have meaning, it is meaningless. Like his sense that he has no choice but to fulfill his father's curse, this speech marks Polyneices' disorientation from the moral necessity of the moment.

The most striking contrast to Oedipus' speech comes from Creon, whose insincerity is apparent from the moment he opens his mouth. Since Ismene has given Oedipus and the audience the information that Creon will be coming to try to inveigle Oedipus back to Thebes—not to bring him home but to control his power on Thebes' border—Creon's words are judged from the start by that knowledge. All the arguments he uses—his appeal to Oedipus' loyalty to Thebes, his claims of respect for Athens, his sense of shame about Antigone's and Oedipus' state, and his desire to hide them away in their home—are all colored by the irony created by his hiding his true motive and our knowing it. Polyneices, by contrast, who comes for the same reason, is quite open about his motivation: "Because—if we're to believe the oracles— / the power lies with those who have you / as their ally" (1460–62 / 1331–32). But Creon tries to gain this goal by the force of his entirely rhetorical arguments, and when they fail he resorts to force, the most definitive evidence of the emptiness of his words, in contrast to Oedipus'. (And his force turns out to be as empty as his words, when the kidnapping of the girls is reversed within minutes of its happening.)

Oedipus' words, by contrast, are untouched by this kind of irony, an irony that Sophocles used so effectively in the *Oedipus Tyrannus* to reveal the limit of Oedipus' understanding. Like the arc of Oedipus' transformation from helpless blind beggar to guide and benefactor of Athens, his language is able to reflect the full range of human experience and, beyond that, his double consciousness of the world of change in which humans live and that larger order with its own rhythm that humans only glimpse, in oracles and seemingly random interventions in the course of their lives.

The power that Oedipus' lived experience and understanding give his language is somehow captured in the Messenger's speech, which reports his last moments. Although the speech is a narrative of what took place, the account moves three times into direct quotation of Oedipus' words and once into quotation of a god's voice addressing Oedipus directly. By this means Sophocles draws an analogy—but only an analogy—between the human and divine voices. The first of Oedipus' words are addressed to Ismene and Antigone in response to their weeping:

> Children, on this day you have no father.
> All that was my life is destroyed on me now:
> You won't ever again have to labor for me
> or look after me as you've always done.
> I know, children, what a hard life it's been.
> But there's one thing can dispel it all,
> one word is enough to wipe hardship away:
> Love, that this man had for you—no man
> can love you more. And now the two of you
> must go on living the rest of your lives
> without him.   (1780–90 / 1611–19)

Oedipus acknowledges the pain both of the loss his death will bring to his daughters and the hardship that living in the world as he has done has caused them—the constant instability and struggle that is an extreme version of the flux of all human life. And he also offers them an expression of the one unchanging truth, the love their life together has created, which is the flip side of his hatred for his sons and their betrayal of that truth. In the second speech the Messenger quotes, he binds Theseus with a promise to do his utmost to protect his daughters: "give these children / the pledge of your hand" (1806–7 / 1632). Here his language acts, as it did in his curse, to overcome its impermanence and fashion a future beyond his death (which we know, from Antigone's story, cannot fully succeed—here is the limit of Oedipus' power). And finally, he orders his daughters to leave with the words "you must be brave now, / and go away from this place, / and not judge it right to see what's forbidden / or hear men say what must not be heard" (1817–20 / 1640–42). His final gift—the secret of his death place—belongs only to Theseus, the words that must not be spoken, that somehow come into contact with an order beyond the human, which human language can approach only by silence.

It is tempting to see the Messenger's report of Oedipus' words as a metaphor for Sophocles' gift to Athens on his death: this play. Sophocles knows that the life of his city will have to change, as all human forms must, and change perhaps radically with the end of the war. But his play captures not only what does not change—the bonds we create with each other that can and must be protected against violation—but also the way we can (with time, experience, character, and openness to the world of change, an ability to learn and listen) come to know simultaneously the rhythm of that change and the rhythm of what is beyond our comprehension but that we experience as "the steady sway of some shaping power" (1977 / 1779). And in the internalization of this knowledge, Oedipus, and the *Oedipus at Colonus*, give us the model for the constancy of self that survives every change in political and social fortune.

RACHEL KITZINGER

CONVENTIONS OF THE
ANCIENT GREEK THEATER

Much of the original experience of Sophocles' audience is lost in encountering a play like the *Oedipus at Colonus* in English instead of Greek and on the page instead of on the stage. Not only is a great deal communicated by the spatial relationships, the physical gestures, the vocal intonations of the actors and the Chorus, and the subtleties particular to the Greek language that are so different from those of English, but the conventions of the ancient theater are so different from our own that we cannot even be confident of the way our imaginations may provide the missing aspects of performance as we read. To orient readers to some aspects of the ancient theater that are particularly important for an understanding of this play, I include here a brief summary of the more important aspects of ancient theater production, as far as we can reconstruct them.

The plays performed in the city of Athens for the City Dionysia, as this one was, took place in the open-air theater of Dionysus, on the southern slope of the Acropolis in the spring. The festival was a great civic occasion, lasting five days. It included, among other things, three days of theatrical contest (or four when the city was not at war). On each of these three days a poet would present three tragedies and a satyr play, followed, in wartime, by a comedy written by a different poet. In times of peace, an extra day was added for the performance of the comedies. The fifteen plays presented in this way were performed once and once only. On very rare occasions a play would be awarded a rerun, sometimes years after its original single performance. The City Dionysia was attended by all sectors of the population of Athens, as well as visitors from elsewhere, and all civic business was suspended during the festival. The poets who competed in the festival were thought of as teachers, and the plays performed were an important element in the creation of Athenian civic identity.

Although the stone structures of the theater of which one can still see some remains date from a period later than the performances of the fifth century, the basic elements of the fifth-century theater, which were made of wood, can be largely reconstructed. The seats for the audience of 15,000 to 17,000 climbed up the south slope of the Acropolis in a semi-circular arrangement. At the base of the seats, on ground level, was the circular orchestra, which may have had an altar at its center. This was the space in which the Chorus performed. There is more uncertainty about the space used by the actors. A likely probability—but only that—is that the actors moved freely between the orchestra and a slightly raised rectangular stage, impinging on the orchestra on its southern edge. Behind the stage rose the skene, which provided the backdrop for the action. We know nothing of the form of the skene at this point in its evolution except that it was a wooden building with a central doorway and a flat roof from which actors, especially those appearing as gods, could deliver lines. In most plays the skene represents a palace, and the central door is one of three ways of entering and exiting the stage. The other two are the *eisodoi*, passageways on stage right and left, between the skene and the edge of the seating. In any given play the right and left *eisodoi* are consistently associated with the direction to different places relevant to the play. In the *Colonus*, for example, one *eisodos* leads to Thebes, the other to Athens, and the central door represents the pathway into the grove of the Eumenides.

These are the basic elements of the physical theater. There was no lighting—performances took place in daylight—and minimal scenery (what there was took the form of painted panels that could be applied to the front of the skene to change it from a palace to another venue). In the *Colonus*, paintings probably transformed the skene into the grove of the Eumenides. Other objects can also help to set the scene. In this play, for example, the statue of the horseman Colonus would have marked the whole theatrical space as Colonus; in addition, there would have been two rock seats for Oedipus, one right up against the skene, which would be understood to be in the grove, the other at the edge of the stage, which would be understood to be just outside the grove. For this play marking those boundaries for the audience is important; these kind of emblematic spatial arrangements are an important dynamic that props create in the ancient theater.

The abstracted physical symbol that the stage can become even stretches, to a certain extent, to the physical presence of the actors. The theater is so large that audience members sitting in the back reaches of the theater are seeing tiny figures below them, over a hundred yards away. Clearly, the effect of the play does not depend on the audience's being able to read minute shifts in body language and facial expression to project the complex idiosyncrasies of a personality, as Western theatrical experience leads us to expect. The actors on the Athenian stage wore masks and elaborately decorated costumes that often covered the whole body. This allowed the three male actors who made up the speaking cast to play multiple roles, both male and female. In this play, for example, the third actor probably came on as the Citizen, Ismene, Theseus, Creon, and Polyneices. In this theatrical situation the words each character delivers give that character a very specific and articulated presence, but the physical appearance is, to a large degree, "generic." The resulting combination lends characters in Greek tragedy compelling paradigmatic force: they are both textured and particular enough to be emotionally compelling, but they are also people involved in making decisions and acting them out in a process and with consequences that any member of the audience—and particularly the male citizens—can see as instructive. Since the setting of the play is almost without exception in the mythical past, and the plot is derived from myth and therefore, in general outline, known to the audience, the experience that the audience has is not derived from the unfolding of the plot per se. Rather, the intensity of the language and the conflicts it plays out combined with the critical distance inherent in the physical circumstances of the theater and the focus on the mythical past creates a theatrical experience that excites, through the imagination, both feeling and thought. The effect of this experience has real consequence for the audience members' understanding of the role they must play in the running of a civic society.

The language of the play was also far from the kind of realistic communication that we are used to. Exchanges between actors are composed in an iambic rhythm, a regular alternation of syllables of shorter and longer duration, usually twelve syllables to a line. Since Greek also had a pitch accent, the sound of these rhythmic lines would to our ear seem more like chanting than conversational speech. The Chorus' songs (referred to as odes, or *stasima*) vary in their rhythms, almost all of which are taken from earlier choral lyric traditions. The fifteen Chorus members sing the odes, and their rhythms determine the choreography of the dance that the Chorus members perform as they sing. The songs were accompanied by a double-reed wind instrument, called an *aulos*, which had particular associations with the worship of the god Dionysus. The play is structured by an alternation between episodes delivered in the iambic rhythm, the poetic rhythm the Greeks considered closest to the rhythm of everyday speech, and choral odes, and were thus multimedia productions. Occasionally, the Chorus and an actor sing together, in responsion not unison (a *kommos*), or the actor performs a solo song. The Chorus leader also exchanges iambic lines with actors during the episodes. The language of tragedy—its diction and sentence formation—is, as far as we can tell, more stylized than that of everyday speech, although there are traditions familiar to the audience from their everyday life that influence tragic forms of speech—for example, arguments delivered in law courts or the public assembly and songs sung in celebration of a god or to accompany certain kinds of work or on ritual occasions such as weddings. The fact that most of the audience did not use a written form of language in the regular course of their lives and were therefore completely attuned to the spoken word made them sophisticated and subtle receivers of the complex poetic language in which the plays were composed.

The actors and the Chorus also, of course, used their bodies to communicate to the audience. Although they had to face the audience more or less frontally to project their voices to the back of the theater, the use of large, expressive gestures, choreography that mimed the images of the songs, the angles of the actors' heads and the subsequent shifts in shading on the mask, and the positioning of bodies in relation to each other had great iconic power in the physical space of the theater and created a dynamic complement to the effect of the words. In this play, for example, it is easy to imagine the communicative significance of the simple act of Oedipus' rising from the stone on which he has been sitting throughout the play and walking without help into the central door of the skene to the accompaniment of thunder (they used a thunder machine) to bring the play to its concluding moments.

Perhaps the greatest difference—among many—between this theater and many contemporary theatrical traditions is the function the plays performed in creating civic identity. The production was paid for by wealthy citizens as a form of taxation; the festival was run and carefully controlled by Athenian magistrates; various rules were established to ensure that the contest between the three playwrights who competed at the festival was as fair as possible; the judges who chose the winner were selected by lot from citizenship rolls; young male citizens performed as the choruses of the plays; and the penalty for anyone disrupting or corrupting the festival's procedures was death. Why did the city expend so much energy on what is to us a form of entertainment? Not only was the theater festival a form of worship of the god Dionysus and thus had strong religious dimensions to it, but the content of the plays drama-tized, in a mythical setting, contemporary issues that were very important for citizens and others members of the community of Athens to think about and debate. The combination of the emotional power of the plays and the formal and abstract qualities of their production effectively engaged the audience in a unique combination of emotional and intellectual turmoil that generated serious thought and debate. The conflicts of the plays revolve around issues that were essential for members of the community to struggle to understand and to debate with each other. The familiarity of the stories, which formed both the informal and formal basis of every citizen's education, gave the audience the opportunity to encounter themselves and rethink their collective identity. And the ambiguities and unresolved conflicts, the ironies and multiple points of view that the play gives voice to gave the citizens whose decisions and actions governed the state—and its empire—an intense awareness of the difficult process of taking action in complex human situations.

RACHEL KITZINGER

ON THE TRANSLATION

> Theoretically, it is impossible. One has to try.
> W. H. AUDEN, on translation

Translators should probably say nothing about their work, since whatever they say will most likely sound defensive or, at best, like special pleading. Ideally, the translation should speak for itself, embodying the translator's particular "theories" (too specific a word for what are so often ad hoc determinations, choices of a moment and determined by many factors, including personal taste and linguistic capacity), rather than making them explicit. For if they are explicit they open themselves distractingly to opposition and/or dismissal as either betraying the original in unforgivable ways or as simply inadequate. Still, a little foreword is probably useful, if only to suggest that the translation has been performed by someone with opinions and certain commitments, and not by a value-neutral machine.

Echoing the title of a poem by Yeats ("The Fascination of What's Difficult"), one of the most accomplished and satisfying modern translators of the *Oedipus at Colonus* speaks of "the fascination of what is, strictly speaking, impossible." (One has only to consider the dynamically operatic pitch- and cadence-play of the original Greek, impossible to duplicate in English, to recognize the truth of this more or less universal sentiment.) What Robert Fitzgerald (whose edition of the play first appeared in 1941, revised 1956) was referring to was the translator's obligation to write in "the English of Sophocles," remembering, I guess, Holderlin's pithy ambition as a translator of Pindar, "to write Greek in German." This present version tries to perform the same impossible task. For me, it has been a task made easier (if no less impossible) by the fact that it is the result of a collaboration with Rachel

Kitzinger, whose exacting lexical and semantic scrupulosity, as well as her scholarly and practical knowledge of the play's language, dramaturgy, and relevant contexts made it possible or at least more plausible for me, lacking knowledge of the language, to attempt this task of translation (what Ezra Pound calls "a thankless and desolate undertaking") in the first place.

What Rachel and I have tried for is a readable and, more important, a speakable text. In doing that, we have not wanted a transformation into a contemporary colloquial manner—inventing an English that would be out of tune with the plain dignity and rhythmic buoyancy, speed, and at the same time solidity of the original. Instead, we have sought an idiomatic English without either antiquarian effects, on the one hand, or too contemporary, colloquial a feel, on the other. To speak only for myself, my purpose was to remain as true as I could to what she offered as the literal (and/or possible) meanings of the words, the lines, and the speeches, while at the same time trying to enact these meanings in an English that had the capacity to be plain, blunt, passionate, and lyrical by turns: to be an instrument capable of conducting an exchange of information, managing an outburst of anger or grief, directing a narrative tale. In addition, I wanted it to be capable of ascending in as natural a manner as possible to a register of something nearer song or chant than "ordinary" speech—as it has to do (in different ways) in the choruses and in those various moments where, in Sophocles' text, the characters themselves shift from the register of speech to that of metrical song.

And while I might have imagined an Irish-accented countryman speaking the lines of the Citizen at the start and the Messenger at the end, and imagined a smoothly (if sinisterly) fluent Creon, a solidly rational Theseus, a young, "heroic," and confused Polyneices, an emotionally quick and sympathetic Antigone, a chorus more tense and ritualized than any character, and an Oedipus as volatile in his self-certain mood swings as Lear or Prospero, none of these imaginings (phantom voices in my head) prompted me to turn any of Sophocles' *personae* into an idiosyncratic speech manner. What I sought in the end was a language that might achieve a different level of rhythmic intensity as it moved from character to character and from episode to episode, neither ascending to too-obviously rhetorical heights nor descending into overly colloquial, contemporary familiarity. In that way, I hoped that anyone who had to speak the lines on stage or radio would feel neither embarrassment nor disgust. The intention was to compose a "literary script" capable of being competently acted or read with pleasure.

I have not, however, tried to make the choral odes, epodes, or the choral dialogues "songs" in any overt way. (Although an imaginative composer/choreographer could perhaps give the odes, in particular, some effective musical accompaniment. Yeats' Chorus, for example, with anachronistic Yeatsian bravura, chanted in the Gregorian mode.) While Fitzgerald reluctantly chose rhyme and/or regularly patterned stanzas to do this work for him, this seemed to me to sacrifice the strangeness and speed of the Greek to a very different and more light-weight (and over-regulated) kind of lyrical effect. And Robert Fagles' choice (in his 1982 edition) to give the choruses an obviously lyrical *content*, but in free-verse lines that have little appeal to the ear, also seems to me to miss something of the Greek effect, its rhythmic and sonic sense of ritualized utterance. What I have done is try to make the expression of these parts of the play different in effect from the various extended speeches and stichomythic passages. I have done this by giving them what I hope is a more pronounced lyrical feel and rhythmic presence than the roughly iambic/roughly pentameter/roughly natural speech pattern of the rest. (I reiterate "roughly" here since I haven't tried anywhere in the play to establish a consistency of any English meter nor to duplicate the metrics of the original, either of which choices would ensure, at least for me, spectacular failure. In fact, in the latest drafts, I chose to loosen considerably the sense of the line, unsettling its—even phantom—iambic beat and lengthening or shorten-ing it as the sense and speech occasion seemed to demand.) In the choral parts of the play, however (whether belonging solely to the Chorus or shared with one or more characters), I have tried to enhance the sense of the rhythmic unit of the *line*, whereas in the passages of speech the rhythmic sense of the line is more absorbed—though I hope not too diluted—by the sense units of the *sentences*. This accounts in the "song" passages for the deliberate elimination of most punctuation, for the lines being slightly indented, and for their being set in italics. The aim, whatever the outcome, was to give a separate rhythmic feel to these choral utterances (and to those passages where, in the original, the characters move into metric song), thinking this might help the director of a production (whether a performance on stage or on radio) to realize this unique and, for a contemporary audience, perhaps strangest ele-ment in the drama as a whole.

One other choice needs a brief word. Whenever I read a translation of a Greek play, I always feel that the expressions of passionate distress (in Greek, *oimoi, oimoi talaina, pheu pheu*, and other such ejaculations), which seem to me simply full-throated utterances of emotion—acoustic units of pure feeling rather than explicitly semantic units—are clumsily rendered by phrases such as "Alas!" or "Misery!" or even "Oh!" or "Ah!" or some variants of these. So to translate *oimoi* as "Alas!" in fact weakens rather than strengthens the emotional effect, makes bland and prissily mannered what should be passionate, unleashed, extra-lexical. English is peculiarly poor in these ejaculative bits of diction—words that are emotive sounds. (Only in comic books, the convention being intact, do they appear with any frequency or conviction—where Ugh!, Aaargh!, and so on are part of the convention.) In her translation of the *Electra*, Ann Carson deals with this problem by leaving such utterances (often in that play the cries and screams of its heroine) in their Greek form. While we found this an interesting strategy, and not without theatrical possibility, such a choice finally seemed too arbitrary, the sudden invasion of the English text by these Greek words too unnatural, too much of the wrong kind of surprise. The choice we came to, therefore, was two fold: to substitute a stage direction at these points, stating With *a loud groan* or With *a cry of terror* or With *a wail of despair* and following it with a more or less innocuously generic *Ohhh!* or *Aaahhh!* Each of these then needs to be, in performance, rhythmically integrated into the relevant passage. This passes on to the actor and director the task of inventing the particular register of vocal utterance to fit the particular moment, one that belongs to the production in question. The reader, meanwhile, is not irritated by the use of old-fashioned locutions such as "Alack!" or "Alas!" That, at least, is the intention. As with other aspects of translation, it is at best an imperfect solution to a problem that seems, finally, insoluble.

When Ezra Pound speaks (in the *Cantos*) of "the hard Sophoclean light," he refers both to meanings (those poignantly difficult truths enunciated and, more generally, summoned into being by the plays in their text and performance) and to style. For all the interrogative shadows inherent in its moral implications, there is always an unflinching clarity in Sophocles' expression, a clarity of expression that lets us experience not only the most difficult human facts of physical, earthbound existence—hate, betrayal, and violence as well as love, loyalty, and tenderness—but also the ineffable, ineluctable presence of mystery. Of course, such "functional clarity" (as William Arrowsmith called it), in two plays centered on a blind man's painful pilgrimage into the light, is peculiarly appropriate both as theme and as medium. In the *Oedipus at Colonus* (a play that takes place in the here and now of last things; that begins with a particular question and ends with a universal assertion), both the mysterious and the mundane are equally bathed in this hard light, and it is something of this clarity that I've tried to convey in the translation. I am, in other words, trying to make sure that the language

I've used doesn't get in the way of the dramatic content by drawing undue attention to itself.

In Sophocles' text, moreover, such clarity endures despite a range and a fabric of allusion that form a large part of the play's texture and its semantic implication. Both Rachel Kitzinger and I agreed that these allusions should be held on to in the translated version and neither softened (by explanatory paraphrase) nor erased. Some glossing notes have been included to illuminate such of them (mainly proper names and places) as may especially darken the text for modern readers. We also decided to keep stage directions at a minimum, confining them to entrances, exits, and very occasionally a bare description of an action, where this is necessary to give the reader a minimal sense of what's taking place (when this may not be entirely clear from the text). Such a practice accorded with our sense that what we were providing was a text for readers, yes, but also a text that would be suitable for performance. Had we been over-explicit in our stage directions—attempting to indicate where and how any movements might take place, as well as how an actor might interpret any particular passage or moment—we would be getting in the way of the reader, whose imaginative response risked being limited to our interpretation. Furthermore, there are no surviving stage directions in the original, so any we might add would be of necessity interpretive and ill-suited to a play written under and out of such different theatrical conditions. We decided, therefore, that stage directions, beyond the most rudimentary, were not really our business but rightly the concern of a director interested in giving the play an effective contemporary staging. Our wish is to see the text as a thing in itself, capable of many actual renderings on the stage or in the mind. Being as spare as possible with such directions lets the play as a textual experience possess a fluency that would be damaged by the intrusion of too many and too fussy intrusions on the purely textual action. For this reason, too, we decided to confine to a note those headings that in some editions divide the play into its component Choral Odes—their strophes and antistrophes—and Episodes. Within the text itself, such divisions are only a distraction to the general reader, and without them the play flows much more efficiently and pleasingly as an organic unit.

There's always a collaborative aspect to translation (aside from the obvious one in this present case and in the series to which it belongs). One must take into account—either to quarrel with or to be confirmed by—some at least of one's predecessors. I have mentioned two modern translators whose versions I admire: those of Robert Fagles and Robert Fitzgerald. Although the formal and interpretive choices made by Rachel Kitzinger and me differ from theirs, often in crucial respects,

I still have to acknowledge—as someone knowing almost no Greek—the degree to which their translations became part of my own intellectual and imaginative fodder as a translator engaged in the same "strictly speaking, impossible task." Other nourishment was provided by the Loeb prose version by Hugh Lloyd-Jones and the nineteenth-century version by R. C. Jebb. The somewhat freer translation by Paul Roche (1959, revised 1991) was also one I returned to with interest, having admired it (and used it in the classroom) years ago. It remains a lively and imaginative rendering. I decided not to consult the version by Yeats, which is, if memory serves, too free to be useful, as well as, in terms of its rhetoric and its verse, too dominantly Yeatsian to be anything but a fatal temptation to my own ear. It is an enviable re-creation—not in "the English of Sophocles," however, but in that, most decisively, of Yeats.

In the end, a translation—indispensable as it may be—is only a version of the original ("versions of possibilities," as Hans Magnus Enzensberger has said). In some ways, it resembles the Messenger's speech in this play, attempting to present in a secondary language what defies explanation or adequate representation. Like the performance of a play or a piece of music, a translation is a "reading" of the given text, and as such is provisional, absolutely provisional. All one can hope for it is that it brings that foreign thing (script, score, text) somehow home to those who encounter it in the new medium, the new language. The Messenger's speech, after all, does let the old men of the Chorus share, at a distance, the ineffable, mysterious facts he has scrupulously witnessed. In our case, the hope is that this version in English brings home to those without Greek or to those English-speakers who may be students of Greek an experience that allows them to feel they have been brought into some enabling contact with the play: that they have had in the reading of it or in attending it as performance (aural or theatrical) some—otherwise unavailable—experience of its inexhaustible presence, sense, and meanings.

EAMON GRENNAN

This translation is based on the Greek text of the play edited by H. Lloyd-Jones and N. Wilson, published by Oxford University Press, 1990. In only a few instances have we chosen an alternate reading.

OEDIPUS AT COLONUS

Translated by

EAMON GRENNAN

and

RACHEL KITZINGER

CHARACTERS

OEDIPUS father and brother of Antigone, Ismene, Polyneices, and Eteocles; husband and son of Jocasta; former king of Thebes but now an exile

ANTIGONE daughter and sister of Oedipus who has accompanied him in his years of exile

STRANGER a citizen of Colonus

CHORUS of elderly citizens of Colonus

ISMENE sister and daughter of Oedipus who has remained in Thebes after Oedipus' exile

THESEUS legendary king of Athens

CREON brother of Jocasta, uncle and brother-in-law of Oedipus

POLYNEICES son and brother of Oedipus, brother of Ismene, Antigone, and Eteocles, son-in-law of King Adrastos of Argos

Line numbers in the right-hand margin of the text refer to the English translation only, and the Notes beginning at p. 405 are keyed to these lines. The bracketed line numbers in the running heads refer to the Greek text.

A grove near Athens, in the district of Colonus. Entrance, stage left, leads to Athens, entrance stage right to Thebes. The grove stretches across the back of the stage. A large unhewn rock lies just inside the grove. Toward the front of the stage there is a rock ledge. On one side stands an equestrian statue. From the direction of Thebes, enter OEDIPUS *slowly, leaning on* ANTIGONE, *both in ragged clothing. They stop at the unhewn rock in the grove.*

OEDIPUS What country is this? Antigone, child
of a blind old man: Whose city is it?
Who'll offer any pitiful gift today
to wandering Oedipus, the homeless man?
He asks little and gets less, though even less
than little is enough—since the long
companionship of time, and bitter trouble,
and beyond that the manner I was born to, teach me
to be easy with whatever happens. But child, if
    you find
any resting place on this traveled road   10
or in some grove set apart for the gods, lead me
and seat me in safety there, so we
may find out where we are. As strangers
we've learned how to listen to the natives of a place
and to act according to what we hear.

ANTIGONE Father, poor Oedipus, unhappy man:
I can see the roof-towers of the city a long way off,
but I'm sure this place we're in is holy ground.
It's thick with olive trees, laurel, and bending vines   20
and—listen!—nightingales—richly feathered
and filling the air with their sweet voices.
Rest yourself. Set down your body
on this rough rock. For old as you are
you've been a long time traveling.

OEDIPUS So . . . help me sit down. Mind the blind man!

                                    He sits on the rock.

ANTIGONE No need to tell me. Time has taught me that.

OEDIPUS Do you know then, and can *you* teach *me*
what this place is we've stopped in?

ANTIGONE I can't. But I know that's Athens over there.

OEDIPUS Yes. Everyone we met said *Athens . . . Athens*.   30

ANTIGONE Should I go and see what place this is?

OEDIPUS Do, child, if there's anyone living here.

ANTIGONE I'm sure there is. . . . But no need to go:
I see someone; he's not far off.

OEDIPUS Coming this way? Has he set out in our direction?

Enter STRANGER *(citizen of Colonus) from direction of
Athens.*

ANTIGONE He's here, father, right beside us. Now ask
whatever you think fitting for the moment. Here he is.

OEDIPUS Stranger, this woman, who is my eyes
as well as her own, says you've come looking
just in time to enlighten—   40

STRANGER Not another word! Get up from there—there where
you're sitting—
that's holy ground! It isn't lawful to walk there.

OEDIPUS What ground? And which gods? Whose sacred place?

STRANGER It mustn't be entered; no one can live there. It
belongs to
the Goddesses—the daughters of the earth, of
the dark!

338

OEDIPUS What's their name? I'd say a prayer to them if I
              heard it.

STRANGER Here we call them the all-seeing Eumenides. In
               other places
            they rightly have other names.

OEDIPUS May they look on their suppliant kindly—
            for I'll never leave this sanctified place.   50

STRANGER What's that you're saying?

OEDIPUS The password for what's to come.

STRANGER It's not for me to move you without permission from
               the city;
            first, I'll let them know what you're doing.

OEDIPUS For the gods' sake, stranger, beggar as I am—
            don't dishonor me by refusing what I ask.

STRANGER Ask then. I'll tell you what I can. I'll not
               dishonor you.

OEDIPUS What is this place we've come to?

STRANGER Listen, I'll tell you what I know. For one thing,
            every bit of this place is holy: 60
            Blessed Poseidon has a home here,
            and the god who brought us fire, the Titan
               Prometheus.
            That very spot you've stepped into
            we call the bulwark of Athens—this country's
            Bronze-footed Threshold. And all these fields
            were laid out by that horseman there, Colonus,
            and carry their founder's name, and
            the people who live here still hold it in common.
            So you see, stranger, since you ask how it is:
            It's a place made famous by no fine stories,   70

only we live together here
and honor the presence of these divinities.

OEDIPUS You say there are people living here?

STRANGER Indeed there are. Bearing this hero's name.

OEDIPUS Have they a ruler? Or are the laws
made by the people themselves?

STRANGER The lord of the city is lord of this place, too.

OEDIPUS Who is this lord of kingly strength and speech?

STRANGER His name, stranger, is Theseus—old King Aegeus's
son.

OEDIPUS Could you send a messenger to him?   80

STRANGER Why? To come and speak to you? For what?

OEDIPUS So, with a small service, he'd gain a great good.

STRANGER What good could a blind man offer?

OEDIPUS Words. When I speak
they will see everything.

STRANGER Do you know, stranger, what you need do now
to be safe here and stay within the law?
I'll tell you, since, in spite of what you've suffered,
I see something noble in you. Stay there,
there where you first appeared, while I   90
go to the citizens (who live *here*, not in the city)
and tell them what's happened. For they will decide
to take you in or send you away.

Exit STRANGER, *in direction of Athens.*

OEDIPUS Has the stranger gone, child? Are we alone?

ANTIGONE He's gone, father; you can talk in peace now:
There's nobody near—no one but me.

OEDIPUS Dread Ladies, before whose faces men bow down:
Since I've brought my body first to this grove of yours,
don't be deaf to my prayers, nor to Phoebus
    himself, who
when he foretold the horrors that lay ahead   100
said that in the fullness of time I'd find rest
when I reached a country I could stop in at last
in a shelter for strangers, a sanctuary
of the Holy Ones. And I could settle then
my wretched life—for the good of those
who would let me live there, and to the ruin
of those who drove me into exile.
And Apollo said there would be signs:
earthquake or thunder, or the bolts of Zeus
lighting up the sky in flashes. I see now   110
it must have been your sure prompting
led me to this grove, or else
I'd never have come upon you here first—
    my abstinence
matching your rites without wine. And I'd never
have set my body on this holy seat
in the rough rock itself. But now grant me, Goddesses,
in keeping with the voice of Apollo,
some limit, some end
to my life's journey, unless
I seem of little or no account, although   120
I've been subject to greater hardships
than any that have tried any man in the world. Come,
sweet children of the ancient dark! Come,
city of Athens—called the city of Pallas,
    of great Athena;
called the most honored city of all—
show pity for Oedipus; show your pity

to this poor phantom of a man. For this, surely,
is not the body I began with.

ANTIGONE Quiet! There are men, old men—
the guardians of this place you've stopped in.   130

OEDIPUS I'll be quiet. Hide me in the grove somewhere,
off the beaten path. Hide me, till I hear
what these men have to say. That
is the kind of knowledge right action depends on.

Enter CHORUS *from direction of Athens.*

CHORUS *Look about you!*
Who was the man? Where is he gone?
What secret spot has he scurried to now?
Seek this rashest most reckless of men!
Shout out loud! Search every corner! Find him!
A tramp—an old tramp—not of this place   140
or he'd never have entered the virgin grove
of these implacable Maidens whose very name
makes us tremble to say it.
So with eyes averted we slip by them in silence
letting them hear without words
the reverence alive in our minds.
But now people say someone's burst in here
showing no fear and no respect.
But though I look all over this godly grove
I still can't see where he's come to rest.   150

OEDIPUS Here! I am he. I am here!
By wordsound, as they say, I see.

CHORUS   (*with a rhythmical common cry of horror*)
Aaahhh! Awful the sight of him! Awful his voice!

OEDIPUS I beseech you, don't see in me a lawless man.

CHORUS Zeus protect us! Who is this old man?

OEDIPUS One whose fortune, protectors of this place,
         wasn't so good that you'd call him blessed.
         Were it otherwise—look!—I'd not be
         making my way with someone else's eyes;
         nor, big man that I am,   160
         anchoring myself on these slight arms.

CHORUS   (With a rhythmical common cry of distress)
         Aaaieee! Blind eyes!
         Were you born like this? Born for this?
         It seems you've had a long hard life—
         but you won't bring down this curse of yours
         on us, too, if I can help it.
         You've gone too far now out of bounds—
         so go no farther in that grassy silent grove
         where bright water in the flowing bowl
         streams into a stream of honey.   170
         Move! Stand off! Step away from where you are!
         Toil-worn wanderer you hear what we say?
         If it's talk you want
         walk off forbidden ground
         and speak your mind where it's lawful for all.
         Until you do that hold your tongue.

OEDIPUS Daughter, what now? What should we do?

ANTIGONE Be as careful, father, as those who live here:
         we should yield to what's needed: we should listen.

OEDIPUS Take hold of me, so.   180

ANTIGONE Here's my hand. Touching you. Here.

OEDIPUS Don't let any harm come to me, strangers,
         now I've trusted you and moved as you asked.

CHORUS *Old man—from this place of rest*
       no one will move you against your will.

In what follows, OEDIPUS moves slowly forward
from the grove to the rock ledge.

OEDIPUS *So? Farther?*

CHORUS *Come a little forward. On. Forward.*

OEDIPUS *Farther? So?*

CHORUS *Keep leading him, child.*
Forward. Farther forward. You see what we mean.   190

ANTIGONE *Come, father. Now follow me.*
With feeble unseeing steps
follow where I lead you.

CHORUS *Long-suffering man*
leaning on a stranger in this strange land:
be ready to hate what this city's learned to hate
and to hold in high esteem what it holds dear.

OEDIPUS *Child—now lead me,*
so we may stand on lawful ground
where we may speak, and listen, too.   200
Let us not struggle against necessity.

CHORUS *Here now. Here. Not a step*
beyond this rocky platform.

OEDIPUS *Like this?*

CHORUS *Yes. Far enough. You hear what we say.*

OEDIPUS *Should I sit now?*

CHORUS *Yes—to the side. Set yourself down*
here at the rock's edge: here.

ANTIGONE *Dear father let me guide you. It is my task*
to fit your footstep to my steady step.   210

OEDIPUS   Groans with the effort.
Ohhh!

ANTIGONE *Lean your old body on my loving arm.*

OEDIPUS   Groans aloud.
　　　Ohhh! Ruin! Destruction!

　　　　　　He sits at the very edge of the rock ledge.

CHORUS *Suffering man—you're settled now. So speak.*
　　　What nature were you born to?
　　　Who's led like this in so much pain?
　　　What country do you bring news of?

OEDIPUS *Ah strangers! I have no city. But do not—*

CHORUS *What is it you forbid, old man?*

OEDIPUS *Do not ask who I am.*   220
　　　Don't seek. Don't explore. Go no farther.

CHORUS *Why no farther?*

OEDIPUS *A terrible birth—*

CHORUS *Speak! Say!*

OEDIPUS *Child! What should I say?*

CHORUS *What seed do you come from?*
　　　Speak, stranger! What father?

OEDIPUS   With a cry of despair.
　　　Aaahhh me! Aaahhh! Child!
　　　What suffering is in store for me now?

CHORUS *Speak since you've come to the very brink.*   230

OEDIPUS *I'll speak. I've nowhere to hide.*

CHORUS *Why this holding back? Go on!*

OEDIPUS *A son . . . you must know . . . of Laius . . .*

CHORUS   With a great groan of distress.
　　　Aahhh!

OEDIPUS *. . . the family of Labdacus . . .*

CHORUS *O Zeus!*

OEDIPUS *. . . wretched Oedipus—*

CHORUS   *You mean you are he?*

OEDIPUS   *Don't be afraid of all I tell you.*

CHORUS   With a cry of horror.
         Aaahhh!   240

OEDIPUS   *Ill-fated . . .*

CHORUS   With an angry shout.
         Ohhh! Ohhh!

OEDIPUS   *Daughter:*
         what's happening?

CHORUS   *Out! Farther off! Get away from this land!*

OEDIPUS   *But how will you keep your promise, then?*

CHORUS   *No man when avenging a wrong—*
         matching one deceit with another
         and giving back not kindness but a blow—
         can rightly receive revenge in return.
         So unanchor from this seat and quit my land   250
         for fear you'd fasten on my city
         some graver obligation.

ANTIGONE   *Ah strangers—men of honor and respect!*
         Though you may not endure this old man my father
         —hearing what he did against his will—
         yet I entreat you strangers to pity me
         for this sad suffering father.
         Appearing like one of your own before you
         I gaze with seeing eyes on your faces
         that this wretched man may win your respect.   260
         Look! In our sufferings
         we depend on you as we depend
         on the power of a god. Come! Show some favor!
         I can't expect to get what I ask
         yet I implore you by whatever you cherish:
         your wife—your child—your land—your god!
         For you know well
         you could never lay eyes on any man
         who could escape if a god leads him.

CHORUS LEADER Know, daughter of Oedipus,   270
               because of your fortune we pity you both
               in equal measure. Yet we tremble at what the gods
                    send us,
               and wouldn't have the strength to say
               anything we haven't said to you already.

OEDIPUS Then what's become of reputation? What good is
         a good name if it fades like morning dew?
         What good is it if Athens stands alone, as they say,
         a god-fearing city—alone able to save
         the sick, afflicted stranger. Where is the good in this
              for me,
         seeing—since my name alone makes you tremble—   280
         you'll drag me from this sanctuary here
         and drive me away? It's not my body you fear
         nor what I've done. For know, I suffered
         more than ever I acted, as you'd see
         if I spoke those things of my father and mother
         which make you afraid of me. I'm well aware of this.
         But how am I bad in my own nature? I only
         returned an action I suffered,
         so even had my eyes been wide open
         I couldn't, with justice, be accused of wrongdoing.   290
         But in *ignorance* I came where I did and
         I suffered; but those at whose hands I suffered,
         I was *knowingly* destroyed by them.
         In light of this, strangers, I am, in the god's name,
         your suppliant. Since in your piety
         you've made me quit this holy place,
         now protect me. Don't honor the gods
         and then make light of them. Think
         how they look on good men and on bad,
         how the unrighteous one never escapes them.   300
         Don't darken bright Athens, that happy city,
         with unrighteous acts. As here you received me
         a suppliant with my pledge, now shield me, now
         watch over me. Don't dishonor this body
         just because it's hard to look at. For I've come
         in reverence, under the gods' protection, to bring

a gift to the citizens of this city. When your leader
gets here, the one you look up to, you'll hear all,
then you'll know everything. Till that happens,
I pray you, do no wrong.   310

CHORUS LEADER Old man, it's impossible not to respect this
grave argument of yours: there's nothing light
about the words you offer. But the lord of this land
will be able to ponder them for us.

OEDIPUS And where is the lord of this land, strangers?

CHORUS LEADER Here in this country, in his father's city:
That look-out who brought us has gone to get him.

OEDIPUS And do you think he'll feel concern for a blind man?
So he'd come himself, in his own person?

CHORUS LEADER Yes—all the more when he knows your name.   320

OEDIPUS But who will bring him that name?

CHORUS LEADER It's a long road: many travelers' tales
wander about on it. When our lord hears, be sure
he'll be here. For your name, old man,
is on all men's tongues; so even if
he's sleeping on some slow journey,
when he hears of you he'll come with all speed.

OEDIPUS Let him come, then, with good fortune
for his city and me. For what good man
is not a friend to himself?   330

ANTIGONE   *Looking toward the entrance from Thebes.*
Oh Zeus! What should I say? Father, what should
        I think?

OEDIPUS What, Antigone? What is it, child?

348

ANTIGONE A woman, coming this way: she's riding
          a Sicilian pony, and shading her face
          with a broad-brimmed sun-hat you'd find in Thessaly.
          What can I say? What *should* I say?
          Is it she or not? Am I wandering in my mind?
          I say *Yes!* I say *No!* But I cannot . . .
          poor wretch, poor woman, *it is!*
          She draws nearer now, and I can see   340
          her eyes brightening in a sign of welcome
          that says—there's no doubt!—it's Ismene!

                        Enter ISMENE *from direction of Thebes.*

          Ismene herself! Ismene!

OEDIPUS Child, what do you mean?

ANTIGONE Your daughter, the sister who shares my blood,
          she's right here before our eyes!
          And you'll know it now by the sound of her voice.

ISMENE Father! Sister! These two names sweetest to my ears!
        With labor and pain I've found the two of you,
        and now how painful it is to look at you.   350

OEDIPUS My child! You've come?

ISMENE Oh father, father! Poor battered man! Father!

OEDIPUS My child, you're here?

ISMENE I've traveled a hard road to find you.

OEDIPUS Touch me, my child.

ISMENE I touch you both at once.

OEDIPUS Ah—children of the same blood.

ISMENE Look! The wretched clutch of us!

OEDIPUS You mean this girl and me?

ISMENE And me, a woeful third.   360

OEDIPUS Daughter, why have you come?

ISMENE For your sake, father.

OEDIPUS Out of longing, is it?

ISMENE And as my own messenger—
along with the only servant I could trust.

OEDIPUS But the young men of our blood—where are they?
What are they doing?

ISMENE They are . . . wherever they are. Terrible
what lies between them now.

OEDIPUS Ach, those two! In their nature, in their way of life,   370
they mimic Egyptian habits. For the men of Egypt
sit indoors weaving, while their wives
go out every day in the world
to provide what they need. So here you both are,
while those fit for the task do housework
like maids. The two of you do their work, this
          hard work—
caring for my suffering self. This girl here,
since she grew from a child into a woman's
          strong body
has tramped through misfortune, leading an old man.
Often barefoot, often hungry,   380
she's crossed wild woodland, and often
under scorching sun or drenching rain
she's toiled in patience, not giving a thought
to home or comfort or food for herself—
so long as her father has enough to eat.
And you, my child [to ISMENE], years ago you reached
          your father
with all those prophecies; traveling in secret

so the people of Thebes would know nothing—
all those prophecies about my body. And when I was
driven out in the world, it was you   390
who made yourself my faithful guardian.
And now, Ismene, have you come once more
with some new story for your father? This time
what mission drove you from home? For you've come
for some reason, haven't you, with some fearful news?

ISMENE What I suffered, searching for you, father—
asking where you lived, what life you led—I'll not
        mention,
for I've no wish to feel that pain twice over
in the doing and the telling. But the bad news I've
        brought
concerns those two, your ill-fated sons.   400
At first they were content to surrender
the throne to Creon, and not pollute the city—
        mindful
of the ruin, begun long ago with their ancestors,
which destroyed your unhappy house.
But now—with a god behind it, and willful wildness—
bitter strife has sprung up between these
two thrice-miserable men, each one hungry
for power, each wanting to rule on his own.
The younger, in temper as well as in years, pushes
the older, Polyneices, from the royal throne,   410
exiling him from his fatherland. And now
the tale is on every man's tongue,
that having fled to the hollow plain of Argos
he adopts a new family, makes a warlike alliance,
and plans to conquer his own land of Cadmus
with honor, or fall in battle and fly to the heavens.
This isn't just words, father,
but dreadful deeds. And I don't know how
the gods will pity your bitter troubles.

OEDIPUS Did you hope somehow, some day, the gods   420
would look on me kindly, and I might be
made whole?

ISMENE I did, father. Because of recent prophecies.

OEDIPUS Prophecies, child? What has been prophesied?

ISMENE That the men of Thebes would seek you out one day,
     living or dead, to ensure their prosperity.

OEDIPUS Look at me. Who'd be better off because of such
          a man?

ISMENE They say their power lies in you. They've found
          this out.

OEDIPUS So when I am no longer, then I'm a man?

ISMENE Yes. For now the gods who ruined you
     have begun to restore you, to raise you up.   430

OEDIPUS To raise up an old man is a silly business—an
          old man
     who in his youth took a fall.

ISMENE But because of these prophecies, very soon now,
     Creon will be here.

OEDIPUS And means to do what, daughter? Explain it to me.

ISMENE To settle you near the land of Cadmus, so they
     can control you, without you crossing their borders.

OEDIPUS What good will they get if I'm lying before their gates?

ISMENE Any harm to your tomb means disaster for them.

OEDIPUS Common sense would tell you that; no need
          for a god.   440

ISMENE That's why they wish to keep you
     near their land, but with no power of your own.

OEDIPUS   And after I'm dead, will they scatter
          even the shadow of Theban dust over me?

ISMENE   No, father; your father's blood will not allow it.

OEDIPUS   Then they'll never take me into their power!

ISMENE   Then this will be a bitter trouble to the Cadmeians.

OEDIPUS   When, child? What events will come together to bring
          that about?

ISMENE   Your rage, when they stand at your grave.

OEDIPUS   Where have you heard all this, my child?   450

ISMENE   From the envoys who returned from the altars
          at Delphi.

OEDIPUS   And Apollo has spoken such words of me?

ISMENE   That's what they said when they returned to Thebes.

OEDIPUS   Did either of my sons hear any of this?

ISMENE   Both heard it, all of it, and understood it well.

OEDIPUS   And even when they heard all this—wicked men!—
          they let power-hunger come before all feeling for me?

ISMENE   It saddens me to hear you say it, but that's
          my message.

OEDIPUS   Well then, let the gods not quench this
          ill-fated quarrel of theirs! And in the battle
          between them,   460
          which grips them as tightly as they their own spears,
          may the end of it depend on me. Then
          the one who now holds scepter and throne would

353

not remain in the state he's in, and the one driven out
would never get back. For they neither
guarded nor defended me—me who gave them life!—
when I was driven in dishonor from my
        father's country,
although I was cast out before their eyes
and declared an exile. Will you say the city then
acted fairly, giving me what I craved?   470
No! Again no! What's true
is that in those first days—my spirit in flames
and I longing for the comfort of death, wanting
        the people
to stone me to death—not one man came forward
to grant my wish. But then
when my troubles were no longer young
and I began to see my passion had pushed me too far,
that I'd blamed myself too much for my mistakes,
then, after all that time, the city
chose to use force and drive me out. And they—   480
sons of their father, able to help their father—
were unwilling to act. So, for want of a word,
I became an exile; with their knowledge and consent
a wanderer forever. But these young women—
        innocent
of the world—have given me all they can; from them
I get nourishment, protection, a secure place
without fear, while those men bartered their father
for a scepter's power, to be sole rulers
of that country. But they'll not win
me as an ally, and they'll get no good   490
from their rule in the land of Cadmus.
I know this, for I hear the prophecies
this girl utters, and remember those
once delivered by Phoebus himself. Let them send
Creon, or any other man of power in that city,
to seek me out. For if you, strangers,
along with the Goddesses present in this place,
are willing to defend me, you'll bring
a great savior to your city, and bitter trouble
        to my enemies.

CHORUS LEADER Oedipus, you're a man who deserves our pity,   500
                as these do, your loyal daughters. But since
                you say you're the savior of this land
                I want to advise you for your own good.

OEDIPUS My friend, since you know I'll do all you ask,
          be my guide now and give me good counsel.

CHORUS LEADER You should perform the purification rite
                of those Goddesses whose presence you entered
                and on whose holy ground you walked.

OEDIPUS How should I do it? Teach me, strangers.

CHORUS LEADER First, in purified hands, you should bring   510
                sacred libations from the ever-flowing stream.

OEDIPUS And when I've drawn this undefiled water?

CHORUS LEADER You'll find mixing bowls, made by a cunning
                            craftsman:
                wreathe these bowls on their rims and handles.

OEDIPUS With branches, or woven wool, or some other way?

CHORUS LEADER With the fleece of a newborn lamb, freshly shorn.

OEDIPUS Be it so. And then? How should I finish the ritual?

CHORUS LEADER Facing where the sun comes up, pour your libations.

OEDIPUS With the bowls, then, I should pour my libations?

CHORUS LEADER Exactly, those bowls. There will be three streams.   520
                Let the last bowl flow till it's empty.

OEDIPUS And this last, filled with what? Go on with
                    your lesson.

CHORUS LEADER Honey and water. You must not add wine.

OEDIPUS   And when dark-leaved earth receives these libations?

CHORUS LEADER   Place three times nine olive branches on it.
Use your two hands. And say these prayers—

OEDIPUS   I long to hear them: they have great power.

CHORUS LEADER   As we call them Eumenides, the Kindly Ones, pray
they receive their suppliant with a kindly heart
and be his savior. Ask this or let another   530
ask it for you. Pray with unheard words, do not
cry aloud. Then leave backwards, don't turn around.
If you do all this, stranger, I'll risk
standing by you. Otherwise, I'd fear for you.

OEDIPUS   Daughters, do you hear these local people,
these strangers?

ISMENE   We heard. Now say, you, what has to be done.

OEDIPUS   I can't move on my own; my lack of strength
and sight
is a twin affliction. But one of you go
and do as they've said. For one living soul, I believe,
is as good as ten thousand to pay the debt   540
fulfilled by this ritual, if that one is there
with good intent. But do it quickly
and don't leave me alone: infirm as I am,
I can't move without a guide.

ISMENE   Father, I'll go to perform this rite.

(*to* CHORUS)

Where is the place it has to be done?

CHORUS LEADER   On the far side of this grove, stranger.
If you need anything, someone there will instruct you.

ISMENE   I'll go and do it. Stay here, Antigone,
and take care of our father. When one labors
for a parent,   550

one should never remember the trouble—
it shouldn't feel like labor at all.

                          Exit ISMENE, *through the grove.*

CHORUS *Stranger: it's terrible to bring to life a pain*
long laid to rest. Yet I long to ask—

OEDIPUS *What?*

CHORUS *About that shattering sorrow you wrestled with—*
ungovernable as the sea.

OEDIPUS *I beg by the bonds of hospitality*
don't recklessly open
the wounds which to my shame I've suffered.   560

CHORUS *Told over and over the story's well known.*
But I'd like the simple truth of it.

OEDIPUS   With a groan.
       Ohhh!

CHORUS *Be easy I beseech you.*

OEDIPUS   With a gasp of despairing resignation.
       Aahhh! Aahhh!

CHORUS *Hear me.*
For I have heard what you desire.

OEDIPUS *Misery stranger! And as the god is my witness*
I bore it willingly.
But nothing that happened was of my choosing.   570

CHORUS *What was it?*

OEDIPUS *In a misery-laden bed the city*
locked me into a ruinous marriage.
I knew nothing.

CHORUS *Was it lying with your mother as I hear*
you filled the bed with the awful name?

OEDIPUS   With a groan.
       Aahh! Stranger! These words are death.
       And out of my loins these two girls—

CHORUS *What are you saying?*

OEDIPUS *This double ruin—*   580

CHORUS *O Zeus!*

OEDIPUS *I planted in my mother's shared womb.*

CHORUS *So they're yours? Offspring and—*

OEDIPUS *Yes. From one source. Sisters to their father.*

CHORUS   *With a cry of horror.*
    Aaahhh!

OEDIPUS *Aaahhh! Indeed! Pain*
    of a million wounds torn open again.

CHORUS *You've suffered—*

OEDIPUS *Things not to be forgotten.*

CHORUS *You did—*   590

OEDIPUS *No not did!*

CHORUS *Then what?*

OEDIPUS *I received a gift for the help I gave.*
    Would I'd never taken it—
    man as I am with a heart that suffers.

CHORUS *Miserable man what more? You murdered—*

OEDIPUS *What are you saying? What do you want to know?*

CHORUS *—your father!*

OEDIPUS   *Gives a cry of pain.*
    Aaahhh! Wound upon wound! A second blow!

CHORUS *You killed!*   600

OEDIPUS *Yes, I killed. But on my side—*

CHORUS *What?*

OEDIPUS *Some justice.*

CHORUS *What do you mean?*

358

OEDIPUS *I'll tell you what I mean.*
    In the grip of disaster I destroyed and murdered.
    But I came to it innocent in law:
    I knew nothing.

               Enter THESEUS, *from the direction of Athens.*

CHORUS LEADER But look, here's our king: Theseus, son of Aegeus.
    He's come in answer to your message.   610

THESUS I've often heard over the years
    of the bloody destruction of your eyes,
    and so I know you, son of Laius.
    And having heard more on my way here,
    I now understand even more,
    for your tattered clothes and shattered face
    tell us who you are. And in pity I'd
    ask you, ill-fated Oedipus, what you want
    of my city and me—you and your ill-fated guide.
    Teach me that. For I know   620
    it would have to be some act beyond telling
    to make me want to turn away. Like you,
    I was raised an exile, far from home,
    and often, on my own, I had to face
    mortal danger. So I could never turn aside
    and not try to save any stranger
    in the state I find you in now. For I know
    I'm a man, and know
    I've no greater claim on tomorrow than you.

OEDIPUS Your generosity, Theseus, in so few words,   630
    leaves me with little to explain. For you
    are in possession of who I am, who my father was,
    and the country I've come from. There
    is nothing left for me to say—except
    what I desire, and then I'm done.

THESEUS Teach me that, so I'll know all there is to know.

OEDIPUS I've come to give you, as a gift, my own
miserable body. It's little enough to look at,
but it's worth more than beauty itself.

THESEUS What makes it worth your coming here? 640

OEDIPUS In time you may learn that, but not now.

THESEUS When will this offering come to light?

OEDIPUS When I die, and you lay out a grave for me.

THESEUS What you ask for is life's last act. But you forget
what will happen before that end.
Or do you think that's of no importance?

OEDIPUS I do. The last act brings all that with it.

THESEUS Then it's soon told, this favor you're asking.

OEDIPUS Mind what you say! This is no small contest!

THESEUS Do you mean your sons' doings? Or whose? 650

OEDIPUS All those who'll force me to go back.

THESEUS But if you went willingly? Exile's no good for you.

OEDIPUS True. But when I wanted to stay, they refused!

THESEUS But this is foolish. What good is passion
in the midst of misfortune?

OEDIPUS When you hear my story, then give your advice.
For the moment, let be.

THESEUS Instruct me, then. I mustn't blame before
I understand.

OEDIPUS I've suffered, Theseus. One horror on top of another.

THESEUS   You mean the ancient misfortunes of your family?   660

OEDIPUS   No! All Greece tosses that story about.

THESEUS   Then what greater sickness has a grip on you?

OEDIPUS   Here's how it is: by my own flesh and blood
          I was driven from my country, and as a father-killer
          I can never go back.

THESEUS   How could they send for you, then, and still keep you
                    far off?

OEDIPUS   The voice of a god will force them.

THESEUS   What sufferings will the oracle make them afraid of?

OEDIPUS   That otherwise they must be struck down, here.

THESEUS   But how could their rancor spread to me?   670

OEDIPUS   Dearest son of Aegeus, none but the gods
          escape old age and death; all else
          time in its relentless flood sweeps away.
          The strength of earth and of the body fades,
          trust dies and distrust flourishes,
          and the same spirit never endures
          between friend and friend, city and city.
          For some now, for others later,
          joy becomes bitter, then bitterness joy. So
          if fair weather is what holds now   680
          between you and Thebes, boundless time
          in its motion gives birth to nights and days
          beyond number, and in their course
          this concord between you will grow to discord
          over a word, a little word, and war
          will shatter it. And where this happens,
          my cold corpse—asleep, unseen—will drink
          their warm blood, if Zeus is still Zeus,
          and his son, Phoebus Apollo, speaks the pure truth.

But hard, secret words like these   690
aren't sweet in the mouth, so leave me
there where I started, and just look after
your own good faith. You'll never say—unless
the gods deceive me—that in this grove
you received in Oedipus a worthless guest.

CHORUS LEADER My lord, for some time now this man
has been making our country promises like this.

THESEUS Indeed? But who would turn away the friendship
of such a man? First, our alliance
always assures us a hearth in common.   700
Then, coming as a suppliant of the gods,
he promises in return, to my country and me,
a great recompense. These are things I respect,
and I'd never spurn what he offers
but offer in return a home in this country.
And if this is the place it now pleases
our friend the stranger to remain in,
I'll make you his guardians—
or if he wishes he may come with me.
Whatever you like, Oedipus: you can make your
        own choice   710
of what I offer and I'll accept it.

OEDIPUS May Zeus send blessings to such men!

THESEUS So what is your wish? To go to my home?

OEDIPUS If it were right. But *here* is the place.

THESEUS Where you'll do what? I'll not oppose it.

OEDIPUS Triumph over those who drove me out.

THESEUS It's a great thing, this gift?
Your being here with us?

OEDIPUS That depends on how you keep the bargain.

THESEUS Of me be certain: I'll not betray you.

OEDIPUS And I'll not bind you with an oath, like a coward.   720

THESEUS Even if you did, you'd get no more than when I
                 gave my word.

OEDIPUS But what will you do?

THESEUS What's your fear?

OEDIPUS Men will come—

THESEUS These men will deal with them.

OEDIPUS Beware, if you leave me—

THESEUS Don't teach me my duty.

OEDIPUS I can't help it. I'm afraid.

THESEUS In *my* heart there's no fear.

OEDIPUS You don't know the threats, the—   730

THESEUS What I know is that no one will take you
                 against my will. Even were they strong enough
                 to think of forcing you from here, I know they'll
                     soon see
                 how an ocean rolls between them and their deed
                 and there's no easy crossing. But even if
                 you pay no heed to my judgment, take heart—
                 if Phoebus indeed has led you here. And if I
                 am absent myself, no matter, for I know
                 my name alone is enough to protect you.

                          Exit THESEUS *in direction of Athens.*

CHORUS *Welcome, stranger: in this country rich in horses*   740
    you've come to the strongest dwellings in the world.
    Here is bright-shining white Colonus. Here
    the sweet-throated nightingale throngs with song
    glades the wind or sun won't touch.
    The wine-flecked ivy grows
    in these thick untrodden groves of the god.
    Fruit trees are free here from frigid winter
    and here with his immortal nurses roams the
        roistering Dionysus.

    Bathed in the dew of the sky
    here the narcissus never withers—ever weaving an
        ancient garland   750
    for the brows of the two Great Goddesses—and here
        grows the golden crocus.
    Streams that flow here from the wide Cephisus
    never sleep and never empty:
    ever-running—never dry—day by day
    this pure water floods the plain
    and livens miles of fertile earth.
    Not even the Muses shun this place—nor golden-
        reined Aphrodite.

    And something grows here
    that never grows—they say—in the fields of Asia
    or the famous Doric isle of Pelops: a tree seeding
        itself by nature.   760
    Self-creating. Fearsome even
    to the weapons of our enemies:
    here the gray-leafed olive flourishes—nourisher
        of children.
    Young or old—no man can lay a fatal hand on it
    for ever-waking Zeus protects it—patron
    of the Sacred Olive—and his gray-eyed child Athena.

    And here's one praise more for our mother city:
    it's this country's proudest boast—a present from the
        god himself—

god of horses colts and shining ocean.
Son of Cronos: Lord Poseidon: it was you who raised
*   the city with this gift*   770
so we boast of it today. You gave us the
*   bridle-harness*
that heals horses of their wildness and on these
*   roads first transformed them.*
And you gave another wonder: oar-blades to tame
*   the waves*
and gallop flashing in the sea-nymphs' wake—
*   the Nereids*
on their hundred dancing feet.

                                A noise of many men arriving.

ANTIGONE   O land praised with such high praises, now
           you'll have to make these words shine in deeds.

OEDIPUS   Child, what's happening?

ANTIGONE   Creon, father, he's coming, and many with him.

OEDIPUS   Now, old men, dearest elders—this   780
          may test your safe-keeping to its limit.

           Enter, from direction of Thebes, CREON *with soldiers.*

CHORUS LEADER   Have courage, we'll keep you. For though I'm old,
                our country's strength has not grown old.

CREON   Men of this country, well-born natives:
        I clearly see in your eyes that you feel
        some fear at my coming among you. But
        you mustn't shrink from me or speak harsh words:
        I don't come like a man with big ambitions,
        since I'm old now and know I've come
        to a city as strong as any in Greece.   790
        But I've been sent, old as I am, to persuade this man
        to come to the land of the Cadmeians,

not just because one man demanded it,
but because all the citizens prompted me to it—
since, in the whole city, I and my family
grieved most for the sufferings of this man.
But wretched Oedipus, listen, and come home!
All the people of Thebes justly call you back,
and I more than any. For I, old man, am the one
who feels most deeply your afflictions—seeing
    you here   800
an unhappy exile, forever a beggar wandering
    without means
and depending on a girl I'd never have thought could
descend into such degradation (it grieves me to say it)
as she's fallen into, this unluckiest of girls: always
looking after you and the needs of your body;
poor, unmarried, a prey for any passing man.
And is this not a shocking reproach I've flung at you
in my distress, and at myself
and my whole family? But I may not hide
what's plain to see. So now, Oedipus, by the gods of
    our fathers   810
be persuaded by me: purge this shame.
Come willingly with me to the city of your birth;
follow me back to your father's house; give this city
a farewell blessing—she's earned it. But
you should show more respect to your native city,
which long ago gave you life.

OEDIPUS Oh you, you who'd stop at nothing,
twisting any just sentence into crooked sense.
Why try to lay hands on me a second time—
here like this, when I'd feel most grief?   820
Years ago, when I was stricken
with misfortunes that cut me to the quick—
so it would have been a joy to be cast out from my
    native place—
you were never willing to grant me this favor,
no matter how much I craved it. But when my
rage was spent at last, and I was glad to live
the rest of my days undisturbed in my own house,

then you wanted nothing but to cast me into exile
and drive me away. Then our kinship
meant nothing to you. But now, when you see
          this city   830
turn its face to me in friendship
and its citizens welcome me into their family,
now you try to draw me away from here, speaking
sour truths in your honeyed words. What good
is there in this? in this show of love
when it's not wanted? Just as if someone
would offer you nothing, no helping hand when you
          need it most,
but then, when your spirit is as full as you could wish,
only then would he give it, granting a useless favor.
Wouldn't this be a hollow pleasure? But this   840
is what you offer me—honorable words
and dishonorable deeds. But I'll proclaim you
to these men here, and let them see you
for the villain you are: You've come here
to take me away, but not to bring me home. You'll
          settle me
in some place nearby, keeping your city
free from harm, suffering nothing at the hands
          of Athens.
You'll not succeed in this. But I'll give you
something else: my vengeance
living forever in your country. And this   850
for my sons: they'll inherit just enough land
to stretch their bodies on in death.
Do I not understand what goes on in Thebes
better than you? Yes, much better,
because I hear more clearly than you
the words of Zeus and his son, Phoebus Apollo.
So here you are, with your traitor's mouth and
          brazen tongue!
But—though I can never convince you of this—
          your words
will only make trouble for you, not safe-keeping.
Go then, and leave us here to live our lives. Left
          to our   860

own will and pleasure, we won't live badly,
even as we're living now.

CREON Do you think it's me you hurt with these words,
or will they wound your own wounded condition?

OEDIPUS My greatest pleasure will be your failure
to win over me or these men with me here.

CREON Miserable man! Can't the years give you sense?
Are you just living to bring contempt on old age?

OEDIPUS You're good with your tongue, but I know
no good man
can contrive a just argument for every cause. 870

CREON To speak a lot and speak to the point are
not the same.

OEDIPUS As if the little you say were to the point.

CREON Not to someone with a mind like yours.

OEDIPUS Away! Go! Now I speak for these men, too:
Don't stand in my way there like a guard
blockading the place where I'm to live.

CREON I call on these men, not you, to witness
all you've said to me, your kinsman. If ever I
take you...

OEDIPUS Who could force me from these allies?

CREON Even without that, I swear you'll suffer. 880

OEDIPUS What sort of threat is that?

CREON Your two girls—I've seized one already
and sent her away. Now I'll take the other.

OEDIPUS   *With a loud moan.*
    Ohhh!

CREON You'll soon have more than that to moan over.

OEDIPUS You have my child?

CREON I have, and in no time this one, too.

OEDIPUS Friends, what will you do? Will you betray me?
    Not drive this blasphemous man from your land?

CHORUS LEADER Go, stranger! Away! Now!   890
    There's no justice in what you do,
    and none in what you've done already.

CREON   *To his men.*
    Now's the moment—*now!*—to bring this one away;
    if she doesn't come willingly, force her!

ANTIGONE   *With a shout of misery.*
    Aahhh! Where can I fly to? What help can I get
    from gods or from men?

CHORUS LEADER What do you think you're doing, stranger?

CREON I won't touch this man. But the girl is mine!

OEDIPUS Lords of this land!

CHORUS LEADER This isn't justice, stranger.   900

CREON Yes, justice!

CHORUS LEADER How justice?

CREON I take what is mine!

OEDIPUS   *With a cry of horror.*
    Ohhh! *City!*

CHORUS   *Stranger! What are you doing?*
         Won't you release her?
         You'll meet—and soon—a test of strength.

CREON   *Back! Stay back!*

CHORUS   *Not from you—with these intentions.*

CREON   *Injure me and face my city in battle!*   910

OEDIPUS   *Isn't this what I told you?*

CHORUS   *Take your hands off her! Now!*

CREON   *Don't try giving orders where you have no power!*

CHORUS   *I say let go!*

CREON   To his men.
        And I say Go!

CHORUS   *Men of this land come quickly quickly!*
         Violent hands are laid on the city! My city!
         Come! Come quickly!

ANTIGONE   Strangers, friends, they're taking me away!

OEDIPUS   Where are you, child?   920

ANTIGONE   I'm being dragged away!

OEDIPUS   My child, reach me your hand.

ANTIGONE   I can't, I haven't the strength.

CREON   Take her away!

The men drag ANTIGONE *off in the direction of Thebes.*

OEDIPUS   Oh wretched! *Wretched!*

CREON   You'll go no farther on these two crutches.
        But since you want to triumph over fatherland
                and friends,

whose orders, though I'm ruler, I carry out,
triumph away! In time I know you'll see the truth:
You're not doing yourself any good now, 930
and you haven't done any good in the past—the way
you oppose your friends, give free rein to your rage.
But it's yourself you make contemptible in the end.

CHORUS LEADER Hold, stranger!

CREON I tell you, don't touch me!

CHORUS LEADER If I don't get these girls back, I won't let you go.

CREON Then you'll soon pay my city a heavier fine!
I won't take only these women.

CHORUS LEADER What will you do?

CREON Seize this man and take him away with me. 940

CHORUS LEADER A terrible thing to say.

CREON And unless the ruler of this land prevents me,
this terrible thing will now be *done*.

OEDIPUS Shameless tongue! You say you'll lay hands on me?

CREON I say, *Be silent!*

OEDIPUS No! I will speak! May these divinities
yet permit me to utter this curse
on you, most craven of men, on you
who have violently taken this helpless girl
who is the only eyes I have: so you double the blow 950
struck years ago at my own two eyes. For this
may all-seeing Helios give you, and your kin,
a life like the life I've led in old age.

CREON Citizens, do you see this?

OEDIPUS Yes, they see you and me—me wounded by deeds,
               defending myself with words.

CREON Well then, I won't swallow my fury:
               Alone as I am, and slowed by age,
               I'll take this man by force!

OEDIPUS   *With a cry of despair.*
               Ohhh! *Misery!*   960

CHORUS *Stranger! What an insolent spirit you have*
               if you come here and think you'll do as you say.

CREON *I think so—yes.*

CHORUS *Then I count this city a city no longer.*

CREON *The weak man if his cause be just*
               still can overpower and cast down the strong.

OEDIPUS *You hear what he says?*

CHORUS *Zeus knows he won't bring this about.*

CREON *Zeus may know but you don't!*

CHORUS *Isn't this insolence?*   970

CREON *Yes, insolence! And you have to take it!*

CHORUS *O people and chief men of the country:*
               these men are breaking bounds—crossing
                   our borders!
               Come! Come running!

                  Enter THESEUS *from the direction of Athens.*

THESEUS What's this cry? What's happening? What fear
               halted my sacrifice at the sea-god's altar, guardian
                   of Colonus?
               Speak, so I'll know what there is to know.
               I've taxed my strength, hurrying here.

OEDIPUS Dearest lord—for I can tell it's you by your voice—
          how bitter my sufferings were just now   980
          at this man's hands.

THESEUS What sufferings? Who has hurt you? Speak.

OEDIPUS This one! Creon. You see him: he's going,
          and he's taken my only two children from me.

THESEUS What do you mean?

OEDIPUS That's what I've suffered.

THESEUS Let one of my men run to the altar
          with all speed. Tell all who are there
          to race from the sacrifice on horseback or on foot
          straight for the place where the two highways meet,   990
          so those girls may go no farther
          and I, bested by this brutish deed of his,
          not become a mockery to this stranger. So go,
          go quickly! Were I in a fury, as he deserves,
          he'd never escape unscathed. But now
          the laws, the laws he came here to uphold,
          will bring him to order.
                              You should know
          you'll not leave this country of ours
          till you bring these two girls back before me.
          You've acted in a manner unworthy of me, unworthy   1000
          of your ancestors and the land that bore you.
          You've come to a city that practices justice,
          where nothing is determined outside the law,
          yet you've wantonly flouted the authority
          of this country—bursting in like this
          and taking what you want, bringing your own
          force to bear. You think there are
          no men here or, if there are, you think
          they're slaves. And you think I'm nobody,
          I count for nothing. Yet Thebes   1010
          didn't bring you up to be bad: it's not her way
          to raise lawless men; she wouldn't condone

anything you've done, if she knew you'd
raided my property like this and
plundered what belongs to the gods, laying
violent hands on these two suppliants, these
wretched girls. Even with all the justification
   in the world,
I'd never cross over into your country
if I lacked permission from the rulers there.
And I'd never snatch away anyone or anything—   1020
because I know how a stranger should behave, always,
in a foreign city, among its citizens. But you,
you bring shame on a blameless city, you shame
your native place: the years have made you
both old and stupid. So, I've said it once
and I'll say it again: have someone
return these girls right away, unless you wish
to reside here by force against your will. In this
my thoughts and my words are one.

CHORUS LEADER   Now you see where you've got to, stranger: 1030
   Coming from that city you seem a just man,
   but your actions show you're a bad one.

CREON   I don't say, son of Aegeus, that your city
   is lacking in manhood. And no bad counsel,
      as you say,
   drove me to these actions. But I knew your people
   would never feel such zeal for my relatives here
   that they'd support them with violence
   against me. And in my heart I knew
   they'd never give shelter to a man
   who murdered his own father. A polluted man,   1040
   a man whose marriage—with all its intimacies—
   was nothing but a sacrilege, the grossest offense.
   And I knew your Council—that makes its home on
      Ares' hill—
   was founded on order, and would never
   permit vagrants like these to settle in the city.
   Believing all this, I took hold of my prey—
   and I'd never have done even that

had he not flung curses at me and my family.
What I suffered, I believe, made it just
for me to act as I've acted here.   1050
In face of all this, you may do as you wish,
since even if there's justice in what I say
I'm nothing in your eyes, being alone. But
old as I am, when the time is ripe
I'll strike whoever strikes me, blow for blow.

OEDIPUS Shameless arrogance! Whom do you think you wound
with these words? Me in my old age
or you in yours? You who've spewed out
murders and marriages and misfortunes, which I
in my wretchedness endured against my will. That   1060
was what pleased the gods—from some old
        anger, perhaps,
against my family. For if it were a question
of me alone, you couldn't with any justice
        reproach me
for any wrongdoing I paid for
by grievously wronging myself and mine.
So teach me, then: if a certain decree of the oracle
was hanging over my father's head, that said
he'd meet his death at the hands of his children,
how in justice blame me for this—I then
unfathered, unmothered, still unborn? And
        beyond that,   1070
if the light I was born to was the light of misery,
and I came to blows with my father and killed him—
knowing nothing of whom I fought, of what I did—
how could you blame me for an act
done in ignorance? And, wretch that you are,
you feel no shame in forcing me to speak—
as speak I will—of this marriage
to my mother, your own blood sister? You lack
all piety and let your tongue run away with you.
So yes, I'll speak now, I won't be silent: 1080
She gave birth to me, and she who bore me—*Aahh!*
the horror of it: I didn't know, she didn't know—
to her bitter shame conceived children with me.

Yet there's one thing I do know: that you
mouth these things willingly against me, against her,
while I, not willing it, wed her
and must speak of it now, though I've no wish to.
But I'll not hear myself called evil for this: neither
for the marriage nor for the murder—that
    bitter reproach
always in your mouth. Just answer me   1090
one question, it will settle everything:
if someone—anyone standing here this minute—
tried to kill you, you the just man, would you
stop to inquire if he was your father
or would you strike back to revenge the blow?
If you love your life, I think you'd quickly
repay in kind the one who struck first
and not look for the justice in it. And, with the gods
guiding me, that was exactly the trouble
that I walked into. So I think even my father's spirit,   1100
were he living, would have no reason
to argue against me. But you—you who are unjust
and think it right to say anything speakable or
    unspeakable—
you reproach me with such things in front of
    these men
and choose to flatter Theseus to his face, and
Athens, too, praising her good order.
But though you're lavish in flattery
you forget this praise: that of all countries
this one knows best how to reverence the gods—
this land here from which you intended to   1110
snatch me away, an old man and a suppliant,
and tried to lay hands on me, and took my daughters.
To answer all this I call on the Goddesses,
and I beseech them and pray they will be my allies
and come to my aid, so you can learn
just what sort of men are guarding this city.

CHORUS LEADER My lord, this stranger is a good man.
We can see his misfortunes are calamitous,
but they deserve our protection.

THESEUS No more talk. At this moment the captors are
                    speeding away,   1120
               while we, the injured, stand still as stones.

CREON Feeble as I am, what will you have me do?

THESEUS Lead the way to where these girls are. I alone
               will be your escort. I know
               you didn't come on your own or unprepared
               for the great violence and daring you've shown here.
                    You've relied
               on someone or something—which I must look to
               and not let the city be weaker than a single man.
               So lead me: if you're keeping these
               girls of ours, you can show me yourself.   1130
               But if their abductors have taken flight already
               we need do nothing: there are others
               racing ahead of us, from whom they'll never escape
               to give thanks to the gods. Lead on, then, and know
               that though you hold, you are held—
               you the hunter Fortune has trapped. For you see,
               things taken by unlawful deceit
               are never safe with those who take them.
               Do you understand this? Or does all I've said
               seem as useless as what *you* said   1140
               when you schemed and plotted to come here?

CREON Since you're here, I can fault nothing you say to me.
            But, once home, we'll know what action to take.

THESEUS Threaten all you like—so long as you go. Now!

                    Exit CREON *and soldiers in direction of Thebes.*

               Oedipus, I ask you to stay here in peace for my sake.
               And trust that if I myself don't die
               I won't rest till I've restored your daughters.

OEDIPUS For this nobility may you prosper, Theseus:
for this even-handed care you show us.

          Exit THESEUS *in the direction of Thebes.*

CHORUS *Would I could be where the men of war*   1150
will soon turn—turn and wade into
the brazen clash of the war-god's battle!
Either on Apollo's sandy shore
or the torchlit strand where the Great Goddesses
foster the rites of mortal creatures
whose tongues are sealed by the golden key of
the ministers there—children of Eumolpus.
Here I can see that battle-rouser Theseus
and these two captive virgin sisters
will come together at the sound of his war-shout—   1160
his sign of triumph.

On horseback in chariots I see them charging
in headlong flight from the pastures of Oea
to a place just west of the snow-white rocks.
He will be defeated!
Terrible the battle-rage of the men who live here—
terrible the might of Theseus' men.
Each bit and bridle flashes like lightning:
each rider gallops flat to the neck of his horse.
Horsemen who honor Athena of the horses   1170
and that earth-encircling son of Rhea—
beloved son—god of the sea.

Do they press on? Do they pull back?
With trust now I beg that these two girls
who have endured dreadful discoveries
and suffered dread things at the hands of their kin—
that all their agonies may soon be over.
This day Zeus will accomplish something—
he'll accomplish something!
I am the prophet of this great contest: O
     that I could   1180

like a dove that is swift as the wind
soar to the clouds: see the strife from on high.

All-seeing Zeus! Overlord of the gods!
In this ambush may you open a path
for the men of this country to catch their prey—
victorious with powerful hands.
And may you, Athena—revered daughter—
clear the way. And I pray
for the help of Apollo the hunter
and his sister who runs with the speckled fleet deer: 1190
may the two of them come
to aid this country and its citizens.

Friend, wandering man, you'll not say now
the watcher is a false prophet. For I see those
daughters again, your two girls, and they're in
        good company.

OEDIPUS Where? What are you saying? What do you mean?

              Enter, from the direction of Thebes, THESEUS *with*
                          ANTIGONE *and* ISMENE.

ANTIGONE Oh father, father! Which god might grant you
        the gift of seeing this man—this best of men!—
        who has brought us back to you?

OEDIPUS My child! Are the two of you here?   1200

ANTIGONE We are, father, we're here—because Theseus saved us
        with his own good hands and those of his men.

OEDIPUS Come, child, come to your father. Come,
        let me touch
        what I'd never hoped to touch again.

ANTIGONE You'll get your wish: for the gift we give
        is what we long for.

OEDIPUS   Where are you—the two of you?

ANTIGONE   Here, together. Right beside you.

OEDIPUS   Little ones, dearest green shoots!

ANTIGONE   Dear to our father!   1210

OEDIPUS   Props for a man—

ANTIGONE   Ill-fated props for a man of misfortune.

OEDIPUS   These dear ones, I hold them close.
           If I should die this very instant, I wouldn't
           be completely wretched, for these two
           are here beside me. Children, give me your support—
           one on each side—and take root
           in the man who planted you. Let both of you
           give him, abandoned till now, some rest from
           his straying and wandering.
                                   And now   1220
           tell me what happened. Be as brief as you can:
           A short speech is always enough for younger women.

ANTIGONE   Here's the man who saved us, father: it's him
           you must listen to; it was he who did it.
           So any speech of mine will be brief, as you say.

OEDIPUS   My friend, don't be amazed that I insist on
           talking on like this with my children, who
           against all hope have come to light here.
           I know there's no cause except yourself
           for my fierce joy in these young ones of mine: 1230
           you made the light that shines on us here;
           it was you, no one else, who saved them.
           And may the gods provide for you as I'd wish,
           both you yourself and this your country.
           For only in you, all of you, have I found
           respect, right manners, and no false words.
           And now, with these words, I recognize

and repay your deeds. It's thanks to you and no other
that I have what I have.
Reach me your right hand, my lord,   1240
so I may, if it's proper, touch it and kiss you.
—But what am I saying? How could *I*, most wretched,
want *you* to touch a man
who wears the stain of every wrong? How could I
wish such a thing on you? No! I won't
let it happen! For none but those
who have lived through what I've lived through
can share what I've suffered. So receive
and return my greeting there where you stand,
and deal justly with me, as you've done this day.   1250

THESEUS I'm not at all amazed, Oedipus,
that you've lingered over the joy you find
in feeling these two children beside you.
Nor do I think it strange you've seized
on their words before words of mine.
This doesn't trouble me at all. For it's
not with words that we wish to make life
luminous, but with our deeds. I myself, old man,
am proof of this. I've not broken a single word
of the oath I swore: these women here, I
          bring them back   1260
alive, unharmed, untouched by the danger
          they were in.
There's no need to boast with empty words
how we won this hard-fought battle; you'll learn
          all about it
in the company of these two daughters. But here's
          a report now
come to my hands by chance as I hurried back:
tell me what you think of it. In words it's brief,
but still surprising. And a man should never
          take lightly
anything that happens.

OEDIPUS What is it, son of Aegeus? Tell me.
I know nothing of what you're asking.   1270

THESEUS They say that some man, some kin of yours but not a
           fellow-citizen,
       came running out of nowhere
       and is this minute sitting at that altar of Poseidon
       where I was sacrificing before I set out.

OEDIPUS Where is he from? What does he hope for, taking
           that seat?

THESEUS This is all I know: they tell me
       he only wants a short talk with you, and no
           trouble in it.

OEDIPUS What sort of talk? His sitting like that, there
       at the altar—it must be something of importance.

THESEUS They say he just wants to talk with you face to face   1280
       and then go away, unharmed by his coming.

OEDIPUS Who could he be, come to the altar like this?

THESEUS Think—have you any kinsman in Argos
       who might want a favor like this from you?

OEDIPUS My dear friend, stop where you are!

THESEUS What is it?

OEDIPUS Do not ask it of me.

THESEUS Ask what? Tell me.

OEDIPUS From your words I can tell exactly who it is
       there like that, supplicating the gods.   1290

THESEUS Who, then? Who is this man I might find fault with?

OEDIPUS My son! It's my son, my lord. I despise him.
His words would cause me more pain
than those of any other man.

THESEUS Why? Is it not possible simply to listen
and not do anything you don't wish to do?
Why is it so painful to hear him out?

OEDIPUS This voice, my lord, is the most loathed voice
that could ever find its way to a father's ear.
Don't force me to yield in this.   1300

THESEUS But if his sitting in supplication asks it of you?
Mustn't you remember your respect for the god?

ANTIGONE Father, I'm young, a woman, but listen to me:
let Theseus give to his own heart and to the god
the satisfaction of what he wishes. And for
          our sakes, too,
let this brother come. For if what he says
will do you no good, you can be sure
it won't drag you from the path you've chosen.
What harm, then, to listen to words? Speech
can bring to light evil intentions. Even if he did you   1310
most grievous wrong, it wouldn't be right
to give ill for ill: he is your child; show him
some understanding. Other men have bad children
and feel deep anger; but rebuked
by the gentle appeals of those dear to them,
they soften their hearts. You, you especially,
don't look to the present,
but consider those pains you yourself suffered
because of your father and your mother.
If you look at them, I know you'll see   1320
how a bad intent in turn ends in bad. Undeniable
the reminders you have of this,
deprived as you are of your two eyes.
So let us have our way, give us what we ask.
It isn't good to have to beg for what's right—

for a man who has been treated kindly
not to know how to answer in kind.

OEDIPUS Your words, child, have won a heavy pleasure.
So since you want it so much, let it be.

                                    To THESEUS.

Only, my friend, if that man is to come here,   1330
you mustn't let anyone take charge of my life.

THESEUS Only once, old man, do I need to hear
the words you've spoken. I've no wish to boast,
but know you are safe, if a god keeps me so.

                    Exit THESEUS, *in the direction of Athens.*

CHORUS *For me the man*
who wants more life than his measured lot
will be revealed in the end for all to see
shielding a life bent out of shape.
For the long days hold in store
many things to steer us nearer to pain   1340
and it's in vain we look for pleasure
in a life spun out past its given span.
And when Hades comes to play his part
helping all to the one end
no wedding-songs then no lyre no dancing
only death at the end of all.

Never to be born is the best story.
But when one has come to the light of day
second-best is to leave and go back
quick as you can back where you came from.   1350
For in his giddy light-headed youth
what sharp blow isn't far from a man? What
    affliction—
strife death dissension the ache of envy—
isn't close by? And in the end
his lot is to lack all power:
despised and cast out in friendless old age

where a man lives with nothing
but one hardship topping another.

I'm not alone in this: this wretch here—
as a northern shore lashed by sea and storm   1360
is battered flat from every side
so wave after wave of ruin and destruction
batter at this wretched man.
And they keep on coming:
from the place of the setting sun and its rising—
from the bright mid-point of day they come
and the bleak northern peaks of midnight.

ANTIGONE And here's the stranger, father, or so it seems.
He's alone at least, and as he makes his way toward us
his two eyes overflow with tears.   1370

OEDIPUS Who is it?

Enter, from the direction of Athens, POLYNEICES.

ANTIGONE The man we've had all this while in our thoughts:
Polyneices. He's here.

POLYNEICES   *With a moan.*
Ohhh! What am I to do? Should I weep, sisters,
first, for my own sorrows or, seeing his sufferings,
let my tears fall
for this old man, my father, whom I find
here with the two of you, banished
to this place of strangers? Dressed in filthy
old rags that have rotted his flesh;   1380
and the matted hair of his head—his eyeless head!—
tangled by every breeze; and his pouch
no different, the one he carries
for food scraps to fill his miserable belly.
To my shame I've come too late
to see all this. But now I myself
bear witness against myself: in caring for you

I've been the worst of men; there's no need to
    hear this
from another's tongue. But since Compassion
shares the throne with Zeus in all he does,   1390
let her stand beside you also, father—
for the wrongs that are done have some cure
and they're over now, there'll be no more of them.
Why are you silent?
Make some sound, father, don't turn your back
    on me.
Can you not offer a single word? Will you
treat me with contempt? Will you send me away
in silence again, with no explanation
even for your rage?
                     Daughters of this man, sisters
of my blood: try to liven his mouth   1400
that's silent as a stone, there's no moving it.
I beg you: don't let him spurn me like this—
while I stand a suppliant, at least to the god.
Not one answering word?

ANTIGONE Unhappy man: tell him yourself why you've come.
    Sometimes
words can draw a voice from silence, either for
some pleasure they bring, or by prompting
those who hear them to anger or pity.

POLYNEICES That's good advice: I'll speak out. But first
I call on the god to help me, from whose shrine   1410
the lord of this land led me, and gave me leave
to speak and listen, and to have safe passage
away from here. And strangers, I'd have this
from you, too, and the promise of it
from my father and sisters.
                  Now, father,
I want to tell you what I've come for:
I've been driven from my native land into exile
because I claimed the right, as the eldest born,
to sit on your throne and be sole ruler. Eteocles then,

though younger, answered by driving me out
    of the country.   1420
He defeated me not in any test of words or
    feat of arms
but by winning the city to his side. And I'm sure
that lurking behind all this is the Fury
who pursues you. Then, when I'd gone to Doric Argos
and taken Lord Adrastos there as my father-in-law,
I made sworn allies of all the chief men
among the Peloponnesian people—honored
    warriors all.
With their help I gathered against Thebes
a great force spearheaded by seven captains,
so I'd either perish there in a just battle   1430
or drive out of that land
those who have done these wicked deeds.
Let that be. But now, why am I here? Full
of suppliant prayers I've come to you, father—
my own prayers and those of my allies, camped now
with their seven spears and seven armies
across the great plain of Thebes. Men like
spear-shaking Amphiareus, first among warriors
and first, too, for reading signs
in the flight of birds. Second, the Aitolian son   1440
of Oineus, Tydeus he's called. Third,
Eteoclos, by birth an Argive. Hippomedon
is fourth, sent by his father, Telaos.
Fifth among them is Capaneus, who boasts
how he'll ravage the city of Thebes with fire
and fling it to destruction. Sixth
is an Arcadian, Parthenopaeus, who surges to battle
bearing a name that honors the virgin Atalanta,
she who in time became his mother; he
is her trusted son. And I, your son—   1450
or if not your son then a man conceived by
some awful destiny and deemed yours—
I lead this fearless army of Argives
against Thebes. These, father, all of us,
now beg you—as you value these children

and your own life—to let go
the fierce anger you feel against me,
as I march out now to repay my brother
who cast me away with nothing, stripped me
of my fatherland. Because—if we're to believe
         the oracles—   1460
the power lies with those who have you
as their ally. So now I implore you, by the
clear springs and the gods of our family—be
persuaded: give in to my words. Because we
are exiles and beggars, you are a stranger,
and we survive by fawning on others, the two of us
who have the one destiny. But—the thought
sickens me!—he who remains sole ruler
in our house, and lives in luxury, mocks
both of us in the same way. But I'll smash him   1470
into little pieces with ease
if you're my ally and think as I do.
And once I've driven him out,
I'll bring you home and settle you in your house,
and settle myself there, too. But I can
make such a boast only if you join
your will to mine, for without you I know
I won't even have the strength to come back alive.

CHORUS LEADER Oedipus, for the sake of the one who sent him,
tell the man what you think is right,   1480
then send him on his way.

OEDIPUS Well then, you men who live here and guard
         this land—
if Theseus hadn't sent this man to me
judging it right that he receive my answer,
he'd never hear the sound of my voice. But now
since he's been deemed worthy, he'll go away
having heard things which won't bring his life
much joy.
              Most vicious of men! When
you held scepter and throne in the city of Thebes
where your brother now rules alone, it was you   1490

who drove your own father away, making him
stateless, a homeless man. And you put
these clothes on him, which now you see and
now you weep at, now you've been caught out
in the same storm of sufferings as myself. But this
isn't something to spill a few tears over:
this has to be endured, endured by me
as long as I live, and with the memory of you
as my destroyer. It was you who gave me
this bitter bread. You who cast me out. Because
    of you   1500
I wander from day to day a beggar, begging
what I need to get through each day.
If I hadn't conceived these girls, these children
who take care of me, I'd not be alive at all,
for all the good *you've* done me. As it is,
these women keep me alive: they nurse
all my needs—these women
who are men, not women at all, in the way
they've shared the troubles I've had. But you
and your brother! The pair of you   1510
are sons of some other man, not mine. So
now your destiny gazes at you, but it does not
stare you straight in the face—as it will very soon
if those gathered armies march on Thebes.
For there's not the smallest chance in the world
you'll destroy that city. Before that happens,
you and your brother will fall in battle—fall
and lie stained and polluted in your own blood.
Such are the curses I once laid on you, and now
I summon these same curses to come   1520
as my ally, so you may think it worthwhile
to respect those who conceived you, and so
you may not escape the dishonor of behaving
as you've behaved to a sightless father. These girls
never did such things! So these curses of mine—
they smother your supplication, and your throne, too,
if Justice herself, ancient in name,
shares by ancient law the seat of Zeus.
Away! I spit you out! I disown you! You

are worst of the wicked! Take   1530
these curses I call down on you:
Never to conquer your native land
with the spear of victory! Never
to get home safe to the plains of Argos,
but to kill, and die with, him who expelled you!
This is my curse, and I call on Tartarus,
the hateful, all-fathering dark itself, to take you
to another home! And I call on these Goddesses
and Ares himself—that god of war
who has driven the two of you to terrible hate!   1540
So hear this, and go. Go tell the Argives and your
            trusted allies
that Oedipus has given his own sons
such gifts as these, such honors!

CHORUS LEADER Polyneices, I take no pleasure in your journey here.
So go, quickly, back where you came from.

POLYNEICES   *Groaning.*
Aahhh! Such a journey it's been! And to fail like this!
Ohhh! I grieve for my comrades: what an end
to the march from Argos we all rallied for.
To come to such an end sickens my heart.
Ohhh! And I can speak of it   1550
to none of my companions, nor can I shy from it,
but must meet in silence whatever happens.
Sisters, you who share this man's blood with me:
Since you hear my father fling bitter curses,
you—you at least—if the curses of our father
            bear fruit,
and you get back to your home in Thebes,
do not revile and dishonor me
but bury me yourselves with funeral offerings,
so the praise you now win from our father
for all the hard ways you take care of him   1560
will have one more praise added, just as true,
because of what you'll do for me.

ANTIGONE Polyneices, I beg you, please, listen to me!

POLYNEICES What is it, dearest Antigone? Tell me.

ANTIGONE Turn your army; lead it back to Argos. Right away.
Don't destroy yourself and that city.

POLYNEICES I can't.
How could I lead the same force there again,
if I'd shown them, even once, that I was afraid?

ANTIGONE But why there again? Why such anger? What good is
          it to you   1570
to destroy your country?

POLYNEICES It's shameful for me to run away. Shameful
for me the elder to be mocked by my brother.

ANTIGONE Don't you see then how you fulfill
the prophecies of this man here
who bellows death on both of you at each
          other's hands?

POLYNEICES Yes, that's what he wants. Mustn't we go along
          with it?

ANTIGONE   *With a groan of misery.*
Aahhh! Who will follow you
when he hears the doom our father predicted?

POLYNEICES But I won't report the darker details.   1580
The role of any true leader
is to give only good news, nothing less.

ANTIGONE That's your decision?

POLYNEICES It is; don't stop me. But for myself, this journey
must now be all my thought. Thanks
to my father and his Furies it's doomed
and bound for disaster. But may Zeus grant
          the two of you
his favor, if you do what I've asked.

Let me go now. Farewell. You'll never see me again
while I'm alive to see you.   1590

ANTIGONE   *With a keening cry.*
Ohh! Ohh! Ohh!

POLYNEICES No, don't weep for me.

ANTIGONE But brother, who would not weep for you,
seeing you rush open-eyed toward Hades?

POLYNEICES If it must be, then I'll die.

ANTIGONE Don't die! Listen to me!

POLYNEICES Don't argue me into what must not be.

ANTIGONE My heart is broken, then, if I'm to lose you.

POLYNEICES Whether things go one way or the other
is in the hands of the gods. But I pray   1600
that you two meet no disaster. The world knows
you don't deserve misfortune.

                    Exit POLYNEICES *in the direction of Thebes.*

CHORUS *From some new source*
I see strange things coming:
horrors heavy with death from the sightless stranger
or destiny itself reaching its end here.
For I can say whatever the gods think worthwhile
will never come to nothing. Time
holds all things always in its eye:
some it pitches down   1610
and next day raises others from the dust.
                                    Sound of thunder.
Thunder in the air! Ah Zeus!

OEDIPUS Children! Children! If there's anyone here,
send them for Theseus, that peerless man!

ANTIGONE Why do you summon him, father? For what
                   good purpose?

OEDIPUS Soon Zeus' thunderbolt will take me to Hades.
         But send for him, quickly!

                                         Sound of thunder.

CHORUS *Again! Look! Huge the flashing crash of it!*
        Clamor unspeakable! This hurled bolt!
        Fear slithers to the roots of my hair: 1620
        like a frighted creature my spirit is shivering.
        Lightning sets fire to the heavens again!
        What end will he unleash upon us?
        I fear it. For lightning never flashes to no purpose—
        never without some misfortune or other.
        Oh! Endless sky! Ah! Zeus!

OEDIPUS It's come, children: the end of my life as the
                   gods foretold.
         And now there's no turning it away.

ANTIGONE How do you know? What sign makes you think so?

OEDIPUS I know it well. But for my sake now   1630
         send someone to the lord of this land
         and bring him to me.

                                         Sound of thunder.

CHORUS   With a cry of terror.
        Aaahhh! See! Again!
        All around us ear-splitting din!
        Mercy mighty power show mercy!
        Mercy if you're bringing down some
        dark invisible thing to mother earth!
        Let me find you just
        and not—because I've looked at a man accursed—
        reap a reward that has no good in it.   1640
        To you I cry—Lord Zeus!

OEDIPUS Children, is he coming yet? Will he find me
         still alive and in my right mind?

ANTIGONE What is it you want to keep your mind clear for?

OEDIPUS To give them, as I promised, a fulfilling favor,
         in return for the good I got from them.

                                        Sound of thunder.

CHORUS   *With a pleading cry.*
         Ohh! Ohh! *Come! Come my son!*
         Even if you're sacrificing to Poseidon
         —making his high hearth holy with the blood
            of cattle—
         come to us here! For this stranger   1650
         thinks you your friends and this our city
         worth honoring with fair recompense
         for all the favor he's had here. Oh
         come, Lord! Hurry! Come! Come running!

                        Enter THESEUS, *from the direction of Athens.*

THESEUS What's this uproar?
          I can hear your voices in it and the voice of
              the stranger.
         Because of Zeus' own thunderbolt, is it?
         Or his hailstones hammering down? It's possible
         to imagine anything when a god comes storming.

OEDIPUS My lord, you've come as I've wished! Some god   1660
         has given your journey a fortunate end.

THESEUS What's happened, son of Laius?

OEDIPUS My life's balance is dipping. I don't want to die
         false to my promise to you and your city.

THESEUS What tells you you're about to die?

OEDIPUS The gods themselves tell me.
Not one of the promised signs was false.

THESEUS How are these things made clear, old man?

OEDIPUS By divine thunder rolling over and over,
bolt after flaming bolt from an almighty hand.   1670

THESEUS I believe you, for I see you've foretold much
and not spoken falsely. Tell me what I must do.

OEDIPUS I will teach you, son of Aegeus, things
which age can never spoil, things that now
will lie in store for this city. And soon,
without the touch of any guide, I'll take you
to the place where I shall die. Don't ever
show this place to anyone: keep the region secret,
along with the ground where this burial-site
lies hidden. So year after year this spot may be   1680
a defense mightier than a multitude of shields,
stronger than the spears of neighboring mercenaries.
And the sacred things I cannot speak of, when you go
alone to that place, you'll understand them: for I may
not reveal them to any of these citizens, nor even
to my own daughters, however much I love them.
So be sure to keep them safe always,
and when the time comes for you to die
give these signs to the chief man among you,
and let him reveal them to his successor,   1690
and so let it go on forever. That way
you will live in an unscathed city
which the dragon-seed men will never ravage.
For countless cities—however well ordered
        some may be—
turn easily to violence. But no matter how late,
the clear-sighted gods see when someone
turns away from them and embraces madness.
Son of Aegeus, don't ever wish
to experience this. But I teach such things

to one who knows them already. Let us go, then: 1700
for this sign from the gods now urges me
on to that place: let nothing any longer hold us back.
Children,

                                                            He rises.

follow me. For, strange as it seems,
now it is I who am your guide, just as you
have always guided your father. Come.
                                        He slowly moves toward the grove.
And lay no hand on me. Let me be.
Let me discover all on my own
the blessed tomb where it is my lot
to be hidden away in the earth at last.   1710
This way, come. Come this way. This is the way
the guide Hermes leads me, and the Goddess
who dwells below. O light invisible! Once, somehow,
you belonged to me. But now my body
feels your touch for the last time: I go now
to hide my life, at its end, in sightless Hades.
But you, dear man, dearest of strangers,
may you yourself, this land, and your people
flourish and prosper. And when I'm dead,
in your well-being remember me.   1720
And may good fortune be with you forever.

          He moves purposefully into the grove, THESEUS, ISMENE,
                              ANTIGONE, *others following.*

CHORUS *If it's right for me to show reverence with prayers*
        to the unseen Goddess and to you—
        master of those who dwell in darkness: Aidoneus!
          Aidoneus!—
        I pray that the stranger may without pain
        without a death that draws deep lamentation
        reach the plains of the dead that hide everything
        and the house of Styx.
        For though he's suffered greatly and to no purpose
        a just power may exalt him again.   1730

                                        Peal of thunder.

O Goddesses of earth! And you
invincible creature who lie down to sleep
before those gates which greet many strangers—you
who whimper before that cave—indomitable
guard they say at the entrance to Hades—
I beseech this son of Earth and Tartarus
to make a safe passage for the stranger
as he hurries headlong
toward Hades and the plains of the dead.
You I call on—Lord of endless sleep!   1740

Enter MESSENGER *from the direction of Athens.*

MESSENGER Men of the city! The quickest way I could tell
      my story
would be to say, "Oedipus is dead!" But no
      short speech
could explain what happened, nor even
could the deeds themselves, many as they were.

CHORUS LEADER Then he's dead, the unfortunate man?

MESSENGER Know this for sure: he's left this daily life of ours.

CHORUS LEADER Unhappy man! How did it happen?
Was his end painless? Was it god-ordained?

MESSENGER Indeed it was, which makes the wonder of it.
You were here, and you know already   1750
how he went forward from this place
with none of his dear ones guiding him, but
      he himself
guiding us all. But then, when he neared
the threshold there—steep as a cliff, with its great
bronze steps rooted in the earth—then he stood still
on one path where the path divides, just there
where a stone bowl marks the pact, everlasting,
between Theseus and Peirithous. And there—
halfway between that and Thoricos Rock, between
the hollow pear tree and the tomb of stone—   1760

he sat down. Then, unwinding his filthy rags, those
clothes he wore, he shouted orders to his children
to bring water from the near stream
for washing and making a libation.
So right away the two of them ran
to Demeter's stony rise, which stood in full view—
Demeter, mother of all young plants. Then,
with no more delay they brought him back
all he asked for, preparing him, as the custom is,
by bathing him and changing his garments.   1770
Then, when he'd done all he wished to do
and every one of his desires was met,
earth-dwelling Zeus thundered out
and the two young women shuddered at the sound
and fell at their father's knee in tears
and kept beating their breasts and wouldn't give up
their loud wailing cries. But he,
when he heard their sudden bitter cries,
folded them both in his arms, and he said:
Children, on this day you have no father.   1780
All that was my life is destroyed on me now:
you won't ever again have to labor for me
or look after me as you've always done.
I know, children, what a hard life it's been.
But there's one thing can dispel it all,
one word is enough to wipe hardship away:
Love, that this man had for you—no man
can love you more. And now the two of you
must go on living the rest of your lives
without him. So he spoke, and the three of them
     together   1790
embraced each other, sobbing and crying.
But when they'd shed their last tear at last
and no more loud cries were filling the air,
then there was silence.

        Then, all of a sudden,
a voice, some voice, someone
was summoning him. And every one of us
felt the hair stand up on our heads with fear.
For again and again a god calls him,

echoing from every direction at once:
You! You there! Oedipus! Why   1800
do we put off our departure like this? What
a long delay you're making! Then,
when he heard himself called by the god,
he asked that Theseus, lord of this land, should
          draw near.
And when Theseus had approached, he said:
Friend of my heart, give these children
the pledge of your hand, that time-honored pledge.
And you, children, give your hands to this man.
Promise me you'll never give up these women
willingly to anyone. Promise me   1810
you'll always do what your heart tells you
is for their good. Then Theseus, that
          large-hearted man,
without pity or tears promised under oath
that for the stranger he'd do all he was asked.
And when all this was finished, Oedipus
laid both his blind hands on his two children:
Children, he said, *you must be brave now,*
and go away from this place,
and not judge it right to see what's forbidden
or hear men say what must not be heard.   1820
So go now. Go quickly away.
Let Theseus alone, who has authority here, remain
to learn the things that are done in this place.
All of us there, we heard him say this,
and with those two young women—in tears,
with loud moans—we moved away. But soon
we turned, and from far off
we saw that man was nowhere to be seen,
and the king himself was holding his hand up
to shade his eyes, as if there appeared some   1830
awesome terror, and he couldn't bear the sight.
Then, in a little while, we see him, in silence,
making a grave and stately bow
at once to the earth and Olympus of the gods.
But what sort of death took that man's life
no mortal tongue could tell, except

Theseus himself, that dear lord. No flaming
thunderbolt from god dispatched him,
and he wasn't snatched by a sudden sea-squall—
but it was either some escort from the gods in heaven   1840
or those below in the land of the dead,
or the dark deep earth itself breaking open
with kindness. For the man was taken
with no groaning, nor the pain of any sickness on him:
his death a wonder, surely, if any man's death is.
All I've spoken may seem mad to you,
but I make no apology nor seek to be excused
by anyone here who thinks me mad indeed.

CHORUS LEADER   Where are his children?
And the friends who went with them?   1850

MESSENGER   The girls aren't far off.

                                        Sound of keening.
There, that's the sound of their crying: they're close at
      hand.

                        Enter ANTIGONE *and* ISMENE *from the direction
                                        of Athens.*

ANTIGONE   With a wail of despair.
            Aaahhh! For us it is for us indeed
            two ill-fated women to bewail
            not once or twice but forever and ever
            the indelibly cursed blood of a father
            filling our veins!
            Once his life was a hardship to us
            a heavy everlasting trouble—
            but now at the end we'll carry away   1860
            things we can't account for at all
            although we've seen and suffered them.

CHORUS   *What? What has happened?*

ANTIGONE   *Friends—you can guess.*

CHORUS *He's gone?*

ANTIGONE *Gone—and just as you'd hope:*
For how could you ever think otherwise
and he not taken by Ares or the surging sea
but snatched off to the Invisible Fields.
   Carried away
by a death that's secret and strange.   1870
Poor sister!
Death-dealing night has settled on our eyes!
Wandering in a far-off land
or over the waves of some distant sea
how shall we weather this hard life at all?

ISMENE *I don't know. May fatal Hades take me*
down to my father: to die
in my misery with him old as he was—
for the life to come isn't worth living.

CHORUS *Best pair of children:*   1880
Try to bear bravely what the god gives.
Don't let the blaze of these feelings inflame you.
There's nothing to blame in what you've come to.

ANTIGONE *But one can even long to have hardship back:*
for what's not dear was dear to me
when I held him in these two arms.
Oh father! Dear father! You who now
wear darkness under the earth forever: even there
you'll never lose her love or mine.

CHORUS *He fared—*   1890

ANTIGONE *As he wished.*

CHORUS *What do you mean?*

ANTIGONE *Dying in the foreign land he longed for*
and now he has his bed
below in the kindly shade forever
and the grief he left behind finds tears.
For father I grieve for you indeed—these eyes

401

> *overflow with tears—and sorrowstruck I don't*
> > *know how*
> *to make such grief go away.*

                                              With a groan.

> *Ohhh!*   1900
> *Your wish was to die in a foreign land*
> *but you died like this—*
> *far from me. All alone.*

ISMENE   With a keening cry.

> *Ohhh! And what fate*
> *waits for me a wretched girl*
> *or dear sister waits for you*
> *now our father has deserted us?*

CHORUS *But since at last*
> *he was content to let his life go—*
> *dear girls cease grieving:*   1910
> *misfortune easily seizes men.*

ANTIGONE *Sister, let's fly back—*

ISMENE *To do what?*

ANTIGONE *I'm caught by a wild desire.*

ISMENE *What desire?*

ANTIGONE *To see the home there in the earth—*

ISMENE *Whose home?*

ANTIGONE *My heart is broken! Our father's home!*

ISMENE *But how could it be right? Don't you see that?*   1920

ANTIGONE *Why do you rebuke me?*

ISMENE *And this, too—*

ANTIGONE *Again! What is it?*

ISMENE *That he fell*
> *far from everyone.*
> *There is no tomb!*

ANTIGONE   *Take me there—*
            then kill me, too!

ISMENE   With a wail of despair.
            Aaahhh!
            Wretched life! How will I live?   1930
            Abandoned again! Helpless! Poor!

CHORUS   *Dear girls have no fear.*

ANTIGONE   *But where can I escape to?*

CHORUS   *You both escaped before.*

ANTIGONE   *What?*

CHORUS   *You fell into no harm.*

ANTIGONE   *Yet I'm thinking—*

CHORUS   *What are you thinking?*

ANTIGONE   *We can't get home.*

CHORUS   *Don't try.*   1940

ANTIGONE   *Trouble holds us hard.*

CHORUS   *That was so before.*

ANTIGONE   *Hard then. Impossible now.*

CHORUS   *A sea of troubles has been your lot.*

ANTIGONE   *Yes! Yes!*

CHORUS   *That's what I say, too.*

ANTIGONE   With a gasp of despairing resignation.
            Aaahhh! Zeus! Where can we go?
            Toward what hope now
            will the god-force drive me?

                                        Enter THESEUS *from the grove.*

THESEUS   Girls, cease your lamentations, wipe away your tears.   1950
           For when earth's darkness is given to one as a gift,
                a grace,
           let there be no grieving: it tempts the gods' anger.

ANTIGONE Son of Aegeus, we fall at your knees.

THESEUS For what, my children? What can I give you?

ANTIGONE With our own eyes
we would see the place where our father is buried.

THESEUS But it isn't lawful or right to go there.

ANTIGONE Lord of Athens, what do you mean?

THESEUS He forbade me this very thing, children,
that anyone should ever go near that place   1960
or break the silence of that blessed sanctuary
where he abides. And he told me
if I followed his words I'd keep this country forever
free of suffering and harm. And the god
heard us, and so did Oath, Zeus' son,
who hears all we say.

ANTIGONE If this indeed was his final wish, we must be satisfied.
But send us back now to Thebes, land of
              our ancestors:
we may yet, somehow,
stop the slaughter rushing toward our brothers.   1970

THESEUS I'll do that, and whatever else would in any way
              serve you,
and please him who has gone just now
under earth's lid. I must be always ready for this,
and never grow weary.

CHORUS LEADER But cease now, cease your keening:
for in every way these things stand under
the steady sway of some shaping power.

NOTES

The numbers in bold refer to the line numbers in the translation; they are followed by the line numbers in the Greek text of the play edited by H. Lloyd-Jones and N. Wilson and published by Oxford University Press (1990; hereafter Oxford Classical Text, or OCT).

1–134 / 1–116 *Prologue* In this section of the play before the entrance of the Chorus, Sophocles establishes the physical setting and introduces the question: where does Oedipus belong?

47–48 / 43 *In other places they rightly have other names* The Eumenides are also referred to as Furies, Erinyes, the Dread Ladies, Holy Ones, or Implacable Maidens.

65 / 57 It is possible that the *Bronze-footed Threshold* marked an entrance to the underworld.

135–269 / 117–253 *Parodos* The entrance song of the Chorus. The Chorus enters from the direction of Athens. They are elderly citizens of Colonus who have heard that someone has entered the grove of the Furies, and they have come to protect the grove and themselves from this transgression. Choruses in Greek tragedy, made up of a group of fifteen men who sing and dance in the orchestra (the circular space in the theater between the semi-circular seating for the audience and the stage and skene) are the oldest element in the evolutionary growth of the genre. We know little about the choreography of their dance, but the words of their songs reveal to us the rhythms to which they danced. Very often their opening song or chant is set to an anapaestic rhythm—short beat, short beat, long beat—to which it is easy to process slowly onto the stage. In this case the

Chorus comes hurrying in to a livelier rhythmical pattern because it has heard the news of a stranger's intrusion into the grove. Choral songs create, by the difference in the way they are performed and in what they say, a contrast with the episodes, or conversations among actors. Although the Chorus is given a group character appropriate to the action of the play, it is never fully immersed in the action of the play. Aeschylus, Sophocles, and Euripides use their choruses differently not only from each other but often from play to play. In this play the contrast between choral songs and episodes is somewhat modified by Sophocles' frequent use of the *kommos*, or sung exchange between chorus and an actor or actors, in place of the choral song. For example, after line 150 (137) Oedipus joins the Chorus' song, first chanting anapaests with them and then at line 186 (179) sharing their song, as does Antigone at line 191 (182).

270–739 / 254–667 *First episode* The episode falls into two parts, divided by a *kommos* between Oedipus and the Chorus (553–608 / 510–48). In the first part Oedipus' daughter/sister Ismene arrives from Thebes to give Oedipus news of recent oracles concerning him; in the second part Theseus enters, in response to Oedipus' request, and offers Oedipus a home in Athens.

292–93 / 274 *but those at whose hands I suffered / I was knowingly destroyed by them.* Oedipus here refers to Jocasta's and Laius' decision to leave him exposed in the wild as an infant, with his ankles pierced, because they had received a prophecy that he was destined to kill his father.

295 / 275 Supplication was a ritual act that often had serious consequences for both those who supplicated and those who received the suppliant; a number of Greek tragedies dramatize those consequences. If someone in need made himself or herself a suppliant to another with the power to help, both parties were bound by rules of behavior that the Greeks believed were enforced by Zeus Hikesios (Zeus of the Suppliants).

371ff. / 337ff. Oedipus' reference to "Egyptian habits" reflects an assumption common to many Greeks that Egyptian culture was a mirror image of their own, substituting "normal" practices with their opposites. However, educated Greeks (such as the historian Herodotos) also had a deep respect for Egyptian culture, recognizing it as older than their own and having had a deep influence on it.

387 / 354 *with all those prophecies* These earlier prophecies gave Oedipus the knowledge he refers to in his earlier conversation with the Stranger, that he would find his final resting place in the grove of the Eumenides and that his presence would constitute a gift to those who received him in their land.

402–3 / 367–69 Creon, Oedipus' uncle and brother-in-law and Jocasta's brother, became king after Oedipus discovered that his patricide and incest were the cause of the plague destroying Thebes and consequently blinded himself. Oedipus' family is descended from Cadmus, the founder of Thebes. The myth of this family, like many mythical families, includes several instances of violence committed against family members by family members in a struggle for power.

438–39 / 401–2 The prophecies seem to indicate that whoever protects and controls Oedipus' tomb will receive protection from it. The Thebans cannot bury Oedipus within their walls, because he killed his father, but they can hope to watch over the tomb and receive its protection if he is brought back to Thebes and, when he dies, is buried just outside the walls.

506ff. / 466ff. The description that follows gives us a very immediate sense of how a purification ritual was performed. Sophocles' inclusion of such a full description marks the importance he gives in the play to the laws by which humans order their lives and also to their limits. For example, the careful description of this ritual makes it clear that it belongs to a particular place and group of people; it is the kind of thing Oedipus must learn anew each time he comes to a new place. Yet Oedipus seems to invest it with a meaning that transcends its local practice (for further discussion, see the Introduction, pp. 310, 313).

569 / 521ff. The manuscript here reads "I bore it unwillingly or unknowingly," but there must be a corruption in the text, because the manuscript reading is metrically impossible. We follow the Oxford Classical Text's (OCT) reading "willingly" (accepted by many other editors) and assume that Oedipus is here making a reference both to his self-blinding and his acceptance of exile.

572 / 525 Oedipus refers to the reward he received for answering the riddle of the Sphinx: the kingship and Jocasta's hand in marriage. The offspring of this incestuous union are Antigone, Ismene, Eteocles, and Polyneices.

606 / 547 *In the grip of disaster I destroyed and murdered* is the translation of the line as emended by H. Lloyd-Jones in the OCT. The manuscript reading, "I murdered and destroyed others," doesn't make sense in the context, so an emendation is necessary. It is interesting that the text of the play is corrupt in several places where the issue of Oedipus' guilt or innocence is being discussed, clear evidence that this question troubled generations of readers and scribes copying the play.

623 / 562 Theseus was raised in his mother's birthplace, Troezen, without knowledge that his father was Aegeus, king of Athens. Like Oedipus, he learned his true parentage only as an adult.

699 / 632 *our alliance* Theseus seems here to refer to a military alliance that has existed over the generations between the rulers of Athens and the rulers of Thebes. It cannot be an alliance specifically between Oedipus and Theseus, since they did not know each other prior to this meeting.

705 / 637 Here again, a possible corruption in the text has frustrated scholars who wish to determine exactly what kind of legal status Theseus is offering Oedipus. Whether or not Theseus' idea is to incorporate Oedipus fully into Athens as a citizen, it is clear at least that he is offering him a home and the readiness to protect him as if he were a citizen.

732 / 658–60 The OCT here brackets three lines in which Theseus personifies and belittles the threats Oedipus fears. These lines were first deleted by a German scholar in the nineteenth century, and the OCT follows his lead, on aesthetic grounds rather than because of any corruption in the text.

740–75 / 668–719 *First stasimon* the first of the independent choral songs composed with pairs of stanzas (strophe and antistrophe), each member of the pair having an identical rhythmical pattern.

751 / 683 The *two Great Goddesses* are Demeter and Persephone, mother and daughter, who were the patron goddesses of the Eleusinian Mysteries; these were an extremely popular mystery cult in nearby Eleusis that seems to have offered its initiates a vision of some kind of afterlife, contrary to the commonly held belief that death was the negation of life and the dead were shapeless, empty shadows—nothingness—in the underworld. One of the many beauties of this song to Colonus, Sophocles' birthplace, and by extension to Athens, is its evocation of an eternal city dependent only

on this song and the hearts and minds of those who hear it for its existence.

758ff. / 694ff. The last two stanzas celebrate the olive, the bridle, and the oar, evoking Athens' foundation myth, in which Athena and Poseidon give these things to Athens in a competition to become its patron god.

760 / 695 The Doric isle of Pelops is the Peloponnese, the southern mainland of Greece, whose most famous city was Sparta, against which Athens has been waging a war and by which it is about to be defeated (see the Introduction). Sparta was founded by Dorians, whose ethnicity the Athenians considered, seemingly correctly, to be different from their own. The Athenians and Spartans spoke different dialects of Greek that were mutually comprehensible but aurally very distinct.

773ff. / 715ff. The text of the last lines of this ode is corrupt, but the image seems clear. In honoring Poseidon for the gift of the oar that allows man to travel over his realm, the Chorus evokes the image of the little waves that the oars make as they dip into the water and sees the "white caps" that also rise on the surface of the sea as the footsteps of the Nereids, nymphs of the sea, accompanying the ship.

776–1149 / 720–1043 *Second episode* Creon, Oedipus' brother-in-law and uncle, arrives from Thebes to persuade Oedipus to return with him. When Oedipus refuses, Creon tries to force him first by revealing that he has already captured Ismene and then by seizing Antigone. Theseus arrives to stop Creon from dragging Oedipus away also and demands that Creon take him to Antigone and Ismene so that he can restore them to Oedipus. The episode is broken at two points (904–18 / 833–43, 960–74 / 876–86) by a strophe and antistrophe in which the Chorus, Oedipus, and Creon, we may suppose, sing and mime the action of seizure and resistance.

811 / 757 *purge this shame* The manuscripts preserve here the imperative "hide!" The editors of the OCT mark the verb as corrupt but do not suggest an emendation. The difficulty with the manuscript reading is both that Creon has just said, "I may not hide what is plain to see," so the command to hide seems contradictory, and that there is no object for the verb "hide." However, Creon clearly wants Oedipus to remove himself from the possibility of the world's censure and the shame it brings the family. Hence our "purge this shame."

845–47 / 784–86 Oedipus accuses Creon of pretending that he will allow Oedipus back into Thebes and will eventually allow him to be buried there. Creon's real motive is to keep Oedipus out of Thebes because, as a patricide, he may pollute the city, but ensure that no one else—and particularly not Athens—can receive the protection of his tomb by harboring him and burying him within the boundaries of their city.

893ff. / 826ff. It is exciting to try to imagine how this struggle would have been choreographed in the original production. It is my feeling that, after Antigone is removed bodily from the stage, there is very little physical contact among Creon, Oedipus, and the Chorus. Rather, one might imagine a stylized and choreographed struggle between Creon and the Chorus that would represent first the Chorus' failed attempt to block Antigone's departure and then their successful attempt to keep Creon away from Oedipus. The rhythmic pattern of the lines is excited iambic trimeter, with one character breaking in and completing another's line, alternating with two stanzas of sung lyrics in which Creon, Oedipus, and the Chorus snatch the song from each other in short spurts.

968 / 882 The words *Zeus knows* were suggested by the great English editor and commentator on Sophocles, R. Jebb, to fill out a part of this line that had been lost. There are several other suggestions; the OCT offers "Zeus will not bring this about, I know." We prefer Jebb's emendation.

1043 / 947 *your Council—that makes its home on Ares' hill* Creon is referring to the area at the foot of the Acropolis called the Areopagus (Hill of Ares) and the council that met there. One of the oldest governmental institutions to survive into the fourth century, the council changed in both function and membership from its aristrocratic beginnings in the sixth century. Aeschylus' *Oresteia* dramatizes the establishment of the council as a civic replacement for the Furies' role as avengers of crimes against the family, and particularly homicide. This function the council retained throughout its history, but at other times it also was responsible for ensuring that the laws by which the Athenians ruled themselves were upheld.

1050 / 954–55 The OCT follows the editor Blaydes in deleting two of Creon's lines here that seem out of place and inappropriate to Creon's character.

1124–28 / 1028–33 These lines follow, in the manuscript tradition, line 1138 / 1027, where they do not make easy sense. A. E. Housman, whose life and scholarship have recently been dramatized in Tom Stoppard's play *The Invention of Love*, suggested their transposition to the place where the OCT prints them and we have translated them.

1126ff. / 1031ff. Theseus suspects that Creon is being aided in his attempt to remove Oedipus by Athenians who would support Thebes against Athens, if they came into conflict. The remark would resonate strongly with the audience, for whom the issue of Athenian supporters of Sparta against Athenian interests was an immediate reality. It also characterizes Theseus as a careful ruler who is watchful over the good of the whole city, rather than the interest of a faction. In this way, although portrayed as a monarch, Theseus also has a democratic bent to his leadership.

1150–92 / 1044–95 *Second stasimon* The Chorus imagines in its song the struggle over Ismene and Antigone between Theseus and Creon's men. They picture it taking place at some point along the path from Athens to Eleusis, the site of the Eleusinian Mysteries. In this way Theseus' recovery of Ismene and Antigone echoes, however subtly and remotely, Demeter's journey to recover Persephone from the Underworld, which the Eleusinian Mysteries commemorate. The children of Eumolpus are members of the family who, generation after generation, administered the Mysteries as chief priests. The second stanza of this song suggests a different route that the Thebans may have taken that would not bring them to Eleusis.

1193–1334 / 1096–210 *Third episode* After Theseus returns Antigone and Ismene to Oedipus, he reports the presence of a suppliant at the altar of Poseidon who wishes to speak to Oedipus. Once Oedipus realizes that this is his son/brother Polyneices, he refuses to speak to him, until Antigone persuades him at least to hear what Polyneices has to say.

1242 / 1132 Greeks believed that a man who has committed patricide is polluted and that the stain of his pollution can spread, through contact, to another individual or a community. Exile was a common form of purification and punishment for such pollution, and, in exile, the murderer can commune with others without endangering them. However, the sense Oedipus has here, and that the Chorus had earlier, that even in exile he is a danger to those with whom he comes in contact, derives from a less formalistic or legalistic sense of his state as a polluted being. Sophocles dramatizes in this moment Oedipus' paradoxical being as both polluted and powerful.

1275 / 1160 To sit upon an altar is to place yourself as a suppliant under the protection of the god and the people within that god's purview. Oedipus therefore knows that the man Theseus is talking about is in need but does not know the nature of the need.

1335–67 / 1211–48 *Third stasimon* The Chorus expresses a pessimistic view of the value of human life in light of the evidence of Oedipus' suffering.

1368–1721 / 1249–555 *Fourth episode* Polyneices asks Oedipus to join him in his attack on Thebes to depose his brother, Eteocles. Oedipus curses Polyneices and Eteocles, and Polyneices leaves to lead his six allies against Thebes, knowing that the expedition is doomed to failure. Before he leaves he secures from Antigone a promise to bury his body. Between Polyneices' departure and the climactic movement of Oedipus into the grove of the Furies, the Chorus sings two pairs of stanzas, **1603–54 / 1447–99**, in which it responds to the thunder and lightning that follow Polyneices' departure as omens of some new and strange thing. Between each stanza Oedipus urgently insists that Theseus be summoned, as he knows the thunder and lightning announce his own imminent death. Theseus arrives, and Oedipus rises from his seat unaided and leads Antigone, Ismene, and Theseus into the grove of the Furies.

1389–90 / 1267–68 *But since Compassion shares the throne with Zeus* The word we here translate as Compassion, *Aidos*, appears also at line **260 / 247**, where we translate it as *respect*. It also appears as a verb at line **1312–13 / 1192**, where we translate it as *show him / some understanding*. *Aidos* is an important concept for understanding the way the Greeks regulated their social behavior. People judged their own behavior by the way they imagined others would view it. *Aidos* could be described as the quality that makes one conscious of, and concerned about, others' opinions of one's behavior. In the first use Antigone is asking the members of the Chorus, who are in a position to give or to deny Oedipus what he wants, to be aware of how others will judge their treatment of him if they abuse that power and do not show him respect. At lines **1312–16 / 1192–94**, Antigone is appealing to Oedipus to treat Polyneices as other fathers who are angry at their sons do. In this passage Polyneices, who also fears that Oedipus will not give him what he needs, appeals to Oedipus' awareness of how he will be viewed as a father. Antigone, too, has attempted to persuade Oedipus to see Polyneices by warning him of seeming too harsh toward his son.

1436 / 1305 Polyneices describes the alliance of the seven heroes who joined together to attack Thebes under his leadership. The story of the "Seven against Thebes," each hero stationed at one of Thebes' seven gates, was a part of the Oedipus myth that had its own narrative tradition in both epic and drama. Aeschylus' play *The Seven against Thebes* and Euripides' *Suppliants* both treat aspects of this story, for example.

1447 / 1320 Parthenopaeus' name contains the word *parthenos*, which means unmarried girl, virgin. Atalanta, Parthenopaeus' mother, resisted marriage by insisting that only a man who could beat her in a footrace could marry her. She killed those she could overtake. She was finally defeated by Melanion, who distracted her in the race with golden apples given to him by Aphrodite. Their son was Parthenopaeus.

1519 / 1375 Presumably, Oedipus here refers to curses he made against his sons when he was first exiled.

1558 / 1410 Polyneices' request of Antigone to bury his body when he dies at Thebes had provided Sophocles, thirty-five years earlier, with the subject for his *Antigone*. His reference to the events of that play here reminds the audience that Oedipus' curse on his sons is the indirect cause of his beloved Antigone's death. Thus Oedipus, despite his great power, is also seen to be subject to a rhythm of events outside his control.

1577 / 1426 Polyneices' inability to act in defiance of Oedipus' curse is the flip side of his refusal to respond to Oedipus' desire when he was being exiled. Both the refusal and the submission characterize Polyneices as a figure who is unable successfully to establish his own independence in the face of the controlling forces of his life.

1586 / 1434 *my father and his Furies* This phrase is ambiguous, and our understanding of Polyneices differs considerably depending on what we think he means here. By the reference to Oedipus' Furies, Polyneices may be blaming Oedipus' own terrible past for Polyneices' own terrible future, or he may refer to Oedipus' curse as his Furies—the punishment he has been able to evoke for Polyneices' treatment of him.

1623 / 1468 *What end will he unleash upon us?* is a translation of the text as transmitted by the manuscripts, understanding Zeus, or possibly Oedipus, as the subject. Alternatively, one could understand the lightning as the subject

("What end will it unleash upon us?"), but then the objection of the editors of the OCT that it is hard to understand how lightning might produce an "end" seems valid. The editors of the OCT emend the text to read "Truly, he will release his weapon." We have chosen to keep the manuscript reading and understand Zeus as the subject. Zeus' sending of the lightning can be seen as the sign of the end to which he is bringing Oedipus.

1678–81 / 1522–25 The place where Oedipus dies becomes the site of a hero cult that was still a place of worship in Sophocles' time.

1693 / 1534 The dragon-seed men are the Thebans, whose ancestors sprang from dragon's teeth sowed in the earth by Cadmus.

1703 / 1542 This spectacular moment, when Oedipus rises and leads the others through the central door of the skene unaided, corresponds dramatically to the scene at the beginning of the play when Antigone helps Oedipus move with great difficulty from the grove to the rock where he has been sitting throughout the play, until this moment. The transformation of Oedipus that is implied in the contrast between these two moments lies at the center of the play's mystery (see the Introduction, pp. 305–9, for further discussion).

1712 / 1548 The *guide Hermes* is a reference to the god Hermes' function as the psychopomp, the leader of the dead down into the underworld; the goddess "who dwells beneath" is Persephone, Demeter's and Zeus' daughter and wife of Hades.

1722–40 / 1556–78 *Fourth stasimon* The song that the Chorus sings, wishing for an easy death for Oedipus, makes reference to the gods of the dead, Persephone (the "unseen Goddess") and Hades ("the master of those who dwell in darkness, Aidoneus"). Aidoneus is another name for the god of the dead. The "goddesses of earth" are the Eumenides, and the "invincible crea-ture" asleep at the entrance of Hades is the three-headed dog Cerberus, whose presence at the entrance to the underworld keeps the living from descending and the dead from ascending.

1741–977 / 1579–779 *Exodos* A messenger describes the ritual preparation of Oedipus for his death, his farewell to his daughters, the voice of a god summoning him, and his final mysterious disappearance that only Theseus witnesses. The Messenger speech is a rich dramatic device frequently used by Sophocles and Euripides. It allows the playwright to narrate action that would be impossible to represent on stage. Both Sophocles and Euripides incorporate detailed visual information into these speeches in order to let the audience "see" what has happened offstage. In this case Sophocles has included very precise geographical markers that would, we suppose, evoke a landscape known in reality to the audience. Of course, none of the details of the landscape has survived, so that we cannot know how close to reality Sophocles has made this description.

1853–949 / 1670–750 The final *kommos* of the play takes the form of a lament for the dead. Antigone and Ismene as the surviving female members of the family would, under normal circumstances, perform a ritual lament at the tomb of their father. Here, since they cannot approach the place of Oedipus' death, their song must have given the audience a powerful sense of unanchored dislocation. Antigone echoes this sense of dislocation when she asks first to be taken to Oedipus' tomb and then to be allowed to go home to Thebes. The lack of spatial focus at the end of the play is an important coda to the intense certainty of Oedipus' movement toward and knowledge of his death place and leaves the audience with a sense of disorienting uncertainty. The meter of the *kommos* incorporates a fair number of iambic lines that we have printed as part of the sung lyrics, although it is possible that these lines were spoken or chanted rather than sung.

1869 / (1681) *Invisible Fields* is a reference to the underworld, where all things lose form and substance.

1950–77 / 1751–79 The final lines of the play, a conversation between Theseus and Antigone in anapaestic rhythm, start the action narrated in Sophocles' play *Antigone*, as Theseus promises to secure Antigone's return to Thebes, where she hopes to stop her brothers' civil war. This final ironic twist, after Theseus' promise to Oedipus to protect Antigone and Ismene, returns the audience, after the mystery of Oedipus' death, to the tension between power and powerlessness that Oedipus—and all mankind—never escapes.

1964–65 / 1766–77 *And the god / heard us* Sophocles does not specify which god is meant here, just as it is unclear which god speaks to Oedipus just before he dies. In both cases he seems to evoke a nameless divine power attending the end of Oedipus' life to deepen the mystery of that end. That Oath, too, is present marks the paramount importance of the binding pact between Theseus and Oedipus that ensures Athens a future "free of suffering," the form of which is also shrouded in mystery.

GLOSSARY

ABAI: Small site northeast of Thebes with an oracle of Apollo.

ADRASTOS: The king of Argos; Polyneices married his daughter in order
to make a military alliance with Argos against Thebes.

AIDONEUS: Another name for Hades, god of the dead.

AKHERON: River in Epirus in northwestern Greece, supposed to lead to
the Underworld. Popular etymology connected it with the
Greek word *akhos* ("woe") as the "river of sorrow."

AMPHION: Early mythical king of Thebes, who helped build the city by
the power of his magical lyre, which caused the stones to leap
spontaneously into their places in the walls. He was husband of
Niobe.

ANTIGONE: Daughter (and sister) of Oedipus, and of his wife (and
mother) Jocasta, and sister of Ismene, Eteokles, and Polyneices;
betrothed to Creon's son, Haimon.

APHRODITE: Olympian goddess of erotic passion; often regarded as the
mother of the god Eros, the personified force of sexual desire.

APOLLO: The god of prophecy, light, and healing whose temple at
Delphi is, through the inspired intermediary of his priestess
(the Pythia), the source of the prophecies that center on the
family of Laios. He is called "Lycian"—an ambiguous epithet
whose meaning suggests the "destroyer"—and Phoebus.

ARES: Olympian god of war, son of Zeus and Hera, sometimes associated by the early Greeks with Thrace and the warlike Thracians. In *Oedipus the King*, Ares is uniquely called the god of plague.

ARGIVE: Adjective from Argos.

ARGOS: A major city of northern Peloponnesos and allied with Polyneices in his attempt to overthrow his brother, Eteocles, and win back the throne of Thebes. In the fifth century, Argos' allegiances in the Peloponnesian War wavered.

ARTEMIS: Daughter of Zeus and Leto, sister of Apollo, a goddess associated with animals, mountains, and the hunt.

ATALANTA: A mythic figure who resisted marriage by challenging all her suitors to a foot race. When she was beaten by Hippomenes, she married him and gave birth to Parthenopaeus, one of the six leaders who join Polyneices in his attack on Thebes.

ATHENA: Virgin daughter of Zeus, also called Pallas; goddess of intelligence, and as a warrior goddess, patron goddess of Athens.

BACCHUS: Another name for Dionysos. Thebes, the place where he vindicated his claim over Greece, is given the epithet "Bacchic."

BAKKHAI (BACCHAE): Female worshipers of Dionysos, particularly in the excited, ecstatic dances and processions that form a part of his cult.

BOREAS: God of the north wind, whose abode is in Thrace. He carries off the Athenian princess Oreithyia to be his wife, by whom he has a daughter, Kleopatra; for her story, see PHINEUS.

BOSPOROS: A narrow channel in Thrace separating what is now European from Asian Turkey and connecting the Sea of Marmara (ancient Propontis) with the Black Sea.

CADMUS: The founder of Thebes; Thebans are sometimes called Cadmeians or dragon-seed men, because of the story that Cadmus created the first inhabitants of his city by sowing the teeth of the Serpent, the dragon he had slain in the earth.

CEPHISUS: River in Attica that was said rarely to run dry, as most Greek rivers did and do in the hot summer months.

CREON (KREON): Successor of Oedipus as king of Thebes; brother of Jokasta and so the maternal uncle of Antigone, Ismene, Eteokles, and Polyneikes. Creon's son Haimon is betrothed to Antigone.

DANAE: Daughter of King Akrisios of Argos, who, learning of a prophecy that her child will kill him, imprisons her in a tower of bronze. Zeus, however, visits her in a shower of gold and fathers Perseus, who eventually fulfills the prophecy.

DAULIA: In Phocis (the region of Delphi), just off the road from Thebes to Delphi to the north.

DELPHI: In the mountains above the north coast of the gulf of Corinth; the site of the greatest prophetic shrine in Greece with its temple to Apollo and his oracle.

DEMETER: Olympian goddess of fertility and particularly of the fertile earth, the harvest, and grain. She is the mother, by Zeus, of Persephone, who is carried away by Hades to be his queen in the Underworld. Demeter brings her back to the upper world for part of the year by withholding crops until Zeus accedes to her demand. See also ELEUSIS, IAKHOS, PERSEPHONE.

DIRKE: A famous spring at Thebes where Kadmos, first king of Thebes, killed a huge serpent guarding the water and thereby founded the city. See also CADMUS.

DIONYSOS: Divine son of Zeus and the Theban princess Semele, he is a complex and multifaceted god, associated with wine, fertility, festive dance and song, the mask, and drama, but also with ecstatic possession, illusion, and madness. He is often dangerous and vengeful in establishing his cult among those who resist him (see DRYAS). Frequently represented in processions of wildly dancing women followers, his maenads (*mainades*, literally, "mad women"), he is sometimes escorted also by satyrs and wild animals. Dionysos is sometimes associated with the Eleusinian goddesses Demeter and Persephone; see IAKKHOS.

DRYAS: Son of King Lykourgos of Thrace. Lykourgos refuses to accept the cult of Dionysos and, in revenge, the god drives him mad so that he thinks his son is Dionysos' vine and chops him into pieces with an axe. In some versions, this act of bloodshed causes a plague, and Lykourgos is then imprisoned in a cave.

EDONIANS: Warlike Thracian people northeast of Greece, in the area of modern Bulgaria.

ELEUSIS: Town south of Athens, the site of the Eleusinian Mysteries, an important cult in honor of Demeter and Persephone that revolves around the story of Persphone's return from Hades to the world above, offering hope of a happy afterlife to those who were initiated into the rites at special ceremonies that were kept secret. The cult, though localized at Eleusis, was open to all and attracted initiates from all over Greece.

EREKHTHEIDS: Royal family of Athens, descended from the early king Erekhtheus.

ERINYES: See FURIES, EUMENIDES.

EROS: Personification of the power of erotic desire. Sometimes regarded as the son of Aphrodite.

ETEOCLES (ETEOKLES): Son (and brother) of Oedipus and of his wife (and mother) Jokasta; brother of Antigone, Ismene, and Polyneices. He holds the throne of Thebes after the death of Oedipus and refuses to share it, as agreed, with Polyneices. The two die in mutually fratricidal battle at one of the seven gates of Thebes.

EUMENIDES: Another name for the Furies, Erinyes, or Dread Goddesses. The literal meaning of the name is "kindly ones," and it can be regarded as a euphemism or as representing a change in, or expansion of, their functions.

EUMOLPUS: Founder of the family who provided the high priests for the Eleusinian Mysteries.

EURYDIKE: Wife of Creon and mother of Haimon and his brother Megareus.

FURIES: Dreaded vengeful deities of the Underworld (Greek *Erinyes*). They particularly punish crimes of bloodshed within the family, and they often drive their victims mad. See also EUMENIDES.

HADES: God of the Underworld and the dead, he shares the world with his brothers Zeus, the god of the sky, and Poseidon, the god of the sea. Persephone, his queen, shares the subterranean throne and realm. The name Hades is often used as a synonym for the Underworld, which the early Greeks imagined as a grim shadowy place for the lifeless shades of men and women after death.

HAIMON: Surviving son of Creon and Eurydice, betrothed to Antigone.

HELIOS: God of the sun.

HERMES: God who, among many other functions, guides the shades of the dead to the underworld. He is also the god of herdsmen, amed in *Oedipus the King* as the god who rules over Mt. Kyllene in N.E. Arcadia, the place of his birth.

IAKKHOS: A youthful divinity, closely associated with Demeter as the divine child; he has an important place in her mystery cult at Eleusis. Originally distinct from Dionysos, he gradually becomes identified with him. His name may originally have meant "Lord of the shouting," derived from the "shouting" (in Greek *iakkhein*) that attended the processions and rites at Eleusis.

IOKASTE: see JOCASTA.

ISMENE: Daughter (and sister) of Oedipus, and of his wife (and mother) Jocasta, and sister of Antigone, Eteokles, and Polyneikes.

JOCASTA: Wife of King Laius of Thebes and mother of Oedipus, whom she believes killed by exposure, after it was prophesied that the infant would grow up to kill the father, and whom she marries, ignorant of who he really is. This incestuous union produces two sons, Oedipus', successors to the throne of Thebes, Eteocles and Polyneices, and two daughters, Antigone and Ismene. When Jocasta discovers the truth of Oedipus', birth, she hangs herself.

KADMOS: see CADMUS.

KASTALIA: A spring sacred to Apollo at Delphi on Mt. Parnassos. Its water was traditionally considered a source of poetic inspiration.

KITHAIRON: A high, desolate mountain to the south of Thebes.

KORYKIAN NYMPHS: Minor female divinities, worshiped in a cave high on Mt. Parnassos in central Greece, and closely associated with Dionysos.

KREON: See CREON.

LABDACUS (LABDAKOS): Father of King Laius of Thebes and so ancestor of the Theban royal line known as the Labdacids.

LAIUS: Son of Labdacus, husband of Jocasta, and father of Oedipus, whom he exposes as an infant because of a prophecy that his son will kill him. Oedipus, however, survives and, when grown to adulthood, ignorant of his true identity, kills his father at a crossing of roads that lead to Delphi, Thebes, and Corinth.

LYKOURGOS: See DRYAS.

MEGAREUS: Deceased son of Kreon and Eurydike and (probably elder) brother of Haimon. If he is to be identified with the Menoikeus elsewhere in the literary tradition, he has sacrificed himself to save Thebes, and thus (in his wife Eurydike's view at least) Kreon can be blamed for his death.

MEROPE: Queen of Corinth, wife of King Polybos, and adoptive mother of Oedipus.

MUSES: Nine goddesses of song, dance, and poetry, daughters of Zeus and Mnemosyne (Memory), often closely associated with Apollo and with Dionysos in his festive aspect.

NEREIDS: Nymphs of the sea, the fifty daughters of Nereus.

NIOBE: Daughter of the Phrygian king Tantalos and later the wife of Amphion, an early king of Thebes. She boastfully compares her seven sons and seven daughters to the two children of the goddess Leto. She is then punished by Leto's children, Apollo and Artemis, who kill all of hers, whereupon in her grief she is transformed into the rocky face of Mt. Sipylos in Phrygia, which was thought to resemble the face of a weeping woman.

OEDIPUS (OIDIPOUS):   Son of Laius by Jocasta. Exposed to the elements at birth because of a prophecy that he would kill his father, Oedipus survives, then kills his father without knowing who he is. Oedipus succeeds the dead king at Thebes after solving the riddle of the Sphinx, a monster ravaging the city, and marries the queen, not knowing that she is his mother. Oedipus has four children by Jocasta—his sons (and half brothers) Eteokles and Polyneikes, and his daughters (and half sisters) Ismene and Antigone.

OLYMPIA: In Elis near the northwest coast of the Peloponnesus, the greatest center for the worship of Olympian Zeus and seat of an oracle of that god.

OLYMPOS: Mountain in northeastern Greece, the peak of which is traditionally considered the abode of the gods, who are therefore called Olympians.

PALLAS: An epithet of Athena, by which she is sometimes invoked as a protective divinity.

PAN: Greek goat god, whose lower quarters were those of a goat; from his thighs up he resembled a man. He is a god of music, lust, and the mountains.

PARNASSOS: High mountain to the west of Thebes and dominating Delphi to the northeast; the site of Apollo's sanctuary at Delphi, and also associated with the cult of Dionysos.

PERITHOUS: Companion of Theseus in some of his exploits, including a descent to the underworld.

PERSEPHONE: Daughter of Zeus and Demeter, who is carried off to the Underworld by its god, Hades, to be his queen. Her annual return to her mother and the upper world for part of the year formed part of the mythic background to the Eleusinian Mysteries, which offered to initiates hope for a happier afterlife. Along with her mother, Persephone is also worshiped as a goddess of fertility. See also DEMETER, ELEUSIS, IAKKHOS.

PHINEUS: King of the Thracian city of Salmydessos, husband of Kleopatra, daughter of Boreas. He divorces Kleopatra to marry a second wife, named Eidothea or Idaia, and imprisons or otherwise maltreats Kleopatra. His second wife blinds Kleopatra's two children.

PHOEBUS: Another name for Apollo, "the bright one."

PHRYGIA: An area in what is now western Turkey, the location of Mt. Sipylos, where Niobe is transformed into stone.

PLUTO: Another name for Hades, god of the Underworld.

POLYBOS: King of Corinth, the adoptive father of the foundling Oedipus.

POLYNEICES (POLYNEIKES): Son (and brother) of Oedipus and of his wife (and mother) Jokasta; brother of Antigone, Ismene, and Eteocles. He holds the throne of Thebes after the death of Oedipus and refuses to share it, as agreed, with Eteocles. Driven into exile by Eteocles, he forms an alliance with the king of Argos to attack Thebes and take back the throne. The two die in mutually fratricidal battle at one of the seven gates of Thebes. Creon then forbids the burial of Polyneices' body.

POSEIDON: Brother of Zeus and Hades, with whom, as god of the sea, he divides rule of all the world; a patron god of Athens.

PYTHIA: The priestess of Apollo in his temple at Delphi. Possessed by the god, she pronounces or sings poetic responses to the questions of the visitors to the oracle of Apollo.

RHEA: Ancient earth goddess, mother of Zeus, Poseidon, Hades, and Ares.

SALMYDESSOS: A Thracian city on the southwestern shore of the Black Sea.

SERPENT: See CADMUS.

SIPYLOS: Mountain in Phrygia whose shape suggested to the ancients the face of a weeping woman. Niobe, in her grief for her dead children, is turned into the stony shape of this mountain.

SPHINX: Demonic creature of three forms: the head of a woman, the body of a bird, and the hindquarters of a lion. Oedipus solved her riddle about a creature with three forms (first walking on four legs, then two, then three). Her name means the "strangler."

STYX: River that runs through the underworld.

TANTALOS: Mythical king of Phrygia in Asia Minor, father of Niobe. Elsewhere in Greek myth he is one of the sinners punished in Hades for sharing the gods' divine food, ambrosia, with mortals after he has been invited to a feast on Olympos.

TARTARUS: A name for the underworld.

TEIRESIAS: Aged, blind seer of Thebes who plays an important role in several Theban myths and most of the surviving Greek tragedies set in Thebes.

THEBES: City in central Greece, founded by Cadmus from Phoenicia, and later ruled by the Labdacids (see LABDACUS), the family of Oedipus. It was guarded by a massive wall with seven gates, at one of which Oedipus' two sons, Polyneikes and Eteokles, rivals for the throne of Thebes, killed each other.

THESEUS: The legendary king of Athens, son of Aegeus, and slayer of the Minotaur in the labyrinth in Crete.

THRACE: Area to the northeast of Greece, extending north into what is roughly modern Bulgaria and along the eastern shores of the Black Sea. It was regarded by the early Greeks as a remote and savage place, inhabited by warlike tribes.

THYIADS: Female worshipers of Dionysos who accompany the god in processions marked by ecstatic dances and singing.

ZEUS: King of the Olympian gods and divine ruler of the world. Initially a sky god associated with celestial phenomena like lightning and thunder, thought of as sharing rule with his brothers Poseidon (lord of the sea) and Hades (lord of the underworld), he later comes to be considered the administrator of cosmic order and the guardian of law and justice. In one of his many cults, he is also worshiped as guardian of the family, Zeus Herkeios, an image of which stood in the courtyard or enclosure (*herkos*) in front of the house.

FOR FURTHER READING

SOPHOCLES

Mary Whitlock Blundell. *Helping Friends and Harming Enemies:
A Study in Sophocles and Greek Ethics*. Cambridge: Cambridge University Press, 1989. A lucid exploration of choices
and decisions made in the tragedies of Sophocles, with reference to the traditional moral code referred to in the title of this
book.

James Morwood. *The Tragedies of Sophocles*. Exeter, UK: Bristol
Phoenix Press, 2008. A useful introduction to each of Sophocles'
surviving plays, including a chapter surveying selected versions
and adaptations.

Karl Reinhardt. *Sophocles*. Translated by H. and D. Harvey. Oxford:
Blackwell, 1989. A classic reading of the Sophoclean tragic
hero.

Charles Segal. *Tragedy and Civilization: An Interpretation of Sophocles*.
Cambridge, MA: Harvard University Press, 1981; reprinted with
new preface, 1999. A detailed and insightful structuralist reading of the tragedies.

R. P. Winnington-Ingram. *Sophocles: An Interpretation*. Cambridge:
Cambridge University Press, 1980. Humane and thought-
provoking studies.

ANTIGONE

Peter Burian. "Gender and the City: *Antigone* from Hegel to Butler and Back." In J. P Euben and K. Bassi, eds. *When Worlds Elide: Classics, Politics, Culture*. Lanham, MD: Lexington, 2010. Considers the interpretative tradition that extends from the pioneering exegesis of Hegel and offers a reading of the play that connects family and political thematics.

Helene Foley. *Female Acts in Greek Tragedy*, especially Chapters I ("The Politics of Tragic Lamentation") and III.3 ("Antigone as Moral Agent"). Princeton: Princeton University Press, 2001. A study of female moral agency in Greek tragedy, with useful results for *Antigone*.

OEDIPUS THE KING

Peter Burian. "Inconclusive Conclusion: The Ending(s) of 'Oedipus Tyrannus.' " In S. Goldhill and E. Hall, eds., *Sophocles and the Tragic Tradition*. Cambridge: Cambridge University Press, 2009. An attempt to understand the play in the light of its unexpectedly open and ambiguous ending.

Charles Segal. *Oedipus Tyrannus: Tragic Heroism and the Limits of Knowledge*, 2nd ed. New York: Oxford University Press, 2001. A comprehensive introduction to the play, its interpretation, and its afterlife, with useful bibliography.

OEDIPUS AT COLONUS

Adrian Kelly. *Sophocles: "Oedipus at Colonus."* London: Duckworth, 2009. A volume in the useful series Companions to Greek and Roman Tragedy, providing a critical introduction and up-to-date bibliography.

Andreas Markantonatos. *Tragic Narrative: A Narratological Study of Sophocles' "Oedipus at Colonus."* Berlin: de Gruyter, 2002. A specialized but revealing study that demonstrates the importance to our understanding of the way Oedipus narrates his own story.